DIABETIC COOKBOOK FOR BEGINNERS

Easy-to-Make Tasty Meals to Help You Manage Type 2 Diabetes - Includes Over 600 Healthy Recipes and 28-Day Meal Plan (Tips & Tricks to Plan Your Diet)

By Amanda Smith

Legal Disclaimer The information contained in this book and its contents is not designed to replace any form of medical or professional advice; and is not meant to replace the need for independent medical, financial, legal, or other professional advice or service that may require. The content and information in this book have been provided for educational and entertainment purposes only.

The content and information contained in this book have been compiled from sources deemed reliable, and they are accurate to the best of the Author's knowledge, information and belief. However, the Author cannot guarantee its accuracy and validity and therefore cannot be held liable for any errors and/or omissions.

Further, changes are periodically made to this book as needed. Where appropriate and/or necessary, you must consult a professional (including but not limited to your doctor, attorney, financial advisor, or other such professional) before using any of the suggested remedies, techniques, and/or information in this book.

Upon using this book's contents and information, you agree to hold harmless the Author from any damaged, costs and expenses, including any legal fees potentially resulting from the application of any of the information in this book. This disclaimer applies to any loss, damages, or injury caused by the use and application of this book's content, whether directly and indirectly, whether for breach of contract, tort, negligence, personal injury, criminal intent, or under any other circumstances.

You agree to accept all risks of using the information presented in this book. You agree that by continuing to read this book, where appropriate and/or necessary, you shall consult a professional (including but not limited to your doctor, attorney, financial advisor, or other such professional) before remedies, techniques, and/or information in this book.

Table of Contents

INTRODUCTION....................................15

CHAPTER 1 UNDERSTANDING TYPE 2 DIABETES..16

How to Prevent Diabetes and Control Sugar Level 16

CHAPTER 2 FOOD CHOICES..............22

15 WORST FOOD FOR DIABETES..........23

CHAPTER 3 Breakfast...........................25

1. Pumpkin-Peanut Butter Single-Serve Muffins 25
2. Breakfast Sausage Casserole.........25
3. Crustless Broccoli Cheese Quiche.26
4. Fruits Breakfast Salad 26
5. Pesto Egg Casserole........................26
6. Kiwi Shake 26
7. Greek Toast 27
8. Mushrooms Bites.............................27
9. Melon Shake 27
10. German Pancakes........................27
11. Vegetables Omelet.......................28
12. Breakfast Bagels..........................28
13. Tex-Mex Omelet 29
14. Mediterranean Toast 29
15. Tomatoes Eggs.............................29
16. Breakfast Burrito.........................29
17. Mushroom and Red Pepper Omelet 30
18. Broccoli Frittata with Ham and Peppers...30
19. Fruits Bowl....................................30
20. Crispy Tofu....................................31
21. Spinach Muffins 31
22. Breakfast Sandwich 31
23. Chia Seeds Breakfast..................31
24. Green Breakfast Soup 32
25. Sweet Porridge 32
26. Hungarian Porridge 32
27. Nuts Porridge 32
28. Healthy Granola Bowl.................33
29. Scrambled Eggs 33
30. Peach Berry Parfait......................33
31. Buckwheat Granola......................33
32. French Crêpes 34
33. Mushrooms Tofu Bowl................34
34. Coconut Pancakes.......................34
35. French Toast................................35
36. Savory Muffins............................35
37. Classical Pancakes 35
38. Homemade Rice Milk..................36
39. Blueberry Muffins........................36
40. Ginger and Lemon Iced-Tea 36

41. **Tropical Juice** 36

42. **Berries Milkshake** 37

43. **Veggie Cheese Omelet** 37

44. **Spicy Corn Burritos** 37

45. **Thai Chicken and Vegetable Curry** 38

46. **Lentil and Zucchini Omelet** 38

47. **Brussels Sprouts and Egg Scramble** 38

48. **Berries Smoothie** 39

49. **Greek Yogurt Bowl** 39

50. **Pumpkin Walnut Bowl** 39

51. **Low-Carb Peanut Butter Pancakes** 39

52. **Broccoli and Shiitake Omelet** 40

53. **Sausage and Pepper Breakfast Burrito** 40

54. **Crepe Cakes** 41

55. **Zucchini Bread** 41

56. **Walnut Granola** 41

57. **Goat Cheese Toast** 42

58. **Cheesy Spinach Artichoke Casserole** 42

59. **Fuits & Nuts Oatmeal** 42

60. **Berry Oat Muffins** 43

61. **Yogurt Sundae** 43

62. **Apple and Bran Muffins** 43

63. **Coconut and Berry Oatmeal** 44

64. **Apple Pumpkin Waffles** 44

65. **Cranberry Grits** 44

66. **Cottage Cheese Pancakes** 45

67. **Huevos Rancheros** 45

68. **Coconut Pancakes** 46

69. **Spanakopita Omelet** 46

70. **Pita and Bacon** 47

71. **Shrimp with Scallion Grits** 47

CHAPTER 4 Appetizers and Snacks ***48***

72. **Fresh Dill Dip** 48

73. **Original Hummus** 48

74. **Chicken Fingers** 48

75. **Tuna Salad Wraps** 48

76. **Tortilla Chips** 49

77. **Fresh Figs and ricotta** 49

78. **Tuna Sandwich** 49

79. **Potatoes Croquettes** 50

80. **Carrots and Cinnamon Bread** 50

81. **Apple and Fennel Salad** 50

82. **Chicken Salad Sandwich** 51

83. **Pasta and Sun-dried Tomatoes** . 51

84. **Lettuce with Dressing** 51

85. **Paprika Carrots** 52

86. **Roasted Beet & Sardine Salad** ... 52

87. **Celery and Aragula Salad** 52

88. **Chicken & Zucchini Hot Salad** 52

89. **Tuna Salad** 53

90. **Ginger-Lime Grilled Shrimp** 53

91. **Kale Chips** 53

92. **Red Pepper Hummus** 54

93. **Buffalo Cauliflower Bites with Ranch Dressing** 54

94. **Baked Cream Cheese Crab Dip** .. 55

95. **Philly Cheese Steak Stuffed Mushrooms** 55

96. **Greek Cookies** 55

97. **Flavored Potatoes Mix** 56

98. Corn Bread 56
99. Kale Popcorn 56
100. Peas Hummus 57
101. Vegetable Rolls..................................57
102. Omelet with Penne 57
103. Grilled Zucchini Hummus...........58
104. Peach and Pita 58
105. Fruit Compote 58
106. Zucchini Tots 59
107. Roasted Cabbage..............................59
108. Stuffed Mushrooms..........................59
109. Tasty Herb Dip 60
110. Rutabaga Wedges 60
111. Tasty Broccoli Nuggets 60
112. Onion Dip 60
113. Crab-Filled Mushrooms 61
114. Artichoke Dip....................................61
115. Chilled Shrimp...................................61
116. Chicken Kabobs 62
117. Broiled Shrimps 62
118. Creamy Cheese Dip 63
119. Baked Scallops...................................63
120. Monterey Jack Cheese Quiche...63
121. Cucumber Pâté...................................64
122. Gruyère Apple Spread 64

CHAPTER 5 Salads.....................................*65*

123. Mozzarella and Tomato Salad....65
124. Energy Salad.......................................65
125. Squash and Broccoli Barley Salad 66
126. Pear and Spinach Salad 66
127. Chicken , Spinach , and Berry Salad 66
128. Blueberry Chicken Salad............67
129. Butterscotch Apple Salad 67
130. Berries salad..67
131. Asian taste salad 68
132. Beet Salad...68
133. Cranberry Cabbage Slaw 68
134. Chestnut Noodle Salad................68
135. Cranberry Broccoli Salad 69
136. Balsamic Beet Salad 69
137. Daikon Salad 69
138. Shrimp Salad 69
139. Chicken Cranberry Sauce Salad 70
140. Egg Celery Salad..........................70
141. Papaya Salad.....................................70
142. Slow cooker Corn Salad 71
143. Chicken Orange Salad 71
144. Almond Pasta Salad 71
145. Pineapple Berry Salad 71
146. Garden fantasy salad...................72
147. Autumn Green salad 72
148. Avocado and Mango salad..........72
149. Green & Yellow Bean Salad........72
150. Carrot Zucchini Salad 73
151. BBQ Salad 73
152. Cheese and Walnut Salad...........73
153. Figs and Aragula Salad................74
154. Spicy Beef Salad 74
155. Broccoli Lettuce Salad.................75
156. Pepper Cabbage Salad 75

157. Lettuce and Carrot Salad with Vinaigrette 75
158. Strawberry Watercress Salad with Dressing 75
159. Cucumber and Cabbage Salad ... 76
160. Lettuce , Asparagus and berries Salad 76
161. Waldorf Salad with Variation 76
162. Asian Pear Salad 77
163. Beet Feta Salad 77
164. Cucumber Salad 77
165. Red Potatoes Salad 78
166. Greek Salad 78
167. Mixed Broccoli Salad 78
168. Cabbage and Pear Salad 78
169. Couscous Salad with Spicy Dressing 79
170. Farfalle Confetti Salad 79
171. Tarragon and Pepper Pasta Salad 80
172. Zucchini and Crispy Salmon Salad 80
173. Brie and Apple Salad 80
174. Sofrito Steak Salad 80
175. Tomato and Peach Salad 81
176. Cucumber Tomato Avocado Salad 81
177. Garlic and Bean Salad 81
178. Quinoa , Salmon , and Asparagus Salad 82
179. Blackberry Goat Cheese Salad ... 82
180. Kale and Cabbage Salad 83
181. Strawberry Spelt Salad 83
182. Chicken, Melon Salad 84
183. Black Bean and Tomato Salad ... 84
184. Rice Salad with Cranberries and Almonds 84
185. Pecan Pear Salad 85
186. Rainbow Cauli Salad 85
187. Veggie Salad 85
188. Asian Style Noodle Salad 86
189. Spinach and Pear Salad 86
190. Caprese Salad 86
191. Creamy Crab Slaw 87
192. Broccoli and Bacon Salad 87
193. Pomegranate and Brussels Sprouts Salad 87
194. Melon and Serrano Ham Salad .. 87
195. Watermelon and Feta Salad 88

CHAPTER 6 Soups and Stews *89*

196. Miso Pork and Apple Soup 89
197. French Onion Soup 89
198. Eggplant and Red Pepper Soup. 90
199. Chicken Pho 90
200. Herbed Cabbage Stew 90
201. Vegetable Lentil Soup 91
202. Veggie Soup 91
203. French Onion Soup 92
204. Classic Chicken Soup 92
205. Pumpkin and Quinoa 92
206. Green Veggies Stew 93
207. Creamy Broccoli Soup 93
208. Onion Soup 93
209. Sorrel Soup 94
210. Cauliflower Soup 94
211. Crab Soup 94

212. **Butternut Squash Soup** 95
213. **Sirloin Carrot Soup** 95
214. **Carrot and Spice Soup** 95
215. **Peach Stew** 95
216. **Chicken and Dill Soup** 96
217. **Berries Soup** 96
218. **Cheese Soup** 96
219. **Wonton Soup** 96
220. **Lentil and lemon Soup** 97
221. **Carrot Coriander Soup** 97
222. **Lettuce and Lovage Soup** 97
223. **Jerusalem Artichoke and Carrot Soup** 97
224. **Russian Vegetable Soup** 98
225. **Cream of Celeriac Soup** 98
226. **Pumpkin and Coconut Soup** 98
227. **Chicory Soup** 99
228. **Black Bean Soup** 99
229. **Cherry Stew** 99
230. **Tofu Soup** 99
231. **Pumpkin and Rosemary Soup** .. 100
232. **Curry , Carrot and Coconut Soup** 100
233. **Buttercup Squash Soup** 100
234. **Turkey and Barley Soup** 101
235. **Cauliflower Leek Soup** 101
236. **Beef Soup** 102
237. **Lime Chicken Soup** 102
238. **Tomato Kale Soup** 103
239. **Cheeseburger Soup** 103
240. **Taco Beef Soup** 103
241. **Beans and Butternut Squash Stew** 104
242. **Sweet Potato and Pumpkin Soup** 104
243. **Carrot Soup** 105
244. **Thai Shrimps Soup** 105
245. **Calabaza Squash Soup** 106
246. **Pork Meatball Soup** 106
247. **Roasted Tomato and Bell Pepper Soup** 106
248. **Savory Cabbage Soup** 107
249. **Spiced Lamb Stew** 107
250. **Seafood Stew** 108
251. **Lamb and Sweet Potato Stew** . 108
252. **Beef Zoodle Stew** 109
253. **Traditional Mexican Beef Stew** 109
254. **African Holiday Stew** 110
255. **Hearty Bell Pepper Stew** 110
256. **Tasty Seafood Stew** 111

CHAPTER 7 Meatless Mains ***112***

257. **Lemony Spinach-Tofu Bake** 112
258. **Grilled Vegetables on White Bean Hummus** 112
259. **Sweet Potato and Chickpea Bowl** 113
260. **Black Bean Enchilada Skillet** 113
261. **Mushroom Cutlets with Creamy Sauce** 114
262. **French Ratatouille** 114
263. **Zucchini Boats** 115
264. **Tofu and Bean Chili** 115
265. **Cauliflower Steaks** 115
266. **Mushroom Pesto Flatbread** 116
267. **Stuffed Squash with Cheese and Artichokes** 116

268. Kale and Mushroom Bread Pudding 117

269. Chickpea Coconut Curry 117

270. Apple Pita Pockets 118

271. Beans and Brown Rice 118

272. Quinoa Veggie Skillet 118

273. Spinach Mini Quiches 119

274. Tempeh Wraps 119

275. Tex Mex Vegetarian Bake 119

276. Party Casserole 120

277. Roasted Cauliflower 120

278. Chili Rellenos Casserole 121

279. Simply Eggplant Parmesan 121

280. Collard Greens and Tomato 121

281. Mushroom and Pesto Flatbreads 122

282. Italian Pasta with Sauce 122

283. Cauliflower and Mushroom Risotto 122

284. BBQ Tofu Veggie Skewers 123

285. Stuffed Sweet Potato 123

286. Veggie and Olives Nachos 124

287. Portobello Mushroom Pizza 124

288. Cauliflower and Cheese 125

289. Marinara Spaghetti Squash 125

290. Eggplant Lasagna 126

291. Mock and Cheese 127

CHAPTER 8 Sides *128*

292. Spaghetti Squash 128

293. Roasted Peppers and Eggplants 128

294. Sautéed Spinach with Parmesan 129

295. Braised Carrots and Kale 129

296. Butternut Squash Hummus 129

297. Zucchini mini cakes 130

298. Chickpeas Veggie Burger 130

299. Quinoa and Fruits Salad 130

300. Boiles Sweet Potatoes 131

301. Caramelized Onions 131

302. Roasted White Bean Dip 132

303. Rosemary Endives 132

304. Sage Carrots 132

305. Braised Cabbage 133

306. Sweet Zucchini Bowl 133

307. Cabbage Quiche 133

308. Lemony Asparagus 134

309. Eggs and Beans 134

310. Oven-Fried Yucca 134

311. Roasted Onion Dip 135

312. Crab Dip 135

313. Glazed Snap Peas 135

314. Cauliflower Hash Brown 136

315. Baked Eggplant Slices 136

316. Veggie Garam Masala 136

317. Mushroom Tacos 137

318. Baby Spinach Salad 137

319. Sweet Potato Puree 137

320. Vegan Chili 137

321. Spinach and Chickpeas Salad .. 138

322. Classical Greek Salad 138

323. Vegan Tortilla 139

324. Curried Okra 139

325. Cauliflower and Herbs Tortilla. 139

326. Broccoli with Pine Nuts 140

327. Green Beans and Peppers 140
328. Asparagus with Sweet Peppers 141
329. Mashed Cauliflower 141
330. Sweet-and-Sour Slaw................ 141
331. Zucchini and Pine Nuts Ribbons 142
332. Broiled Tomatoes with Cheese 142
333. Braised Kale with Ginger 142
334. Garlic Fettuccine........................ 142
335. Linguine with Pesto 143
336. Pasta with Peppers 143
337. Vegetable Clam Sauce Shells... 143
338. Fettuccine with Peppers and Broccoli 144
339. Veggie Lo Mein........................... 144
340. Asian Stir-Fried Rice 145
341. Rainbow Rice Casserole........... 145
342. Brown Rice with Spinach.......... 145
343. Curried Rice with Broccoli 146
344. Zucchini Pasta with Mango-Kiwi Sauce 146
345. Beans Burger.............................. 146
346. Barley Veggie Bowl 147
347. Roasted Eggplant with Feta Dip 147
348. Vegetable Potpie 148
349. Marsala Roasted Carrots 148
350. Cajun Asparagus........................ 149

CHAPTER 9 Fish and Seafood........... 150

351. Cajun-Spiced Tilapia................. 150
352. Open-Faced Tuna Melts 150
353. Grilled Cod 150
354. Cod and Green Bean Curry....... 151
355. Calamari Salad 151
356. Salmon and Veggie Soup.......... 151
357. White Fish Soup......................... 152
358. Onion Dijon Crusted Catfish 152
359. Herb Baked Tuna 152
360. Cilantro Lime Salmon 153
361. Tuna and Potato Salad 153
362. Oven-Fried Catfish 153
363. Asian Ginger tuna...................... 154
364. Cheesy Tuna Chowder.............. 154
365. Fish with Mushrooms 155
366. Salmon with Spicy Honey......... 155
367. Salmon with Maple Glaze 155
368. Dijon Mustard and Marinated Shrimp 156
369. Fish and Veggie Stew 156
370. Baked Cod Crusted with Herbs 156
371. Salmon Meal 157
372. Tangy Orange Shrimp............... 157
373. Shrimp Italian Pasta................. 158
374. Salmon and Cauliflower........... 158
375. Shrimp and Greens 158
376. Seared Herbed Scallops 159
377. Almond-Crusted Sole................ 159
378. Breaded Baked Sole.................. 159
379. Roasted Tilapia with Garlic Butter 160
380. Pesto-Crusted Tilapia 160
381. Lime Baked Haddock 161
382. Fish Tacos with Vegetable Slaw 161
383. Dill Relish on White Sea Bass .. 161

384. **Tilapia with Lemon Garlic Sauce** 162

385. **Spinach with White Beans and Shrimps** ... 162

386. **Bagel with Salmon and Egg** ... 162

387. **Salmon Stuffed Pasta** ... 163

388. **Cod and Green Bean risotto** ... 163

389. **Citrus Glazed Salmon** ... 164

390. **Broiled Salmon Fillets** ... 164

391. **Grilled Lemony Cod** ... 165

392. **Marinated Salmon Steak** ... 165

393. **Tuna with honey Glaze** ... 165

394. **Stuffed Mushrooms** ... 165

395. **Crispy Fish Fillets** ... 166

396. **Simple Soup** ... 166

397. **Lime-Marinated Salmon** ... 166

398. **Tuna with Pineapple** ... 167

399. **Tangy Glazed Black Cod** ... 167

400. **Spicy Lime and Basil Grilled Fish** 168

401. **Shrimp Paella** ... 168

402. **Shrimp Scampi** ... 168

403. **Salmon & Pesto Salad** ... 169

404. **Baked Fennel & Garlic Sea Bass** 169

405. **Lemon Cilantro & Tuna and Rice** 170

406. **Red Cod Risotto** ... 170

407. **Sardine Fish Cakes** ... 170

408. **Cajun Catfish** ... 171

409. **4-Ingredients Salmon Fillet** ... 171

410. **Tuna and Shallot** ... 171

411. **Brazilian Fish Stew** ... 171

412. **Spanish Cod in Sauce** ... 172

413. **Fish Shakshuka** ... 172

414. **Ginger Shrimp** ... 172

415. **Monk-fish Curry** ... 173

416. **Steamed Fish with Garlic** ... 173

417. **Baked Haddock** ... 174

418. **Sauté Fillets** ... 174

419. **Lemon Scallops** ... 174

420. **Tuna Casserole** ... 175

421. **Lemon Pepper Salmon** ... 175

422. **Tilapia with Mango Salsa** ... 175

423. **Honey Roasted Salmon** ... 176

424. **Halibut with Green Beans** ... 176

425. **Salmon with Brussels Sprouts** . 177

426. **Simply Sole Piccata** ... 177

427. **Crusted Halibut** ... 177

428. **Curried Tuna Salad Wraps** ... 178

429. **Veggie-Stuffed Trout** ... 178

430. **Lemony Cod with Asparagus** ... 179

431. **Cajun Catfish** ... 179

432. **BBQ Tuna Steaks** ... 179

433. **Rosemary Trout** ... 179

434. **Lemony White Fish Fillets** ... 180

435. **Greek Scampi** ... 180

436. **Scallops with Asparagus** ... 181

437. **Shrimp Burgers with Mango** ... 181

438. **Cajun Shrimp Casserole** ... 182

439. **Original Cioppino** ... 182

440. **Orange Scallops** ... 183

441. **Shrimp with Feta** ... 183

442. **Jambalaya** ... 183

443. **Traditional Paella** ... 184

444. **Seafood Enchiladas**.................... 185

445. **Steamed Mussels**........................ 185

446. **Breaded Scallop Patties**............ 186

447. **Panko-Crusted Coconut Shrimp** 186

CHAPTER 10 Poultry............................ *188*

448. **Chicken Grilled Cheese**............. 188

449. **Braised Chicken with Apple Slaw** 188

450. **One-Pan Chicken Meal** 189

451. **Coconut Lime Chicken**............... 189

452. **Slow Chicken Curry**.................... 190

453. Apple & Cinnamon Spiced Pork loin.. 190

454. Lemon & herb turkey breasts 190

455. Orange Grilled Chicken..................... 191

456. **Roasted Citrus Chicken**............. 191

457. **Chicken Vegetable Curry** 192

458. **Chicken Paella**............................ 192

459. **Chicken Rigatoni** 192

460. **Easy Chicken Fajitas**.................. 193

461. **Chicken Asian style**.................... 193

462. **Crispy Chicken Rolls** 194

463. **Mango Chicken Stir-Fry** 194

464. **Tuscany Meatballs**...................... 194

465. **Chicken Fried Rice**...................... 195

466. **Turkey Club burger** 195

467. **Chicken Enchiladas** 195

468. **Cheesy Wings**............................. 196

469. **Chicken Salad balsamic** 196

470. **Chicken and Veggie Soup**......... 197

471. **Chicken and Broccoli** 197

472. **Tagine with Meatballs**............... 197

473. **Parmesan Roasted Cauliflower**198

474. **Cabbage Apple Stir-Fry** 198

475. **Mozzarella Salad**........................ 198

476. **Celery and Fennel Salad with berries**.. 199

477. **Red Cabbage Burgers**................ 199

478. **Easy Noodles** 199

479. **Chow Mein** 200

480. **Lemony Roasted Chicken** 200

481. **Chicken and Apples Mix**............ 200

482. **Walnut Turkey and Peaches** 201

483. **Chicken Curry**............................. 201

484. **Chicken Couscous** 201

485. **Roasted Turkey**........................... 202

486. **Smokey Turkey Chili**.................. 202

487. **Homemade Turkey Soup**........... 203

488. **Tropical Chicken salad** 203

489. **Chicken Meatballs**...................... 203

490. **Asian chicken Satay**................... 204

491. **Chicken Creole style** 205

492. **Turkey burger with jalapeno peppers**... 205

493. **Gnocchi and chicken dumplings** 205

494. **Turkey Sausage** 206

495. **Chicken Salad Wrap**................... 206

496. **Chicken Salad with Apples | Grapes**... 206

497. **Chicken Spanish Style**............... 207

498. **Smoky Chicken** 207

499. **Chicken Noodles**......................... 207

500. **Peppered Chicken with Kale**.... 208

501. **Teriyaki Chicken with Broccoli** 208

502. Coconut Chicken Curry.............209
503. Chicken 'Cacciatore'.................209
504. Greek Stuffed Peppers.............210
505. Creole Chicken.........................210
506. Cashew Chicken........................211
507. Citrus Chicken Thighs...............211
508. Chicken Pappardelle.................212
509. Tropical Chicken.......................212
510. Coconut-Encrusted Chicken.....213
511. Turkey and Quinoa Casserole..213
512. Mushroom Stuffed Turkey........214
513. Herbed Whole Turkey Breast...214
514. Herb-Roasted Turkey and Veggies...215
515. Roasted Duck Legs....................215
516. Mexican Turkey Sliders............216
517. Turkey Zoodles with Spaghetti Sauce 216
518. Turkey Tacos.............................216
519. Quick Turkey Potpie..................217

CHAPTER 11 Beef, Pork, and Lamb..218

520. Peppered Beef...........................218
521. Steak Fajita Bake.......................218
522. Beef Veggie Fajita Bowls..........218
523. Beef with Peppercorn Sauce....219
524. Beef Burrito Bowl......................219
525. Marinated Steak........................220
526. Broccoli Beef Stir-Fry...............220
527. Beer Braised Brisket.................221
528. Bunless Sloppy Joes..................221
529. Sunday Pot Roast......................221
530. Classic Stroganoff.....................222
531. Gingered-Pork Stir-Fry.............223
532. Pork Tenderloin Roast with Glaze 223
533. Roasted Pork Loin.....................224
534. Cajun Smothered Pork Chops..224
535. Chipotle Chili Pork Chops.........224
536. Pork Chops with Red Cabbage 225
537. Curried Pork Skewers...............225
538. Mustard Glazed Pork Chops.....226
539. Lamb Kofta Meatballs with Cucumber Salad..................................226
540. Rosemary Lamb Chops.............226
541. Lamb Burgers with Mushrooms 227
542. Lime Lamb Cutlets....................227
543. Lamb and Pomegranate Salad.228

CHAPTER 12 Desserts.........................229

544. Peach Crumb Cobbler...............229
545. Melon Pear Medley....................229
546. Spiced Baked Apples.................229
547. Maple Oatmeal Cookies............230
548. Peach and Almond Meal Fritters 230
549. Tapioca Berry Parfaits..............230
550. Blackberry Yogurt Ice Pops.....231
551. Chocolate Almond Butter Fudge 231
552. Pineapple Nice Cream..............231
553. Grilled Peach and Yogurt Bowls 231
554. Creamy Strawberry Crepes......232
555. Flourless Orange Bundt Cake..232
556. Avocado Chocolate Mousse......233
557. Cottage Cheese Pancakes........233

558. Frozen Chocolate Peanut Butter Bites 233
559. Apple Crunch 234
560. Goat Cheese-Stuffed Pears 234
561. Gingerbread Soufflés 234
562. Crispy Apple Chips 235
563. Blackberry Soufflés 235
564. Carrot Cupcakes 236
565. Spicy Peaches 236
566. Pumpkin Cheesecake bar 236
567. Blueberry Mini Muffins 237
568. Vanilla custard 237
569. Coconut Cream Pie 237
570. Date and Almond Balls with Seeds 238
571. Apricot Soufflé 238
572. Mini Lime Tarts 239
573. Bakery Squares 239
574. Chocolate almond clusters 239
575. Lemon squares 240
576. Peanut butter coconut balls 240
577. Strawberry fluff 241
578. Super light tiramisu 241
579. Apple crisp 241
580. Rich & creamy fudge 242
581. Apple-caramel crunch balls 242
582. Protein cheesecake 242
583. Peanut butter cookies 243

CHAPTER 13 Sauces, Dips and Dressings 244

584. Cranberry Sauce 244
585. Tofu and Lemon Sauce 244
586. Pepper Sauce 244
587. BBQ Sauce 245
588. Easy Peanut Sauce 245
589. Creamy Lemon Sauce 245
590. Greek Tzatziki Sauce 245
591. Roasted Tomato Salsa 246
592. Beet Yogurt Dip 246
593. Quick Pesto 246
594. Guacamole 247
595. Chimichurri 247
596. Ranch Dressing 247
597. Italian Dressing 247
598. Creamy Avocado Dressing 248
599. Greek or Italian Vinaigrette 248
600. Tahini Dressing with Honey 248

CHAPTER 14 28-DAY MEAL PLAN 249

Appendix 1 CONVERSIONS CHART 252

Appendix 2 INDEX 252

INTRODUCTION

I have devoted myself to the study of diabetes for many years and have met many patients who have come to consult me. Through their treatment and my understanding of diabetes, I have summarized some experience in treating this disease. Now I want to give you a brief introduction so that you will have a better understanding of diabetes and some actions to relieve or eliminate the pain caused by diabetes. There are many ways to deal with it, of course, and the main focus of this guide is to reduce and eliminate pain through dietary control. Before introducing the recipes, let me introduce some basic knowledge about diabetes.

CHAPTER 1 UNDERSTANDING TYPE 2 DIABETES

Type 2 diabetes (T2D), formerly known as adult-onset diabetes, is a form of diabetes characterized by high blood sugar, insulin resistance, and relative lack of insulin. Common symptoms include increased thirst, frequent urination, and unexplained weight loss. Symptoms may also include increased hunger, feeling tired, and sores that do not heal. Symptoms often come on slowly. Long-term complications from high blood sugar include heart disease, stroke, diabetic retinopathy that can lead to blindness, kidney failure and poor blood flow in the limbs that can lead to amputations. Sudden onset of a hyperglycemic hyperosmolar state can occur; however, ketoacidosis is uncommon.

Major Causes of Type 2 Diabetes

Insulin is necessary to live as it performs an essential function: it allows glucose in our blood to enter our cells and fuel our bodies.

In the presence of type 2 diabetes, the body continues to break down carbohydrates from food and drink and turns them into glucose. The pancreas responds to this by releasing insulin. But because this insulin cannot work properly, blood sugar levels continue to rise. This means more insulin is released and this may cause a risk of hyperglycaemia.

How to Prevent Diabetes and Control Sugar Level

Type 2 diabetes is a non-communicable disease which is caused when the body is unable to use properly the produced insulin, or the body cannot make enough insulin.

We know the causes of type 2 diabetes so all we need to do is work toward prevention. The aims of a diabetic diet are the following:

- Make sure the blood glucose is at a normal rate
- Improve the health by balanced nutrition
- Allow the body to gain appropriate weight
- Make sure the blood lipid concentration is at an optimal rate

Changes in our lifestyle can significantly help to face diabetes. before you get started with a diabetic diet take note of the following tips that will change your habits and drastically help you to face your dise

20 TIPS TO PREVENT DIABETES

1 REDUCE ALCOHOL
Although many medical experts say that drinking a glass of red wine every night can have positive effects on health it is known that alcohol can interfere with some medications and, like any alcoholic beverage, contains a significant amount of sugar that can increase your glucose to spike. So it is advisable to avoid alcohol as much as possible and choose the less fun but infinitely healthier option called water.

2 GET A GLUCOMETER
If you've been diagnosed with diabetes, chances are your doctor has already told you to purchase this device. And many doctors and nutritionists recommend that type 1 type 2 and even pre-diabetics check their blood sugar levels throughout the day. Knowing your sugar levels can help manage your condition by letting you know if a food you just ate has impacted your levels, and will help you assess what to prepare for your next meal. Many glucometers are sold for less than $50 so while being inexpensive it is a valuable tool to use daily.

3 TAKE A SHORT WALK AFTER EACH MEAL New researches suggest that postprandial walks, that means after meals, can help stabilize your blood sugar levels. Many physical fitness experts and doctors agree that a 20 minute walk can be quite effective, but even only 10 minutes of brisk walking after a meal can still have a positive impact on your glucose levels. In fact, a ten-minute brisk walk after a meal has been shown to be more effective for lowering and balancing blood sugar levels than exercising at different times of the day.

4 LIFT WEIGHTS
weight lifting can help you bulk up but lifting weights can also have dramatic positive effects for your health, not just your appearance. The more muscle you have, the better your insulin will work. Increasing your lean muscle mass means you will burn calories at a faster rate, which can help stabilize your blood sugar levels in a more effective way. And it will make your muscle cells more sensitive to insulin strengthening your muscles can also help you better control your blood pressure, lower your risk of cardiovascular disease, increase your bone density, and improve your cholesterol levels.

5 EXPERIMENTS WITH MEAL FREQUENCY
Most nutritionists believe that you can stabilize your blood sugar levels by eating five or six small meals a day, or two or three larger meals a day.
As it turns out, everyone's body and metabolism are different and what works for one person may not work for another. Many diabetics have reported that eating 4 to 6 small healthy snacks throughout the day works best to help them fight cravings and keep glucose levels steady but it's up to you to experiment and figure out which way of eating will work best for your body

6 LOSE THE SALT
Although salt doesn't negatively affect blood sugar levels, consuming excessive amounts of salt has been shown to increase the risk of high blood pressure, which is linked to heart disease, stroke and diabetes.
Check the salt you add to your meals or take a close look at the nutrition labels of all the food packages you buy. 1 teaspoon 's worth of salt a day is the perfect portion. It corresponds to 6 grams. Tip: To limit salt, it's helpful to avoid packaged foods, cook more meals at home and avoid adding extra salt at restaurants

7 CUT DOWN ON READ MEAT
The latest research shows that eating a diet high in red meats will increase your risk of developing diabetes. There are many factors

for this, one simply being that eating a lot of large portions of red meat portions of red meat can add to your weight. But scientists recently discovered that the high iron contents on red meat may increase oxidative stress in your body, which can lower your insulin sensitivity. Plus additional stress in your body, which can lower your insulin sensitivity. plus additional studies have showed a link between high red meat consumption and certain forms of cancer.
However, red meat can still provide many important nutrients, like protein and vitamin B12. Therefore, while most nutritionists and doctors argue that while red meat can have a place in your diet, you should avoid eating more than 70 grams of red meat per day. That's about the equivalent to 2 sausages.
We recommend limiting your red meat to 2 meals per week.

8 SWITCH TO VEGETABLE BASED PASTAS

you probably know that most traditional pastas are made with flour white and are therefore extremely starchy. They will spike your blood sugar in a few minutes, and they do not provide your body with much on any fiber. Some vegetables, like carrots, squash and even zucchini can be used to create amazing pasta noodles. Using them you will ensure that your plate is loaded with an excellent amount of healthy carbohydrates and fiber and you will cut down on that extra sugar found in flour pastas. All you need is a spiralizer or even just a peeler to create the noodles. In fact, many grocery stores and supermarkets already carry pre-spiralized vegetable based pasta noodles. Instead of boiling your noodles simply saute them with a little bit of olive oil and add a sauce. Creating heart-healthy, nutrient-rich sauces form home, like tomato garlic red sauce.

9 EAT 2 TO 4 SERVINGS OF FRUIT PER DAY fruit is nature's candy. It will give you a strong dose of sugar, but if you pick the right fruits and eat them the right way, you will also be getting a variety of essential vitamins, antioxidants, and fiber. Whole fruits are low-calories, but they will help you feel fuller, quicker. Some fruits, like pears, may raise your blood sugar levels higher and quicker than other fruits, like apples, For example, some studies have concluded that eating grapes, blueberries, and apples can help you lower your risk for developing type2 diabetes. In general most fruits, eaten whole, without being juiced or added to cereals or bread, will have positive health benefits, like helping with weight management, reducing cardiovascular disease risk, and lowering your blood pressure. So, in general, fruits can be added to your plate for most every meal. Simply go for about 2 to 4 serving of fruits per day, because overdoing it on the fruit can supply your body with an overabundance of carbs. An apple or other fruits that are about the size of your fist like a peach or a pear, for example, count as one serving. Larger fruits, like mangos, will count as 2 servings. But you can eat up to 4 strawberries or 16 grapes and count those as one serving of fruits.

10 ADD ANTI-OXIDANT RICH SPICES AND HERBS TO YOUR MEAL

you can dramatically better your nutrition simply by adding a few pinches of spice to your meals. Ginger, turmeric, garlic, cinnamon and many others spices and herbs can help you manage glucose levels, fight against oxidative damage, and improve your heart health. Ginger has been shown to improve insulin sensitivity and cholesterol levels. (Try a teaspoon of grated ginger in your soups or stir fries or make yourself some ginger tea). Turmeric can help you control high blood sugar and it has excellent anti-inflammatory properties use a pinch or two on your chicken, or add a bit to your scrambles eggs. You can also include turmeric in a variety of teas or veggie smoothies, Garlic can also help you better control your glucose levels and fight against free radical damage.

Add minced garlic to a wide variety of soup, salsa, or other meals.

11 SWITCH TO 100% WHOLE GRAIN OR SPROUNTED GRAIN BREADS

Many nutritionists suggest to consume whole-grain or sprouted grain breads instead of white sliced bread. They contain beneficial nutrients and good amounts of fiber to slow your insulin response. Another option is pumpernickel or sourdough breads as well. Sourdough is long-germented which produces acetic acid. Acetic acid has been shown to help lower blood sugar. Pumpernickel is created by using a sourdough starter, so it may provide some positive health benefits as well. Just make sure to check the labels of these breads first to avoid added sugars or other hidden ingredients.

12 BUY SEASONAL PRODUCE

Most people realize that fruits and especially vegetables are essential for every meal.
However is not easy to have a good amount of them always available at a reasonable price. For that reason you could try to use better the freezer. You can find amazing produce at unbeatable prices, as long as you buy them in season, and store them in the freezer for future consumptions. So seek out the most competitively priced farmers market stalls or organic produce stores in your area and buy extra kale, spinach, broccoli, sweet potatoes, chopped onions, apples, berries, and much more, then bag up your extras and toss them in your freezer.
Now you will have healthy low-cost produce for months to come.

13 USE A MEAL KIT DELIVERY SERVICE

Most of these services offer you a variety of weekly meal plans meant to feed the entire family, all with quality produce and other natural ingredients. This will allow you to satisfy your family needs but also avoid waste of foods and allow to saving money. In fact with food kit delivery services, they supply the exact amount of produce you will need. Plus, avoiding your trips to the grocery store, you will reduce the amount of unhealthy high sugar snack foods you may inevitably be tempted to normally purchase.

14 COUNT YOUR CARBS

counting calories or amounts of food sounds unsustainable. But this habit can help you learn which foods negatively affect your blood sugar the most and can help you better manage both your glucose levels and your weight. Counting carbs is especially important if you are type 1 diabetic so you can accurately just your insulin depending on what you eat. Many doctors say to keep your total carb count per meal to between 45 and 60 grams or about 20 grams per snack. If you are about to consume a package product just check the total carbohydrate number listed on the nutritional label. If you are eating unpackaged fruits or vegetables, you can quickly look up their specific carb counts online. But in simple terms, any single serving of a veggie fruits or milk will be about 15 grams -worth of carbs.

15 30 MINUTES OF PHYSICAL ACTIVITY PER DAY

new research shown that there doesn't seem to be much added health benefit to adding extra time to your normal workout routine. 30 minutes or so of moderate to heavy aerobic or anaerobic exercise each day will let you get the results you want. Many doctors believe a total of 150 minutes of physical activity per week is enough for anyone to properly increase heart health, strengthen your muscles, expand your lung capacity, aid in better sleep, improve your memory, and even help you feel happy. But recent studies show that 30 minutes of moderate physical activity works just as well as doing a full hour of exercise, when it comes to weight loss.
Simply go for 30 continuous minutes of brisk walking, swimming, cycling even dancing or

completing some house chores can do the trick.

16 EAT OILY, OMEGA 3-RICH FISH AT LEAST TWICE A WEEK

omega eating -3 fatty acid rich foods on a regular basis has been shown to increase insulin sensitivity, as well as many other health benefits, from reducing the risk of cardiovascular disease, to fighting against inflammation, to lowering rates of depression. And oily lean protein fish, like salmon, tuna, and mackerel, are excellent at delivering those omega-3 fats to your body. Furthermore they are a source of VITAMIN D. Nutritionists and doctors recommend that type 2 diabetics eat at least two portions of these types of fish per week.

17 EAT HALF A PLATE OF NON-STARCHY VEGETABLES IN EACH MEAL

This is essential to bettering your health and fighting diabetes. Non-starchy vegetables, like broccoli, cauliflower, asparagus and cabbage, contain about 25 calories and 5 grams of carbs. But they also provide 3 grams of fiber and up to 2 grams of protein per cup. By filling half of your plates with these nutrient-dense veggies controlling your daily calories will be easier. Try to eat three servings of one cup of raw or half a cup of cooked vegetables each day and definitely stock up on your non-starchy veggies at the peaks of their seasons. Saute them in a bit of olive oil and freeze extras to have them always available.

18 ALLOW YOURSELF SMALL TREATS ONCE A WEEK

Sugary treats will negatively affect your glucose levels, and can add on the pounds. But most doctors and nutritionists agree that no matter your diabetes diagnosis, you need to allow yourself small indulgences every once in a blue moon. The trick is to find unprocessed on-packaged sweets where possible and watch your portions and the frequency of eating these treats. So it's allowed to consume a few pieces of pineapple or some unsweetened Greek yogurt with berries or a small sizes piece of dark chocolate, up to few times per week. once you have a portion of sweets remember to pair your sweets with some protein like chicken, fish, or even some string cheese to lessen your insulin response. In other words, have your small indulgences, but eat them responsibly and after a healthy meal. The goal is to keep your cravings in check and avoid to find yourself binging on these high sugar foods. So avoid the chips, crackers, and other package products and preferably choose some other sweets.

19 CUT DOWN ON PROCESSED SUGAR INTAKE

Even though we recommend allowing yourself those small snacks every once in a while, your true aim is to dramatically cut back on your processed sugar intake in general. That means avoiding the soda, potato chips, and cookies aisles but also skip the white breads, and just say no to those empty calorie fast food meals. Habit changing is extremely difficult, so if you need to wean yourself off a diet high in packaged added -sugar products, give yourself a month to gradually lower the amount of these foods. Eventually your body will adjust to your healthier, more natural lifestyle. And soon you will be craving whole fruits, vegetables, natural sources of fat and protein, and you will leave those old high-sugar food cravings for good.

20 WATCH YOUR PORTIONS

average sizes of our plates, and our food have ballooned. In fact the average frozen pizza size has increased from 200grams to 250 grams in the last 2 decades alone. Potato chip bags, muffin sizes, even your average bagel has increased the size within the last few years. doctors and nutritionists agree that the key to balancing your blood sugar, losing weight and maintaining a healthy lifestyle is the amount of food more which food you eat. Sometimes someone can eat the best quality, most wholesome foods and still be overweight. this happens because they are eating too much food, so we recommend limiting your meal portions to only one plate of food. For example, if you are filling your entire plate with rice, that is just too much, a single serving of pasta should be no larger than ½ a tennis ball, and one serving of meat should actually be no larger or thicker than a deck of cards. That may prove difficult for you at first but our bodies are resilient and they learn. If you cut back on your portions, your firs few meals may leave you feeling hungry, but soon your stomach will adjust and you will begin to feel fuller quicken in no time at all.

CHAPTER 2 FOOD CHOICES

For a healthy and balanced diet it is essential to eat fruit every day. But there are some fruits that contain a unhealthy amount of sugar that cause a spike in blood sugar levels. Choosing diabetes-friendly fruits will hel keep your blood sugar in the healthy range. The following list will direct you to healthy choices:

FRUITS OPTIONS

GOOD FRUITS

Blueberries : they are superfoods loaded with vitamins, minerals and antioxidants. In general all berries are highly recommended.

Peaches: they are low in calories and a great source of fiber, potassium and vitamins. they are a super healthy addiction to daily meals. The antioxidants and vitamin C content help in fighting off free radicals and makes your skin and hair look healthier and softer.

Apricots: they come loaded with beneficial vitamin A, C, potassium, copper and manganese. Their low glycemic index and nutrient content help regulates diabetes.

Apples: they contain fiber that neutralize carb intake and maintain blood sugar levels.

Oranges: they contain vitamin C but also vitamin A and iron. These nutrients reduce inflammation and also protect the heart. The folate and potassium helps in controlling diabetes.

Kiwi: rich in antioxidants they keep immune system strong and also keep heart health. They are the perfect addition to a diabetic meal plan.

Pears: they have a low glycemic index and they are dense is nutrients and vitamins; they get several health benefits like fighting inflammatic and helping with digestion.

Cherries: they have inflammation reducin properties. They also contain melatonin to favor good sleep. They are low in GI index that essential to maintain blood sugar levels.

FRUITS TO AVOID

Pineapple: extremely high on the GI index, contains high amounts of sugar that cause spikes i blood sugar. In case you want to eat these fruit remember to watch your total carb intake to avoi to exceed.

Mango: loaded with a variety of vitamins an minerals they also contain loads of calories, suga and carbs that increase blood sugar.

Watermelons: they contain several healthy benefit and also vitamins and minerals (vitamin A, B, C an folate, fiber, magnesium) but also tons of sugar

Banana: excellent for morning breakfast to sta active throughout the day. They contain high level of carbs, sugar and calories.

Grapes: they help in boosting the immune system and make your hair and skin healthier but contain too much sugar for diabetics.

Raisins: they contain antioxidants and are low in calories but they contain tons of sugar. Enoy them in moderation.

Dates: being dried and processed they are highly concentrated with calories and sugar. Absolutely to avoid!

15 WORST FOOD FOR DIABETES

The relationship between diabetes and nutrition is multifaceted and involves our body's ability to use carbohydrates | protein | and fat: for energy.

As follows a list to help you choosing your meals and avoid the 15 worst foods fo diabetics

15 LOW-FAT PACKAGED FOOD

Even if this food is low-fat often is full of sugar (ex low-fat yogurt, low-fat chips, low-fat crackers, low-fat cereals have actually 25% pure sugar)and often full of the worst kind of sugars that is HIGH FRUCTOSE CORN SYRUP

14 PACKAGED SAUCES

if you check the nutrition labels of these sauces you will discover how much hidden sugar is added to these products. Furthermore many of these products contain a long list of unhealthy chemicals and preservatives (to keep these items sit on shelves for months at a time) also they contain high amount of salt

13 BBQ SAUCES

they are delicious because basically are full of pure sugar -1 TABLESPOON of store-bought bbq sauce contains 7 grams of sugar.

12 PACKAGED SALAD DRESSINGS

Salads are healthy but high-sugar and high carbs dressings totally defeat the purpose of the healthy salad (from ranch to vinaigrette all the dressings contain lots of sugar and low-fat ones even more)

Try making your own dressing at home (1 tbsp olive oil -1/3 tbsp balsamic vinegar-1 lemon juice) to avoid extra and unneeded sugar

11 PACKAGED SOUPS

Sounds nutrition but contain high fructose corn syrup or other sugars such as dextrose or sucrose; if you really want a warm comfort food try to prepare it at home with vegetable or chicken

10 CANNED FRUITS

they are meant to sit on shelves for months and these cans are filled to the brim with sugar-loaded syrups – it works as preservatives but you will eat them

furthermore, the process of canning fresh food remove most of the vitamin C FROM THOSE FRUITS.

9 PROTEIN BARS

Even if they seems to be a source of health and quick of energy actually most of these products contain up to 30 grams of added sugar that means they are the same as a candy bar.

If you are looking for protein sources before work out take natural sources of proteins like chicken, fish and nuts

8 SPORTS AND MINERAL DRINKS

They are usually added with HIGH FRUCTOSE CORN SYRUP instead try calorie-free sparkling water added with pieces of fresh fruits or vegetables to give flavor and nutrition

7 SMOOTHIE

often contain more than just fruits such as high-fat ice cream, sugary yogurt or syrup. Consume smoothie will let you consume more than 2 serving per day because fruits are condensed. Furthermore a smoothie contains fiber that have been shredded in a blender becoming less effective for your body, with the effect that you will become hungry sooner.

6 FRUITS JUICES

Are basically pure sugar

5 FRENCH FRIES

First they come from potatoes that contain 40grams of carbs each -it's a high glycemic food. Second deep fried potatoes will spike your blood sugar and add a ton of calories to your meal. Try to make your baked potatoes home and try sweet potatoes that are less starchy than potatoes.

4 PACKAGED SWEET TREATS

Cookies, desserts, snack bars are all full of highly processed sugars

3 WHITE BREAD, WHITE RICE, AND WHITE FLOUR PASTAS

Are made from high starchy carbs that means they will supply you with a large helping of simple sugars but not much fiber. Try to switch to whole or brown grain and your body will be able to process the sugars from brown rice much more effectively.

2 POTATO CHIPS

Even if they are claiming to be low-fat or low-sodium we have to remember they come from starchy potatoes added with additives, preservatives but overall they are basically designed to addict you to that food after just tone bite. That's why it seems so hard to stop eating after the first chip

1 SOFT DRINKS

Each of them contain 7 teaspoons of added sugar. Totally to avoid!

CHAPTER 3 Breakfast

1. Pumpkin-Peanut Butter Single-Serve Muffins

Cooking time: 25 mins | Servings: 2

INGREDIENTS:

- 1 ½ cup canned pumpkin
- 2 tbsp powdered peanut butter
- 2 tbsp coconut flour
- 2 tbsp finely ground flaxseed
- ½ tsp baking powder
- 1 tbsp dried cranberries
- ½ cup water
- 2 large eggs
- ½ tsp vanilla extract
- olive oil cooking spray

DIRECTIONS:

1. Preheat the oven to 350°F.
2. In a medium bowl, stir together the powdered peanut butter, coconut flour, flaxseed, baking powder, dried cranberries, and water.
3. In a separate medium bowl, whisk together the pumpkin and eggs until smooth.
4. Add the pumpkin mixture to the dry ingredients. Stir to combine.
5. Add the vanilla. Mix together well.
6. Spray 2 (8-ounce) ramekins with cooking spray.
7. Spoon half of the batter into each ramekin.
8. Place the ramekins on a baking and carefully transfer the sheet to the preheated oven. Bake for 25 minutes or until a toothpick in the center comes out clean.

NUTRITION: calories 219, fat 99g, protein 13g, carbs 24g, sugars 9g , fiber 10g , sodium 137mg

2. Breakfast Sausage Casserole

Cooking Time: 3h 10 mins | Servings: 6

INGREDIENTS:

- 1 lb. pork sausage
- 1 tbsp garlic powder
- 1 tbsp dried thyme
- 1 tbsp rubbed sage
- ½ tbsp salt
- ½ cup green bell pepper
- ½ cup red bell pepper
- ½ cup red onion
- 1 tbsp ghee
- 12 eggs
- ½ cup coconut milk
- 1 tbsp nutritional yeast

DIRECTIONS:

1. Heat cast-iron pot for about 2 mins over medium heat then cut sausages into small pieces. Add them to the pot to cook for 3 mins.
2. Add in garlic, thyme, sage, and salt to the pot and cook for 5 more mins. Turn off the heat, stir in bell peppers and chopped onion.
3. Grease the slow cooker with ghee. Pour the pork mixture into the bottom of your slow cooker.
4. In another large mixing bowl, mix eggs , milk and nutritional yeast until well combined.
5. Pour the egg mixture over the pork mixture then cover to cook 2-3hours or until the eggs are completely cooked
6. Serve and enjoy when hot.

NUTRITION: calories 484, fat 38g, carbs 5g, proteins 29g, fiber 1.7g, sodium 129mg

3. Crustless Broccoli Cheese Quiche

Cooking Time: 2h 15 mins| Servings: 8

INGREDIENTS:

- 3 cups broccoli
- 9 eggs
- 1 tbsp olive oil
- ¾ tbsp salt and pepper
- ¼ powder onion
- 18 oz cream cheese
- 2 cups colby-jack cheese, shredded

DIRECTIONS:

1. Heat a large skillet with water over the stove to boil, add broccoli once the water starts to boil.
2. Cook for about 3 mins then drain and rinse it with cold water.
3. In a bowl add eggs, pepper , salt , onion powder and cheese. Mix using a hand mixture until the cream cheese and eggs are well incorporated.
4. Grease the slow cooker with olive oil, add broccoli at the bottom then sprinkle over ½ cup of cheese.
5. Pour over the egg mixture on the broccoli.
6. Cover and cook on high for about 2 hours 15 mins. Don't open the lid when cooking.
7. Sprinkle the remaining cheese and cover again for about 10 mins for cheese to melt. Serve!

NUTRITION: calories 297, fat 24g, carbs 4g, protein 16g, fiber 1g, potassium 246mg, sodium 552mg

4. Fruits Breakfast Salad

Cooking Time: 0 mins | Servings:2

INGREDIENTS:

- 1 cored and cubed pear
- ½ tsp cinnamon powder
- 1 peeled and sliced pear
- 2 oz toasted pepitas
- ½ lime juice

DIRECTIONS:

In a bowl, combine the pear using the pear, lime juice, cinnamon and pepitas, toss, divide between small plates and serve enjoying.

NUTRITION: calories 186, fat 4g, carbs 16g ,proteins 9g, fiber 3g, potassium 203mg, sodium 118mg

5. Pesto Egg Casserole

Cooking Time: 2 h 5 mins | Servings:8

INGREDIENTS:

- 10 eggs, beaten
- 1 cup mozzarella, shredded
- 1 tbsp garlic, minced
- alt & pepper to taste
- 8-10 basil leaves, chopped
- 1 cup grape tomatoes, sliced and salted
- 8 oz mozzarella, fresh and cubed
- 6 oz pesto

DIRECTIONS:

1. Mix eggs, mozzarella cheese, minced garlic , salt , and pepper to taste in a mixing bowl.
2. Pour the mixture in a greased slow cooker.
3. Add basil, tomatoes, and mozzarella on top then cook on low for 2 hours.
4. Top with pesto, serve and enjoy.

NUTRITION: calories 416, fat 36g, carbs 5g, protein 18g, fiber 1g, sodium 558mg , potassium 180mg

6. Kiwi Shake

Cooking Time: 0 mins | Servings:1

INGREDIENTS:

- 2 cups kiwi cubed
- 1 pear, peeled and sliced
- 2 oranges , peeled and quartered

- 12-16 ice cubes , crushed

DIRECTIONS:

Place kiwi, pear, oranges, and ice in a blender container.

Blend until smooth. Pour into glasses and serve.

NUTRITION: calories 139 , fat 15g , carbs 36g , protein 2g , fiber 1g , sodium 168mg , potassium 111mg

7. Greek Toast

Cooking Time: 0 mins | Servings:6

INGREDIENTS:

- 1 ½ tsp. reduced-Fat: crumbled feta
- 3 sliced Greek olives
- ¼ mashed avocado
- 1 slice whole wheat bread
- 1 tbsp roasted red pepper hummus
- 1 sliced hardboiled egg
- 3 sliced cherry tomatoes

DIRECTIONS:

1. First , toast the bread and top it with ¼ mashed avocado and 1 tbsp hummus.
2. Add the cherry tomatoes, olives, hardboiled egg and feta.

NUTRITION: calories 333, fat 17g, carbs 33g , protein 16g, fiber 1g, sodium 296mg , potassium 125mg

8. Mushrooms Bites

Cooking Time: 0 mins | Servings:2

INGREDIENTS:

- 4 Portobello mushroom caps
- 3 tbsp coconut aminos
- 2 tbsp sesame oil
- 1 tbsp fresh ginger , minced
- 1 small garlic clove , minced

DIRECTIONS:

1. Set your broiler to low, keeping the rack 6 inches from the heating source
2. Wash mushrooms under cold water and transfer them to a baking sheet
3. Take a bowl and mix in sesame oil, garlic , coconut aminos , ginger and pour the mixture over the mushroom tops
4. Cook for 10 mins

NUTRITION: calories 196, fat 14g , carbs 14g , protein 7g , sg , fiber 1g , sodium 58mg , potassium 131mg

9. Melon Shake

Cooking Time: 0 mins | Servings:1

INGREDIENTS:

- 2 cups chopped melon (cantaloupe, honeydew)
- 2 cups cold water

DIRECTIONS:

Place all ingredients in a blender container. Blend until smooth.

NUTRITION: calories 29, fat 0g, carbs 7g , protein 2g, fiber 1g, sodium 88mg , potassium 111mg

10. German Pancakes

Cooking Time: 15 mins | Servings:10

INGREDIENTS:

- 2/3 cup wholemeal flour
- ¼ tsp vanilla extract , unsweetened
- 1 tbsp brown sugar
- 1 cup milk, low-fat
- 4 eggs
- 1 ¼ cup cream cheese , softened
- 1/3 cup fruit jam for serving, sugar-free

DIRECTIONS:

1. Prepare the batter by taking a medium-sized bowl, add flour in it along with sugar, stir until mixed, whisk in eggs until blended, and then whisk in vanilla and milk until smooth.
2. Take a skillet pan, about 8 inches, spray it with oil and when hot, add 3 tbsps of the prepared batter, tilt the pan to spread the batter evenly, and cook for 45 seconds, or until the bottom is browned.
3. Flip the pancake , continue cooking for 45 seconds until the other side is

browned , and when done , transfer pancake to a plate.

4. Cook nine more pancakes in the same manner and, when done, spread 2 tbsp of cream cheese on one side of the pancake, fold it, and then serve with 1 tbsp of fruit jam.

NUTRITION: calories 74, fat 2g, carbs 10g, protein 16.1g, fiber 0.9g , potassium 146mg , sodium 252mg

11. Vegetables Omelet

Cooking Time: 2 mins | Servings: 8

INGREDIENTS:

- 4 egg whites
- 2 oz goat cheese
- 2 tbsp olive oil
- 2 whole eggs
- 3 cup spinach , fresh
- Cooking spray
- 10 sliced baby Bella mushrooms
- 8 tbsp Sliced red onion

DIRECTIONS:

1. Place a skillet over medium-high heat and add olive.
2. Add the sliced red onions to the pan and stir until translucent. Then, add your mushrooms to the pan and keep stirring until they are slightly brown.
3. Add spinach and stir until they wilted. Season with a tiny bit of pepper and salt. Remove from heat.
4. Spray a small pan with cooking spray and Place over medium heat.
5. Break 2 whole eggs in a small bowl. Add 4 egg whites and whisk to combine.
6. Pour the whisked eggs into the small skillet and allow the mixture to sit for a minute.
7. Use a spatula to gently work your way around the skillet's edges. Raise the skillet and tip it down and around in a circular style to allow the runny eggs to reach the center and cook around the edges of the skillet.
8. Add crumbled goat cheese to a side of the omelet top with your mushroom mixture.
9. Then, gently fold the other side of the omelet over the mushroom side with the spatula.
10. Allowing cooking for thirty seconds. Then, transfer the omelet to a plate.

NUTRITION: calories 412, fat 29g, carbs 18g, protein 25g, fiber 0.9g, potassium 87mg, sodium 105mg

12. Breakfast Bagels

Cooking Time: 2 mins | Servings: 8

INGREDIENTS:

- 1 ¼ cup whole bread flour
- 2 cup whole wheat flour
- 2 tbsp Honey
- 2 tsp Yeast
- 1 ½ cup warm water
- 1 ½ tbsp Olive oil
- 1 tbsp vinegar

DIRECTIONS:

1. In a bread machine, mix all ingredients , and then process on dough cycle.
2. Once done, create 8 pieces shaped like a flattened ball.
3. Make a hole in the center of each ball using your thumb then create a donut shape.
4. In a greased baking sheet, place donut-shaped dough then cover and let it rise about ½ hour.
5. Prepare about 2 inches of water to boil in a large pan.
6. In a boiling water, drop one at a time the bagels and boil for 1 minute, then turn them once.
7. Remove them and return to baking sheet and bake at 350°F for about 20 to 25 mins until golden brown.

NUTRITION: calories 228, fat 4g, carbs 41g , protein 6g, fiber 0.9g, potassium 96mg, sodium 112mg

13. Tex-Mex Omelet

Cooking Time: 0 mins | Servings: 2

INGREDIENTS:

- ¼ cup low-fat mexican cheese
- 2 tbsp water
- 1 tsp organic olive oil
- ¼ tsp black pepper
- 2 eggs
- ¼ cup chunky salsa

DIRECTIONS:

1. In a bowl, combine the eggs with all the water, cheese, salsa and pepper and whisk well.
2. Heat up a pan with all the oil over medium-high heat, add the eggs mix , spread in for the pan , cook for 3 mins , flip , cook for 3 more mins , divide between plates and serve.

NUTRITION: calories 220, fat 4g , carbs 12g , protein 7g, fiber 1g, sodium 279mg , potassium 144mg

14. Mediterranean Toast

Cooking Time: 3 mins | Servings: 6

INGREDIENTS:

- 1 ½ tsp. reduced-fat crumbled feta
- 3 sliced greek olives
- ¼ mashed avocado
- 1 slice good whole wheat bread
- 1 tbsp roasted red pepper hummus
- 1 sliced hardboiled egg
- 3 sliced cherry tomatoes

DIRECTIONS:

1. First , toast the bread and top it with ¼ mashed avocado and 1 tbsp hummus.
2. Add the cherry tomatoes, olives, hardboiled egg and feta.

NUTRITION: calories 333 , fat 17g , carbs 33g , protein 16g , sodium 258mg , potassium 180mg

15. Tomatoes Eggs

Cooking Time: 3 mins | Servings: 2

INGREDIENTS:

- 2 whole eggs
- ½ cup canned tomatoes
- ½ cup canned tomatoes
- ¼ cup fresh basil leaves, roughly chopped
- ½ garlic clove , minced
- ¼ tsp chili powder
- ¼ tsp sunflower seeds
- ½ tsp olive oil

DIRECTIONS:

1. Preheat your oven to 375°F
2. Take a small baking dish and grease with olive oil
3. Add garlic , basil , tomatoes chili , olive oil into a dish and stir
4. Crack eggs into a dish, keeping space between the two
5. Sprinkle the whole dish with sunflower seeds and pepper
6. Place in oven and cook for 12 mins until eggs are set and tomatoes are bubbling
7. Serve with basil on top

NUTRITION: calories 235, fat 18g, carbs 7g , protein 15g, fiber 1g, sodium 248g, potassium 123mg

16. Breakfast Burrito

Cooking Time: 3 mins | Servings: 2

INGREDIENTS:

- 4 eggs
- 2 flour tortillas, burrito size
- 3 tbsps green chiles , diced
- ½ tsp hot pepper sauce
- ¼ tsp ground cumin

DIRECTIONS:

1. Take a medium-sized skillet pan, place it over medium heat , grease it with oil , and let it get hot.
2. Crack eggs in a bowl, add chilies, hot sauce, and cumin, whisk until combined, then pour the egg mixture in the hot skillet and cook for 2 minutes, or until

eggs have been cooked to the desired level.

3. Meanwhile, heat the tortillas by microwaving them for 20 seconds until hot.
4. When eggs have cooked, distribute evenly between hot tortillas, and roll it up like a burrito.

NUTRITION: calories 366, fat 18g, carbs 33g , protein 18g, sodium 179mg, potassium 144mg

17. Mushroom and Red Pepper Omelet

Cooking Time: 12 mins | Servings: 2

INGREDIENTS:

- ¼ cup sweet red peppers , diced
- ½ cup mushrooms , diced
- 2 tbsps white onion , diced
- ¼ tsp ground black pepper
- 1 tsp Worcestershire sauce
- 2 tsps unsalted butter
- 3 eggs
- 2 tbsps whipped cream cheese

DIRECTIONS:

1. Take a medium-sized skillet pan , place it over medium heat , add 1 tsp butter and when it melts , add onions and mushrooms. Cook for 5 mins , or until onions are tender.
2. Stir in red pepper, then transfer vegetables to
3. a plate and set aside until needed.
4. Crack the eggs in a bowl, add Worcestershire sauce , and whisk until combined.
5. Return skillet pan over medium heat, add remaining butter and when it melts , pour in the egg mixture , and cook for 2 mins , or until omelet is partially cooked.
6. Then top cooked vegetables on one side of the omelet, top with cream cheese, and continue cooking until omelet is cooked completely.
7. When done, remove the pan from the heat, cover the filling of the omelet by folding the other half of the omelet , sprinkle it with black pepper , and then divide the omelet into two.

NUTRITION: calories 199, fat 15g, carbs 4g , protein 11g, sodium 239mg, potassium 124mg

18. Broccoli Frittata with Ham and Peppers

Cooking Time: 4 hours | Servings: 4

INGREDIENTS:

- 1 cup sliced sweet peppers
- 8 oz cubed ham
- 2 cups broccoli, frozen
- 1 cup half and half
- 4 eggs
- 2 tbsp pepper , ground
- 1 tbsp salt
- 1 cup cheddar cheese, shredded

DIRECTIONS:

1. Grease a pan, 6x3, with butter then arrange sweet peppers to the pan bottom.
2. Place ham over the sweet peppers and cover with broccoli.
3. Meanwhile, whisk together half and half, eggs , ground pepper , and salt in a bowl.
4. Stir cheese into the egg mixture then pour over ham and vegetables. Cover with a silicone lid.
5. Pour 2 cups water into inner liner of a slow cooker with a steamer rack inside.
6. Place the pan on top of the steamer rack then cook for about 4 hours on high.
7. Transfer the frittata to a plate.

NUTRITION: calories 418, fat 30g, carbs 9g, proteins 28g, sodium 246mg, potassium 569mg

19. Fruits Bowl

Cooking Time: 5 mins | Servings: 2

INGREDIENTS:

- 1 cup chopped melon
- 1 sliced pear
- 1 cup chopped oranges

- 1 cup almond milk

DIRECTIONS:

In a bowl, combine the mango with all the current pear, pineapple and almond milk, stir, divide into smaller bowls and serve each day.

NUTRITION: calories 185, fat 2g, carbs 12g, proteins 6g, sodium 106mg, potassium 159mg

20. Crispy Tofu

Cooking Time: 30 mins | Servings: 8

INGREDIENTS:

- 1 lb extra-firm tofu, drained and sliced
- 2 tbsp olive oil
- 1 cup almond meal
- 1 tbsp yeast
- ½ tsp onion powder
- ½ tsp oregano

DIRECTIONS:

1. Add all ingredients except tofu and olive oil in a shallow bowl and mix well
2. Preheat your oven to 400°F
3. In a wide bowl, add the almond meal and mix well
4. Brush tofu with olive oil, dip into the mix and coat well
5. Line a baking sheet with parchment paper
6. Transfer coated tofu to the baking sheet
7. Bake for 20-30 minutes, making sure to flip once until golden brown

NUTRITION: calories 285, fat 20g, carbs 9g, proteins 16g, sodium 86mg, potassium 148mg

21. Spinach Muffins

Cooking Time: 30 mins | Servings: 6

INGREDIENTS:

- 4 oz spinach
- ½ cup non-fat milk
- cooking spray
- 6 eggs
- 1 cup crumbled low-fat cheese
- ½ cup chopped roasted red pepper

DIRECTIONS:

1. In a bowl, combine the eggs using the milk , cheese , spinach , red pepper and whisk well.
2. Grease a muffin tray with cooking spray, divide the muffin mix, introduce within the oven and bake at 350°F for around 30 minutes.
3. Divide between plates and serve enjoying

NUTRITION: calories 155, fat 10g, carbs 9g, proteins 10g , sodium 186mg , potassium 349mg

22. Breakfast Sandwich

Cooking Time: 5 mins | Servings: 2

INGREDIENTS:

- 1 multigrain bagel, halved
- 2 tbsps cream cheese , divided
- 2 slices tomato
- 1 slice red onion
- 1 cup microgreens

DIRECTIONS:

1. Toast the bagel in a toaster lightly.
2. Spread the cream cheese on each of the bagel halves, then top each half with 1 slice of tomato and a couple of onion rings.
3. Season with the black pepper.
4. Top each half with ½ cup of microgreens and serve.

NUTRITION: calories 156, fat 6g, carbs 22g , proteins 5g, sodium 195mg , potassium 163mg

23. Chia Seeds Breakfast

Cooking Time: 5 mins | Servings: 4

INGREDIENTS:

- 3 cup coconut milk
- 1 tsp grated lemon zest
- 4 tbsp Chia seeds
- 1 cup blueberries
- 4 tbsp coconut sugar
- 2 cup old-fashioned oats

DIRECTIONS:

In a bowl, combine the oats with chia seeds, sugar, milk, lemon zest and blueberries , stir , and divide into cups whilst within the fridge for 8 hours. am over the sweet peppers and cover with broccoli.

NUTRITION: calories 283, fat 12g , carbs 13g , proteins 15g , sodium 125mg , potassium 63mg

24. Green Breakfast Soup

Cooking Time: 5 mins | Servings: 2

INGREDIENTS:

- 2 cups of spinach
- 1 avocado, halved
- 2 cups of low-Sodium vegetable or chicken broth
- 1 tsp of ground coriander
- 1 tsp of ground cumin
- 1 tsp of ground turmeric
- Freshly ground black pepper

DIRECTIONS:

1. Using a food processor, add the spinach, avocado, broth, coriander, cumin, and turmeric. Process until smooth.
2. Transfer the mixture to a small saucepan over medium heat , and cook until heated through , 2 to 3 mins—season with pepper.
3. **Lower Sodium tip:** If you want to lower the Sodium further, consider making your own Simple Chicken Broth for more control over the ingredients. Freeze the broth in 2-cup portions so you can make quick soups when needed.

NUTRITION: calories 221, fat 18g , carbs 15g , proteins 5g, sodium 170mg, potassium 551mg

25. Sweet Porridge

Cooking Time: 0 mins | Servings: 2

INGREDIENTS:

- 2 tbsps coconut flour
- 2 tbsps vanilla protein powder
- 3 tbsps golden flaxseed meal
- 1 ½ cups almond milk , unsweetened
- powdered erythritol

DIRECTIONS:

1. Take a bowl and mix in flaxseed meal, Protein powder, coconut flour and mix well.
2. Add mix to the saucepan (placed over medium heat).
3. Add almond milk and stir, let the mixture thicken.
4. Add your desired amount of sweetener and serve.

NUTRITION: calories 259, fat 13g , carbs 5g , proteins 16g , sodium 31mg , potassium 124mg

26. Hungarian Porridge

Cooking Time: 8 mins | Servings: 2

INGREDIENTS:

- 1/3 cup coconut cream
- 1 tbsp chia seeds
- 1 tbsp ground flaxseed
- ½ cup of water
- 1 tsp vanilla extract
- 1 tbsp almond butter

DIRECTIONS:

1. Add chia seeds, coconut cream, flaxseed , water , and vanilla to a small pot.
2. Stir and let it sit for 5 mins. Add butter and place pot over low heat.
3. Keep stirring as butter melts. Once the porridge is hot/not boiling, pour into a bowl.
4. Add a few berries or a dash of cream for extra flavor.

NUTRITION: calories 410, fat 38g, carbs 10g, proteins 6g , sodium 11mg , potassium 100mg

27. Nuts Porridge

Cooking Time: 15 mins | Servings: 2

INGREDIENTS:

- 1 cup cashew nuts, raw and unsalted
- 1 cup pecan, halved
- 2 tbsps stevia

- 4 tsps coconut oil, melted
- 2 cups of water

DIRECTIONS:

1. Chop the nuts in a food processor and form a smooth paste.
2. Add water, oil, stevia to the nut paste and transfer the mix to a saucepan.
3. Stir cook for 5 mins on high heat.
4. Reduce heat to low and simmer for 10 mins.

NUTRITION: calories 260 , fat 22g , carbs 13g , proteins 6g , sodium 30mg , potassium 124mg

28. Healthy Granola Bowl

Cooking Time: 25 mins | Servings: 6

INGREDIENTS:

- 1-once porridge oats
- 2 tsp maple syrup
- 4 medium pears
- 4 pots of cream cheese
- 5 oz fresh berries
- ¼ oz pumpkin /sunflower /dry chia seeds
- ¼ oz dehydrated coconut

DIRECTIONS:

1. Preheat your oven to 300° F
2. Take a baking tray and line with baking paper
3. Add oats , maple syrup , and seeds in a large bowl
5. Spread mix on a baking tray. Spray coconut oil on top and bake for 20 minutes, making sure to keep stirring from time to time
6. Sprinkle coconut after the first 15 mins
7. Remove from oven and let it cool
8. Take a bowl and layer sliced pears on top of cream cheese
9. Spread the cooled granola mix on top and serve with a topping of berries

NUTRITION: calories 446, fat 29, carbs 37g , proteins 13g, sugars 4g, sodium 145mg, potassium 389mg

29. Scrambled Eggs

Cooking Time: 10 mins | Servings: 1

INGREDIENTS:

- ½ cup cream cheese
- ¼ cup unsweetened almond or rice milk
- 3 eggs
- 2 egg whites
- 1 tbsp finely chopped scallion , green part only
- 2 tbsps unsalted butter

DIRECTIONS:

1. In a mixing bowl, whisk eggs and whites. Add cream cheese, milk , scallions , and tarragon. Combine to mix well with each other.
2. Take a medium saucepan or skillet, add butter. Heat over medium heat.
3. Add egg mixture and stir-cook for 4-5 mins until eggs are scrambled evenly.

NUTRITION: calories 238 , fat 17g , carbs 3g , proteins 8g , sodium 211mg , potassium 152mg

30. Peach Berry Parfait

Cooking Time: 5 mins | Servings: 2

INGREDIENTS:

- 1 cup of plain, unsweetened yogurt, divided
- 1 tsp of vanilla extract
- 1 small peach , diced
- ½ cup of blueberries
- 2 tbsps of walnut pieces

DIRECTIONS:

1. Add the yogurt and vanilla in a bowl together , then add 2 tbsps of yogurt to each of 2 cups. Divide the diced peach and the blueberries between the cups, and top with the remaining yogurt.
2. Sprinkle each cup with 1 tbsp of walnut pieces.
3. **Cooking tip:** Make these up to three days in advance, cover, and refrigerate until ready to eat.

NUTRITION: calories 191, fat 10g, carbs 14g ,proteins 12g, sodium 40mg, potassium 327mg

31. Buckwheat Granola

Cooking Time: 45 mins | Servings: 1

INGREDIENTS:

- 2 cups oats
- 1 cup buckwheat
- 1 cup sunflower seeds
- 1 cup pumpkin seeds
- ½ cup dates , pitted and chopped
- 1 cup apple puree
- 6 tbsps coconut oil
- 5 tbsps cocoa powder
- 1 tsp fresh grated ginger

DIRECTIONS:

1. In a large bowl, mix the oats with the buckwheat, sunflower seeds , pumpkin seeds , dates , apple puree , oil , cocoa powder , and ginger then stir well.
2. Spread on a lined baking sheet, press well, and place in the oven at 360°F for 45 mins. Leave the granola to cool down, slice, and serve for breakfast.

NUTRITION: calories 161, fat 3g, carbs 11g , proteins 8g, sodium 31mg, potassium 14mg

32. French Crêpes

Cooking Time: 10 mins | Servings: 1

INGREDIENTS:

- 2 eggs
- 1 tsp vanilla extract
- ½ cup almond milk , unsweetened
- ½ cup water
- 2 tbsps agave nectar
- 1 cup coconut flour
- 3 tbsps coconut oil, melted

DIRECTIONS:

1. In a bowl, whisk the eggs with the vanilla extract, almond milk, water, and agave nectar.
2. Add the flour and 2 tbsps oil gradually and stir until you obtain a smooth batter.
3. Heat a pan with the rest of the oil over medium heat, add some of the batter, spread into the pan , and cook the crepe until it's golden on both sides then transfer to a plate.
4. Repeat with the rest of the batter and serve the crepes.

NUTRITION: calories 121, fat 3g, carbs 14g , proteins 6g , sodium 31mg , potassium 94mg

33. Mushrooms Tofu Bowl

Cooking Time: 10 mins | Servings: 2

INGREDIENTS:

- 1 tbsp of chopped shallots
- ½ cup of sliced white mushrooms
- ⅓ cup medium-firm tofu , crumbled
- ⅓ tsp turmeric
- 1 tsp of cumin
- ⅓ tsp of smoked paprika
- 3 tbsps of vegetable oil

DIRECTIONS:

1. Take a medium saucepan or skillet, add oil. Heat over medium heat.
2. Add shallots, mushrooms, and stir-cook until they become softened for 3-4 mins.
3. Add tofu, salt, spices, and stir-cook until tofu is tender and cooked well.
4. Serve warm.

NUTRITION: calories 217, fat 21g, carbs 11g , proteins 8g , sodium 301mg, potassium 147mg

34. Coconut Pancakes

Cooking Time: 10 mins | Servings: 2

INGREDIENTS:

- 2 egg whites
- 2 tbsps wholemeal flour
- 3 tbsp. of coconut shavings
- 2 tbsp. of coconut milk (optional)
- 1 tbsp. of coconut oil

DIRECTIONS:

1. Get a bowl and combine all the ingredients.
2. Mix well until you get a thick batter.
3. Heat a skillet on medium heat and heat the coconut oil.

4. Pour half the mixture to the center of the pan, forming a pancake and cook through for 3-4 mins on each side.

5. Serve with your choice of berries on the top.

NUTRITION: calories 177, fat 13g , carbs 12g , proteins 5g, sodium 133mg, potassium 135mg

35. French Toast

Cooking Time: 8 mins | Servings: 4

INGREDIENTS:

- 4 slices of whole bread, cut in half diagonally
- 3 whole eggs and 1 egg white
- 1 cup of plain almond milk
- 2 tbsp. of canola oil
- 1 tsp. of cinnamon

DIRECTIONS:

1. Preheat your oven to 400°F
2. Beat the eggs and the almond milk.
3. Heat the oil in a pan.
4. Dip each bread slice/triangle into the egg and almond milk mixture.
5. Fry in the pan until golden brown on each side.
6. Place the toasts in a baking sheet and let cook in the oven for another 5 mins.
7. Serve warm and drizzle with some honey, icing sugar, or cinnamon on top.

NUTRITION: calories 291, fat 16g, carbs 25g , proteins 9.2g, sodium 211mg, potassium 97mg

36. Savory Muffins

Cooking Time: 35 mins | Servings: 12

INGREDIENTS:

- 2 cups of corn flakes
- ½ cup almond milk
- 4 large eggs
- 2 tbsp. of olive oil
- ½ cup of almond milk
- 1 medium white onion , sliced
- 1 cup of plain Greek yogurt
- ¼ cup of pecans , chopped
- 1 tbsp. mixed seasoning blend

DIRECTIONS:

1. Preheat the oven at 350°F.
2. Heat the olive oil in the pan. Saute the onions with the pecans and seasoning blend for a couple of mins.
3. Add the rest of the ingredients and toss well.
4. Split the mixture into 12 small muffin cups (lightly greased) and bake for 30–35 mins or until an inserted knife or toothpick is coming out clean.
5. Serve warm or keep at room temperature for a couple of days.

NUTRITION: calories 106, fat 5g, carbs 8.5g , proteins 4.7g , sodium 52mg, potassium 87mg

37. Classical Pancakes

Cooking Time: 20 mins | Servings: 10

INGREDIENTS:

- 2/3 cups whole wheat flour
- 4 large eggs
- 2 tbsp. of sugar
- ½ tsp. of lemon zest
- 1 cup of low-fat milk
- ¼ tsp. of vanilla extract

DIRECTIONS:

1. Mix flour and sugar, then whisk in the eggs and combine well in a medium.
2. Put then the milk, vanilla, and lemon zest to the mix and whisk well.
3. Spray a small 8–10-inch pan with cooking spray and pour around 4 tbsp. of the mixture and distribute evenly by tilting the pan from one side to another.
4. Cook until the batter is solid and light golden brown (around 50 seconds on each side). Flip.
5. Repeat the above two steps until all the batter has finished.

NUTRITION: calories 74, fat 2g, carbs 10.5g , proteins 4.7g, sodium 39mg, potassium 73mg

38. Homemade Rice Milk

Cooking Time: 0 | Servings: 4

INGREDIENTS:

- 1 cup brown rice
- 4 cups of water
- ½ tsp of vanilla extract (optional)

DIRECTIONS:

1. In a dry skillet, set at medium heat, toast the rice until lightly browned, about 5 mins.
2. Transfer the rice to a jar or bowl, and add the water. Cover, refrigerate and soak overnight.
3. In a blender, add the rice and water, along with the vanilla (if using), and process until smooth.
4. Place a fine-mesh strainer over a glass jar or bowl, and pour the milk into it. Serve immediately, or cover, refrigerate and serve within three days. Shake before using it.

NUTRITION: calories 112, fat 0g , carbs 24g , proteins 0g , sodium 80mg , potassium 55mg

39. Blueberry Muffins

Cooking Time: 35 mins | Servings: 5

INGREDIENTS:

- 3 egg whites
- 1/4 cup whole wheat flour
- 1 tbsp. of coconut flour
- 1 tsp. of baking soda
- 1 tbsp. of nutmeg , grated
- 1 tsp. of vanilla extract
- 1 tsp. of stevia
- 1/4 cup of fresh blueberries

DIRECTIONS:

1. Set the oven 325°F for preheating.
2. Add all the ingredients in a bowl.
3. Divide the batter into 4 and spoon into a lightly oiled muffin tin.
4. Bake in the oven for 15–20 mins or until cooked through.
5. Your knife should pull out clean from the middle of the muffin once done.
6. Allow to cool on a wired rack before serving.

NUTRITION: calories 48, fat 1g, carbs 8g , proteins 2g , sodium 288mg , potassium 44mg

40. Ginger and Lemon Iced-Tea

Cooking Time: 0 | Servings: 2

INGREDIENTS:

- 2 cups of concentrated green or matcha tea, served hot
- 1 lemon , cut into wedges
- 1/4 cup of crystallized ginger, chopped into fine pieces

DIRECTIONS:

1. Get a glass container and mix the tea with the ginger and then cover and chill for 3 hours.
2. Strain and pour into serving glasses on top of ice if you wish.
3. Garnish with a wedge of lemon to serve.

NUTRITION: calories 20, fat 0g , carbs 5g, proteins 1g , sodium 4mg, potassium 106mg

41. Tropical Juice

Cooking Time: 0 | Servings: 2

INGREDIENTS:

- 2 cups of melon, chunks.
- 1 cup strawberries
- 1/2 cup of low-fat coconut milk
- 1 cup of water

DIRECTIONS:

In a blender, combine all the ingredients. Process until smooth.

Tip: You can use, non-dairy milk, such as almond.

NUTRITION: calories 55, fat 9g, carbs 6g , proteins 7g , sodium 111mg , potassium 129mg

42. Berries Milkshake

Cooking Time: 0 | Servings: 4

INGREDIENTS:

- 1 cup of rice milk
- ½ cup blueberries
- ½ cup of blackberries
- 2 or 3 ice cubes

DIRECTIONS:

Add ingredients together in a blender, blending until smooth , and then serve in tall glasses.

NUTRITION: calories 45, fat 1g , carbs 7g , proteins 2g , sodium 29 mg , potassium 118mg

43. Veggie Cheese Omelet

Cooking Time: 2 hours | Servings: 4

INGREDIENTS:

- 6 eggs
- ⅛ tbsp chili powder
- ¼ tbsp salt and pepper
- ⅛ tbsp garlic powder
- 1 cup broccoli florets
- 1 finely chopped yellow onion , small
- 1 thinly sliced red bell pepper
- 1 minced garlic clove
- ½ cup milk
- 1 cup cheddar cheese , shredded
- *for garnish:*
- chopped onions
- chopped tomatoes
- fresh parsley

DIRECTIONS:

1. Grease slow cooker inside lightly with cooking spray then set aside.
2. Combine eggs , chili powder , pepper , salt, and garlic powder in a mixing bowl. Whisk the mixture using eggbeaters until well combined.
3. Add broccoli florets, onions, sliced peppers , and garlic to the egg mixture , stir.
4. Pour the mixture to the slow cooker, cover and cook for about 2 hours on high. Start to Check on the omelet at 1 hour 30 mins. When eggs are set the omelet is done.
5. Splash with cheese the cover again for about 2-3 mins until cheese melts. Turn the slow cooker off.
6. Cut into 8 wedges then transfer to a plate , serving.
7. Garnish with chopped onions, chopped tomatoes , and fresh parsley.
8. Serve and enjoy.

NUTRITION: calories 134, fat 8g, carbs 4g , protein 12g, sodium 573mg, potassium 315mg

44. Spicy Corn Burritos

Cooking Time: 20 mins | Servings: 4

INGREDIENTS:

- 3 tbsps of olive oil , divided
- 1 (10-ounce) package of frozen cooked brown rice
- 1½ cups of frozen yellow corn
- 1 tbsp of chili powder
- 1 cup of shredded pepper jack cheese
- 4 large or 6 small corn tortillas

DIRECTIONS:

1. Put the skillet in over medium heat and put 2 tbsps of olive oil. Add the rice , corn , and chili powder and cook for 4 to 6 mins , or until the ingredients are hot.
2. transfer the ingredients from the pan into a medium bowl. Let cool for 15 mins.
3. Stir the cheese into the rice mixture.
4. Heat the tortillas using the directions from the package to make them pliable. Fill the corn tortillas with the rice mixture , then roll them up.
5. At this point , you can serve them as is , or you can fry them first. Heat the remaining tbsp of olive oil in a large skillet. Fry the burritos, seam-side down at first, turning once , until they are brown and crisp , about 4 to 6 mins per side , then serve.

NUTRITION: calories 388, carbs 41g, protein 13g , fat 24g , phosphorus 304mg , potassium 282mg , sodium 510mg

45. Thai Chicken and Vegetable Curry

Cooking Time: 20 mins | Servings: 4

INGREDIENTS:

- 1 lb chicken breasts
- 1 ½ cups cauliflower florets
- 1 clove garlic , minced
- 1 cup light coconut milk
- 1 cup low Sodium chicken broth
- 1 medium bell pepper , julienned
- 1 medium onion , halved and sliced
- 1 tbsp fish sauce or low Sodium soy sauce
- 1 tbsp fresh ginger , minced
- 1 tbsp lime juice
- 1 tsp light brown sugar
- 1 tsp red curry paste
- 2 cups baby spinach
- 2 tsp olive oil
- Lime wedges

DIRECTIONS:

1. Heat oil in a skillet over medium high flame.
2. Sauté the onion and bell pepper for four mins or until soft.
3. Add the ginger | garlic and curry paste. Mix then add the chicken. Sauté for two mins before adding the coconut milk | broth | brown sugar and fish sauce
4. Add the cauliflowers and reduce the heat to medium low.
5. Simmer and stir the mixture occasionally until the chicken is cooked through.
6. Add the spinach and lime juice and cook until the spinach has wilted.
7. Serve immediately with lime wedges.

NUTRITION: calories 394 , carbs 11g , protein 29g , fat 28g , phosphorus: 316mg , potassium 745mg , sodium 252

46. Lentil and Zucchini Omelet

Cooking time: 45 mins | Servings: 2

INGREDIENTS:

- 1/3 cup dried lentils, picked over , rinsed , and drained
- 1 cup water
- olive oil cooking spray
- 1 medium zucchini, thinly sliced
- ½ cup grape tomatoes, coarsely chopped
- 1 garlic clove, chopped
- 2 tbsp chopped fresh chives
- 2 large eggs
- 2 tbsp nonfat: milk

DIRECTIONS:

1. Preheat the oven to 350°F.
2. In a small saucepan set over high heat , heat the water until it boils.
3. Add the lentils. Reduce the heat to low. Simmer for about 15 mins , or until most of the liquid has been absorbed. In a colander , drain and set aside.
4. Lightly coat an 8- or 9-inch nonstick skillet with cooking spray. Place the skillet over medium-high heat.
5. Add the zucchini, tomatoes, garlic , and chives. Sauté for 5 to 10 mins , stirring frequently , or until soft.
6. Add the lentils to the skillet.
7. In a medium bowl, beat together the eggs and milk with a fork.
8. Lightly coat a small casserole or

NUTRITION: calories 304, carbs 15g , protein 27g , fat 22g

47. Brussels Sprouts and Egg Scramble

Cooking time: 20 mins | Servings: 4

INGREDIENTS:

- 8 large eggs
- avocado oil cooking spray
- 4 slices turkey bacon
- 20 brussels sprouts, halved lengthwise
- ¼ cup crumbled feta, for garnish

DIRECTIONS:

1. Heat a large skillet over medium heat. When hot, coat the cooking surface with cooking spray and cook the bacon to your liking.
2. Carefully remove the bacon from the pan and set it on a plate lined with a paper towel to drain and cool.
3. Place the Brussels sprouts in the skillet cut-side down , and cook for 3 mins.
4. Reduce the heat to medium-low. Flip the Brussels sprouts , move them to one side of the skillet , and cover. Cook for another 3 mins.
5. Uncover. Cook the eggs to over-medium alongside the Brussels sprouts , or to your liking.
6. Crumble the bacon once it has cooled.
7. Divide the Brussels sprouts into 4 portions and top each portion with one-quarter of the crumbled bacon and 2 eggs. Add 1 tbsp of feta to each portion.

NUTRITION: calories 253 , fat 15g , protein 21g , carbs 10g , sugars 4g , fiber 4g , sodium 343mg

48. Berries Smoothie

Cooking time: 0 mins | Servings: 4

INGREDIENTS:

- 2 cups frozen berries of choice
- 1 cup plain low-fat greek yogurt
- 1 cup unsweetened vanilla almond milk
- ½ cup natural almond butter

DIRECTIONS:

1. Put the berries , yogurt , almond milk , and almond butter into a blender and blend until smooth. If the smoothie is too thick , add more almond milk to thin.

NUTRITION: calories 277, fat 18g , protein 13g , carbs 19g , sugars 11g , fiber 6g , sodium 140mg

49. Greek Yogurt Bowl

Cooking time: 0 mins | Servings: 2

INGREDIENTS:

- 1½ cups plain low-fat: Greek yogurt
- 2 kiwis | peeled and sliced
- 2 tbsp shredded coconut flakes
- 2 tbsp halved walnuts
- 1 tbsp chia seeds
- 2 tsps honey | divided (optional)

DIRECTIONS:

1. Divide the yogurt between two small bowls.
2. Top each serving of yogurt with half of the kiwi slices , coconut flakes , walnuts , chia seeds , and honey (if using).

NUTRITION: calories 260, fat 9g , protein 21g , carbs 23g, sugars 14g, fiber 6g , sodium 83mg

50. Pumpkin Walnut Bowl

Cooking time: 0 mins | Servings: 2

INGREDIENTS:

- 1 cup plain Greek yogurt
- ½ cup canned pumpkin purée (not pumpkin pie mix)
- 1 tsp pumpkin pie spice
- 2 (1-gram) packets stevia
- ½ tsp vanilla extract
- Pinch sea salt
- ½ cup chopped walnuts

DIRECTIONS:

1. In a bowl, whisk together the yogurt , pumpkin purée , pumpkin pie spice , stevia , vanilla , and salt (or blend in a blender).
2. Spoon into two bowls. Serve topped with the chopped walnuts.

NUTRITION: calories 292 , fat 23g , protein 9g , carbs 15g , sugars 6g , fiber 4g , sodium 85mg

51. Low-Carb Peanut Butter Pancakes

Cooking time: 10 mins | Servings: 2

INGREDIENTS:

- 1 cup almond flour
- ½ tsp baking soda
- 2 large eggs
- Pinch sea salt
- ¼ cup sparkling water

- 2 tbsp canola oil, plus more for cooking
- 4 tbsp peanut butter

DIRECTIONS:

1. Heat a nonstick griddle over medium-high heat.
2. In a small bowl, whisk together the almond flour , baking soda , and salt.
3. In a glass measuring cup, whisk together the eggs , water , and oil.
4. Pour the liquid ingredients into the dry ingredients and mix gently until just combined.
5. Brush a small amount of canola oil onto the griddle.
6. Using all the batter, spoon four pancakes onto the griddle.
7. Cook until set on one side, about 3 mins. Flip with a spatula and continue cooking on the other side.
8. Before serving, spread each pancake with 1 tbsp of the peanut butter.

NUTRITION: calories 454, fat 41g , protein 17g , carbs 8g , sugars 3g, fiber 3g, sodium 408mg

52. Broccoli and Shiitake Omelet

Cooking time: 10 mins | Servings: 4

INGREDIENTS:

- 1 cup broccoli florets
- 1 cup sliced shiitake mushrooms
- 2 tbsp olive oil
- ½ onion, finely chopped
- 1 garlic clove , minced
- 8 large eggs , beaten
- ½ tsp sea salt
- ½ cup grated Parmesan cheese

DIRECTIONS:

1. Preheat the oven broiler on high.
2. In a medium ovenproof skillet over medium-high heat, heat the olive oil until it shimmers.
3. Add the onion, broccoli, and mushrooms, and cook, stirring occasionally , until the vegetables start to brown , about 5 mins. Add the garlic and cook , stirring constantly , for 30 seconds. Arrange the vegetables in an even layer on the bottom of the pan.
4. While the vegetables cook , in a small bowl , whisk together the eggs and salt. Carefully pour the eggs over the vegetables. Cook without stirring , allowing the eggs to set around the vegetables. As the eggs begin to set around the edges , use a spatula to pull the edges away from the sides of the pan. Tilt the pan and allow the uncooked eggs to run into the spaces. Cook 1 to 2 mins more , until it sets around the edges. The eggs will still be runny on top.
5. Sprinkle with the Parmesan and place the pan in the broiler. Broil until brown and puffy , about 3 mins.
6. Cut into wedges to serve.

NUTRITION: calories 280, fat 21g , protein 19g , carbs 7g , sugars 1g , fiber 2g , sodium 654mg

53. Sausage and Pepper Breakfast Burrito

Cooking time: 15 mins | Servings: 4

INGREDIENTS:

- 8 oz bulk pork breakfast sausage
- ½ onion , chopped
- 1 green bell pepper, seeded and chopped
- 8 large eggs , beaten
- 4 (6-inch) low-carb tortillas
- 1 cup shredded pepper Jack cheese
- ½ cup sour cream
- ½ cup prepared salsa

DIRECTIONS:

1. In a large nonstick skillet on medium-high heat, cook the sausage, crumbling it with a spoon, until browned, about 5 mins. Add the onion and bell pepper. Cook , stirring , until the veggies are soft , about 3 mins. Add the eggs and cook , stirring , until eggs are set , about 3 mins more.
2. Spoon the egg mixture onto the 4 tortillas. Top each with the cheese and fold into a burrito shape.
3. Serve with sour cream and salsa , if desired.

NUTRITION: calories 485, fat 36g , protein 32g , carbs 13g , sugars 3g, fiber 8g , sodium 810mg

54. Crepe Cakes

Cooking time: 20 mins | Servings: 4

INGREDIENTS:

- 4 large eggs
- Avocado oil cooking spray
- 4 oz plain cream cheese , softened
- 2 medium pears
- ⅛ tsp salt

DIRECTIONS:

1. Heat a large skillet over low heat. Coat the cooking surface with cooking spray , and allow the pan to heat for another 2 to 3 mins.
2. In a medium bowl , mash the cream cheese and pears together with a fork until combined. The pears can be a little chunky.
3. Add the eggs and salt, and mix well.
4. For each cake, drop 2 tbsp of the batter onto the warmed skillet and use the bottom of a large spoon or ladle to spread it thin. Let it cook for 7 to 9 mins.
5. Flip the cake over and cook briefly, about 1 minute.

NUTRITION: calories 175, fat 9g, protein 9g , carbs 15g , sugars 8g, fiber 2g, sodium 213mg

55. Zucchini Bread

Cooking time: 45 mins | Servings: 24

INGREDIENTS:

- 1½ cups gluten-free flour
- 1 cup almond flour
- ½ cup chickpea flour
- 1 tsp salt
- 1 tsp baking powder
- 1 tsp baking soda
- ½ tsp ground nutmeg
- ½ tsp ground cinnamon
- 3 medium eggs
- ¼ cup sunflower seed oil
- 2 ripe pears , mashed
- 2 zucchini, grated , with water squeezed out

DIRECTIONS:

1. Preheat the oven to 350°F. Line a 9 × 13-inch pan with parchment paper.
2. In a large bowl , use a fork or whisk to combine the gluten-free flour , almond flour , chickpea flour , salt , baking powder , baking soda , nutmeg , and cinnamon.
3. In a separate large bowl , beat the eggs , oil , pears , and zucchini together well.
4. Fold the dry ingredients into the wet ingredients , stir until well combined , and pour into the prepared pan.
5. Transfer the pan to the oven , and bake for 40 to 45 mins , or until a butter knife inserted into the center comes out clean. Remove from the oven , and let the bread rest for 15 mins before serving.

NUTRITION: calories 203, fat 11g , protein 6g , carbs 21g , sugars 4g , fiber 4g , sodium 323mg

56. Walnut Granola

Cooking time: 30 mins | Servings: 16

INGREDIENTS:

- 4 cups rolled oats
- 1 cup walnut pieces
- ¼ tsp salt
- 1 tsp ground cinnamon
- 1 tsp ground ginger
- ½ cup coconut oil , melted
- ½ cup unsweetened applesauce
- 1 tsp vanilla extract
- ½ cup dried cherries

DIRECTIONS:

1. Preheat the oven to 350°F. Line a baking sheet with parchment paper.
2. In a large bowl , toss the oats , walnuts , salt , cinnamon , and ginger.
3. In a large measuring cup , combine the coconut oil , applesauce , and vanilla. Pour over the dry mixture and mix well.
4. Transfer the mixture to the prepared baking sheet. Cook for 30 mins , stirring about halfway through. Remove from the

oven and let the granola sit undisturbed until completely cool. Break the granola into pieces, and stir in the dried cherries.

5. Transfer to an airtight container, and store at room temperature for up to 2 weeks.

NUTRITION: calories 224, fat 15g, protein 5g , carbs 20g , sugars 5g , fiber 3g, sodium 30mg

57. Goat Cheese Toast

Cooking time: 10 mins | Servings: 2

INGREDIENTS:

- 2 slices whole-wheat thin-sliced bread
- ½ avocado
- 2 tbsp crumbled goat cheese
- Salt , to taste

DIRECTIONS:

1. In a toaster or broiler, toast the bread until browned.
2. Remove the flesh from the avocado. In a medium bowl , use a fork to mash the avocado flesh. Spread it onto the toast.
3. Sprinkle with the goat cheese and season lightly with salt.
4. Add any toppings and serve.

NUTRITION: calories 137, fat 6g, protein 5g , carbs 18g , sugars 0g , fiber 5g , sodium 195mg

58. Cheesy Spinach Artichoke Casserole

Cooking time: 35 mins | Servings: 8

INGREDIENTS:

Nonstick cooking spray

- 1 (10-ounce) package frozen spinach
- 1 (14-ounce) can artichoke hearts, drained
- ¼ cup finely chopped red bell pepper
- 2 garlic cloves , minced
- 8 eggs , lightly beaten
- ¼ cup unsweetened almond milk
- ½ tsp salt
- ½ tsp freshly ground black pepper
- ½ cup crumbled goat cheese

DIRECTIONS:

1. Preheat the oven to 375°F. Spray an 8-by-8-inch baking dish with nonstick cooking spray.
2. In a large mixing bowl , combine the spinach , artichoke hearts , bell pepper , garlic , eggs , almond milk , salt , and pepper. Stir well to combine.
3. Transfer the mixture to the baking dish. Sprinkle with the goat cheese.
4. Bake for 35 mins until the eggs are set. Serve warm.

NUTRITION: calories 105 , fat 5g , protein 9g , carbs 6g, sugars 1g, fiber 2g, sodium 488mg

59. Fuits & Nuts Oatmeal

Cooking time: 5 mins | Servings: 4

INGREDIENTS:

- 1 cup steel cut oats
- 1 cup unsweetened almond milk
- 1 ½ cups coconut water or water
- ¾ cup frozen chopped peaches
- ¾ cup frozen mango chunks
- 1 (2-inch) vanilla bean , scraped (seeds and pod)
- Ground cinnamon
- ¼ cup chopped unsalted macadamia nuts

DIRECTIONS:

1. In the electric pressure cooker, combine the oats, almond milk, coconut water, peaches, mango chunks, and vanilla bean seeds and pod. Stir well.
2. Close and lock the lid of the pressure cooker. Set the valve to sealing.
3. Cook on high pressure for 5 mins.
4. When the cooking is complete, allow the pressure to release naturally for 10 mins, then quick release any remaining pressure. Hit Cancel.
5. Once the pin drops, unlock and remove the lid.
6. Discard the vanilla bean pod and stir well.
7. Spoon the oats into 4 bowls. Top each serving with a sprinkle of cinnamon and 1 tbsp of the macadamia nuts.

NUTRITION: calories 127 , fat 7g , protein 2g , carbs 14g, sugars 8g, fiber 3g, sodium 167mg

60. Berry Oat Muffins

Cooking time: 10 mins | Servings: 7

INGREDIENTS:

- ½ cup rolled oats
- 2 large eggs
- ¼ cup whole wheat flour
- ½ tbsp baking powder
- ½ tsp ground cinnamon
- ⅛ tsp salt
- ½ cup plain Greek yogurt
- 2 tbsp pure maple syrup
- 1 tsp olive oil
- ½ tsp vanilla extract
- ½ cup frozen mix berries

DIRECTIONS:

1. In a large bowl, stir together the oats , flour , baking powder , cinnamon , and salt.
2. In a medium bowl , whisk together the eggs , yogurt , maple syrup , oil , and vanilla.
3. Add the egg mixture to oat mixture and stir just until combined. Gently fold in the blueberries.
4. Scoop the batter into each cup of the egg bite mold.
5. Pour 1 cup of water into the electric pressure cooker. Place the egg bite mold on the wire rack and carefully lower it into the pot.
6. Close and lock the lid of the pressure cooker. Set the valve to sealing.
7. Cook on high pressure for 10 mins.
8. When the cooking is complete , allow the pressure to release naturally for 10 mins , then quick release any remaining pressure. Hit Cancel.
9. Lift the wire rack out of the pot and place on a cooling rack for 5 mins. Invert the mold onto the cooling rack to release the muffins.
10. Serve the muffins warm or refrigerate or freeze.

NUTRITION: calories 117, fat 4g, protein 5g , carbs 15g , sugars 4g , fiber 2g, sodium 89mg

61. Yogurt Sundae

Cooking time: 0 mins | Servings: 1

INGREDIENTS:

- ¾ cup plain nonfat greek yogurt
- ¼ cup mixed berries
- 2 tbsp cashew, walnut, or almond pieces
- 1 tbsp ground flaxseed
- 2 fresh mint leaves , shredded

DIRECTIONS:

1. Spoon the yogurt into a small bowl. Top with the berries, nuts, and flaxseed.
2. Garnish with the mint and serve.

NUTRITION: calories 238 , fat 11g , protein 21g , carbs 16g , sugars 9g , fiber 4g , sodium 64mg

62. Apple and Bran Muffins

Cooking time: 20 mins | Servings: 18 muffins

INGREDIENTS:

- 2 cups whole-wheat flour
- 2 eggs
- 1 cup wheat bran
- ⅓ cup granulated sweetener
- 1 tbsp baking powder
- 2 tsps ground cinnamon
- ½ tsp ground ginger
- ¼ tsp ground nutmeg
- 1½ cups skim milk
- ½ cup melted coconut oil
- 2 apples , peeled , cored , and diced

DIRECTIONS:

1. Preheat the oven to 350°F.
2. Line 18 muffin cups with paper liners and set the tray aside.
3. In a large bowl , stir together the flour , bran , sweetener , baking powder , cinnamon , ginger , and nutmeg.
4. In a small bowl , whisk the eggs , milk , and coconut oil until blended.

5. Add the wet ingredients to the dry ingredients , stirring until just blended.
6. Stir in the apples and spoon equal amounts of batter into each muffin cup.
7. Bake the muffins until a toothpick inserted in the center of a muffin comes out clean , about 20 mins.
8. Cool the muffins completely and serve.
9. Store leftover muffins in a sealed container in the refrigerator for up to 3 days or in the freezer for up to 1 month.

NUTRITION: calories 142, fat 7g, protein 4g , carbs 19g, fiber 3g, sugars 6g, sodium 21mg

63. Coconut and Berry Oatmeal

Cooking time: 35 mins | Servings: 6

INGREDIENTS:

- 2 cups rolled oats
- 2 eggs
- ¼ cup shredded unsweetened coconut
- 1 tsp baking powder
- ½ tsp ground cinnamon
- ¼ tsp sea salt
- 2 cups skim milk
- ¼ cup melted coconut oil , plus extra for greasing the baking dish
- 1 tsp pure vanilla extract
- 2 cups fresh blueberries

DIRECTIONS:

1. Preheat the oven to 350°F.
2. Lightly oil a baking dish and set it aside.
3. In a medium bowl, stir together the oats, coconut, baking powder, cinnamon , and salt.
4. In a small bowl, whisk together the milk, oil, egg, and vanilla until well blended.
5. Layer half the dry ingredients in the baking dish , top with half the berries , then spoon the remaining half of the dry ingredients and the rest of the berries on top.
6. Pour the wet ingredients evenly into the baking dish. Tap it lightly on the counter to disperse the wet ingredients throughout.
7. Bake the casserole , uncovered , until the oats are tender , about 35 mins.
8. Serve immediately

NUTRITION: calories 296, fat 17g, protein 10g , carbs 26g, fiber 4g, sugars 10g, sodium 154mg

64. Apple Pumpkin Waffles

Cooking time: 20 mins | Servings: 6

INGREDIENTS:

- 2¼ cups whole-wheat pastry flour
- 3 large eggs
- 2 tbsp granulated sweetener
- 1 tbsp baking powder
- 1 tsp ground cinnamon
- 1 tsp ground nutmeg
- 1¼ cups pumpkin purée
- 1 apple, peeled, cored, and finely chopped
- coconut oil , for cooking

DIRECTIONS:

1. In a large bowl , stir together the flour , sweetener , baking powder , cinnamon , and nutmeg.
2. In a small bowl , whisk together the eggs and pumpkin.
3. Add the wet ingredients to the dry and whisk until smooth.
4. Stir the apple into the batter.
5. Cook the waffles according to the waffle maker directions, brushing your waffle iron with melted coconut oil , until all the batter is gone.
6. Serve immediately.

NUTRITION: calories 232, fat 4g, protein 11g , carbs 40g , fiber 7g , sugars 5g, sodium 52mg

65. Cranberry Grits

Cooking time: 15 mins | Servings: 5

INGREDIENTS:

- ¾ cup stone-ground grits or polenta (not instant)
- ½ cup dried cranberries
- 1 pinch of salt
- 1 tbsp butter
- 1 tbsp half-and-half
- ¼ cup sliced almonds , toasted

DIRECTIONS:

1. In the electric pressure cooker, stir together the grits, cranberries, salt, and 3 cups of water.
2. Close and lock the lid. Set the valve to sealing.
3. Cook on high pressure for 10 mins.
4. When the cooking is complete , hit Cancel and quick release the pressure.
5. Once the pin drops , unlock and remove the lid.
6. Add the butter (if using) and half-and-half. Stir until the mixture is creamy , adding more half-and-half if necessary.
7. Spoon into serving bowls and sprinkle with almonds.

NUTRITION: calories 219 , fat 10g , protein 5g , carbs 32g , fiber 4g , sugars 6g , sodium 30mg

66. Cottage Cheese Pancakes

Cooking time: 10 mins | Servings: 2

INGREDIENTS:

Batter:

- ½ cup low-fat cottage cheese
- ¼ cup oats
- 1/3 cup egg whites (about 2 egg whites)
- 1 tbsp stevia
- 1 tsp vanilla extract
- Olive oil cooking spray
- Berries or sugar-free jam , for topping (optional)

DIRECTIONS:

1. Add the cottage cheese, oats, egg whites , stevia and vanilla extract to a food processor. Pulse into a smooth and thick batter.
2. Coat a large skillet with cooking spray and place it over medium heat.
3. Slowly pour half of the batter into the pan , tilting the pan to spread it evenly. Cook for about 2 to 3 mins until the pancake turns golden brown around the edges. Gently flip the pancake with a spatula and cook for 1 to 2 mins more.
4. Transfer the pancake to a plate and repeat with the remaining batter.
5. Top with the berries or sugar-free jam and serve , if desired.

NUTRITION: calories 188, fat 1g, protein 24g , carbs 18g, fiber 1g, sugars 2g , sodium 258mg

67. Huevos Rancheros

Cooking time: 15 mins | Servings: 4

INGREDIENTS:

Huevos Rancheros:

- 1 cup low-sodium black beans, drained and rinsed
- ½ cup jarred salsa verde
- Avocado oil cooking spray
- 8 large eggs
- 1 cup fresh Pico de Gallo (see below)
- 4 lime wedges

Pico De Gallo:

- 1 tomato , diced
- ½ large white onion, diced
- ½ jalapeño pepper, stemmed , seeded , and diced
- 1 tbsp fresh cilantro , chopped
- 1 tbsp freshly squeezed lime juice
- ⅛ tsp salt

DIRECTIONS:

Make the Huevos Rancheros

1. In a small saucepan, add the black beans and salsa verde. Cover, and cook over low heat for 10 mins until the black beans are heated through.

2. Meantime , heat a skillet over medium-low heat until hot. Coat the skillet with cooking spray.
3. One at a time, crack the eggs into the skillet and fry about 4 to 5 mins , or until the eggs white are opaque and the yolks are firm.
4. Remove the black bean and fried eggs from the heat to a plate.
5. To serve | place ¼ of the cooked black beans and pico de gallo on top of two fried eggs, finished by the juice squeezed from the lime wedges.

Make the Pico De Gallo

6. Mix together the tomato, onion , pepper , cilantro , lime juice , and salt in a bowl. Stir well with a fork to incorporate.

NUTRITION: calories 212, fat 9g, protein 15g , carbs 18g , fiber 5g, sugars 4g, sodium 440mg

68. Coconut Pancakes

Cooking time: 15 mins | Servings: 4

INGREDIENTS:

- ½ cup coconut flour
- 1 tsp baking powder
- ½ tsp ground cinnamon
- ⅛ tsp salt
- 6 large eggs
- 1/3 cup unsweetened almond milk
- 2 tbsp avocado or coconut oil

DIRECTIONS:

1. Stir together the flour, baking powder , cinnamon , and salt in a large bowl. Set aside.
2. Beat the eggs with the almond milk, and oil in a medium bowl until fully mixed.
3. Heat a large nonstick skillet over medium-low heat.
4. Make the pancakes: Pour 1/3 cup of batter into the hot skillet , tilting the pan to spread it evenly. Cook for 3 to 4 mins until bubbles form on the surface. Flip the pancake with a spatula and cook for about 3 minutes, or until the pancake is browned around the edges and cooked through. Repeat with the remaining batter.
5. Serve the pancakes on a plate while warm.

NUTRITION: calories 269, fat 17g, protein 13g, carbs 10g, fiber 5g, sugars 2g, sodium 324mg

69. Spanakopita Omelet

Cooking time: 15 mins | Servings: 4

INGREDIENTS:

- 8 egg whites
- 2 tbsp olive oil
- ½ sweet onion, chopped
- 1 red bell pepper, seeded and chopped
- ½ tsp minced garlic
- ¼ tsp salt and pepper
- 2 cups shredded spinach
- ½ cup crumbled low-sodium feta cheese

DIRECTIONS:

1. Preheat the oven to 375°F.
2. Place a heavy ovenproof skillet over medium-high heat and add the olive oil.
3. Sauté the onion, bell pepper, and garlic until softened, about 5 mins. Season with salt and pepper.
4. Whisk together the egg whites in a medium bowl, then pour them into the skillet and lightly shake the pan to disburse.
5. Cook the vegetables and eggs for 3 mins , without stirring.
6. Scatter the spinach over the eggs and sprinkle the feta cheese evenly over the spinach.
7. Put the skillet in the oven and bake , uncovered , until cooked through and firm , about 10 mins.
8. Loosen the edges of the frittata with a rubber spatula , then invert it onto a plate.
9. Serve.

NUTRITION: calories 146, fat 10g, protein 10g, carbs 3g, fiber 1g, sugars 2g, sodium 292mg

70. Pita and Bacon

Cooking time: 15 mins | Servings: 2

INGREDIENTS:

- 1 (6-inch) whole-grain pita bread
- 2 medium eggs
- 3 tsps olive oil
- 2 bacon slices
- Juice of ½ lemon
- 1 cup microgreens
- 2 tbsp crumbled goat cheese
- Freshly ground black pepper , to taste

DIRECTIONS:

1. Heat a large skillet over medium heat. Cut the pita bread in half and brush each side of both halves with ¼ tsp of olive oil (using a total of 1 tsp oil). Cook for 2 to 3 mins on each side, then remove from the skillet.
2. In the same skillet , heat 1 tsp of oil over medium heat. Crack the eggs into the skillet and cook until the eggs are set , 2 to 3 mins. Remove from the skillet.
3. In the same skillet , cook the Canadian bacon for 3 to 5 mins , flipping once.
4. In a large bowl , whisk together the remaining 1 tsp of oil and the lemon juice. Add the microgreens and toss to combine.
5. Top each pita half with half of the microgreens , 1 piece of bacon , 1 egg , and 1 tbsp of goat cheese. Season with pepper and serve.

NUTRITION: calories 251, fat 13g, protein 13g , carbs 20g, fiber 3g, sugars 1g, sodium 400mg

71. Shrimp with Scallion Grits

Cooking time: 20 mins | Servings: 6 to 8

INGREDIENTS:

- 1 pound medium shrimp, shelled and deveined
- 1½ cups fat-free milk
- 1½ cups water
- 2 bay leaves
- 1 cup stone-ground corn grits
- ¼ cup seafood broth
- 2 garlic cloves , minced
- 2 scallions, white and green parts, thinly sliced
- ½ tsp dried dill
- ½ tsp smoked paprika

DIRECTIONS:

1. In a medium stockpot, combine the milk , water , and bay leaves and bring to a boil over high heat.
2. Gradually add the grits, stirring continuously.
3. Reduce the heat to low, cover , and cook for 5 to 7 mins , stirring often , or until the grits are soft and tender. Remove from the heat and discard the bay leaves.
4. In a small cast iron skillet , bring the broth to a simmer over medium heat.
5. Add the garlic and scallions , and sauté for 3 to 5 mins , or until softened.
6. Add the shrimp, dill, paprika , and cook for about 7 mins , or until the shrimp is light pink but not overcooked.
7. Plate each dish with ¼ cup of grits, topped with shrimp.

NUTRITION: calories 198, fat 1g , protein 20g , carbs 24g , fiber 1g , sugars 3g , sodium 204mg

CHAPTER 4 Appetizers and Snacks

72. Fresh Dill Dip

Cooking time: 5 mins | Servings: 6

INGREDIENTS:

- 1 cup fat-free yogurt
- ¼ tsp salt and pepper
- ¼ cup minced parsley
- 2 tbsp finely chopped fresh chives
- 1 tbsp finely chopped fresh dill
- 1 tbsp apple cider vinegar

DIRECTIONS:

1. In a small bowl, combine all the ingredients. Chill for 2 to 4 hours. Serve with fresh cut vegetables.

NUTRITION: calories 20, fat 0g, protein 2g , carbs 3g, sugars 3g, sodium 125mg

73. Original Hummus

Cooking time: 5 mins | Servings: 12

INGREDIENTS:

- 1 (15-ounce) can chickpeas , drained
- 3 cloves garlic
- Juice of 1 lemon
- 1 tsp olive oil
- 1 tsp ground cumin
- 1 tsp tahini

DIRECTIONS:

1. In a blender or food processor, combine all the ingredients until smooth, adding chickpea liquid or water if necessary to blend , and create a creamy texture.
2. Refrigerate until ready to serve. Serve with crunchy vegetables , crackers , or pita bread.

NUTRITION: calories 40, fat 1g , protein 2g , carbs 6g , sugars 1g , fiber 2g , sodium 40mg

74. Chicken Fingers

Cooking time: 25 mins | Servings: 2

INGREDIENTS:

- 8 oz boneless skinless chicken breasts , sliced into long strips
- 1 egg , lightly beaten
- ½ cup almond flour
- ¼ cup chopped almonds
- 1tsp paprika
- ½ tsp garlic powder
- 1 tsp onion powder
- 1 tsp ground cumin
- ½ tsp salt and black pepper
- olive oil cooking spray

DIRECTIONS:

1. Preheat the oven to 375°F.
2. Spray a baking sheet with cooking spray. Set aside.
3. In a medium bowl, mix together the almond meal, almonds , paprika , garlic powder , onion powder , cumin , salt , and pepper.
4. Working with one piece of chicken at a time , dredge it in the egg and then coat it with the almond mixture. Place it on the prepared baking sheet. Repeat coating the remaining chicken strips by dredging in the egg first then the almond mixture.
5. Place the sheet in the preheated oven. Bake for 20 to 25 mins , or until golden.
6. Serve immediately.

NUTRITION: calories 405, fat 25g, protein 38g, carbs 9g, sugars 1g, fiber 4g, sodium 90mg

75. Tuna Salad Wraps

Cooking time: 0 mins , Servings: 2

INGREDIENTS:

- 1 (5-ounce) can tuna, rinsed and drained
- 1 tsp lemon juice
- ½ medium avocado
- 2 tbsp plain nonfat: Greek yogurt
- ¼ cup carrots
- 1 radish , sliced
- ¼ cup halved green olives
- 2 scallion , diced
- Salt and pepper , to taste
- 2 large green lettuce leaves

DIRECTIONS:

1. To a small bowl, add the tuna. Gently flake with a fork. Drizzle with the lemon juice.
2. In a medium bowl, mash the avocado until creamy. Mix in the yogurt.
3. Add the tuna, carrots , radishes , olives , and scallion to the avocado mixture. Season with salt and pepper. Stir to combine.
4. Top each lettuce leaf with half of the tuna salad. Serve!

NUTRITION: calories 178, fat 7g, protein 25g , carbs 10g , sugars 3g, fiber 6g , sodium 102mg

76. Tortilla Chips

Cooking Time: 25 mins | Servings: 6

INGREDIENTS:

- 12 whole wheat grain tortillas
- ¼ tsp. cayenne
- 2 tbsp organic olive oil
- 1 tbsp chili powder

DIRECTIONS:

1. Spread the tortillas for the lined baking sheet , add the oil , chili powder and cayenne , toss , introduce inside oven and then bake at 350°F for 25 mins.
2. Divide into bowls and serve as a side dish.

NUTRITION: calories 199, fat 3g , carbs 14g , protein 5g

77. Fresh Figs and ricotta

Cooking Time: 5 mins | Servings: 4

INGREDIENTS:

- 8 dried figs , halved
- ¼ cup ricotta cheese
- 16 walnuts , halved
- 1 tbsp honey

DIRECTIONS:

1. Take a skillet and place it over medium heat , add walnuts and toast for 2 mins
2. Top figs with cheese and walnuts
3. Drizzle honey on top.

NUTRITION: calories 204, carbs 15g , fat 16g, protein 4.8g, potassium 255mg, sodium 299mg

78. Tuna Sandwich

Cooking Time: 15 mins | Servings: 4

INGREDIENTS:

- 4 whole wheat bread slices
- 1 tbsp olive oil
- 1 peeled and diced medium cucumber
- 1 tbsp diced onion
- 1 can flavored tuna
- ½ cup shredded spinach

DIRECTIONS:

1. Grab your blender and add the spinach , tuna , onion , oil , salt and pepper in , and pulse for about 10 to 20 seconds.
2. In the meantime , toast your bread and add your diced cucumber to a bowl , which you can pour your tuna mixture in. Carefully mix and add the mixture to the bread once toasted.
3. Slice in half and serve , while storing the remaining mixture in the fridge.

NUTRITION: calories 302 , carbs 35g , fat: 6g , protein 28g , potassium 200mg , sodium 281mg

79. Potatoes Croquettes

Cooking Time: 20 mins | Servings: 4

INGREDIENTS:

- 4 medium "leached" potato, cooked and peeled
- 1 tbsp. of butter
- 1 tbsp. of rice milk
- 1 tsp. of pepper
- 1 beaten egg
- 1 cup of white bread crumbs
- 2 tbsp. of canola oil

DIRECTIONS:

1. Mash potatoes with milk , butter , and pepper.
2. Form cooled potatoes into balls with your hands.
3. Dip balls in beaten egg.
4. Next , roll balls in bread crumbs.
5. Then place balls in a hot oiled skillet and fry until golden brown.

NUTRITION: calories 322 , carbs 75g , fat 36g, protein 7g, potassium 233mg , sodium 399mg

80. Carrots and Cinnamon Bread

Cooking Time: 10 mins | Servings: 2

INGREDIENTS:

- 1-1/2 cups whole wheat flour
- 1 tbsp sugar
- 1 tsp baking powder
- 1/4 tsp baking soda
- 1-1/2 tsps ground cinnamon
- 1/4 tsp ground allspice
- 1 egg , beaten
- 1/2 cup water
- 2 tbsps vegetable oil
- ½ tsp vanilla
- 1-1/2 cups finely shredded carrots
- 1/4 cup chopped pecans
- 1/4 cup golden raisins

DIRECTIONS:

1. Preheat oven to 350°F. Lightly oil a 9x5x3 inch loaf pan.
2. Stir together dry Ingredients: in large mixing bowl. Make a well in center of dry mixture.
3. In separate bowl, mix together remaining ingredients; add this mixture all at once to dry ingredients. Stir just enough to moisten and evenly distribute carrots.
4. Turn into prepared pan. Bake for 50 mins or until toothpick inserted in center comes out clean.
5. Cool 5 mins in pan. Remove from pan and complete cooling on a wire rack before slicing.

NUTRITION: calories 99, fat 3g, carbs 18g , protein 4g , potassium 210mg , sodium 175mg

81. Apple and Fennel Salad

Preparation Time: 15 mins | Servings: 6

INGREDIENTS:

- 1 fennel bulb
- 1 granny smith apple
- 2 tbsp lemon juice
- 3 tbsp olive oil
- 1/3 tsp mustard

DIRECTIONS:

1. Slice the fennel bulb and apples.
2. Mix the mustard and lemon juice in a bowl and add the olive oil , sea salt and black pepper to taste.
3. Combine the apple and fennel slices in a bowl and pour the vinaigrette over. Add salt and pepper again.
4. Serve and garnish with the chopped fennel top.

NUTRITION: calories 248, fat 10g , carbs 36g , protein 6g

82. Chicken Salad Sandwich

Cooking Time: 10 mins | Servings: 2

INGREDIENTS:

- 2 bowls of cooked chicken
- ½ cup of low-fat mayonnaise
- ½ cup of green bell pepper
- ½ cup of pieces pineapple
- 1/3 cup of carrots
- 4 slices of flatbread
- ½ tsp. of black pepper

DIRECTIONS:

1. Prepare aside the diced chicken and drain pineapple, adding green bell pepper , black pepper , and carrots.
2. Combine all in a bowl and refrigerate until chilled.
3. Later on, serve the chicken salad on the flatbread.

NUTRITION: calories 345, fat 18.2g, carbs 23.5g, protein 17.4g, potassium 330mg, sodium 395mg

83. Pasta and Sun-dried Tomatoes

Cooking Time: 20 mins | Servings: 4

INGREDIENTS:

- 1/2 cup sun-fried tomatoes
- 2 tbsp olive oil
- 4 garlic cloves, mashed
- 1/2 cup veggie broth
- 2 cup pasta

INGREDIENTS:

1. Preheat olive oil in a skillet over medium heat.
2. Sauté garlic for 30 seconds. Then add tomatoes and broth.
3. Cover the mixture and then simmer for 10 mins.
4. Fill a pot with water and boil pasta in it for 10 mins until al dente.
5. Drain the pasta and keep it aside.
6. Add parsley and olives to the tomato mixture and mix well.
7. Serve the plate with tomato sauce and add 1 tsp parmesan cheese.

NUTRITION: calories 330, fat 8.2g, carbs 31.5g, protein 7.4g, potassium 230mg , sodium 264mg

84. Lettuce with Dressing

Cooking Time: 0 mins | Servings: 4

INGREDIENTS:

- 1 slice whole wheat-bread
- 2 heads romaine lettuce , rinsed and halved lengthwise
- 4 tsps olive oil
- 4 tsps homemade dressing
- 4 tbsps shredded parmesan cheese
- 16 cherry tomatoes , rinsed and halved

DIRECTIONS:

1. Preheat grill pan on high temperature.
2. Cube the bread. Spread in a single layer on a foil-covered tray for a toaster oven or conventional oven. Toast to a medium-brown color and crunchy texture. Remove. Allow to cool.
3. Brush the cut side of each half of romaine lettuce with 1 tsp of olive oil.
4. Place cut side down on a grill pan on the stovetop. Cook just until grill marks appear and romaine is heated through , about 2–5 mins.
5. Place each romaine half on a large salad plate. Top each with one-fourth of the bread cubes. Drizzle each with 1 tsp of light Caesar dressing. Sprinkle each with 1 tbsp of shredded parmesan cheese. Garnish with eight tomato halves around each plate.

NUTRITION: calories 162 , fat 3.2g , carbs 17.5g , protein 1.4g

85. Paprika Carrots

Cooking Time: 30 mins | Servings: 4

INGREDIENTS:

- 1 lb. trimmed baby carrots
- 1 tbsp sweet paprika
- 1 tsp. lime juice
- ¼ tsp. black pepper
- 3 tbsp olive oil
- 1 tsp. sesame seeds

DIRECTIONS:

1. Arrange the carrots on a lined baking sheet , add the paprika and the other Ingredients: except the sesame seeds , toss , introduce in the oven and bake at 400°F for 30 mins.
2. Divide the carrots between plates , sprinkle sesame seeds on top and serve.

NUTRITION: calories 345, fat 18.2g , carbs 23.5g, protein 17.4g, potassium 330mg, sodium 395mg

86. Roasted Beet & Sardine Salad

Cooking Time: 2 hours | Servings: 4

INGREDIENTS:

- 2 cans sardine
- ½ cup low-fat mayonnaise
- 1 tbsp prepared horseradish
- 2 tbsp fresh dill
- 1 lb beets, stems trimmed
- Butter

DIRECTIONS:

1. Chop the fresh dill.
2. Clean the beets and place them individually in small closed-up foil packets.
3. Place them in a roasting dish and roast for about 45 mins to an hour , until a fork enters the flesh easily. Put on a plate to cool. When cool enough to handle, cut the beets into ½-inch cubes and place in a bowl with 2 tbsp butter. Toss well to coat the beets all over with the fat
4. Mix the mayonnaise, dill and horseradish in a bowl and add salt and pepper to taste.
5. Place a bed of roasted beets on each plate and add the mayonnaise on top. Place the sardines on top of the mayonnaise.

NUTRITION: calories 393 , fat 23.2g , carbs 33.5g , protein 17.4g

87. Celery and Aragula Salad

Cooking Time: 0 mins | Servings: 4

INGREDIENTS:

- 1 shallot, thinly sliced
- 3 celery stalks, cut into 1-inch pieces about ¼ inch thick
- 2 cups of loosely packed arugula
- 1 tbsp of olive oil
- 2 tbsps of white wine vinegar
- freshly ground black pepper
- 2 tbsps of grated Parmesan cheese

DIRECTIONS:

1. In a medium bowl , toss the shallot , celery stalks , and arugula.
2. In a small bowl , whisk the olive oil , vinegar , and pepper.
3. Toss your salad with your dressing.
4. Top with Parmesan cheese and serve.

NUTRITION: calories 45, fat 4.2g, carbs 1.5g, protein 1.4g, potassium 47mg, sodium 70mg

88. Chicken & Zucchini Hot Salad

Cooking Time: 15 mins | Servings: 4

INGREDIENTS:

- 2 ½ lbs chicken breasts
- 5 zucchinis
- 3 tbsp butter
- 1 tbsp oregano
- 1 large onion

- 7 tbsp mayonnaise
- Juice of 2 lemons
- 2 cloves garlic
- Salt and pepper to taste

DIRECTIONS:

1. Cut the chicken breasts and zucchinis into cubes.
2. Mince the garlic and chop the onion.
3. Heat a large frying pan over a medium-high heat | add some butter and cook the chicken cubes and until well cooked. Put on a plate.
4. Add the onion to the same pan and cook about 5 mins. Add the zucchini cubes | oregano | salt and pepper to taste. Cook until soft. Mix the mayonnaise | lemon juice and garlic in a bowl.
5. Add the cooked chicken | onion and zucchini to the sauce and mix well. You may add some lettuce onion.

NUTRITION: calories 76 , fat 3.8g , carbs 10.5g , protein 1.8g

89. Tuna Salad

Cooking Time: 2 mins | Servings: 2

INGREDIENTS:

- 2 can (12 oz) tuna
- 3 tsp mayonnaise
- 2 tsp pickle relish (naturally fermented)
- 2 tsp mustard
- 2 celery stalks
- ½ cup onion
- Pepper to taste

DIRECTIONS:

1. Chop the stalks and onion.
2. Mix everything together in a bowl , adjusting the texture and taste with more or less mustard and mayonnaise.
3. Add only pepper because the canned tuna is salted already

NUTRITION: calories 51 , fat 1g , carbs 9g , phosphorus 19mg , potassium 14mg , sodium 102mg , protein 1g

90. Ginger-Lime Grilled Shrimp

Cooking Time: 6 mins | Servings: 3-4

INGREDIENTS:

- 1-2 pounds large shrimp
- 2 tbsp lime juice
- ¼ tbsp crushed red pepper flakes
- 3 cloves garlic
- 2 tsp freshly-grated ginger
- ¼ tsp salt
- ¼ tsp ground black pepper
- 2 tbsp fresh cilantro leaves
- 1 tbsp olive oil

DIRECTIONS:

1. Mince the garlic and cilantro leaves.
2. Mix lime juice, red pepper flakes, garlic , ginger , salt , black pepper , and cilantro in a bowl , and then drizzle in the oil , stirring constantly.
3. Pierce the shrimp at the head end and carefully cut along the back toward the tail , removing the dark vein.
4. Rinse in running water. Pat dry , and then place in a bowl and mix with the
5. Marinade well. Cover tightly and place into the fridge for 20 mins.
6. Preheat the gas grill on high heat.
7. Thread the shrimp on skewers , leaving a little room between them. Grill for 2-3 mins per side with the lid closed.

NUTRITION: calories 23.5, fat 13g , carbs 0.6g , protein 2g

91. Kale Chips

Cooking Time: 25 mins| Servings: 6

INGREDIENTS:

- 2 cups Kale
- 2 tsp of olive oil

- ¼ tsp of chili powder
- Pinch cayenne pepper

DIRECTIONS:

1. Preheat the oven to 300°F.
2. Line 2 baking sheets with parchment paper; set aside.
3. Remove the stems from the kale and tear the leaves into 2-inch pieces.
4. Wash the kale and dry it completely.
5. Transfer the kale to a large bowl and drizzle with olive oil.
6. Use your hands to toss the kale with oil, taking care to coat each leaf evenly.
7. Season the kale with chili powder and cayenne pepper and toss to combine thoroughly.
8. Spread the seasoned kale in a single layer on each baking sheet. Do not overlap the leaves.
9. Bake the kale rotating the pans once, for 20 to 25 mins until it is crisp and dry.
10. Remove the trays from the oven and allow the chips to cool on the trays for 5 mins.
11. Serve.

NUTRITION: calories 24¸ fat 2g, carbs 2g , phosphorus 21mg, potassium 111mg, sodium 13mg, protein 1g

92. Red Pepper Hummus

Cooking Time: 10 mins | Servings: 8

INGREDIENTS:

- 1 red bell pepper
- 1 (15-ounce) can of chickpeas, drained and rinsed
- Juice of 1 lemon
- 2 tbsps of tahini
- 2 garlic cloves
- 2 tbsps of olive oil

DIRECTIONS:

1. Move the rack of the oven to the highest position. Heat the broiler to high.
2. Core the pepper and cut it into three or four large pieces. Arrange them on a baking sheet, skin-side up.
3. Broil the peppers for 5 to 10 mins, until the skins are charred. Remove from the oven then transfer the peppers to a small bowl. Cover with plastic wrap and let them steam for 10 to 15 mins, until cool enough to handle.
4. Peel the charred skin off the peppers, and place the peppers in a blender.
5. Add the chickpeas , lemon juice , tahini , garlic , and olive oil. Wait until smooth , then add up to 1 tbsp of water to adjust consistency as desired.

NUTRITION: calories 103, fat 6g , carbs 10g , phosphorus 58mg, potassium 91mg, sodium 72mg , protein 3g

93. Buffalo Cauliflower Bites with Ranch Dressing

Cooking Time: 30 mins | Servings: 8 Serves

INGREDIENTS:

- 4 cups of cauliflower florets
- 2 tbsps olive oil
- ¼ tsp of salt and pepper
- ¼ tsp of smoked paprika
- ¼ tsp of garlic powder
- ½ cup of sugar free hot sauce
- 1 cup organic mayonnaise
- ½ cup of Silk unsweetened coconut milk
- 1 tsp of garlic powder
- 1 tsp of onion powder
- 1 tbsp of fresh lemon juice
- ¼ cup fresh chopped parsley

DIRECTIONS:

1. First heat oven to 400°F. Spray baking sheet with nonstick olive oil cooking spray.
2. Place florets in a large bowl and toss with olive oil. In a small bowl mix the salt,paprika and garlic powder together with hot sauce.
3. Add the hot sauce into cauliflower bowl and stir well until well coated. Spread cauliflower out evenly on baking sheet and bake for 30 mins.
4. Whisk ingredients together and pour into a mason jar. Cover and refrigerate until ready to serve with cauli bites.

NUTRITION: calories 123 , fat 16g, carbs 12g , fiber 3g , protein 39g

94. Baked Cream Cheese Crab Dip

Cooking Time: 30 mins | Servings: 12

INGREDIENTS:

- 8 oz. lump crab meat
- 8 oz. cream cheese softened
- ½ cup avocado mayonnaise
- 1 tbsp lemon juice
- 1 tsp Worcestershire sauce
- ½ tsp of garlic powder
- ½ tsp of onion powder
- ½ tsp of salt
- ¼ tsp of dry mustard
- ¼ tsp of black pepper

DIRECTIONS:

Add all ingredients into small baking dish and spread out evenly. Bake at 375°F for about 25 to 30 mins. Serve with low Carbs crackers or vegetables.

NUTRITION: calories 167 , fat 12g , carbs 21g , fiber 2g , protein 31g

95. Philly Cheese Steak Stuffed Mushrooms

Cooking Time: 15 mins | Servings: 2

INGREDIENTS:

- 24 oz. baby bella mushrooms
- 1 cup chopped red pepper
- 1 cup chopped onion
- 2 tbsps butter
- 1 tsp salt divided
- ½ tsp of pepper divided
- 1 pound of beef sirloin shaved or thinly sliced against the grain
- 4 oz cheese

DIRECTIONS:

1. First heat oven to 350°F. Remove stems from mushrooms and place mushrooms on a greased baby sheet. Sprinkle with ½ tsp of salt and ¼ tsp of pepper on both sides and bake for 15 mins. Set aside. Melt 1 tbsp butter in a large skillet and cook pepper and onions until soft. Then season with ½ tsp of salt and ¼ tsp of pepper.
2. Remove from the skillet and set aside. In the same skillet | melt the remaining tbsp of butter and cook the meat to your preference.
3. Add the provolone cheese and stir until completely melted.
4. Return back the veggies. Add mixture into the mushrooms, top with more cheese if you like and bake for 5 mins. Serve and enjoy.

NUTRITION: calories 435 , fat 16g , carbs 27g , fiber 3g , protein 39g

96. Greek Cookies

Cooking Time: 25 mins | Servings: 6

INGREDIENTS:

- ½ cup plain yogurt
- ½ tsp baking powder
- 2 tbsps Erythritol
- 1 tsp almond extract
- ½ tsp ground clove
- ½ tsp orange zest, grated
- 3 tbsps walnuts | chopped
- 1 cup wheat flour
- 1 tsp butter | softened
- 1 tbsp honey

- 3 tbsps water

DIRECTIONS:

1. In the mixing bowl mix up together the plain yogurt, baking powder, Erythritol , almond extract , ground cloves orange zest , flour , and butter.
2. Knead the non-sticky dough. Add olive oil if the dough is very sticky and knead it well.
3. Then make the log from the dough and cut it into small pieces.
4. Roll every piece of dough into the balls and transfer in the lined with baking paper tray.
5. Press the balls gently and bake for 25 mins at 350°F.
6. Meanwhile , heat up together honey and water. Simmer the liquid for 1 minute and remove from the heat.
7. When the cookies are cooked , remove them from the oven and let them cool for 5 mins.
8. Then pour the cookies with sweet honey water and sprinkle with walnuts.
9. Cool the cookies.

NUTRITION: calories 134 , fat 3.4 , fiber 0.9 , carbs 26.1 , protein 4.3

97. Flavored Potatoes Mix

Cooking Time: 25 mins | Servings: 2

INGREDIENTS:

- 4 potatoes , thinly sliced
- 2 tbsps olive oil
- 1 fennel bulb , thinly sliced
- 1 tbsp dill , chopped
- 8 cherry tomatoes , halved
- Salt and black pepper to the taste

DIRECTIONS:

1. Preheat your air fryer to 365°F and add the oil.
2. Add potato slices, fennel, dill , tomatoes , salt and pepper , toss , cover and cook for 25 mins.
3. Divide potato mix between plates and serve.

NUTRITION: calories 240 , fat 3 , fiber 2 , carbs 5 , protein 12

98. Corn Bread

Cooking Time: 20 mins | Servings: 10

INGREDIENTS:

- 2 eggs
- 1 cup unsweetened rice milk
- 1 ¼ cups yellow cornmeal
- ¾ cup whole wheat flour
- 1 tbsp baking soda
- 2 tbsp brown sugar
- cooking spray
- 2 tbsp olive oil

DIRECTIONS:

1. Preheat the oven to 425°F.
2. Lightly spray an 8-by-8-inch baking dish with cooking spray. Set aside.
3. In a medium bowl, stir together the cornmeal, flour, baking soda substitute , and sugar.
4. In a small bowl, whisk together the eggs, rice milk , and olive oil until blended.
5. Add the wet ingredients to the dry ingredients and stir until well combined.
6. Pour the batter into the baking dish and bake for 20 mins or until golden and cooked through.
7. Serve warm.

NUTRITION: calories 198 , fat 5g , carbs 34g , phosphorus 88mg , potassium 94mg , sodium 25mg , protein 4g

99. Kale Popcorn

Cooking Time: 0 mins | Servings: 4

INGREDIENTS:

- 10 cup popped popcorn
- ½ bunch chopped kale
- 2 tsps. grapeseed oil
- 2 tsps. lemon zest

DIRECTIONS:

1. Preheat the oven to 325°F.
2. Pat the kale completely dry with kitchen paper and then coat with olive oil and salt.
3. Place onto the baking sheet and bake for 11 mins until crispy.
4. Stir once or twice halfway through cooking and be careful that the kale does not burn.
5. Remove the kale and let cool.
6. Place the cooled kale into a food processor together with the lemon zest and process into a fine powder.
7. Add this seasoning to the prepared popcorn and serve.

NUTRITION: calories 134, fat 3.4, fiber 0.9 , carbs 22.1 , protein 5.3

100. Peas Hummus

Cooking Time: 0 mins | Servings: 4

INGREDIENTS:

- Juice of ½ lemon
- 2 cup drained chickpeas
- 2 tbsp oil
- 1 clove garlic
- 4 tbsp chopped parsley
- 12 black olives

DIRECTIONS:

Pour the chickpeas and juice in a blender together with garlic and oil. Serve with olives and parsley.

NUTRITION: calories 107, fat 9.4, fiber 0.9, carbs 16.1 , protein 11.3

101. Vegetable Rolls

Cooking Time: 0 mins | Servings: 8

INGREDIENTS:

- ½ cup finely shredded red cabbage
- ½ cup grated carrot
- ¼ cup julienne red bell pepper
- ¼ cup julienned scallion, both green and white parts
- ¼ cup chopped cilantro
- 1 tbsp olive oil
- ¼ tsp ground cumin
- ¼ tsp freshly ground black pepper
- 1 cucumber, sliced very thin

DIRECTIONS:

1. In a bowl, toss together the black pepper, cumin, olive oil, cilantro, scallion, red pepper, carrot, and cabbage. Mix well.
2. Evenly divide the vegetable filling among the cucumber strips, placing the filling close to one end of the strip.
3. Roll up the cucumber strips around the filling and secure with a wooden pick.
4. Repeat with each cucumber strip.

NUTRITION: calories 26, fat 2g , carbs 3g, phosphorus 14mg , potassium 95mg , sodium 7mg , protein 0g

102. Omelet with Penne

Cooking Time: 30 mins | Servings: 4

INGREDIENTS:

- 6 egg whites
- ¼ cup rice milk
- 1 tbsp chopped fresh parsley
- 1 tsp. chopped fresh chives
- ground black pepper
- 2 tsp olive oil
- ¼ small sweet onion,| chopped
- 1 tsp minced garlic
- ½ cup boiled and chopped red bell pepper
- 2 cups cooked penne

DIRECTIONS:

1. Preheat the oven to 350°F.

2. In a bowl , whisk together the egg whites , rice milk , parsley, chives , and pepper.
3. Heat the oil in a skillet.
4. Sauté the onion , garlic , red pepper for 4 mins or until they are softened
5. Add the cooked penne to the skillet.
6. Pour the egg mixture over the pasta and shake the pan to coat the pasta.
7. Leave the skillet on the heat for 1 minute to set the bottom of the frittata and then transfer the skillet to the oven.
8. Bake | the frittata for 25 mins or until it is set and golden brown.
9. Serve.

NUTRITION: calories 170, fat 3g , carbs 25g , phosphorus 62mg , potassium 144mg , sodium 90mg , protein 10g

103. Grilled Zucchini Hummus

Cooking Time: 10 mins | Servings: 4

INGREDIENTS:

- 4 zucchinis, halved
- 1/4 tsp paprika
- 1/4 cup fresh cilantro
- 1 tsp cumin
- 2 1/2 tbsp tahini
- 2 tbsp fresh lemon juice
- 1 tbsp olive oil
- 2 garlic cloves, peeled
- Pepper and Salt

DIRECTIONS:

Season the zucchini with pepper and salt. Arrange zucchini on hot grill and cook for 10 mins. Transfer grilled zucchini along with ingredients into the food processor and process until smooth. Serve and enjoy.

NUTRITION: calories 136, fat 10 g , carbs 9g , protein 4g

104. Peach and Pita

Cooking Time: 1 min | Servings: 4

INGREDIENTS:

- 2 medium whole wheat pita pockets
- 1/4 cup reduced Fat: chunky peanut butter
- ½ apple, cored and thinly sliced
- ½ pear, thinly sliced
- ½ fresh peach, thinly sliced

DIRECTIONS:

1. Cut pitas in half to make 4 pockets and warm in the microwave for about 10 seconds to make them more flexible.
2. Carefully open each pocket and spread a thin layer of peanut butter on the inside walls.
3. Fill with a combination of apple, pear, and peach slices. Serve at room temperature.

NUTRITION: calories 180 , fat 3g , carbs 26g , phosphorus 88mg , potassium 188mg , protein 13g

105. Fruit Compote

Cooking Time: 10 mins | Servings: 8

INGREDIENTS:

- ½ pineapple cored and peeled , cut into 8 slices
- 2 apples peeled and pitted , cut into 8 pieces
- 3 pears peeled , cut into 8 diagonal pieces
- 3/4 cup water
- 1/2 cup sugar
- 2 tsps fresh lemon juice
- 1 piece lemon peel
- 1/2 tsp rum or vanilla extract (optional)

DIRECTIONS:

1. In a saucepan combine 3/4 cup of water with the sugar , lemon juice , and lemon peel (and rum or vanilla

extract if desired). Bring to a boil , then reduce the heat and add the fruit. Cook at a very low heat for 5 mins.

2. Pour the syrup in a cup. Remove the lemon rind and cool the cooked fruit for 2 hours.
3. To serve the compote , arrange the fruit in a serving dish and pour a few tsps of syrup over the fruit. Garnish with mint leaves.
4. Serve with Homemade Sour Cream

NUTRITION: calories 148 , fat 1g , carbs 29g , phosphorus 71g , potassium 188mg , protein 4g

106. Zucchini Tots

Cooking Time: 20 mins | Servings: 4

INGREDIENTS:

- 2 eggs, lightly beaten
- 2 cups zucchini grated and squeeze out all liquid
- ½ cup cheddar cheese, shredded
- 2 tbsp onion, minced
- ½ cup parmesan cheese, grated
- Pepper and Salt

DIRECTIONS:

Preheat the oven to 400°F. Spry mini muffin trays with cooking spray and set aside. Add all ingredients into the bowl and mix until well combined. Pour batter into the prepared muffin tray and bake for 20 mins. Serve and enjoy.

NUTRITION: calories 100, fat 7g, carbs 3g , protein 7g

107. Roasted Cabbage

Cooking Time: 35 mins | Servings: 2

INGREDIENTS:

- 1 green cabbage, cut into 1-inch wedges
- 1 tsp brown sugar
- 1 tbsp balsamic vinegar
- ¼ tsp freshly ground pepper
- 2 tbsp olive oil

DIRECTIONS:

1. Preheat oven to 450°F, with baking pan heating inside.
2. Combine sugar and pepper in a small bowl.
3. Brush cabbage wedges with oil. Sprinkle with pepper and sugar.
4. Put the seasoned wedges on the hot baking sheet. Roast until cabbage is browned and tender for 25 mins.
5. Drizzle with balsamic vinegar

NUTRITION: calories 36 , fat 2 g , carbs 4g , protein 4g , sodium 31 mg , potassium 194mg

108. Stuffed Mushrooms

Cooking Time: 25 mins | Servings: 4

INGREDIENTS:

- 12 mushrooms , clean and cut stems
- 8 oz cream cheese
- 1 tbsp butter
- 3 bacon slices , cooked and chopped
- 2 tbsp chives , chopped
- ½ tsp paprika
- Pepper and Salt

DIRECTIONS:

1. Preheat the oven to 400°F.
2. Finely chop the mushroom stems.
3. Melt butter into the pan over medium heat. Add chopped mushroom stems and sauté for a minute. Remove from heat. In a bowl, mix together cream cheese, bacon, sautéed mushroom stems, chives, paprika , pepper , and salt.
4. Stuff cream cheese mixture into each mushroom and arrange mushrooms in a baking dish. Bake in preheated oven for 20 mins. Serve and enjoy.

NUTRITION: calories 313, fat 28.8g, carbs 3.7g , protein 11.4g

109. Tasty Herb Dip

Cooking Time: 5 mins | Servings: 8

INGREDIENTS:

- 1 cup mayonnaise
- 1 tsp dried dill
- 1 tsp dried parsley
- 1 tsp dried chives
- ½ cup sour cream
- ½ tsp onion powder
- ½ tsp garlic powder

DIRECTIONS:

Add all ingredients into the bowl and mix until well combined. Place in refrigerator for 20 mins. Serve and enjoy.

NUTRITION: calories 143 , fat 12g , carbs 8g , protein 1g

110. Rutabaga Wedges

Cooking Time: 20 mins | Servings: 4

INGREDIENTS:

- 1 lb. rutabaga, peel and cut into wedges
- 3 tbsp olive oil
- 1/2 tsp paprika
- 1/4 tsp garlic powder
- pepper and salt to taste

DIRECTIONS:

1. Preheat the oven to 400°F.
2. Add rutabaga wedges into the mixing bowl. Add remaining ingredients on top and toss to coat.
3. Transfer rutabaga wedges on a baking tray and bake in preheated oven for 20 mins and serve.

NUTRITION: calories 163, fat 14g, carbs 9g, protein 2g

111. Tasty Broccoli Nuggets

Cooking Time: 30 mins | Servings: 4

INGREDIENTS:

- 2 cups broccoli florets
- 2 egg whites
- 1/4 cup almond flour
- 1 cup cheddar cheese, shredded
- Salt

DIRECTIONS:

1. Preheat the oven to 350°F.
2. Add broccoli into the boiling water and cook for 10 mins or until softened. Drain well.
3. Spray a baking tray with cooking spray and set aside.
4. Add cooked broccoli florets into the large bowl and using potato masher mash into small pieces.
5. Add remaining ingredients and mix until well combined.
6. Make small nuggets from mixture place onto the baking tray and bake for 20 mins.
7. Serve and enjoy.

NUTRITION: calories 175, fat 14g, carbs 5g, protein 11g

112. Onion Dip

Cooking Time: 4 h 30 mins | Servings: 12

INGREDIENTS:

- 4 onions, sliced
- 2 tbsp olive oil
- 2 tbsp butter
- ½ cup mozzarella cheese
- 8 oz sour cream
- pepper and salt to taste

DIRECTIONS:

1. Add oil, butter and onions into the crock pot and stir well.
2. Cover and cook on high for 4 hours.
3. Transfer onion mixture into the blender with sour cream, pepper and salt and blend until smooth.

4. Return blended onion mixture into the crock pot.
5. Add mozzarella cheese and stir well and cook on low for 30 mins more.
6. Stir and serve.

NUTRITION: calories 96, fat 8g, carbs 4g, protein 2g

113. Crab-Filled Mushrooms

Cooking time: 25 mins | Servings: 10

INGREDIENTS:

- 20 large fresh mushroom caps
- 6 oz canned crabmeat, rinsed and flaked
- ½ cup crushed whole-wheat crackers
- 1 tbsp chopped fresh parsley
- 1 tbsp finely chopped green onion
- ¼ cup chopped pimiento
- 3 tbsp olive oil
- 5 tbsp wheat germ

DIRECTIONS:

1. Preheat the oven to 350°F. Clean the mushrooms by dusting off any dirt on the cap with a mushroom brush or paper towel; remove the stems.
2. In a small mixing bowl, combine the crabmeat , crackers , parsley , onion , and pepper.
3. Place the mushroom caps in a 13-x-9-x-2-inch baking dish, crown side down. Stuff some of the crabmeat filling into each cap. Place a little pimiento on top of the filling.
4. Drizzle the olive oil over the caps and sprinkle each cap with ½ tbsp wheat germ. Bake for 15 to 17 mins. Transfer to a serving platter and serve hot.

NUTRITION: calories 100, fat 6g , protein 5g , carbs 8g , sugars 2g , fiber 2g , sodium 95mg

114. Artichoke Dip

Cooking time: 20 mins | Servings: 12

INGREDIENTS:

- 2 (9-ounce) packages frozen artichoke hearts | thawed
- 2 cloves garlic
- 2 tbsp olive oil
- 1/3 cup fresh lemon juice
- ¼ tsp hot pepper sauce
- ¼ cup grated fresh Parmesan cheese
- 1½ cups dried whole-wheat bread crumbs
- ¼ cup finely chopped parsley

DIRECTIONS:

1. Preheat the oven to 350°F.
2. In a blender or food processor, combine the artichoke hearts , garlic , olive oil , lemon juice , and hot pepper sauce and purée for 30 seconds.
3. Pour the purée into a large bowl; stir in the cheese, bread crumbs , and parsley. Transfer the mixture to a 1-quart baking dish.
4. Cover the dip and bake at 350°F for 15 mins or until lightly golden brown. Serve warm with crackers or bread.

NUTRITION: calories 45, fat 1g, protein 2g, carbs 6g, sugars 1g, fiber 2g,sodium 25mg

115. Chilled Shrimp

Cooking time: 5 mins | Servings: 10

INGREDIENTS:

- 2 pounds jumbo shrimp , unshelled
- ¼ cup plus 2 tbsp olive oil , divided
- 2 medium lemons , thinly sliced
- 2 tbsp minced garlic
- 2 medium red onions , thinly sliced
- ½ cup minced parsley
- Parsley sprigs (for garnish)

DIRECTIONS:

1. Preheat the oven to 400ºF (205ºC). Peel , and devein shrimp , leaving the tails intact.

2. Arrange the shrimp on a baking sheet and brush with 2 tbsp of the olive oil. Bake the shrimp for 3 mins or until they turn bright pink.
3. Place the lemon slices in a large bowl. Add the remaining ¼ cup of olive oil , garlic , onions , and minced parsley. Add the shrimp and toss vigorously to coat. Cover, and let marinate , refrigerated , for 6 to 8 hours.
4. Just before serving, arrange the shrimp on a serving platter. Garnish with parsley sprigs and some of the red onions and lemons from the bowl.

NUTRITION: calories 90 , fat 2g , protein 16g , carbs 3g , sugars 1g , fiber 0g , sodium 75mg

116. Chicken Kabobs

Cooking time: 20 mins | Servings: 6

INGREDIENTS:

- 1 pound boneless, skinless chicken breast
- 3 tbsp light soy sauce
- 1 (1-inch) cube of fresh ginger root , finely chopped
- 2 tbsp olive oil
- 2 tbsp dry vermouth
- 2 large clove garlic , finely chopped
- ¼ cup arugula
- 2 large lemons , cut into wedges

DIRECTIONS:

1. Cut the chicken into 1-inch cubes and place in a shallow bowl.
2. In a small bowl , combine the soy sauce , ginger root , oil , vermouth , and garlic and pour over the chicken. Cover the chicken and let marinate for at least 1 hour (or overnight).
3. Thread the chicken onto 12 metal or wooden skewers (remember to soak wooden skewers in water before using). Grill or broil 6 inches from the heat source for 8 mins, turning frequently.
4. Arrange the skewers on a platter and garnish with the arugula and lemon wedges. Serve hot with additional soy sauce , if desired.

NUTRITION: calories 110, fat 3g , protein 16g , carbs 2g , sugars 1g , fiber 0g , sodium 110mg

117. Broiled Shrimps

Cooking time: 10 mins | Servings: 12

INGREDIENTS:

- 2 pounds large shrimp , unshelled
- $^1/_3$ cup olive oil
- 2 tbsp lemon juice
- ¼ cup chopped scallions
- 1 tbsp chopped garlic
- 2 tsps freshly ground black pepper
- 1 large lemon, sliced
- 3 tbsp chopped fresh parsley

DIRECTIONS:

1. Set the oven to broil. Shell the uncooked shrimp, but do not remove the tails. With a small knife , split the shrimp down the back , and remove the vein. Wash the shrimp with cool water , and pat dry with paper towels.
2. In a medium skillet , over medium heat , heat the olive oil. Add the lemon juice , scallions , garlic , and pepper. Heat the mixture for 3 mins. Set aside.
3. In a baking dish , arrange the shrimp and pour the olive oil mixture over the shrimp. Broil the shrimp 4 to 5 inches from the heat for 2 mins per side , just until the shrimp turns bright pink. Transfer the shrimp to a platter and garnish with lemon slices and parsley. Pour the juices from the pan over the shrimp.

NUTRITION: calories 100 , fat 6g , protein 10g , carbs 1g , sugars 0g , fiber 0g , sodium

50mg

118. Creamy Cheese Dip

Cooking time: 5 mins | Servings: 40

INGREDIENTS:

- 1 cup fat-free yogurt
- 1 cup fat-free ricotta cheese
- 1 cup low-fat cottage cheese

DIRECTIONS:

1. Combine all the ingredients in a food processor; process until smooth. Place in a covered container and refrigerate until ready to use (this cream cheese can be refrigerated for up to 1 week).

NUTRITION: calories 10 , fat 0g , protein 2g , carbs 1g , sugars 1g , fiber 0g , sodium 30mg

119. Baked Scallops

Cooking time: 10 mins | Servings: 4

INGREDIENTS:

- 12 oz fresh bay or dry sea scallops
- 1½ tsps pickling spices
- ½ cup cider vinegar
- ¼ cup water
- 1 tbsp finely chopped onion
- 1 red bell pepper , cut into thin strips
- 1 head lettuce , rinsed and dried
- 1/3 cup sesame seeds , toasted

DIRECTIONS:

1. Preheat the oven to 350°F. Wash the scallops in cool water and cut any scallops that are too big in half.
2. Spread the scallops out in a large baking dish (be careful not to overlap them). In a small bowl, combine the spices , cider vinegar , water , onion , and pepper; pour the mixture over the scallops. Season with salt, if desired.
3. Cover the baking dish and bake for 7 mins. Remove from the oven and allow the scallops to chill in the refrigerator (leave them in the cooking liquid/vegetable mixture).
4. Just before serving , place the lettuce leaves on individual plates or a platter , and place the scallops and vegetables over the top. Sprinkle with sesame seeds before serving.

NUTRITION: calories 150 , fat 6g , protein 14g , carbs 10g , sugars 2g, fiber 3g , sodium 150mg

120. Monterey Jack Cheese Quiche

Cooking time: 15 mins | Servings: 12

INGREDIENTS:

- 4 egg whites
- 1 cup plus 2 tbsp low-fat cottage cheese
- ¼ cup plus 2 tbsp flour
- ¾ tsp baking powder
- 1 cup shredded Monterey Jack cheese
- 1 red bell pepper, diced
- 1 cup lentils, cooked
- 1 tbsp olive oil

DIRECTIONS:

1. Preheat the oven to 350°F.
2. In a medium bowl, beat the egg whites and cottage cheese for 2 mins , until smooth.
3. Add the flour and baking powder and beat until smooth. Stir in the cheese , red pepper , and lentils.
4. Coat a 9-inch-square pan with the olive oil and pour in the egg mixture. Bake for 30 to 35 mins, until firm.
5. Remove the quiche from the oven and allow to cool for 10 mins (it will be easier to cut). Cut into 12 squares and transfer to a platter and serve.

NUTRITION: calories 100, fat 3g, protein 8g , carbs 9g , sugars 2g , fiber 2g, sodium 210mg

121. Cucumber Pâté

Cooking time: 20 mins | Servings: 12

INGREDIENTS:

- 1 large cucumber , peeled , seeded , and quartered
- 1 small green bell pepper , seeded and quartered
- 2 stalks celery, quartered
- 1 medium onion, quartered
- 1 cup low-fat: cottage cheese
- ½ cup plain nonfat: Greek yogurt
- 1 package unflavored gelatin
- ¼ cup boiling water
- ¼ cup cold water

DIRECTIONS:

1. Spray a 5-cup mold or a 1½-quart mixing bowl with nonstick cooking spray.
2. In a food processor , coarsely chop the cucumber , green pepper , celery , and onion. Remove the vegetables from the food processor and set aside.
3. In a food processor , combine the cottage cheese and yogurt , and blend until smooth.
4. In a medium bowl , dissolve the gelatin in the boiling water; slowly stir in the cold water. Add the chopped vegetables and cottage cheese mixture and mix thoroughly.
5. Pour the mixture into the prepared mold and refrigerate overnight or until firm. To serve, carefully invert the mold onto a serving plate, and remove the mold. Surround the pâté with assorted crackers and serve.

NUTRITION: calories 30, fat 0g, protein 4g , carbs 3g, sugars 2g, fiber 1g, sodium 95mg

122. Gruyère Apple Spread

Cooking time: 5 mins | Servings: 10

INGREDIENTS:

- 2 oz fat-free cream cheese softened
- ¼ cup low-fat: cottage cheese
- 2 oz Gruyere cheese
- ¼ tsp dry mustard
- ⅛ tsp freshly ground black pepper
- ½ cup shredded apple (unpeeled)
- 1 tbsp finely chopped pecans
- 1 tsp minced fresh chives

DIRECTIONS:

1. Place the cheeses in a food processor , and blend until smooth. Add the mustard and pepper , and blend for 30 seconds.
2. Transfer the mixture to a serving bowl , and fold in the apple and pecans. Sprinkle the dip with chives.
3. Cover , and refrigerate the mixture for 1 to 2 hours. Serve chilled with crackers , or stuff into celery stalks.

NUTRITION : calories 40, fat 2g, protein 3g , carbs 1g , sugars 1g , fiber 0g , sodium 100mg

CHAPTER 5 Salads

123. Mozzarella and Tomato Salad

Cooking time: 0 mins | Servings: 2

INGREDIENTS:

- 2 oz mozzarella cheese , cut into ¾-inch cubes
- ½ cup cherry tomatoes , halved
- ½ cup cannellini beans , drained and rinsed
- ½ cup artichoke hearts , drained
- ¼ cup jarred roasted red peppers
- ¼ cup chopped scallions
- 1 tbsp minced fresh basil
- 1 tbsp olive oil
- 2 tsps balsamic vinegar
- ⅛ tsp salt
- 4 cups baby spinach , divided

DIRECTIONS:

1. In a small bowl , stir together the mozzarella cheese , tomatoes , beans , artichoke hearts , red peppers , and scallions.
2. In another small bowl , whisk the basil , olive oil , balsamic vinegar , and salt until combined.
3. Drizzle the dressing over the cheese and vegetables. Toss to coat. Chill for 15 mins.
4. Using 2 plates , arrange 2 cups of spinach on each. Top with half of the cheese and vegetable mixture.
5. Serve immediately.

NUTRITION: calories 207, fat 5g, protein 17g , carbs 25g , sugars 3g, fiber 8g , sodium 251mg

124. Energy Salad

Cooking time: 0 mins | Servings: 2

INGREDIENTS:

Salad:

- 6 cups mixed baby greens
- 1 cup shelled edamame
- 1 cup chopped red cabbage
- 1 cup chopped red bell pepper
- 1 cup sliced fresh button mushrooms
- ½ cup sliced avocado
- 1 cup pea shoots, divided

Dressing:

- 1 tbsp olive oil
- 1 tbsp freshly squeezed lemon juice
- 1 tbsp balsamic vinegar
- 1 tbsp chia seeds
- Pinch salt and pepper

DIRECTIONS:

Make the Dressing

1. In a small bowl, whisk together the olive oil , lemon juice , balsamic vinegar , chia seeds until well combined. Season with salt and pepper.

Make the Salad

2. In a large bowl, toss together the mixed greens , edamame , red cabbage , red bell pepper , mushrooms , and avocado. Drizzle the dressing over the salad. Toss again to coat well.
3. Divide the salad between 2 plates. Top each with ½ cup of pea shoots and serve.

NUTRITION: calories 435, fat 24g, protein

21g, carbs 38g , sugars 9g, fiber 12g, sodium 136mg

125. Squash and Broccoli Barley Salad

Cooking time: 40 mins | Servings: 4

INGREDIENTS:

- ½ butternut squash
- 1 tsp plus 2 tbsp olive oil | divided
- 1 cup broccoli florets
- 1 cup barley
- ½ cup toasted chopped walnuts
- 1 cup baby kale
- ½ red onion | sliced
- 2 tbsp balsamic vinegar
- 2 garlic cloves | minced
- ½ tsp salt
- ¼ tsp freshly ground black pepper

DIRECTIONS:

1. Preheat the oven to 400°F. Line a baking sheet with parchment paper.
2. Peel and seed the squash, and cut it into dice. In a large bowl , toss the squash with 2 tsps of olive oil. Transfer to the prepared baking sheet and roast for 20 mins.
3. While the squash is roasting , toss the broccoli in the same bowl with 1 tsp of olive oil. After 20 mins , flip the squash and push it to one side of the baking sheet. Add the broccoli to the other side and continue to roast for 20 more mins until tender.
4. While the veggies are roasting , in a medium pot , cover the barley with several inches of water. Bring to a boil , then reduce the heat , cover , and simmer for 30 mins until tender. Drain and rinse.
5. Transfer the barley to a large bowl , and toss with the cooked squash and broccoli , walnuts , kale , and onion.
6. In a small bowl , mix the remaining 2 tbsp of olive oil , balsamic vinegar , garlic , salt , and pepper. Toss the salad with the dressing and serve.

NUTRITION: calories 275, fat 15g, protein 6g, carbs 32g, sugars 3g, fiber 7g , sodium 144mg

126. Pear and Spinach Salad

Cooking time: 0 mins | Servings 2

INGREDIENTS:

- 4 cups baby spinach
- ½ pear, cored , peeled , and chopped
- ¼ cup whole walnuts , chopped
- 2 tbsp apple cider vinegar
- 2 tbsp olive oil
- ½ tsp Dijon mustard
- ½ tsp sea salt

DIRECTIONS:

1. Layer the spinach on the bottom of two mason jars. Top with the pear and walnuts.
2. In a small bowl , whisk together the vinegar , oil , mustard , and salt. Put in another lidded container.
3. Shake the dressing before serving and add it to the mason jars. Close the jars and shake to distribute the dressing.

NUTRITION: calories 254, fat 23g, protein 4g, carbs 10g, sugars 4g, fiber 4g, sodium 340mg

127. Chicken , Spinach , and Berry Salad

Cooking time 0 mins | Servings 4

INGREDIENTS:

Salad

- 6 cups baby spinach
- 2 cups shredded roast chicken
- ½ cup sliced berries
- ½ cup sliced almonds
- 1 avocado , sliced
- ¼ cup crumbled feta (optional)

Dressing

- 2 tbsp olive oil

- 2 tsps honey
- 2 tsps balsamic vinegar

DIRECTIONS:

Make the Salad

1. In a large bowl , combine the spinach , chicken, strawberries, and almonds.
2. Pour the dressing over the salad and lightly toss.
3. Divide into four equal portions and top each with sliced avocado and 1 tbsp of crumbled feta (if using).

Make the Dressing

1. In a small bowl, whisk together the olive oil, honey, and balsamic vinegar.

NUTRITION: calories 339, fat 22g , protein 25g, carbs 13g, sugars 6g, fiber 6g , sodium 132mg

128. Blueberry Chicken Salad

Cooking time 0 mins | Servings 4

INGREDIENTS:

- 2 cups chopped cooked chicken
- ½ cup fresh blueberries
- ¼ cup finely chopped almonds
- 1 celery stalk , finely chopped
- ¼ cup finely chopped red onion
- 1 tbsp chopped fresh basil
- ½ cup plain , nonfat Greek yogurt
- ¼ tsp salt and black pepper
- 6 cups salad greens (baby spinach, spicy greens , romaine)

DIRECTIONS:

1. In a large mixing bowl, combine the chicken, blueberries , almonds , onion , and basil. Toss gently to mix.
2. In a small bowl, combine the yogurt , salt , and pepper. Add to the chicken salad and stir to combine.
3. Arrange 2 cups of salad greens on each of 4 plates and divide the chicken salad among the plates to serve.

NUTRITION: calories 207, fat 6g, protein 28g , carbs 11g, sugars 6g, fiber 3g , sodium 235mg

129. Butterscotch Apple Salad

Cooking Time 0 mins | Servings 6

INGREDIENTS:

- 3 cups apples , chopped
- 2 cups kiwi
- 8 oz. whipped topping
- 1/2 cup butterscotch topping
- 1/3 cup almonds
- 1/4 cup butterscotch chips

DIRECTIONS:

1. Put all the salad ingredients into a suitable salad bowl.
2. Toss them well and refrigerate for 1 hour. Serve.

NUTRITION: calories 293, fat 12g**,** sodium 152mg, carbs 45g, fiber 4.2g, protein 4.2g, phosphorus 202mg , potassium 296mg

130. Berries salad

Cooking time 0 mins | Servings 4

INGREDIENTS:

- 1 lb. of hulled and quartered strawberries
- 3 tbsp. of balsamic vinegar
- 2 tbsp. of honey
- dash of ground cardamom
- ground pepper
- 1 pint of blueberries
- 1 sprig mint leaves roughly torn

DIRECTIONS:

1. Whisk together in a large bowl the vinegar, honey, pepper, and cardamom.
2. Tumble in the berries and mint leaves. Serve chilled.

NUTRITION: calories 143, fat 14.3 g , carbs 4.5g , protein 1.8 g , sodium 51.5 mg

131. Asian taste salad

Cooking time 0 mins | Servings 4

INGREDIENTS:

- 2 sliced pear peppers
- 1/2 cup of diced radishes
- 4 tsp. of red diced onion
- 4 tsp. of mirin
- 1 tsp. of sesame oil
- 1/2 tsp. of fresh ginger minced
- 2 tsp. of rice wine vinegar
- 4 cups of cucumbers partially peeled cut into thin slices
- 1 green onion sliced thin
- 1 tsp. of pepper

DIRECTIONS:

1. In a large bowl , toss together peppers , radishes , and red onions.
2. In a separate bowl , whisk together Mirin , sesame oil , ginger , vinegar , and pepper.
3. Pour dressing over cucumber medley and refrigerate for 2 hours or overnight.
4. Serve with a sprinkling of green onions.

NUTRITION: calories 34 , fat 12.3 g , carbs 4.7g , protein 0.9 g , sodium 50.5 mg

132. Beet Salad

Cooking Time 30 mins | Servings 4

INGREDIENTS:

- 6 medium sized beets
- 1 tbsp olive oil
- freshly ground black pepper
- 1 cup water
- 1 tbsp balsamic vinegar

DIRECTIONS:

1. Wash the beets carefully and trim them to ½ inch portions
2. Add 1 cup of water to the pot
3. Place a steamer on top and arrange the beets on top of the steamer
4. Lock up the lid and cook on HIGH pressure for 1 minute
5. Release the pressure naturally and allow the beet to cool
6. Slice the top of the skin carefully
7. Slice up the beets in uniform portions and season with vinegar and pepper
8. Allow them to marinate for 30 mins
9. Add a bit of olive oil and serve!

NUTRITION: calories 123, fat 7.3 g , carbs14.5g , protein 1.8 g, sodium 65.5 mg

133. Cranberry Cabbage Slaw

Cooking Time 0 mins | Servings 4

INGREDIENTS:

- ½ medium cabbage head , shredded
- 1 medium red apple , shredded
- 2 tbsps onion , sliced
- ½ cup dried cranberries
- 1/4 cup almonds , toasted sliced
- ½ cup olive oil
- ¼ tsp stevia
- 1/4 cup cider vinegar
- ½ tbsp celery seed
- ½ tsp dry mustard
- ½ cup cream

DIRECTIONS:

1. Take a suitable salad bowl.
2. Start tossing in all the ingredients.
3. Mix well and serve.

NUTRITION: calories 308, fat 24.5g, sodium 23mg, carbs 13.5g, fiber 3.2g, protein 2.6g, phosphorus 257mg, potassium 219mg

134. Chestnut Noodle Salad

Cooking Time 0 mins | Servings 6

INGREDIENTS:

- 8 cups cabbage , shredded
- ½ cup canned chestnuts , sliced
- 6 green onions , chopped
- 1/4 cup olive oil
- 1/4 cup apple cider vinegar
- 3/4 tsp stevia
- 1/8 tsp black pepper
- 1 cup chow Mein noodles , cooked

DIRECTIONS:

1. Take a suitable salad bowl.
2. Start tossing in all the ingredients.
3. Mix well and serve.

NUTRITION: calories 191, fat 13g, sodium 78mg , carbs 5.8g, fiber 3.4g, protein 4.2g , phosphorus 188mg , potassium 302mg

135. Cranberry Broccoli Salad

Cooking Time 0 mins | Servings 4

INGREDIENTS:

- 3/4 cup plain Greek yogurt
- 1/4 cup mayonnaise
- 2 tbsps maple syrup
- 2 tbsps apple cider vinegar
- 4 cups broccoli florets
- 1 medium apple , chopped
- ½ cup red onion , sliced
- 1/4 cup parsley , chopped
- ½ cup dried cranberries
- 1/4 cup pecans

DIRECTIONS:

1. Put all the salad ingredients into a suitable salad bowl.
2. Toss them well and refrigerate for 1 hour. Serve.

NUTRITION: calories 252, fat 10g , sodium 157mg, carbs 34g, fiber 5g, protein 9.4g, phosphorus 291mg, potassium 480mg

136. Balsamic Beet Salad

Cooking Time 0 mins | Servings 2

INGREDIENTS:

- 1 cucumber , peeled and sliced
- 15 oz. canned low-Sodium beets, sliced
- 4 tsp balsamic vinegar
- 2 tsp sesame oil
- 2 tbsps zola cheese

DIRECTIONS:

1. Take a suitable salad bowl.
2. Start tossing in all the ingredients.
3. Mix well and serve.

NUTRITION: calories 145, fat 7.8g, sodium 426mg, carbs 16.4g, fiber 3.8g, protein 5g , phosphorus 79mg , potassium 229mg

137. Daikon Salad

Cooking Time 5 mins | Servings 2

INGREDIENTS:

- ¼ peeled and grated pumpkin
- 2 tbsp lemon juice
- 2 peeled and grated daikons
- 3 tbsp olive oil
- 2 cup minced parsley

DIRECTIONS:

1. Combine all the ingredients in a salad bowl.
2. Sprinkle with olive oil and lemon juice.

NUTRITION: calories 237, fat 2.3, carbs 13g, fiber 3.4g, protein 4.2g, phosphorus 158mg , potassium 212mg

138. Shrimp Salad

Cooking Time 0 mins | Servings 4

INGREDIENTS:

- 1 lb. shrimp , boiled and chopped
- 1 hardboiled egg , chopped
- 1 tbsp celery , chopped
- 1 tbsp green pepper , chopped
- 1 tbsp onion , chopped
- 2 tbsps mayonnaise
- 1 tsp lemon juice
- ½ tsp chili powder
- ⅛ tsp hot sauce
- ½ tsp dry mustard

- Lettuce , chopped or shredded

DIRECTIONS:

1. Take a suitable salad bowl.
2. Start tossing in all the ingredients. Mix well and serve.

NUTRITION: calories 184, fat 5.7g, sodium 381mg, carbs 4g, fiber 0.3g , protein 27.5g , phosphorus 249mg , potassium 233mg

139. Chicken Cranberry Sauce Salad

Cooking Time 0 mins | Servings 6

INGREDIENTS:

- 3 cups of chicken meat , cooked , cubed
- 1 cup grapes
- 2 cups daikon salad carrots , shredded
- 1/4 red onion , chopped
- 1 large yellow bell pepper , chopped
- 1/4 cup mayonnaise
- 1/2 cup cranberry sauce

DIRECTIONS:

1. Put all the salad ingredients into a suitable salad bowl.
2. Toss them well and refrigerate for 1 hour. Serve.

NUTRITION: calories 240, fat 8.6g, sodium 161mg , carbs 19g, fiber 1.4g, protein 21g , phosphorus 260mg , potassium 351mg

140. Egg Celery Salad

Cooking Time 0 mins | Servings 4

INGREDIENTS:

- 4 eggs , boiled , peeled and chopped
- 1/4 cup celery , chopped
- ½ cup sweet onion , chopped
- 2 tbsps sweet pickle , chopped
- 3 tbsps mayonnaise
- 1 tbsp mustard

DIRECTIONS:

1. Put all the salad ingredients into a suitable salad bowl.
2. Toss them well and refrigerate for 1 hour. Serve.

NUTRITION: calories 134, fat 8g, sodium 259mg , carbs 7.4g¸ fiber 0.6g, protein 6.8g , phosphorus 357mg , potassium 113mg

141. Papaya Salad

Cooking Time 0 mins | Servings 6

INGREDIENTS:

- 10 small shrimps , dried
- 2 small red Thai Chilies
- 1 garlic clove , peeled
- ¼ cup tamarind juice
- 1 tbsp Thai fish sauce , low Sodium
- 1 lime , cut into 1 inch pieces
- 4 cherry tomatoes , halved
- 3 long beans, trimmed into 1 inch pieces
- 1 carrot , coarsely shredded
- ½ cucumber, coarsely chopped and seeded
- 1/6 a small green cabbage , cored and thinly sliced
- 1 lb unripe green papaya, quartered , seeded and shredded using mandolin
- 3 tbsps unsalted roasted peanuts

DIRECTIONS:

1. Take a mortar and pestle and crush your shrimp alongside garlic , chills
2. Add tamarind juice, fish sauce and palm sugar
3. Squeeze 3 quarts of lime pieces over the mortar
4. Grind to make a dressing, keep the dressing on the side
5. Take a bowl add the remaining ingredients (excluding the peanut), making sure to add the papaya last
6. Use a spoon and stir in the dressing
7. Mix the vegetable and fruit and coat them well

8. Transfer to your serving dish
9. Garnish with some peanuts and lime pieces

NUTRITION: calories 183, fat 1g , sodium 161mg, carbs 51g, fiber 1.4g, protein 2g , phosphorus 260mg, potassium 351mg

142. Slow cooker Corn Salad

Cooking Time 2 hours | Servings 6

INGREDIENTS:

- 2 oz ham, cut into strips
- 1 tsp olive oil
- 2 cups corn
- 1/2 cup salt –free tomato sauce
- 1 tsp garlic , minced
- 1 green bell pepper , chopped

DIRECTIONS:

1. Grease your Slow Cooker with oil
2. Add corn , prosciutto , garlic , tomato sauce , bell pepper to your Slow Cooker
3. Stir and place lid
4. Cook on HIGH for 2 hours

NUTRITION: calories 157, fat 1.6g, sodium 151mg, carbs 11g, fiber 1.1g sugars 7.2g protein 26g

143. Chicken Orange Salad

Cooking Time 0 mins | Servings 4

INGREDIENTS:

- 1 ½ cup chicken , cooked and diced
- ½ cup celery , diced
- ½ cup green pepper , chopped
- ¼ cup onion , sliced
- 1 cup orange, peeled and cut into segments
- ¼ cup mayonnaise
- ½ tsp black pepper

DIRECTIONS:

1. Take a suitable salad bowl.
2. Start tossing in all the ingredients. Mix well and serve.

NUTRITION: calories 167, fat 6.6g, sodium 151mg, carbs 11.2g, fiber 1.1g ,protein 16g , phosphorus 211mg , potassium 249mg

144. Almond Pasta Salad

Cooking Time 0 mins | Servings 14

INGREDIENTS:

- 1 lb. elbow macaroni , cooked
- 1/2 cup sun-dried tomatoes , diced
- 1 (15 oz.) can whole artichokes , diced
- 1 orange bell pepper , diced
- 3 green onions , sliced
- 2 tbsps basil , sliced
- 2 oz. slivered almonds

Dressing

- 1 garlic clove , minced
- 1 tbsp Dijon mustard
- 1 tbsp raw honey
- 1/4 cup white balsamic vinegar
- 1/3 cup olive oil

DIRECTIONS:

1. Take a suitable salad bowl.
2. Start tossing in all the ingredients. Mix well and serve.

NUTRITION: calories 260, fat 7.7g, sodium 143mg, carbs 41g, fiber 9.5g, protein 9.6g , phosphorus 39mg , potassium 585mg

145. Pineapple Berry Salad

Cooking Time 0 mins | Servings 4

INGREDIENTS:

- 4 cups pineapple , peeled and cubed
- 3 cups strawberries , chopped
- 1/4 cup honey
- 1/2 cup basil leaves
- 1 tbsp lemon zest
- 1/2 cup blueberries

DIRECTIONS:

1. Take a suitable salad bowl.
2. Start tossing in all the ingredients; mix well and serve.

NUTRITION: calories 128, fat 0.6g, sodium 3mg, carbs 33.1g, fiber 5.2g, protein 1.8g , phosphorus 151mg , potassium 362mg

146. Garden fantasy salad

Cooking time 0 mins | Servings 6

INGREDIENTS:

- 2 cups of peeled and shredded carrots
- 1½ cups of shredded green cabbage
- 1½ cups of shredded purple cabbage
- 1 cup of chopped cucumber
- 2 chopped large scallions
- ¼ cup of chopped fresh parsley leaves

For Dressing

- 2 tbsp. of olive oil
- 2 tbsp. of fresh lemon juice
- 1 tsp. of finely grated fresh lemon zest
- Pinch of salt

DIRECTIONS:

1. In a large serving bowl, add all salad ingredients
2. In another bowl, all dressing ingredients and mix till well combined.
3. Pour dressing over salad and toss to coat well. Serve immediately.

NUTRITION: calories 71, fat 17.1 g , carbs 7.2g , protein 1.1 g , sodium 63 mg

147. Autumn Green salad

Cooking time 0 mins | Servings 4

INGREDIENTS:

For Dressing

- 1 tbsp. of shallot , minced
- 1/3 cup of olive oil
- 2 tbsp. of fresh lemon juice
- 1 tsp. of honey

For Salad

- 1½ cups of chopped broccoli florets
- 1½ cups of shredded cabbage
- 4 cups of chopped lettuce

DIRECTIONS:

1. In a bowl, add all dressing ingredients and beat till well combined. Keep aside.
2. In another large bowl, mix all salad ingredients.
3. Add dressing and gently toss to coat well. Serve immediately.

NUTRITION: calories 179, fat 17.1g, carbs 7.8g , protein 1.7 g, sodium 21 mg

148. Avocado and Mango salad

Cooking time 0 mins | Servings 4

INGREDIENTS:

- 1 chopped lettuce
- 1 avocado
- 1 apple, chopped
- 1 pinch of pepper
- 1 tbsp of White wine vinegar
- 1 tbsp of olive oil
- 2 tbsp of chopped toasted almonds
- 2 tbsp of dried cranberries

DIRECTIONS:

1. Peel and chop the vegetables.
2. Put the lettuce, apple, avocado , almonds , and cranberries in a bowl.
3. On the other hand , mix the oil with the vinegar and add pepper.
4. Pour over the salad and mix. Serve on plates and enjoy.

NUTRITION: calories 179, fat 17.1 g , carbs 7.8g , protein 1.7 g, sodium 21 mg

149. Green & Yellow Bean Salad

Cooking Time 0 mins | Servings 4

INGREDIENTS:

- 1 cup green beans , fresh
- 1 cup yellow beans , fresh
- 1/3 cup onion , sliced

- 1/3 cup green pepper , sliced
- ¼ cup olive oil
- ¼ cup vinegar
- ½ tsp basil , dried
- 1 tsp parsley , dried
- ¼ tsp black pepper

DIRECTIONS:

1. Take a suitable salad bowl.
2. Start tossing in all the ingredients. Mix well and serve.

NUTRITION: calories 189, fat 13.1g , sodium 5mg, carbs 14g, fiber 5.9g, protein 4.8g, phosphorus 147mg, potassium 243mg

150. Carrot Zucchini Salad

Cooking Time 0 mins | Servings 2

INGREDIENTS:

- 1/4 cup rice vinegar
- 1/8 tsp stevia
- 1/2 tsp olive oil
- 1/8 tsp black pepper
- 1/2 zucchini, peeled and julienned
- 1 cup carrots , julienned
- 2 tbsps red bell pepper , julienned

DIRECTIONS:

1. Take a suitable salad bowl.
2. Start tossing in all the ingredients; mix well and serve.

NUTRITION: calories 92, fat 1.6g, sodium 43mg, carbs 6.1g, fiber 3.5g, protein 2.3g , phosphorus 147mg, potassium 529mg

151. BBQ Salad

Cooking Time 1 h + 30 mins | Servings 1

INGREDIENTS:

- 2 yellow peppers , large
- 4 boneless , skinless chicken breasts
- 1 tsp soy sauce
- 2 tbsp cilantro
- 2 tbsp olive oil
- 2 cloves garlic
- 1 tbsp ginger, minced
- ½ tsp hot red chili pepper flakes
- 5 ½ cups mixed salad greens
- 3 tbsps rice vinegar

DIRECTIONS:

1. Mince fresh cilantro.
2. Whisk together pepper flakes , garlic , ginger , cilantro , and half of the oil in a large bowl.
3. Add chicken breasts and coat well. Cover and refrigerate for 30 mins.
4. Cut peppers into quarters.
5. Over medium-high heat , grill pepper until they start to blacken , for about fifteen mins. Remove them to plate.
6. Grill chicken breasts for 15 mins per side , until done.
7. Chop chicken and warm grilled peppers into ½ inch wide strips. Toss peppers and chicken with remaining vinegar and oil and greens.

NUTRITION: calories 171, fat 5.1g , sodium 35mg , carbs 5g , fiber 5.9g , protein 24.8g , phosphorus 60mg , potassium 64mg

152. Cheese and Walnut Salad

Cooking Time 5 mins | Servings 1

INGREDIENTS:

- 1 oz Feta cheese , crumbled
- 2 oz walnuts , chopped
- 1 cup fresh parsley , chopped
- 1 cup cucumbers , chopped
- ½ cup tomatoes , chopped
- ½ red onion , sliced
- 2 tbsps sesame oil
- 1 tbsp lemon juice

DIRECTIONS:

1. Make the dressing by mixing Italian seasoning, lemon juice, and sesame oil.
2. Then in the salad bowl combine crumbled Feta cheese, walnuts,

parsley, cucumbers, tomatoes , and onion.

3. Drizzle the dressing over the salad and mix it up with the help of two spatulas.

NUTRITION: calories 126, fat 111.6g , sodium 23mg , carbs 4.1g, fiber 3.5g, protein 2.3g , phosphorus 47mg , potassium 59mg

153. Figs and Aragula Salad

Cooking Time 5 mins | Servings 1

INGREDIENTS:

- 3 figs , sliced
- 2 oz Feta cheese , crumbled
- 1 tbsp balsamic vinegar
- 1 tsp canola oil
- 2 tbsps almonds , sliced
- 2 cups fresh parsley
- 1 cup fresh arugula
- ½ tsp salt
- ½ tsp honey

DIRECTIONS:

1. Make the salad dressing by mixing balsamic vinegar , canola oil , salt , and honey.
2. Then put sliced almonds and figs in the big bowl.
3. Chop the parsley and add in the fig mixture too.
4. After this , tear arugula.
5. Combine arugula with fig mixture.
6. Add salad dressing and shake the salad well.

NUTRITION: calories 116, fat 6.5g , sodium 22mg , carbs 14.8g , fiber 2.8g , protein 4.8g , phosphorus 45mg , potassium 69mg

154. Spicy Beef Salad

Cooking Time 35 mins | Servings 1

INGREDIENTS:

- 8 cups torn romaine lettuce
- ½ cup each julienned cucumber, sweet yellow pepper, and red onion
- 4 tsp olive oil
- ½ cup of halved grape tomatoes
- Chili-lime vinaigrette
- ¼ cup fresh lime juice
- 1 tsp of grated lime rind
- 1 tbsp honey
- 1 tbsp Asian chili sauce
- 2 tbsp rice vinegar
- 1 tbsp minced ginger root
- 1 tbsp fresh lime juice
- 1 tbsp cornstarch
- 1 tsp Asian chili sauce
- 2 cloves garlic , minced
- 1 lb. beef strip loin, top sirloin or flank steak , thinly sliced

DIRECTIONS:

1. Combine the chili sauce, sesame oil, garlic , lime juice , ginger root , and cornstarch in a medium bowl.
2. Add beef. Toss to coat. Let stand for 10 mins.
3. In a large frypan , heat 1 tsp canola oil.
4. Stir-fry onion, yellow pepper , cucumber , tomatoes until just wilted and hot. Transfer to the clean bowl.
5. Heat the remaining canola oil in the same pan. Stir-fry beef until cooked and browned.
6. Add to wilted vegetables, tossing to combine.
7. Whisk all chili-lime vinaigrette ingredients together.
8. Put chili-lime vinaigrette in the pan. Cook until hot and slightly thickened.
9. Top romaine with veggies and beef and vinaigrette.

NUTRITION: calories 126, fat 4.3g , sodium 32mg , carbs 4.1g, fiber 3.5g, protein 12.3g , phosphorus 37mg , potassium 199mg

155. Broccoli Lettuce Salad

Cooking Time 0 mins | Servings 2

INGREDIENTS:

- 1 cup lettuce , chopped
- ¼ zucchini , peeled and cubed
- 4 carrots , diced
- 1/4 cup broccoli florets
- 2 tbsps balsamic vinegar
- 1 tsp olive oil

DIRECTIONS:

1. Take a suitable salad bowl.
2. Start tossing in all the ingredients. Mix well and serve.

NUTRITION: calories 43, fat 2.5g , sodium 22mg , carbs 4.8g, fiber 1.2g , protein 0.8g , phosphorus 200mg , potassium 188mg

156. Pepper Cabbage Salad

Cooking Time 0 mins| Servings 4

INGREDIENTS:

- 1 small cabbage head , shredded
- 1 medium green bell pepper , shredded
- 2 medium carrots , shredded
- 1/3 tbsp stevia
- 1/2 cup vinegar
- 1/2 cup water
- 2 tsps celery seed

DIRECTIONS:

1. Take a suitable salad bowl.
2. Start tossing in all the ingredients. Mix well and serve.

NUTRITION: calories 168, fat 0.5g , sodium 58mg , carbs 27.9g, fiber 5.7g , protein 3g , phosphorus 133mg , potassium 493mg

157. Lettuce and Carrot Salad with Vinaigrette

Cooking Time 0 mins | Servings 4

INGREDIENTS:

For the vinaigrette

- ½ cup olive oil
- 4 tbsp balsamic vinegar
- 2 tbsp chopped fresh oregano
- Pinch red pepper flakes
- Ground black pepper

For the salad

- 4 cups shredded green leaf lettuce
- 1 carrot , shredded
- ¾ cup fresh green beans , cut into 1-inch pieces
- 3 large radishes , sliced thinly

DIRECTIONS:

1. To make the vinaigrette place the ingredients in a bowl and whisk.
2. To make the salad in a bowl , toss together the carrot , lettuce , green beans , and radishes.
3. Add the vinaigrette to the vegetables and toss to coat.
4. Arrange the salad on plates and serve.

NUTRITION: calories 273 , fat 27g , carbs 7g , phosphorus 30mg , potassium 197mg , sodium 27mg , protein 1g

158. Strawberry Watercress Salad with Dressing

Cooking Time 0 mins | Servings 6

INGREDIENTS:

For the dressing

- ¼ cup olive oil
- ¼ cup rice vinegar
- 1 tbsp honey
- ¼ tsp pure almond extract
- ¼ tsp ground mustard
- ground black pepper

For the salad

- 2 cups chopped watercress
- 2 cups shredded green leaf lettuce
- ½ red onion , sliced very thin
- ½ english cucumber , chopped
- 1 cup sliced strawberries

DIRECTIONS:

1. To make the dressing , in a small bowl , whisk together the olive oil and rice vinegar until mixed.
2. Whisk in the almond extract , honey , mustard , and pepper. Set aside.
3. To make the salad In a large bowl , toss together the watercress , green leaf lettuce , onion , cucumber , and strawberries.
4. Pour the dressing over the salad and toss to combine.

NUTRITION: calories 159 , fat 14g , carbs 9g , phosphorus 34mg, potassium 195mg , sodium 14mg , protein 1g

159. Cucumber and Cabbage Salad

Cooking Time 0 mins | Servings 4

INGREDIENTS:

- ¼ cup heavy cream
- ¼ cup freshly squeezed lemon juice
- 2 tbsp granulated sugar
- 2 tbsp chopped fresh dill
- 2 tbsp finely chopped scallion, green part only
- ¼ tsp ground black pepper
- 1 english cucumber , sliced thinly
- 2 cups shredded green cabbage

DIRECTIONS:

1. In a small bowl, stir together the lemon juice , cream, sugar , dill , scallion , and pepper until well blended.
2. In a large bowl, toss together the cucumber and cabbage.
3. Place the salad in the refrigerator and chill for 1 hour.
4. Stir before serving.

NUTRITION: calories 99, fat 6g , carbs 13g , phosphorus 38mg , potassium 200mg , sodium 14mg , protein 2g

160. Lettuce , Asparagus and berries Salad

Cooking Time 0 mins | Servings 4

INGREDIENTS:

- 2 cups shredded green leaf lettuce
- 1 cup asparagus , cut into long ribbons with a peeler
- 1 scallion , both green and white parts , sliced
- 1 cup raspberries
- 2 tbsp balsamic vinegar
- Ground black pepper to taste

DIRECTIONS:

1. Arrange the lettuce evenly on 4 serving plates.
2. Arrange the asparagus and scallion on top of the greens.
3. Place the raspberries on top of the salads , dividing the berries evenly.
4. Drizzle the salads with balsamic vinegar.
5. Season with pepper.

NUTRITION: calories 36 , fat 0g , carbs 8g , phosphorus 43mg , potassium 200mg , sodium 11mg , protein 2g

161. Waldorf Salad with Variation

Cooking Time 0 mins | Servings 4

INGREDIENTS:

- 3 cups green leaf lettuce, torn into pieces
- 1 cup halved grapes
- 3 celery stalks , chopped
- 1 apple , chopped
- ½ cup light sour cream
- 2 tbsp freshly squeezed lemon juice
- 1 tbsp granulated sugar

DIRECTIONS:

1. Arrange the lettuce evenly on 4 plates. Set aside.
2. In a bowl , stir together the grapes , celery , and apple.

3. In another bowl , stir together the sour cream , lemon juice , and sugar.
4. Add the sour cream mixture to the grape mixture and stir to coat.
5. Spoon the dressed grape mixture onto each plate, dividing the mixture evenly.

NUTRITION: calories 73, fat 2g, carbs 15g , phosphorus 29mg , potassium 194mg , sodium 30mg , protein 1g

162. Asian Pear Salad

Cooking Time 0 mins | Servings 6

INGREDIENTS:

- 2 cups shredded green cabbage
- 1 cup shredded red cabbage
- 2 scallions , both green and white parts , chopped
- 2 celery stalks , chopped
- 1 asian pear , cored and grated
- ½ red bell pepper , boiled and chopped
- ½ cup chopped cilantro
- ¼ cup olive oil
- 1 lime juice
- Zest of 1 lime
- 1 tsp granulated sugar

DIRECTIONS:

1. In a bowl , toss together the green and red cabbage , scallions , celery , pear , red pepper , and cilantro.
2. In a bowl , whisk together the olive oil , lime juice , lime zest , and sugar.
3. Add the dressing to the cabbage mixture and toss to coat.
4. Chill for 1 hour and serve.

NUTRITION: calories 105 , fat 9g , carbs 6g , phosphorus 17mg , potassium 136mg , sodium 48mg , protein 1g

163. Beet Feta Salad

Cooking Time 30 mins | Servings 2

INGREDIENTS:

- 4 cups baby salad greens
- ½ sweet onion , sliced
- 8 small beets , trimmed
- 2 tbsps + 1 tsp olive oil
- 1 tbsp white wine vinegar
- 1 tsp Dijon mustard
- Black pepper (ground) , to taste
- 2 tbsps crumbled feta cheese
- 2 tbsps walnut pieces

DIRECTIONS:

1. Preheat an oven to 400°F. Grease an aluminum foil with some cooking spray.
2. Add beets with 1 tsp of olive oil; combine and wrap foil.
3. Bake for 30 mins until it becomes tender. Cut beets into wedges.
4. In a mixing bowl , add remaining olive oil , vinegar , black pepper , and mustard. Combine to mix well with each other.
5. In a mixing bowl , add salad greens , onion , feta cheese , and walnuts. Combine to mix well with each other.
6. Add half of the prepared vinaigrette and toss well.
7. Add beet and combine well.
8. Drizzle remaining vinaigrette and serve fresh.

NUTRITION: calories 185, fat 9g , carbs 6g , phosphorus 98mg , potassium 601mg , sodium 235mg , protein 4g

164. Cucumber Salad

Cooking Time 5 mins | Servings 2

INGREDIENTS:

- 1 tbsp dried dill
- 1 onion
- ¼ cup water
- 1 cup vinegar
- 3 cucumbers
- ¾ cup white sugar

DIRECTIONS:

In a bowl , toss together all the ingredients and mix well.

NUTRITION: calories 49, fat 0g , carbs 11g , phosphorus 24mg , potassium 171mg , sodium 341mg , protein 2g

165. Red Potatoes Salad

Cooking Time 5 mins | Servings 2

INGREDIENTS:

- 2 cups mayonnaise
- 1 lb. bacon
- 1 stalk celery
- 4 eggs
- 2 lbs. red potatoes
- 1 onion

DIRECTIONS:

1. In a pot add water , potatoes and cook until tender.
2. Remove, drain and set aside.
3. Place eggs in a saucepan, add water , and bring to a boil.
4. Cover and let eggs stand for 10-15 mins.
5. When ready remove , meanwhile in a deep skillet cook bacon on low heat.
6. In a bowl add all ingredients and mix well.

NUTRITION: calories 280, fat 20g , carbs 26g , phosphorus 130mg , potassium 0mg , sodium 180mg , protein 3g

166. Greek Salad

Cooking Time 0 mins | Servings 6

INGREDIENTS:

- 2 cucumbers , diced
- 2 tomatoes , sliced
- 1 green lettuce , cut into thin strips
- 2 red bell peppers , cut
- ½ cup black olives pitted
- 3 and ½ oz feta cheese , cut
- 1 red onion , sliced
- 2 tbsps olive oil
- 2 tbsps lemon juice
- Sunflower seeds and pepper to taste

DIRECTIONS:

1. Dice cucumbers and slice up the tomatoes
2. Tear the lettuce and cut it up into thin strips
3. De-seed and cut the peppers into strips
4. Take a salad bowl and mix in all the listed vegetables, add olives and feta cheese (cut into cubes)
5. Take a small cup and mix in olive oil and lemon juice, season with sunflower seeds and pepper. Pour mixture into the salad and toss well , enjoy!

NUTRITION: calories 155 , fat 1.4g , carbs 16g , phosphorus 130mg , potassium 0mg , sodium 180mg , protein 22g

167. Mixed Broccoli Salad

Cooking Time 5 mins | Servings 2

INGREDIENTS:

- 1 tbsp wine vinegar
- 1 cup cauliflower florets
- ¼ cup white sugar
- 2 cups hard-cooked eggs
- 5 slices bacon
- 1 cup broccoli florets
- 1 cup cheddar cheese
- 1 cup mayonnaise

DIRECTIONS:

In a bowl add all ingredients and mix well.

NUTRITION: calories 89, fat 4.5g , carbs 11g , phosphorus 47mg , potassium 257mg , sodium 51mg , protein 3g

168. Cabbage and Pear Salad

Preparation Time 10 mins +1 h|Servings 1

INGREDIENTS:

- 2 scallions , chopped
- 2 cups finely shredded green cabbage
- 1 cup finely shredded red cabbage
- ½ red bell pepper , boiled and chopped
- ½ cup chopped cilantro
- 2 celery stalks , chopped
- 1 Asian pear , cored and grated
- ¼ cup olive oil
- Juice of 1 lime
- Zest of 1 lime
- 1 tsp granulated sugar

DIRECTIONS:

1. In a mixing bowl , add cabbages , scallions , celery , pear , red pepper , and cilantro. Combine to mix well.
2. Take another mixing bowl; add olive oil , lime juice , lime zest , and sugar. Combine to mix well with each other.
3. Add dressing over and toss well.
4. Refrigerate for 1 hour; serve chilled.

NUTRITION: calories 128 , fat 8g , carbs 2g , phosphorus 25mg , potassium 148mg , sodium 57mg , protein 3g

169. Couscous Salad with Spicy Dressing

Cooking Time 0 mins | Servings 6

INGREDIENTS:

For the dressing

- ¼ cup olive oil
- 3 tbsp grapefruit juice
- 1 lime juice
- Zest of 1 lime
- 1 tbsp chopped fresh parsley
- Pinch cayenne pepper
- Ground black pepper

For the salad

- 3 cups cooked couscous , chilled
- ½ red bell pepper , chopped
- 1 scallion , both white and green parts , chopped
- 1 apple , chopped

DIRECTIONS:

1. To make the dressing, in a bowl , whisk together the grapefruit juice , olive oil , lime juice , lime zest , parsley , and cayenne pepper.
2. Season with black pepper.
3. To make the salad, in a bowl , mix the red pepper , chilled couscous , scallion , and apple.
4. Add the dressing to the couscous mixture and toss to combine.
5. Chill in the refrigerator and serve.

NUTRITION: calories 187, fat 9g , carbs 23g , phosphorus 24mg , potassium 108mg , sodium 5mg , protein 3g

170. Farfalle Confetti Salad

Cooking Time 0 mins | Servings 6

INGREDIENTS:

- 2 cups cooked farfalle pasta
- ¼ cup boiled and finely chopped red bell pepper
- ¼ cup finely chopped cucumber
- ¼ cup grated carrot
- 2 tbsp yellow bell pepper
- ½ scallion, green part only , finely chopped
- ½ cup homemade mayonnaise
- 1 tbsp freshly squeezed lemon juice
- 1 tsp chopped fresh parsley
- ½ tsp granulated sugar
- Freshly ground black pepper

DIRECTIONS:

1. In a bowl , toss together the pasta , red pepper , carrot , cucumber , yellow pepper , and scallion.
2. In a bowl, whisk together the mayonnaise, parsley , lemon juice , and sugar.

3. Add the dressing to the pasta mixture and stir to combine.
4. Season with pepper.
5. Chill for 1 hour and serve.

NUTRITION: calories 119, fat 3g , carbs 20g , phosphorus 51mg, potassium 82mg, sodium 16mg protein 4g

171. Tarragon and Pepper Pasta Salad

Cooking Time 35 mins | Servings 4

INGREDIENTS:

- 2 cups cooked pasta
- 1 red bell pepper , finely diced
- ½ cucumber , finely diced
- ¼ red onion , finely diced
- 1 tsp black pepper
- 2 tbsp olive oil
- 1 tbsp dried tarragon

DIRECTIONS:

1. Cook pasta according to package directions
2. cool and combine the rest of the raw ingredients and mix well.
3. Serve.

NUTRITION: calories 157, fat 8g , carbs 24g , phosphorus 61mg , potassium 95mg , sodium 5mg , protein 11g

172. Zucchini and Crispy Salmon Salad

Cooking Time 15 mins | Servings 2

INGREDIENTS:

- 2 (3 oz. each) Skinless salmon fillets
- ½ cup spinach
- ½ cup zucchini, sliced
- 1 tbsp balsamic vinegar
- 2 tbsp olive oil
- 2 sprigs thyme , torn
- 1 lemon juiced

DIRECTIONS:

1. Preheat the broiler to medium-high heat.
2. Cook the salmon in parchment paper with 1 tbsp. oil , lemon , and pepper for 10 mins.
3. Remove the parchment paper and finish under the broiler for 5 mins until golden brown and crispy. Remove.
4. Heat 1 tbsp. oil in a pan on medium heat.
5. Add the zucchini slices and sauté for 5 to 6 mins.
6. Add the spinach to the pan and allow to wilt for 30 seconds.
7. Add the salmon fillets to a bed of zucchini and spinach , and drizzle with balsamic vinegar and a sprinkle of thyme.

NUTRITION: calories 309 , fat 23g , carbs 5g , phosphorus 294mg, potassium 119mg , sodium 52mg, protein 22g

173. Brie and Apple Salad

Cooking Time 0 mins | Servings 2

INGREDIENTS:

- ½ cup brie , sliced
- ½ apple , peeled , cored and diced
- 1 cup watercress
- 1 tsp white vinegar

DIRECTIONS:

1. Toss watercress in vinegar and scatter with brie and apple.
2. Serve with Melba toast or crackers.

NUTRITION: calories 111, fat 7g , carbs 8g , phosphorus 20mg , potassium 99mg , sodium 7mg , protein 5g

174. Sofrito Steak Salad

Cooking time 15 mins | Servings 4

INGREDIENTS:

- 4 oz recaíto cooking base

- 2 (4-ounce) flank steaks
- 8 cups fresh spinach , loosely packed
- ½ cup sliced red onion
- 2 cups diced tomato
- 2 avocados , diced
- 2 cups diced cucumber
- ⅓ cup crumbled feta

DIRECTIONS:

1. Heat a large skillet over medium-low heat. When hot , pour in the recaíto cooking base , add the steaks , and cover. Cook for 8 to 12 mins.
2. Meanwhile , divide the spinach into four portions. Top each portion with one-quarter of the onion , tomato , avocados , and cucumber.
3. Remove the steak from the skillet , and let it rest for about 2 mins before slicing. Place one-quarter of the steak and feta on top of each portion.

NUTRITION: calories 344, fat 18g, protein 25g , carbs 18g, sugars 6g, fiber 8g, sodium 382mg

175. Tomato and Peach Salad

Cooking time 0 mins | Servings 6

INGREDIENTS:

- 6 cups mixed spring greens
- 4 large ripe plum tomatoes , thinly sliced
- 4 large ripe peaches , pitted and thinly sliced
- ½ onion , thinly sliced
- 1 tbsp balsamic vinegar
- 2 tbsp olive oil
- Freshly ground black pepper , to taste

DIRECTIONS:

1. Put the greens in a large salad bowl , and layer the tomatoes , peaches , and onion on top.
2. Dress with the vinegar and oil , toss together , and season with pepper.

NUTRITION: calories 127, fat 5g , protein 4g , carbs 19g , sugars 13g , fiber 5g , sodium 30mg

176. Cucumber Tomato Avocado Salad

Cooking time 0 mins | Servings 4

INGREDIENTS:

- 1 cup cherry tomatoes , halved
- 1 large cucumber , chopped
- 1 small red onion , thinly sliced
- 1 avocado , diced
- 2 tbsp chopped fresh dill
- 2 tbsp olive oil
- Juice of 1 lemon
- ¼ tsp salt and black pepper

DIRECTIONS:

1. In a large mixing bowl, combine the tomatoes , cucumber , onion , avocado , and dill.
2. In a small bowl, combine the oil , lemon juice , salt , and pepper , and mix well.
3. Drizzle the dressing over the vegetables and toss to combine. Serve.

NUTRITION: calories 151, fat 12g , protein 2g , carbs 11g, sugars 4g, fiber 4g , sodium 128mg

177. Garlic and Bean Salad

Cooking time 0 mins | Servings 8

INGREDIENTS:

- 1 (15-ounce) can chickpeas , drained and rinsed
- 1 (15-ounce) can kidney beans , drained and rinsed
- 1 (15-ounce) can white beans , drained and rinsed
- 1 red bell pepper , seeded and finely chopped
- ¼ cup chopped scallions , both white and green parts
- ¼ cup finely chopped fresh parsley
- 2 garlic cloves , minced
- 2 tbsp olive oil

- 1 tbsp vinegar
- 1 tsp Dijon mustard
- ¼ tsp freshly ground black pepper

DIRECTIONS:

1. In a large mixing bowl, combine the beans , bell pepper , scallions , parsley , and garlic. Toss gently to combine.
2. In a small bowl, combine the olive oil , vinegar , mustard , and pepper. Toss with the salad.
3. Cover and refrigerate for an hour before serving, to allow the flavors to mix.

NUTRITION: calories 193, fat 5g , protein 10g , carbs 29g, sugars 3g, fiber 8g , sodium 246mg

178. Quinoa , Salmon , and Asparagus Salad

Cooking time 20 mins | Servings 4

INGREDIENTS:

- ½ cup quinoa
- 1 cup water
- 4 (4-ounce) salmon fillets
- 1 pound asparagus , trimmed
- 1 tsp olive oil , plus 2 tbsp
- ½ tsp salt and pepper
- ¼ tsp red pepper flakes
- 1 avocado , chopped
- ¼ cup chopped scallions
- ¼ cup chopped fresh cilantro
- Juice of 1 lime

DIRECTIONS:

1. In a small pot , combine the quinoa and water , and bring to a boil over medium-high heat. Cover , reduce the heat , and simmer for 15 mins.
2. Preheat the oven to 425°F. Line a large baking sheet with parchment paper.
3. Arrange the salmon on one side of the prepared baking sheet. Toss the asparagus with 1 tsp of olive oil and arrange on the other side of the baking sheet. Season the salmon and asparagus with ¼ tsp of salt , ¼ tsp of pepper , and the red pepper flakes. Roast for 12 mins until browned and cooked through.
4. While the fish and asparagus are cooking , in a large mixing bowl , gently toss the cooked quinoa , avocado , scallions , and cilantro. Add the remaining 2 tbsp of olive oil and the lime juice, and season with the remaining ¼ tsp of salt and pepper.
5. Break the salmon into pieces, removing the skin and any bones, and chop the asparagus into bite-sized pieces. Fold into the quinoa and serve warm or at room temperature.

NUTRITION: calories 397, fat 22g, protein 29g , carbs 23g, sugars 3g, fiber 8g , sodium 292mg

179. Blackberry Goat Cheese Salad

Cooking time 20 mins | Servings 4

INGREDIENTS:

Salad

- 1 sweet potato , cubed
- 1 tsp olive oil
- 6 cups salad greens (baby spinach , spicy greens , romaine)
- ½ red onion , sliced
- ¼ cup crumbled goat cheese

Vinaigrette

- 1 pint blackberries
- 2 tbsp red wine vinegar
- 1 tbsp honey
- 3 tbsp olive oil
- ¼ tsp salt

DIRECTIONS:

Make the Vinaigrette

1. In a blender jar, combine the blackberries, vinegar , honey , oil , salt , and pepper , and process until smooth. Set aside.

Make the Salad

2. Preheat the oven to 425°F. Line a baking sheet with parchment paper.
3. In a medium mixing bowl, toss the sweet potato with the olive oil. Transfer to the prepared baking sheet and roast for 20 mins, stirring once halfway through , until tender. Remove and cool for a few mins.
4. In a large bowl, toss the greens with the red onion and cooled sweet potato , and drizzle with the vinaigrette. Serve topped with 1 tbsp of goat cheese per serving.

NUTRITION: calories 196 , fat 12g, protein 3g , carbs 21g, sugars 10g, fiber 6g, sodium 184mg

180. Kale and Cabbage Salad

Cooking time 0 mins | Servings 4

INGREDIENTS:

- 1 bunches baby kale , thinly sliced
- ½ head green savoy cabbage , cored and thinly sliced
- ¼ cup apple cider vinegar
- Juice of 1 lemon
- 1 tsp ground cumin
- ¼ tsp smoked paprika
- 1 medium red bell pepper , thinly sliced
- 1 cup toasted peanuts

DIRECTIONS:

1. In a large salad bowl , toss the kale and cabbage together.
2. In a small bowl , to make the dressing , whisk the vinegar , lemon juice, cumin , and paprika together.
3. Pour the dressing over the greens , and gently massage with your hands.
4. Add the pepper, peanuts and toss to combine.

NUTRITION: calories 199, fat 12g, protein 10g , carbs 17g, sugars 4g, fiber 5g, sodium 46mg

181. Strawberry Spelt Salad

Preparation time 17 mins , Cooking time 10 mins | Servings 8

INGREDIENTS:

- 1 cup spelt , rinsed and drained
- ¼ tsp salt

Salad

- 1¼ cups sliced strawberries
- ¼ cup slivered almonds , toasted
- Fresh basil leaves for garnish

Dressing

- 1 tbsp lime juice (from ½ medium lime)
- ½ tbsp balsamic vinegar
- ½ tsp Dijon mustard
- ½ tbsp honey or pure maple syrup
- ¼ cup olive oil

DIRECTIONS:

Make the Spelt

1. In the electric pressure cooker, combine the spelt, salt, and 2 cups of water.
2. Close and lock the lid. Set the valve to sealing.
3. Cook on high pressure for 10 mins.
4. When the cooking is complete, allow the pressure to release naturally for 10 mins, then quick release the remaining pressure. Hit Cancel.
5. Once the pin drops, unlock and remove the lid.
6. Fluff the spelt with a fork and let cool.

Make the Dressing

7. While the spelt is cooking , in a small jar with a screw-top lid , combine the lime juice , balsamic vinegar , mustard , honey , and olive oil. Shake until well combined.

Make the Salad

8. In a large bowl , toss the spelt with the dressing. Stir in the strawberries and almonds.

9. Season with pepper , garnish with basil , and serve.

NUTRITION: (½ cup) calories 176 , fat 9g , protein 3g, carbs 22g, sugars 3g, fiber 2g , sodium 68mg

182. Chicken, Melon Salad

Cooking time 0 mins | Servings 3

INGREDIENTS:

Salad

- 4 cups chopped kale , packed
- 1½ cups diced melon
- 1½ cups shredded rotisserie chicken
- ½ cup sliced almonds
- ¼ cup crumbled feta

Dressing

- 1 tsps honey
- 2 tbsp olive oil
- 2 tsps apple cider vinegar or freshly squeezed lemon juice

DIRECTIONS:

Make the Salad

1. Divide the kale into three portions. Layer 1/3 of the melon, chicken, almonds , and feta on each portion.
2. Drizzle some of the dressing over each portion of salad. Serve immediately.

Make the Dressing

3. In a small bowl , whisk together the honey , olive oil , and vinegar.

NUTRITION: calories 396, fat22 g , protein 27g , carbs 24g, sugars 12g, fiber 4g , sodium 236mg

183. Black Bean and Tomato Salad

Cooking time 0 mins | Servings 5

INGREDIENTS:

- 1 (15-ounce) can black beans , drained and rinsed
- 1 avocado , diced
- 1 cup cherry
- 2 tomatoes , halved
- 1 cup chopped baby spinach
- ½ cup finely chopped red bell pepper
- ½ cup chopped scallions
- 2 tbsp freshly squeezed lime juice
- 1 tbsp olive oil
- 2 garlic cloves , minced
- 1 tsp honey
- ¼ tsp salt and pepper

DIRECTIONS:

1. In a large bowl , combine the black beans , avocado , tomatoes , spinach , bell pepper , and scallions.
2. In a small bowl , mix the lime juice , oil , garlic , honey , salt , and pepper. Add to the salad and toss.
3. Chill for 1 hour before serving.

NUTRITION: calories 169 , fat 7g , protein 6g , carbs 22g, sugars 3g, fiber 9g , sodium 235mg

184. Rice Salad with Cranberries and Almonds

Cooking time 25 mins | Servings 6

INGREDIENTS:

Rice

- 1 cup wild rice blend , rinsed
- 1 tsp salt
- 1½ cups vegetable broth or chicken bone broth

Dressing

- ¼ cup olive oil
- ¼ cup white wine vinegar
- 1½ tsps grated orange zest
- Juice of 1 medium orange (about ¼ cup)
- 1 tsp honey or pure maple syrup

Salad

- ¾ cup dried cranberries
- ¼ cup sliced almonds , toasted
- Freshly ground black pepper , to taste

DIRECTIONS:

Make the Rice

1. In the electric pressure cooker ,

combine the rice , salt , and broth.

2. Close and lock the lid. Set the valve to sealing.
3. Cook on high pressure for 25 mins.
4. When the cooking is complete , hit Cancel and allow the pressure to release naturally for 15 mins , then quick release any remaining pressure.
5. Once the pin drops , unlock and remove the lid.
6. Let the rice cool briefly , then fluff it with a fork.

Make the Dressing

7. While the rice cooks , make the dressing In a small jar with a screw-top lid , combine the olive oil , vinegar , zest , juice , and honey. (If you don't have a jar, whisk the ingredients together in a small bowl.) Shake to combine.

Make the Salad

8. In a large bowl, combine the rice, cranberries , and almonds.
9. Add the dressing and season with pepper.
10. Serve warm or refrigerate.

NUTRITION: (1/3 cup) calories 126, fat 5g , protein 3g, carbs 18g, sugars 2g, fiber 2g , sodium 120mg

185. Pecan Pear Salad

Preparation time 15 mins, Cooking time 0 mins | Servings 4

INGREDIENTS:

- 5 oz mixed greens
- 2 pears , chopped
- ¼ cup blue cheese , crumbled
- 1 cup pecan halves
- ½ cup dried cranberries
- ½ cup olive oil
- 2 tbsp vinegar
- 1 tbsp Dijon mustard
- ¼ tsp salt

DIRECTIONS:

1. In a large bowl combine greens , pears , cranberries and pecans.
2. Whisk remaining ingredients, except blue cheese , together in a small bowl Pour over salad and toss to coat. Serve topped with blue cheese crumbles.

NUTRITION: calories 326, fat 26g , protein 5g , carbs 20g, fiber 6g , sugars 9g , sodium 294mg

186. Rainbow Cauli Salad

Cooking time 0 mins | Servings 6

INGREDIENTS:

- 1 head broccoli, separated into florets
- 1 head cauliflower, separated into florets
- 1 red onion, sliced thin
- 1 cup cherry tomatoes , halved
- ½ cup fat free sour cream
- ½ cup mayonnaise

DIRECTIONS:

1. In a large bowl combine vegetables.
2. In a small bowl , whisk together mayonnaise and sour cream. Pour over vegetables and toss to mix.
3. Cover and refrigerate at least 1 hour before serving.

NUTRITION: calories 153, fat 10g , protein 2g , carbs 12g, fiber 2g, sugars 4g, sodium 264mg

187. Veggie Salad

Cooking time 0 mins | Servings 4

INGREDIENTS:

- 1 cucumber , chopped
- 1 pint cherry tomatoes , cut in half
- 2 radishes , chopped
- 1 yellow bell pepper chopped
- ½ cup fresh parsley , chopped
- 3 tbsp lemon juice
- 1 tbsp olive oil
- Salt, to taste

DIRECTIONS:

1. Place all in a large bowl and toss to combine. Serve immediately or cover and chill until ready to serve.

NUTRITION: calories 71, fat 4g, protein 2g, carbs 9g, fiber 2g , sugars 4g , sodium 98mg

188. Asian Style Noodle Salad

Cooking time 0 mins | Servings 4

INGREDIENTS:

- 2 carrots , sliced thin
- 2 radish , sliced thin
- 1 cucumber , sliced thin
- 1 mango , julienned
- 1 red bell pepper , julienned
- 1 bag tofu Shirataki Fettuccini noodles
- ¼ cup lime juice
- ¼ cup fresh cilantro , chopped
- 2 tbsp fresh mint , chopped
- 2 tbsp rice vinegar
- 2 tbsp chili sauce
- 2 tbsp roasted peanuts finely chopped
- ½ tsp sesame oil

DIRECTIONS:

1. Pickle the vegetables In a large bowl , place radish , cucumbers , and carrots. Add vinegar , and lime juice and stir to coat the vegetables. Cover and chill 15 to 20 mins.
2. Prep the noodles remove the noodles from the package and rinse under cold water. Cut into smaller pieces. Pat dry with paper towels.
3. To assemble the salad. Remove the vegetables from the marinade, reserving marinade , and place in a large mixing bowl. Add noodles, mango , bell pepper , chili , and herbs.
4. In a small bowl, combine 2 tbsp marinade with the chili sauce and sesame oil. Pour over salad and toss to coat. Top with peanuts and serve.

NUTRITION: calories 159, fat 4g, protein 4g, carbs 30g, fiber 6g, sugars 18g , sodium 119mg

189. Spinach and Pear Salad

Cooking time 0 mins | Servings 2

INGREDIENTS:

- 4 cups baby spinach
- ½ pear, cored , peeled , and chopped
- 1 tbsp apple cider vinegar
- 1 tsp peeled and grated fresh ginger
- ½ tsp Dijon mustard
- 2 tbsp olive oil
- ½ tsp sea salt
- ¼ cup chopped walnuts

DIRECTIONS:

1. Combine the vinegar , ginger , mustard , olive oil , and salt in a small bowl. Stir to mix well.
2. Combine the remaining ingredients in a large serving bowl , then toss to combine well.
3. Pour the vinegar dressing in the bowl of salad and toss before serving.

NUTRITION: calories 229, fat 20g, protein 3g , carbs 10g , fiber 3g, sugars 4g , sodium 644mg

190. Caprese Salad

Cooking time 0 mins | Servings 4

INGREDIENTS:

- 3 medium tomatoes , cut into 8 slices
- 2 (1-ounce) slices mozzarella cheese
- ¼ cup fresh basil , sliced thin
- 2 tsps olive oil
- ⅛ tsp salt and pepper

DIRECTIONS:

1. Place tomatoes and cheese on serving plates. Sprinkle with salt and pepper. Drizzle oil over and top with basil. Serve.

NUTRITION: calories 78, fat 5g , protein 5g , carbs 4g, fiber 1g , sugars 1g , sodium 84mg

191. Creamy Crab Slaw

Cooking time 0 mins | Servings 4

INGREDIENTS:

- 2 (6-ounce) cans crabmeat , drained
- ½ pound cabbage , shredded
- ½ pound red cabbage , shredded
- 2 hard-boiled eggs , chopped
- Juice of ½ lemon
- ½ cup mayonnaise
- Salt and ground black pepper , to taste

DIRECTIONS:

1. In a large bowl , combine both kinds of cabbage.
2. In a small bowl , combine mayonnaise and lemon juice. Add to cabbage and toss to coat.
3. Add crab and eggs and toss to mix , season with salt and pepper. Cover and refrigerate 1 hour before serving.

NUTRITION: calories 381, fat 24g, protein 18g , carbs 25g, fiber 8g, sugars 12g, sodium 266mg

192. Broccoli and Bacon Salad

Cooking time 0 mins | Servings 4

INGREDIENTS:

- 2 cups broccoli , separated into florets
- 4 slices bacon , chopped and cooked crisp
- ½ cup cheddar cheese , cubed
- ¼ cup Greek yogurt
- ⅛ cup red onion , diced fine
- ⅛ cup almonds , sliced
- ¼ cup reduced-fat mayonnaise
- 1 tbsp lemon juice
- 1 tbsp apple cider vinegar
- ¼ tsp salt and pepper

DIRECTIONS:

1. In a large bowl, combine broccoli , onion , cheese , bacon , and almonds.
2. In a small bowl, whisk remaining together till combined.
3. Pour dressing over broccoli mixture and stir. Cover and chill at least 1 hour before serving.

NUTRITION: calories 220, fat 14g, protein 11g, carbs 12g, fiber 2g, sugars 5g, sodium 508mg

193. Pomegranate and Brussels Sprouts Salad

Cooking time 0 mins | Servings 6

INGREDIENTS:

- 3 slices bacon , cooked crisp and crumbled
- 3 cup Brussels sprouts , shredded
- 3 cup kale , shredded
- 1½ cup pomegranate seeds
- ¼ cup Parmesan cheese , grated

Vinaigrette

- 1 orange , zested and juiced
- 1 lemon , zested and juiced
- ¼ cup olive oil
- ½ tsp Dijon mustard
- 1 tsp honey
- 1 clove garlic , crushed
- Salt and ground black pepper , to taste

DIRECTIONS:

1. Combine the ingredient for the citrus vinaigrette in a small bowl.
2. Toss the remaining ingredients with the vinaigrette in a large bowl.
3. Serve garnished with more cheese if desired.

NUTRITION: calories 255, fat 18g, protein 9g , carbs 15g, fiber 5g, sugars 4g, sodium 176mg

194. Melon and Serrano Ham

Salad

Cooking time 0 mins | Servings 4

INGREDIENTS:

- 6 mozzarella balls , quartered
- 1 medium melon , peeled and cut into small cubes
- 4 oz serrano ham , sliced
- 1 tbsp fresh lime juice
- 2 tbsp olive oil 1 tsp honey

DIRECTIONS:

1. In a large bowl , whisk together oil , lime juice , and honey. Season with salt and pepper to taste.
2. Add the cantaloupe and mozzarella and toss to combine. Arrange the mixture on a serving plate and add serrano ham. Serve.

NUTRITION: calories 241, fat 16g, protein 18g, carbs 6g, fiber 0g, sugars 3g, sodium 701mg

195. Watermelon and Feta Salad

Cooking time 0 mins | Servings 6

INGREDIENTS:

- 3 cups watermelon, cut in 1-inch cubes
- 2 cups arugula
- 1 lemon , zested
- ½ cup feta cheese , crumbled
- ¼ cup fresh mint , chopped
- 1 tbsp fresh lemon juice
- 3 tbsp olive oil
- Salt and black pepper, to taste

DIRECTIONS:

1. Combine oil, zest , juice and mint in a large bowl. Stir together.
2. Add watermelon and gently toss to coat. Add remaining and toss to combine. Taste and adjust seasoning as desired.
3. Cover and chill at least 1 hour before serving.

NUTRITION: calories 150, fat 11g, protein 4g , carbs 10g, fiber 1g, sugars 6g, sodium 145mg

CHAPTER 6 Soups and Stews

196. Miso Pork and Apple Soup

Cooking time: 10 mins | Servings: 2

INGREDIENTS:

- 6 oz extra-lean ground pork
- 1 cup chicken broth
- 1½ tsps olive oil
- 1 medium sweet onion, chopped
- 2 garlic cloves, minced
- 1apple peeled, cored, and chopped
- 2 cups water
- 2 cups angel hair coleslaw
- 1½ tbsp white miso

DIRECTIONS:

1. In a medium saucepan set over medium-high heat , heat the olive oil.
2. Add the onion and garlic. Sauté for about 2 mins , or until softened.
3. Add the pork. Cook for about 2 mins , stirring occasionally , until no longer pink.
4. Stir in the apple. Cook for about 2 mins more , stirring occasionally , until just beginning to soften.
5. Add the water and chicken broth. Bring to a boil.
6. Add the angel hair coleslaw. Cook for 2 mins until softened.
7. To a small bowl , add the miso.
8. Remove ¼ cup of the cooking liquid from the pan and add it to the miso. Whisk until fully dissolved.
9. Stir the miso mixture back into the soup. Remove from the heat.
10. Serve immediately.

NUTRITION: calories 317, fat 15g, protein 21g, carbs 29g, sugars 12g , fiber 5g , sodium 612mg

197. French Onion Soup

Cooking time: 30 mins | Servings: 2

INGREDIENTS:

- 1 (8-ounce) can chickpeas, drained and rinsed
- 1 tbsp olive oil
- 2 medium onions, sliced
- 2 cups beef broth
- ½ tsp dried thyme
- salt and black pepper to taste
- 4 slices Swiss cheese

DIRECTIONS:

1. In a medium soup pot set over medium-low heat, heat the olive oil.
2. Add the onions. Stir to coat them in oil. Cook for about 10 mins, or until golden brown.
3. Add the beef broth, chickpeas, and thyme. Bring to a simmer.
4. Taste the broth. Season with salt and pepper. Cook for 10 mins more.
5. Preheat the broiler to high.
6. Ladle the soup into 2 ovenproof soup bowls.
7. Top each with 2 slices of Swiss cheese. Place the bowls on a baking sheet. Carefully transfer the sheet to the preheated oven. Melt the cheese under the broiler for 2 mins. Alternately | you can melt the cheese in the microwave (in microwave-safe

bowls) on high in 30-second intervals until melted.

8. Enjoy immediately.

NUTRITION: calories 330, fat 10g , protein 27g, carbs 37g, sugars 11g , fiber 10g , sodium 402mg

198. Eggplant and Red Pepper Soup

Cooking Time: 40 mins | Servings: 4

INGREDIENTS:

- 2 halves red bell peppers
- 2 cups of eggplant , cubed
- 2 garlic cloves , crushed
- 1 tbsp. of olive oil
- 1 small , cut into quarters sweet onion
- 1 cup of chicken stock
- ¼ cup of chopped fresh basil
- black pepper to taste

DIRECTIONS:

1. Preheat the oven to 350°F.
2. Put the onions , red peppers , eggplant , and garlic in a baking sheet.
3. Drizzle the vegetables with the olive oil.
4. Roast the vegetables for 30 mins or until they are slightly charred and soft.
5. Cool the vegetables slightly and remove the skin from the peppers.
6. Puree the vegetables with a hand mixer (with the chicken stock).
7. Transfer the soup to a medium pot and add enough water to reach the desired thickness.
8. Heat the soup to a simmer and add the basil.
9. Season with pepper and serve.

NUTRITION: calories 6, fat 2g, carbs 9g, phosphorus 33mg, potassium 198mg , sodium 98mg , protein 2g

199. Chicken Pho

Cooking Time: 15 mins | Servings: 4

INGREDIENTS:

- 5 cups of chicken broth
- 1-inch piece of ginger , cut lengthwise into 2 or 3 strips
- 1 cup of cooked chicken breast, diced
- several fresh thai basil sprigs
- 1 cup of mung bean sprouts
- 1 lime , cut into wedges
- 1 jalapeño pepper, stemmed , seeded , and thinly sliced
- 1 (16-ounce) package of dried rice vermicelli noodles , cooked according to package
- 4 tbsps (¼ cup) of sliced scallions
- 4 tbsps (¼ cup) of chopped cilantro leaves

DIRECTIONS:

1. In a medium stockpot over medium-high heat, add the broth and ginger , and bring to a simmer. Add the chicken and simmer for 5 mins. Remove the ginger from the pot and discard it.
2. On a plate, arrange the Thai basil , bean sprouts , lime wedges , and jalapeño slices. Distribute the noodles among four bowls. Add 1¼ cups of broth to each bowl. Top with 1 tbsp each of the scallions and cilantro. Serve immediately alongside the plate of garnishes.

NUTRITION: calories 325, fat 3g , carbs 55g , protein 21g, phosphorus 205mg , potassium 389mg , sodium 313mg

200. Herbed Cabbage Stew

Cooking Time: 35 mins | Servings: 6

INGREDIENTS:

- 6 cups of shredded green cabbage
- 1 tsp of unsalted butter
- ½ large sweet onion, chopped
- 1 tsp of minced garlic
- 3 celery stalks, chopped
- 1 scallion, both green and white parts chopped
- 2 tbsps of chopped fresh parsley
- 2 tbsps of freshly squeezed lemon juice
- 1 tbsp of chopped fresh thyme
- 1 tsp of chopped savory herb
- 1 tsp of chopped fresh oregano
- water
- 1 cup green beans, chopped
- freshly ground black pepper

DIRECTIONS:

1. In a medium stockpot over medium-high heat | melt the butter.
2. Sauté the onion and garlic in the melted butter for about 3 mins or until the vegetables are softened.
3. Add the cabbage, celery, scallion, parsley , lemon juice , thyme , savory herb , and oregano to the pot , and add enough water to cover the vegetables by about 4 inches.
4. Bring the soup to a boil, reduce the heat to low, and simmer the soup for about 25 mins or until the vegetables are tender. Add the green beans and simmer 3 mins—season with pepper.

NUTRITION: calories 33, fat 1g, carbs 6g, phosphorus 29mg , potassium 187mg , sodium 20mg , protein 1g

201. Vegetable Lentil Soup

Cooking Time: 25 mins | Servings: 4

INGREDIENTS:

- 5 cups of chicken broth
- ½ sweet onion , diced
- 2 carrots , diced
- 2 celery stalks , diced
- ½ cup of lentils
- 2 cups of sliced chard leaves
- 1 tbsp of olive oil
- 1 lemon

DIRECTIONS:

1. In a medium stockpot over medium-high heat, heat the olive oil.
2. Add the onion and stir until softened, about 3 to 5 mins.
3. Add the carrots, celery, lentils, and broth.
4. Bring to a boil , reduce the heat , and simmer , uncovered , for 15 mins , until the lentils are tender.
5. Add the chard and cook for 3 additional mins , until wilted—season with the pepper and lemon juice.

NUTRITION: calories 19, fat 6g, carbs 25g, protein 13g, phosphorus 228mg, potassium 707mg , sodium 157mg

202. Veggie Soup

Cooking Time: 50 mins | Servings: 8

INGREDIENTS:

- 2 chopped ribs celery
- 2 cubes low-Sodium bouillon
- 8 cup water
- 2 cup uncooked green split peas
- 3 bay leaves
- 2 carrots
- 2 chopped potatoes

DIRECTIONS:

1. In a medium-large pot, put the bouillon cubes, split peas , and water. Stir a bit to break up the bouillon cubes.
2. Next, add the chopped potatoes , celery , and carrots followed with bay leaves.
3. Stir to combine well.
4. Cover and cook for at least 40 mins
5. Add a bit salt and pepper as needed.
6. Before serving, remove the bay leaves and enjoy.

NUTRITION: calories 149, fat 1g, carbs 30g , phosphorus 122mg, potassium 178mg, sodium 64mg , protein 12g

203. French Onion Soup

Cooking Time: 50 mins | Servings: 4

INGREDIENTS:

- 4 onions , sliced thin
- 2 cups of chicken stock
- 2 tbsps of unsalted butter
- 2 cups of water
- 1 tbsp of chopped fresh thyme
- freshly ground black pepper

DIRECTIONS:

1. Set your butter on to melt in a saucepan on medium heat. Add the onions to the saucepan and cook them slowly, frequently stirring, for about 30 mins or until the onions are caramelized and tender.
2. Add the chicken stock and water and bring the soup to a boil. Switch to low heat to simmer for 15 mins. Stir in the thyme and season the soup with pepper. Serve piping hot.

NUTRITION: calories 90, fat 6g, carbs 7g, phosphorus 22mg, potassium 192mg, sodium 57mg , protein 2g

204. Classic Chicken Soup

Cooking Time: 30 mins | Servings: 2

INGREDIENTS:

- 2 cups chopped cooked chicken breast
- 1 cup chicken stock
- 2 tsps minced garlic
- 2 celery stalks , chopped
- 1 tbsp unsalted butter
- ½ sweet onion , diced
- 1 carrot , diced
- 4 cups of water
- 1 tsp chopped fresh thyme
- black pepper (ground), to taste
- 2 tbsps chopped fresh parsley

DIRECTIONS:

1. Take a medium-large cooking pot , heat oil over medium heat.
2. Add onion and stir-cook until it becomes translucent and softened.
3. Add garlic and stir-cook until it becomes fragrant.
4. Add celery, carrot , chicken , chicken stock , and water.
5. Boil the mixture.
6. Over low heat, simmer the mixture for about 25-30 mins until veggies are tender.
7. Mix in thyme and cook for 2 mins. Season to taste with black pepper.

NUTRITION: calories 135, fat 6g, carbs 7g, phosphorus 122mg, potassium 208mg, sodium 74mg, protein 12g

205. Pumpkin and Quinoa

Cooking Time: 30 mins | Servings: 4

INGREDIENTS:

- 2 pieces of pumpkin
- 2 tbsps of olive oil
- 1 tbsp of onion
- 2 carrots cut into strips
- 1 potato , diced
- 1 cup of cooked quinoa
- 1 tsp of curry
- ground bread

DIRECTIONS:

1. Preheat the oven to 350°F.
2. Cut the pumpkin lengthwise and remove the filling place with water in a bowl.
3. Heat over medium heat in a pan , add the oil , quinoa , and onion , add the carrots , potatoes , and cook for 3 mins , and pepper curry.

4. Put the pumpkins in a tray and fill with the filling , place on the ground bread and bake for 10 mins.

NUTRITION: calories 232, fat 6g , carbs 40g, phosphorus 122mg, potassium 258mg, sodium 63mg , protein 8g

206. Green Veggies Stew

Cooking Time: 30 mins | Servings: 2

INGREDIENTS:

- 6 cups shredded green cabbage
- 3 celery stalks , chopped
- 1 tsp unsalted butter
- ½ large sweet onion , chopped
- 1 tsp minced garlic
- 1 scallion , chopped
- 2 tbsps chopped fresh parsley
- 2 tbsps lemon juice
- 1 tsp chopped fresh oregano
- 1 tbsp chopped fresh thyme
- 1 tsp chopped savory
- water
- 1 cup fresh green beans , cut into 1-inch pieces

DIRECTIONS:

1. Take a medium-large cooking pot , heat butter over medium heat.
2. Add onion and stir-cook until it becomes translucent and soft.
3. Add garlic and stir-cook until it becomes fragrant.
4. Add cabbage , celery , scallion , parsley , lemon juice , thyme , savory , and oregano; add water to cover veggies by 3-4 inches.
5. Stir the mixture and boil it.
6. Over low heat, cover , and simmer the mixture for about 25 mins until veggies are tender.
7. Add green beans and cook for 2-3 more mins. Season with black pepper to taste.
8. Serve warm.

NUTRITION: calories 56, fat 1g, carbs 7g ,phosphorus 36mg, potassium 194mg , sodium 31mg , protein 1g

207. Creamy Broccoli Soup

Cooking Time: 15 mins |Servings: 4

INGREDIENTS:

- 2 cups of chopped broccoli
- 1 tsp of olive oil
- ½ sweet onion , roughly chopped
- 4 cups of low-Sodium vegetable broth
- freshly ground black pepper
- 1 cup of rice milk
- ¼ cup of grated Parmesan cheese

DIRECTIONS:

1. In a medium saucepan over medium-high heat, heat the olive oil.
2. Add the onion and cook for 3 to 5 mins ,until it begins to soften. Add the broccoli and broth , and season with pepper.
3. Bring to a boil, reduce the heat , and simmer uncovered for 10 mins , until the broccoli is just tender but still bright green.
4. Transfer the soup mixture to a blender. Add the rice milk, and process until smooth.
5. Return to the saucepan, stir in the Parmesan cheese , and serve.

NUTRITION: calories 88, fat 3g, carbs 12g, protein 4g, phosphorus 87mg, potassium 201mg, sodium 281mg

208. Onion Soup

Cooking Time: 1 hour | Servings: 4

INGREDIENTS:

- 5 yellow onions , cut into halved and sliced
- 2 tbsps avocado oil
- black pepper to taste
- 5 cups beef stock

- 3 thyme sprigs
- 1 tbsp tomato paste

DIRECTIONS:

1. Take a pot and place it over medium high heat
2. Add onion and thyme and stir
3. Lower down heat to low and cook for 30 mins
4. Uncover pot and cook onions for 1 hour , stirring often
5. Add tomato paste , stock and stir
6. Simmer for 30 mins more and then serve

NUTRITION: calories 86, fat 4g, carbs 7g, protein 3g, sugar 10g, fiber 3g, sodium 96 mg, potassium 154mg

209. Sorrel Soup

Cooking Time: 15 mins | Servings: 6

INGREDIENTS:

- 80 oz fresh sorrel leaves
- 1 cup single cream
- 4 cup vegetable stock
- 1 tbsp olive oil
- 1 large onion , chopped
- 1 clove garlic finely chopped

DIRECTIONS:

1. In a large pot, heat oil and cook onion.
2. Add the stock and bring to boil. Stir in the sorrel, cover and cook for 1 min. Put in a blinder. Serve hot or chilled.

NUTRITION: calories 68, fat 6g, carbs 9.2g, protein 4g, phosphorus 57mg, potassium 111mg, sodium 179mg

210. Cauliflower Soup

Cooking Time: 40 mins | Servings: 6

INGREDIENTS:

- 3 cups cauliflower, riced
- 1 bay leaf
- 1 tsp herbs de Provence
- 2 garlic cloves, peeled and diced
- ½ cup coconut milk
- 2 and ½ cups vegetable stock
- 1 tbsp coconut oil
- ½ tsp cracked pepper
- 1 leek, chopped

DIRECTIONS:

1. Take a pot, heat oil into it
2. Sauté the leeks in it for 5 mins
3. Add in the garlic and then stir cook for another minute
4. Add all the remaining ingredients and mix them well
5. Cook for 30 mins
6. Stir occasionally
7. Blend the soup until smooth by using an immersion blender.
8. Serve hot and enjoy!

NUTRITION: calories 68, fat 6g, carbs 11g, protein 4g, phosphorus 97mg, potassium 186mg , sodium 181mg

211. Crab Soup

Cooking Time: 10 mins | Servings: 4

INGREDIENTS:

- 1 cup crabmeat
- ¼ cup basil , chopped
- 2 lbs tomatoes
- 5 cups watermelon , cubed
- ¼ cup wine vinegar
- 2 garlic cloves, minced
- 1 zucchini , chopped
- Pepper to taste

DIRECTIONS:

1. Take your blender and add tomatoes , basil , vinegar, 4 cups watermelon , garlic , 1/3 cup oil, pepper and pulse well
2. Transfer to fridge and chill for 1 hour

3. Divide into bowls and add zucchini, crab and remaining watermelon

NUTRITION: calories 321, fat 5g, carbs 28g, protein 4g, phosphorus 87mg, potassium 151mg, sodium 134g

212. Butternut Squash Soup

Cooking Time: 20 mins | Servings: 6

INGREDIENTS:

- 2 cup diced apple
- 1/8 tsp. ground allspice
- 6 cup diced butternut squash
- 6 cup water
- ½ tsp. ground cinnamon
- 2 cup unsweetened apple juice

DIRECTIONS:

1. Place diced squash and apple into a stockpot, add the water and apple juice , and bring to a boil over high heat. Once boiling, reduce heat to medium-low , cover , and simmer until tender , roughly 20 mins.
2. Remove from heat. Add spices and stir to combine. Purée in a blender or food processor.

NUTRITION: calories 150, fat 0g, carbs 38g, protein 9g, sugar 12g, fiber 3g, sodium 66mg, potassium 175mg

213. Sirloin Carrot Soup

Cooking Time: 20 mins | Servings: 4

INGREDIENTS:

- 1 lb. chopped carrots and celery mix
- 32 oz. low-Sodium beef stock
- 1/3 cup whole-wheat flour
- 1 lb. ground beef sirloin
- 1 tbsp olive oil
- 1 chopped yellow onion

DIRECTIONS:

1. Heat up the olive oil in a saucepan over medium-high flame; add the beef and the flour.
2. Stir well and cook to brown for 4-5 mins.
3. Add the celery, onion, carrots, and stock; stir and bring to a simmer.
4. Turn down the heat to low and cook for 12-15 mins.
5. Serve warm.

NUTRITION: calories 140, fat 4g, carbs 17g, protein 9g, sugar 12g, fiber 3g, sodium 86mg, potassium 184mg

214. Carrot and Spice Soup

Cooking Time: 25 mins | Servings: 6

INGREDIENTS:

- 1 lb carrots roughly chopped
- 1 tbsp olive oil
- 1 medium onion , finely chopped
- 1 garlic clove
- 1 tbsp chopped fresh coriander
- fresh ground pepper
- 4 cup vegetable stock

DIRECTIONS:

1. In a pot , heat olive oil and cook onion and garlic.
2. Add the chopped carrots and stock and cover. Bring to the boil. Once the vegetables are tender cool a little and then put in a blender. Taste and serve.

NUTRITION: calories 122, fat 1.5g, carbs 4.8g, protein 2.4g, phosphorus 145g, potassium 222mg, sodium 134g

215. Peach Stew

Cooking Time: 10 mins | Servings: 6

INGREDIENTS:

- 3 tbsp coconut sugar
- 5 cup peeled and cubed peaches
- 2 cup water
- 1 tsp grated ginger

DIRECTIONS:

In a pot , combine the peaches while using the sugar, ginger and water , toss , provide a boil over medium heat, cook for 10 mins , divide into bowls and serve cold.

NUTRITION: calories 142, fat 1.5g, carbs 7.8g, protein 2.4g, phosphorus 127mg, potassium 199mg, sodium 134g

216. Chicken and Dill Soup

Cooking Time: 1 hour | Servings: 6

INGREDIENTS:

- 1 whole chicken
- 1 lb. sliced carrots
- 1 cup chopped yellow onion
- 6 cup low-Sodium veggie stock
- ½ cup chopped red onion
- 2 tsps. chopped dill

DIRECTIONS:

1. Put chicken in a pot , add water to pay for , give your boil over medium heat , cook first hour , transfer to a cutting board , discard bones , shred the meat , strain the soup , get it back on the pot , heat it over medium heat and add the chicken.
2. Also add the carrots, yellow onion , red onion, a pinch of salt, black pepper and also the dill, cook for fifteen mins , ladle into bowls and serve.

NUTRITION: calories 208, fat 6g, carbs 8g, protein 12g, phosphorus 87mg, potassium 201mg, sodium 91mg

217. Berries Soup

Cooking Time: 15 mins | Servings: 6

INGREDIENTS:

- 1 lb fresh or frozen raspberries
- 3 cup cranberry juice
- 3 tsp arrowroot
- 1 tbsp sugar

DIRECTIONS:

Combine 2/3 of the raspberries with the cranberry juice. Bring to the boil in a saucepan. In a separate bowl mix the arrowroot and the tbsp of cranberry juice until smooth. Mix together and stir over a gentle heat until the soup has thickened.

NUTRITION: calories 157, fat 1g, carbs 7g, protein 6g, sugar 10g, fiber 3g, sodium 75mg, potassium 132mg

218. Cheese Soup

Cooking Time: 35 mins | Servings: 6

INGREDIENTS:

- 1 lb potatoes peeles and chopped
- 4 cup vegetable stock
- 4 oz cheddar cheese grated
- 1 garlic clove
- 1 tsp olive oil
- 1 large onion finely chopped

DIRECTIONS:

In a pan , heat the oil and cook garlic and onion. Add potatoes, stock and bring to the boil. Simmer for about 20 mins. Serve warm.

NUTRITION: calories 257, fat 15g, carbs 11g, protein 12g, fiber 3g, sodium 56mg, potassium 124mg

219. Wonton Soup

Cooking Time: 15 mins | Servings: 8

INGREDIENTS:

- ½ lb. lean ground pork
- 4 sliced scallions
- ¼ tsp. ground white pepper
- 2 cup sliced fresh mushrooms
- 4 minced garlic cloves
- 6 oz. dry whole-grain yolk-free egg noodles
- 1 tbsp minced fresh ginger
- 8 cup low-Sodium chicken broth

DIRECTIONS:

1. Place a stockpot over medium heat. Add the ground pork, ginger, and

garlic and sauté for 5 mins. Drain any excess fat , then return to stovetop.

2. Add the broth and bring to a boil. Once boiling, stir in the mushrooms, noodles , and white pepper. Cover and simmer for 10 mins.
3. Remove pot from heat. Stir in the scallions and serve immediately.

NUTRITION: calories 143, fat 4g, carbs 14g, protein 16g, fiber 3g, sodium 55mg, potassium 125mg

220. Lentil and lemon Soup

Cooking Time: 40 mins | Servings: 4

INGREDIENTS:

- 5 oz red lentils
- 2 tsp tomato puree
- 2 tsp olive oil
- 1 large onion finely chopped
- 1 garlic cloves , peeled
- 1 pint vegetable stock
- 14 oz tin chopped tomatoes
- juice of ½ lemon

DIRECTIONS:

1. Heat the oil and cook onion and garlic for 10 mins. Add the lentils and the stock and bring to the boil.
2. Add the tinned tomatoes and tomato puree and bring back to the boil (covered 15 mins). Taste for seasoning and serve.

NUTRITION: calories 104, fat 12g , carbs 12g , protein 11g

221. Carrot Coriander Soup

Cooking Time: 30 mins | Servings: 6

INGREDIENTS:

- 1 lb carrots roughly chopped
- 14 oz carrots roughly chopped
- 1 oz butter
- 1 large onion finely chopped
- 1 tbsp fresh coriander
- 1 ¾ pint vegetable stock
- ¼ single cream

DIRECTIONS:

1. Melt the butter and cook the onions for 5 mins. Add carrots , stock and a pinch of grated nutmeg.
2. Cover and bring to the boil for 10 mins.
3. Cool a little and then put in a liquidiser. Season and serve.

NUTRITION: calories 132, fat 1g, carbs 10g, protein 8g, fiber 3g, sodium 58mg, potassium 111mg

222. Lettuce and Lovage Soup

Cooking Time: 30 mins | Servings: 6

INGREDIENTS:

- 9 oz potatoes peeled and chopped
- 1 oz butter
- 6 oz chopped onions
- 3 lb iceberg lettuce , finely chopped
- ¾ pint milk
- 1 pint vegetable stock
- 14 oz tin chopped tomatoes
- 3 tsp lemon juice

DIRECTIONS:

1. Melt the butter and cook the onions for 5 mins. Add potatoes , lettuce , stock and lemon juice.
2. Cover and bring to the boil for 15 mins.
3. Cool a little and then put in a liquidiser. Return to a clean pan and stir in the lovage and cover for more 5 mins and then serve.

NUTRITION: calories 144, fat 12g, carbs 22g, protein 15g, sodium 45mg, potassium 128mg

223. Jerusalem Artichoke and Carrot Soup

Cooking Time: 25 mins | Servings: 6

INGREDIENTS:

- 1 oz butter
- 1 large onion finely chopped

- 14 oz Jerusalem Artichokes peeled and chopped
- 14 oz carrots roughly chopped
- ½ stick celery
- 1 pint vegetable stock
- 1 cup milk

DIRECTIONS:

1. Melt the butter and cook the onions for 5 mins. Add the artichokes, carrots and celery and cook gently for 2 mins.
2. Add the vegetable stock and bring to the boil for 20 mins.
3. Cool the soup a little then puree in a liquidizer. Season and serve.

NUTRITION: calories 158, fat 10g, carbs 18g, protein 9g, fiber 3g, sodium 35mg, potassium 185g

224. Russian Vegetable Soup

Cooking Time: 20 mins | Servings: 6

INGREDIENTS:

- 8 oz potatoes peeled and sliced
- 4 oz parsnips , sliced
- 4 oz carrots , sliced
- 2 oz cabbage
- 1 oz butter
- 1 large onion finely chopped
- 2 tbsp chopped parsley
- 2 pints vegetable stock

DIRECTIONS:

1. Melt the butter and cook the vegetables. Add the parsley , herbs and stock.
2. Cover and bring to the boil for 20 mins.
3. Cool a little and then put in a liquidizer. Season and serve.

NUTRITION: calories 155, fat 5g, carbs 13 g, protein 8g, fiber 3g, sodium 88mg, potassium 111mg

225. Cream of Celeriac Soup

Cooking Time: 35 mins | Servings: 6

INGREDIENTS:

- 14 oz celeriac , peeled and chopped
- 4 oz potatoes peeled and sliced
- 1 tbsp olive oil
- 1 pint vegetable stock
- 1 tbsp lemon juice
- ½ milk

DIRECTIONS:

1. Heat the oil and cook the celeriac, potatoes for 5 mins. Add the stock and lemon juice and bring to the boil for 20 mins.
2. Cool a little and then put in a liquidizer. Season and serve.

NUTRITION: calories 110, fat 3g, carbs 10 g, protein 5g, fiber 4g, sodium 28mg, potassium 155g

226. Pumpkin and Coconut Soup

Cooking Time: 30 mins | Servings: 4

INGREDIENTS:

- 1 cup pumpkin , canned
- 6 cups chicken broth
- 1 cup low Fat: coconut almond milk
- 1 tsp sage , chopped
- 3 garlic cloves , peeled
- Sunflower seeds and pepper to taste

DIRECTIONS:

1. Take a stockpot and add all the Ingredients: except coconut almond milk into it.
2. Place stockpot over medium heat.
3. Let it bring to a boil.
4. Reduce heat to simmer for 30 mins.
5. Add the coconut almond milk and stir.

NUTRITION: calories 144, fat 15g, carbs 15g, protein 6g, fiber 3g, sodium 55mg, potassium 145g

227. Chicory Soup

Cooking Time: 40 mins | Servings: 6

INGREDIENTS:

- 2 heads of chicory, sliced
- 1 large onion finely chopped
- 4 oz parsnips , sliced
- 14 oz potatoes peeled and sliced
- 1 tbsp olive oil
- 1 pint vegetable stock
- ½ pint milk
- ¼ pint double cream

DIRECTIONS:

1. Heat the oil and cook the chicory, onion, parsnip and potatoes for 10 mins. Add the stock and bring to the boil for 30 mins.
2. Cool a little and then put in a liquidizer. Add lemon juice, milk , and cream and taste for seasoning.

NUTRITION: calories 100, fat 9g, carbs 15 g, protein 6g, fiber 4g, sodium 38mg, potassium 155g

228. Black Bean Soup

Cooking Time: 20 mins | Servings: 4

INGREDIENTS:

- 1 chopped yellow onion
- 1 chopped sweet potato
- 1 tsp. cinnamon powder
- 32 oz. low-Sodium chicken stock
- 38 oz. no-salt-added, drained and rinsed canned black beans
- 2 tsps. organic olive oil

DIRECTIONS:

1. Heat up a pot using the oil over medium heat, add onion and cinnamon , stir and cook for 6 mins.
2. Add black beans stock and sweet potato , stir , cook for 14 mins , puree utilizing an immersion blender , divide into bowls and serve for lunch.

NUTRITION: calories 221, fat 3g, carbs 15g , protein 8 , fiber 3g , sodium 76mg , potassium 158mg

229. Cherry Stew

Cooking Time: 0 mins | Servings: 6

INGREDIENTS:

- 2 cup water
- ½ cup powered cocoa
- ¼ cup coconut sugar
- 1 lb pitted cherries

DIRECTIONS:

In a pan, combine the cherries with all the water, sugar plus the hot chocolate mix , stir , cook over medium heat for ten mins , divide into bowls and serve cold.

NUTRITION: calories 207, fat 1g, carbs 8g, protein 6g, fiber 3g, sodium 45mg, potassium 122mg

230. Tofu Soup

Cooking Time: 10 mins | Servings: 8

INGREDIENTS:

- 1 lb. cubed extra-firm tofu
- 3 diced medium carrots
- 8 cup low-Sodium vegetable broth
- ½ tsp freshly ground white pepper
- 8 minced garlic cloves
- 6 sliced and divided scallions
- 4 oz sliced mushrooms
- 1-inch minced fresh ginger piece

DIRECTIONS:

1. Pour the broth into a stockpot. Add all of the ingredients except for the tofu and last 2 scallions. Bring to a boil over high heat.
2. Once boiling, add the tofu. Reduce heat to low, cover, and simmer for 5 mins.
3. Remove from heat, ladle soup into bowls, and garnish with the remaining sliced scallions. Serve immediately.

NUTRITION: calories 91, fat 3g, carbs 8g, protein 8, sugar 3g, fiber 3g, sodium 46mg, potassium 116mg

231. Pumpkin and Rosemary Soup

Cooking Time: 25 mins | Servings: 4

INGREDIENTS:

- 1lb pumpkin flesh
- 3 oz pumpkin seeds
- 5 garlic clove
- 2 onions
- 1 tbsp freshly chopped rosemary
- ½ cup olive oil
- 3 cup vegetable stock

DIRECTIONS:

1. Cut the pumpkin in cubes. Peel the cloves of garlic and chop finely.
2. Mix the pumpkin, garlic, onions, pumpkin seeds, rosemary , and olive oil and put everything on a baking tray on a baking sheet.
3. Bake in a preheated oven 350°F for approx. 25 mins, stirring every 10 mins
4. Then put everything in a large saucepan , mix roughly if necessary.
5. Add broth little by little , bring back to boil and cook in small broths for another 5 mins.

NUTRITION: calories 125, fat 8g, carbs 8g, protein 5 , fiber 3g, sodium 79mg, potassium 123mg

232. Curry , Carrot and Coconut Soup

Cooking time: 5 mins | Servings: 6

INGREDIENTS:

- 6 medium carrots , roughly chopped
- 4 cups vegetable broth
- 1 tbsp olive oil
- 1 small onion , coarsely chopped
- 2 celery stalks , coarsely chopped
- 1tsp curry powder
- 1 tsp ground cumin
- 1 tsp minced fresh ginger
- ¼ tsp salt
- 1 cup canned coconut milk
- ¼ tsp freshly ground black pepper
- 1 tbsp chopped fresh cilantro

DIRECTIONS:

1. Heat an Instant Pot to high and add the olive oil.
2. Sauté the onion and celery for 2 to 3 mins. Add the curry powder, cumin, and ginger to the pot and cook until fragrant , about 30 seconds.
3. Add the carrots , vegetable broth , and salt to the pot. Close and seal, and set for 5 mins on high. Allow the pressure to release naturally.
4. In a blender jar, carefully purée the soup in batches and transfer back to the pot.
5. Stir in the coconut milk and pepper , and heat through. Top with the cilantro and serve.

NUTRITION: calories: 145, fat 11g, protein 2g, carbs 13g, sugars 4g, fiber 3g, sodium 238mg

233. Buttercup Squash Soup

Cooking time: 10 mins | Servings: 4

INGREDIENTS:

- 3 cups vegetable broth or chicken bone broth
- 2 tbsp olive oil
- 1 medium onion , chopped
- 1½ pounds buttercup squash , peeled , seeded , and cut into 1-inch chunks
- ½ tsp kosher salt
- ¼ tsp ground white pepper
- whole nutmeg , for grating

DIRECTIONS:

1. Set the electric pressure cooker to the Sauté setting. When the pot is hot , pour in the olive oil.

2. Add the onion and sauté for 3 to 5 mins , until it begins to soften. Hit Cancel.
3. Add the broth, squash, salt, and pepper to the pot and stir. (If you want a thicker soup, use 4 cups of broth. If you want a thinner, drinkable soup, use 5 cups.)
4. Close and lock the lid of the pressure cooker. Set the valve to sealing.
5. Cook on high pressure for 10 mins.
6. When the cooking is complete, hit Cancel and allow the pressure to release naturally.
7. Once the pin drops, unlock and remove the lid.
8. Use an immersion blender to purée the soup right in the pot. If you don't have an immersion blender, transfer the soup to a blender or food processor and purée. (Follow the instructions that came with your machine for blending hot foods.)
9. Pour the soup into serving bowls and grate nutmeg on top.

NUTRITION: (1¹/₃ cups) calories 111 , fat 5g, protein11 g, carbs 18g, sugars 4g, fiber 4g, sodium 166mg

234. Turkey and Barley Soup

Cooking time: 20 mins | Servings: 6

INGREDIENTS:

- 1 pound ground turkey
- 2 cups chicken bone broth, low-sodium store-bought chicken broth , or water
- 1 tbsp avocado oil
- 1 (28-ounce) can diced tomatoes
- 2 tbsp tomato paste
- 2½ cups package frozen chopped carrots
- 2½ cups package frozen peppers and onions
- ¹/₃ cup dry barley
- 1 tsp salt
- ¼ tsp freshly ground black pepper
- 2 bay leaves

DIRECTIONS:

1. Set the electric pressure cooker to the Sauté/More setting. When the pot is hot , pour in the avocado oil.
2. Add the turkey to the pot and sauté , stirring frequently to break up the meat , for about 7 mins or until the turkey is no longer pink. Hit Cancel.
3. Add the broth, tomatoes and their juices, and tomato paste. Stir in the carrots, peppers and onions , barley , salt , pepper , and bay leaves.
4. Close and lock the lid of the pressure cooker. Set the valve to sealing.
5. Cook on high pressure for 20 mins.
6. When the cooking is complete, hit Cancel and allow the pressure to release naturally for 10 mins, then quick release any remaining pressure.
7. Once the pin drops, unlock and remove the lid. Discard the bay leaves.
8. Spoon into bowls and serve.

NUTRITION: (1¼ cups) calories 253 , fat 12g, protein 19g, carbs21 g, sugars 7g, fiber 7g, sodium 560mg

235. Cauliflower Leek Soup

Cooking time: 20 mins | Servings: 2

INGREDIENTS:

- 2 cups chopped leeks (2 to 3 leeks)
- 2 cups cauliflower florets
- 1 garlic clove , peeled
- ¹/₃ cup vegetable broth
- ½ cup half-and-half
- ¼ tsp salt and pepper
- Avocado oil cooking spray

DIRECTIONS:

1. Heat a large stockpot over medium-low heat. When hot, coat the cooking

surface with cooking spray. Put the leeks and cauliflower into the pot.

2. Increase the heat to medium and cover the pan. Cook for 10 mins, stirring halfway through.
3. Add the garlic and cook for 5 mins.
4. Add the broth and deglaze the pan , stirring to scrape up the browned bits from the bottom.
5. Transfer the broth and vegetables to a food processor or blender and add the half-and-half, salt, and pepper. Blend well.

NUTRITION: calories 173, fat 7g, protein 6g, carbs 24g, sugars 8g, fiber 5g, sodium 487mg

236. Beef Soup

Cooking time: 15 mins | Servings: 4

INGREDIENTS:

- 1 pound ground beef
- 1 onion , chopped
- 2 celery stalks , chopped
- 2 carrot , chopped
- 1 tsp dried rosemary
- 5 cups beef or chicken broth
- ½ tsp sea salt and pepper
- 1 cup peas

DIRECTIONS:

1. In a large pot over medium-high heat , cook the ground beef , crumbling with the side of a spoon , until browned , about 5 mins.
2. Add the onion, celery, carrot, and rosemary. Cook, stirring occasionally, until the vegetables start to soften , about 5 mins.
3. Add the broth, salt, pepper , and peas. Bring to a simmer. Reduce the heat and simmer, stirring, until warmed through, about 5 mins more.

NUTRITION: calories 355, fat 17g, protein 34g, carbs 18g, sugars 6g, fiber 5g, sodium 362mg

237. Lime Chicken Soup

Cooking time: 35 mins | Servings: 4

INGREDIENTS

- 2 boneless , skinless chicken breasts
- 2 cups chicken broth
- ½ cup water
- 1 tbsp olive oil
- 1 onion , thinly sliced
- 1 garlic clove , minced
- 1 jalapeño pepper , diced
- 1 Roma tomato , diced
- ½ tsp salt
- 2 (6-inch) corn tortillas , cut into thin strips
- Juice of 1 lime
- ¼ cup shredded cheddar cheese , for garnish
- Nonstick cooking spray

DIRECTIONS:

1. In a medium pot, heat the oil over medium-high heat. Add the onion and cook for 3 to 5 mins until it begins to soften. Add the garlic and jalapeño, and cook until fragrant, about 1 minute more.
2. Add the chicken, chicken broth, tomato , and salt to the pot and bring to a boil. Reduce the heat to medium and simmer gently for 20 to 25 mins until the chicken breasts are cooked through. Remove the chicken from the pot and set aside.
3. Preheat a broiler to high.
4. Spray the tortilla strips with nonstick cooking spray and toss to coat. Spread in a single layer on a baking sheet and broil for 3 to 5 mins , flipping once , until crisp.
5. When the chicken is cool enough to handle, shred it with two forks and return to the pot.

6. Season the soup with the lime juice. Serve hot, garnished with cilantro , cheese , and tortilla strips.

NUTRITION: calories 191, fat 8g, protein 19g, carbs 13g, sugars 2g, fiber 2g, sodium 482mg

238. Tomato Kale Soup

Cooking time: 15 mins | Servings: 4

INGREDIENTS:

- 3 cups chopped baby kale leaves
- 3 cups low-sodium vegetable broth
- 1 (28-ounce) can crushed tomatoes
- 1 tbsp olive oil
- 1 onion , chopped
- 2 carrots, finely chopped
- 2 garlic cloves, minced
- ½ tsp dried oregano
- ¼ tsp dried basil
- ¼ tsp salt

DIRECTIONS:

1. In a large pot, heat the oil over medium heat. Add the onion and carrots to the pan. Sauté for 3 to 5 mins until they begin to soften. Add the garlic and sauté for 30 seconds more, until fragrant.
2. Add the vegetable broth, tomatoes , oregano , and basil to the pot and bring to a boil. Reduce the heat to low and simmer for 5 mins.
3. Using an immersion blender, purée the soup.
4. Add the kale and simmer for 3 more mins. Season with the salt. Serve immediately.

NUTRITION: calories 172, fat 5g, protein 6g, carbs 30g, sugars 13g, fiber 8g, sodium 601mg

239. Cheeseburger Soup

Cooking time: 25 mins | Servings: 4

INGREDIENTS:

- 1 pound lean ground beef
- 1 (15-ounce) can diced tomatoes
- 2 cups beef or vegetable broth
- ½ cup diced white onion
- ½ cup diced celery
- ½ cup sliced portobello mushrooms
- 1/3 cup single cream
- ¾ cup shredded sharp cheddar cheese
- Avocado oil cooking spray

DIRECTIONS:

1. Heat a large stockpot over medium-low heat. When hot, coat the cooking surface with cooking spray. Put the onion, celery , and mushrooms into the pot. Cook for 7 mins , stirring occasionally.
2. Add the ground beef and cook for 5 mins , stirring and breaking apart as needed.
3. Add the diced tomatoes with their juices and the broth. Increase the heat to medium-high and simmer for 10 mins.
4. Remove the pot from the heat and stir in the half-and-half.
5. Serve topped with the cheese.

NUTRITION: calories 330, fat 18g, protein 33g, carbs 9g, sugars 5g, fiber 2g, sodium 321mg

240. Taco Beef Soup

Cooking time: 20 mins | Servings: 4

INGREDIENTS:

- 1 pound 93% lean ground beef
- 2 cups beef or vegetable broth
- 1 (15-ounce) can diced tomatoes
- 1 red bell pepper, chopped
- ½ cup chopped yellow onion
- 1 tsp ground cumin
- ½ tsp salt
- ½ tsp chili flakes
- ½ tsp garlic powder
- 1½ cups frozen corn
- 1/3 cup half and half
- Avocado oil cooking spray

DIRECTIONS:

1. Heat a large stockpot over medium-low heat. When hot, coat the cooking surface with cooking spray. Put the pepper and onion in the pan and cook for 5 mins.
2. Add the ground beef, cumin, salt, chili powder , and garlic powder. Cook for 5 to 7 mins, stirring and breaking apart the beef as needed.
3. Add the broth, diced tomatoes with their juices, and corn. Increase the heat to medium-high and simmer for 10 mins.
4. Remove from the heat and stir in the half-and-half.

NUTRITION: calories 320, fat 12g, protein 30g, carbs 23g, sugars 7g, fiber 4g, sodium 456mg

241. Beans and Butternut Squash Stew

Cooking time: 7 mins | Servings: 6

INGREDIENTS:

- 1 pound butternut squash, peeled, seeded , and cut into 1-inch cubes
- 2 ½ cups vegetable broth or water
- 1 (15-ounce) can diced tomatoes
- 1 (15-ounce) can white beans, rinsed and drained
- 1 avocado, chopped just before serving
- 1 tbsp olive oil
- 1 tbsp chili powder
- 1 tsp dried oregano
- 1 tsp ground cumin
- 1 tbsp garlic powder
- ½ tsp salt

DIRECTIONS:

1. In the electric pressure cooker, toss the squash with the olive oil, chili powder, oregano, cumin, garlic pepper , and salt.
2. Stir in the broth, and tomatoes and their juices.
3. Close and lock the lid of the pressure cooker. Set the valve to sealing.
4. Cook on high pressure for 7 mins.
5. When the cooking is complete, hit Cancel and quick release the pressure.
6. Once the pin drops, unlock and remove the lid.
7. Stir in the beans and let the stew sit for about 5 mins to let the beans warm up.
8. Use an immersion blender to purée about one-third of the stew right in the pot. (I like to leave some chunks of squash and whole beans for more texture.)
9. Spoon into serving bowls and top with the avocado.

NUTRITION: (1 cup) calories 196, fat 6g, protein 7g, carbs 31g, sugars 4g, fiber 8g, sodium 332mg

242. Sweet Potato and Pumpkin Soup

Cooking time: 45 mins | Servings: 8 to 10

INGREDIENTS:

- 3 cups vegetable broth, divided
- 1 celery stalk, roughly chopped
- 1 cup roughly chopped tomato
- 1 red bell pepper, chopped
- 1 large sweet potato, peeled and cut into 2-inch cubes
- 1 small pumpkin, peeled and cut into 2-inch cubes
- 1 bay leaf
- 1 tsp paprika
- 2 cups roasted unsalted peanuts
- Baby sage leaves (optional)

DIRECTIONS:

1. In a large pan, bring 1 cup of broth to a simmer over medium heat.

2. Add the celery, tomato, and bell pepper and cook for 5 to 7 mins , or until softened.
3. Add the sweet potato , pumpkin , bay leaf , paprika , and the remaining 2 cups of broth. Cover and cook for 30 mins , or until the sweet potato and pumpkin are soft.
4. Add the peanuts and cook for 5 mins , or until the peanuts become less crunchy. Discard the bay leaf.
5. Transfer to a heat-safe blender , and pulse until the soup has a batter-like consistency.
6. Serve and garnish with baby sage leaves.

NUTRITION: calories 266, fat 18g, protein 12g, carbs 19g, sugars 6g, fiber 5g, sodium 50mg

243. Carrot Soup

Cooking time: 25 mins | Servings: 6

INGREDIENTS:

- 1 pound carrots, peeled and halved
- 3 cups vegetable broth, divided
- 2 celery stalks, halved
- 1 small yellow onion , roughly chopped
- ½ fennel bulb, cored and roughly chopped
- 1 (1-inch) piece fresh ginger, peeled and chopped
- 2 tsps ground cumin
- 1 garlic clove , peeled

DIRECTIONS:

1. Select the Sauté setting on an electric pressure cooker, and combine ½ cup of broth , the celery , onion , fennel , and ginger. Cook for 5 mins , or until the vegetables are tender.
2. Add the carrots, cumin , garlic , and the remaining 3½ cups of broth.
3. Close and lock the lid, and set the pressure valve to sealing.
4. Change to the manual setting, and cook for 15 mins.
5. Once cooking is complete, quick-release the pressure. Carefully remove the lid , and let cool for 5 mins.
6. Using a stand mixer or an immersion blender, carefully purée the soup. Serve with a heaping plate of greens.

NUTRITION: calories 82, fat 2g, protein 3g, carbs 13g, sugars 5g, fiber 3g, sodium 121mg

244. Thai Shrimps Soup

Cooking time: 10 mins | Servings: 4

INGREDIENTS:

- ½ pound shrimp , peeled and deveined
- 3 cups fish or vegetable broth
- 2 cups chopped carrots
- 1 tbsp coconut oil
- 1 tbsp Thai red curry paste
- ½ onion , sliced
- 2 garlic cloves , minced
- ½ cup whole unsalted peanuts
- 1 can coconut milk
- Minced fresh cilantro , for garnish

DIRECTIONS:

1. In a large pan, heat the oil over medium-high heat until shimmering.
2. Add the curry paste and cook , stirring constantly , for 1 minute. Add the onion, garlic , carrots , and peanuts to the pan , and continue to cook for 2 to 3 mins until the onion begins to soften.
3. Add the broth and bring to a boil. Reduce the heat to low and simmer for 5 to 6 mins until the carrots are tender.
4. Using an immersion blender or in a blender, purée the soup until smooth and return it to the pot. With the heat still on low, add the coconut milk and stir to combine. Add the shrimp to the

pot and cook for 2 to 3 mins until cooked through.

5. Garnish with cilantro and serve.

NUTRITION: calories 237, fat 14g, protein 14g, carbs 17g, sugars 6g, fiber 5g, sodium 619mg

245. Calabaza Squash Soup

Cooking time: 45 mins | Servings: 4

INGREDIENTS:

- 1 pound calabaza squash, peeled and chopped
- 1 tomato , chopped
- 4 cups vegetable broth
- 1 medium onion, chopped
- 1 medium green bell pepper, chopped
- 4 scallions , chopped
- 1 tbsp fresh thyme
- 1 tbsp minced ginger root
- Juice of 1 lime
- ¼ cup chopped cilantro
- salt , to taste
- ¼ cup toasted pepitas

DIRECTIONS:

1. Put the calabaza squash, tomato, onion , bell pepper, scallions, thyme, and ginger roots in a saucepan , then pour in the vegetable broth.
2. Bring to a boil over medium-high heat. Reduce the heat to low, then simmer for 45 mins or until the vegetables are soft. Stir constantly.
3. Add the lime juice, cilantro, and salt. Pour the soup in a large bowl , then add the thyme and garnish with pepitas before serving.

NUTRITION: calories 50, fat 0g, protein 2g, carbs 12g, fiber 4g, sugars 5g, sodium 20mg

246. Pork Meatball Soup

Cooking time: 5 hours | Servings: 4

INGREDIENTS:

- ½ pound ground pork
- 3 cup chicken broth
- 3 cup mustard greens, torn
- 2 scallions, sliced thin
- 2 tsps fresh ginger, peeled and grated fine
- 1 tbsp soy sauce
- 1 tbsp vegetable oil
- 2 cloves garlic , diced fine
- 1 tsp peppercorns , crushed
- 1 tsp fish sauce
- ¾ tsp red pepper flakes
- ½ tsp cumin seeds, chopped coarse
- Sea salt and black pepper , to taste

DIRECTIONS:

1. In a large bowl, combine pork , garlic , ginger , and spices. Season with salt and pepper. Use your hands to combine all thoroughly.
2. Heat oil in a large skillet over medium heat. Form pork into 1-inch balls and cook in oil till brown on all sides. Use a slotted spoon to transfer the meatballs to a crock pot.
3. Add remaining and stir. Cover and cook on low for 4 to 5 hours or until meatballs are cooked through. Serve.

NUTRITION: calories 157, fat 6g, protein 19g, carbs 7g, fiber 2g, sugars 2g, sodium 571mg

247. Roasted Tomato and Bell Pepper Soup

Preparation time: 20 mins | Cooking time: 35 mins | Servings: 6

INGREDIENTS:

- 12 plum tomatoes, cored and halved
- 2 oz goat cheese, grated
- 4 cups chicken broth
- 1 cup water

- 2 tbsp olive oil , plus more for coating the baking dish
- 3 celery stalks , coarsely chopped
- 3 red bell peppers, seeded , halved
- 2 garlic cloves, lightly crushed
- 1 sweet onion, cut into eighths
- salt and black pepper , to taste
- 2 tbsp chopped fresh basil

DIRECTIONS:

1. Preheat the oven to 400°F. Coat a large baking dish lightly with olive oil.
2. Put the tomatoes in the oiled dish, cut-side down. Scatter the celery, bell peppers, garlic , and onion on top of the tomatoes. Drizzle with 2 tbsp of olive oil and season with salt and pepper.
3. Roast in the preheated oven for about 30 mins, or until the vegetables are fork-tender and slightly charred.
4. Remove the vegetables from the oven. Let them rest for a few mins until cooled slightly.
5. Transfer to a food processor, along with the chicken broth , and purée until fully mixed and smooth.
6. Pour the purée soup into a medium saucepan and bring it to a simmer over medium-high heat.
7. Sprinkle the basil and grated cheese on top before serving.

NUTRITION: calories 187, fat 9g, protein 7g, carbs 21g, fiber 6g, sugars 14g, sodium 825mg

248. Savory Cabbage Soup

Cooking time: 6 hours | Servings: 6

INGREDIENTS:

- 6 bacon strips, cut into 1-inch pieces
- 2 cup cauliflower, separated into florets
- 2 cup cabbage, sliced thin
- 2 celery stalks, peeled and diced
- 1 onion, diced
- 1 carrot, peeled and diced
- 3 cup chicken or vegetable broth
- 2 cloves garlic, diced fine
- ¼ tsp thyme

DIRECTIONS:

1. Cook bacon in a large skillet over medium-high heat until almost crisp. Remove from skillet and place on paper towels to drain.
2. Add the celery , garlic , and onion to the skillet and cook , stirring frequently , about 5 mins. Use a slotted spoon to transfer to the crock pot.
3. Add the bacon , broth , cabbage , carrot , and thyme to the crock pot. Cover and cook on low for 4 to 5 hours or until the carrots are tender.
4. Add the cauliflower and cook until tender , about 1 to 2 hours. Serve.

NUTRITION: calories 150, fat 8g, protein 10g, carbs 8g, fiber 3g, sugars 3g, sodium 216mg

249. Spiced Lamb Stew

Cooking time: 2 h 15 mins | Servings: 4

INGREDIENTS:

- 1½ pounds lamb shoulder , cut into 1-inch chunks
- 2 sweet potatoes , peeled , diced
- 2 cups beef or vegetable broth
- 2 tbsp olive oil
- ½ sweet onion , chopped
- 1 tbsp grated fresh ginger
- 1 tsp minced garlic
- 1 tsp ground cinnamon
- 1 tsp ground cumin
- ¼ tsp ground cloves
- Sea salt and freshly ground back pepper , to taste
- 2 tsps chopped fresh parsley , for garnish

DIRECTIONS:

1. Preheat the oven to 300°F.

2. Place a large ovenproof skillet over medium-high heat and add the olive oil.
3. Brown the lamb, stirring occasionally , for about 6 mins.
4. Add the onion, ginger, garlic, cinnamon , cumin, and cloves , and sauté for 5 mins.
5. Add the sweet potatoes and broth and bring the stew to a boil.
6. Cover the skillet and transfer the lamb to the oven. Braise, stirring until the lamb is very tender , about 2 hours.
7. Remove the stew from the oven and season with salt and pepper.
8. Serve garnished with the parsley.

NUTRITION: calories 544, fat 35g, protein 32g, carbs 16g, sugars 4g, fiber 2g, sodium 395mg

250. Seafood Stew

Cooking time: 30 mins | Servings: 6

INGREDIENTS:

- 2 (4-ounce) haddock fillets , cut into 1-inch chunks
- 1 tbsp olive oil
- 1 sweet onion , chopped
- 2 tsps minced garlic
- 3 celery stalks , chopped
- 2 carrots , peeled and chopped
- 1 (28-ounce) can sodium-free diced tomatoes , undrained
- 3 cups low-sodium chicken broth
- ½ cup clam juice
- ¼ cup dry white wine
- 2 tsps chopped fresh basil
- 2 tsps chopped fresh oregano
- 1 pound mussels, scrubbed, debearded
- 8 oz shrimp, peeled, deveined, quartered
- Sea salt and pepper , to taste
- 2 tbsp chopped fresh parsley

DIRECTIONS:

1. Place a large saucepan over medium-high heat and add the olive oil.
2. Sauté the onion and garlic until softened and translucent, about 3 mins.
3. Stir in the celery and carrots and sauté for 4 mins.
4. Stir in the tomatoes, chicken broth , clam juice , white wine , basil , and oregano.
5. Bring the sauce to a boil, then reduce the heat to low. Simmer for 15 mins.
6. Add the fish and mussels , cover , and cook until the mussels open , about 5 mins.
7. Discard any unopened mussels. Add the shrimp to the pan and cook until the shrimp are opaque , about 2 mins.
8. Season with salt and pepper. Serve garnished with the chopped parsley.

NUTRITION: calories 248, fat 7g, protein 28g, carbs 19g, sugars 7g, fiber 2g, sodium 577mg

251. Lamb and Sweet Potato Stew

Cooking time: 2 h 15 mins | Servings: 4

INGREDIENTS:

- 1½ pounds lamb shoulder , cut into 1-inch chunks
- 1 tsp ground cinnamon
- 1 tsp ground cumin
- 1 tbsp fresh ginger , grated
- 2 tsps garlic , minced
- ¼ tsp ground cloves
- 2 tbsp olive oil
- ½ sweet onion , chopped
- 2 cups low-sodium beef broth
- 2 sweet potatoes , peeled , diced
- 2 tsps chopped fresh parsley , for garnish

- salt and pepper, to taste

DIRECTIONS:

1. Preheat the oven to 300°F.
2. Heat the olive oil in an oven-safe skillet over medium-high heat.
3. Brown the lamb shoulder in the skillet for 6 mins. Shake the skillet periodically.
4. Add the cinnamon, cumin, ginger, garlic, cloves, and onion to the skillet and sauté for 5 mins or until aromatic.
5. Add the beef broth and sweet potatoes to the skillet. Bring to a boil. Stir constantly.
6. Put the skillet lid on and cook in the preheated oven for 2 hours until the lamb is fork-tender.
7. Divide the stew among four bowls , then top with parsley , salt , and pepper. Give it a stir before serving.

NUTRITION: calories 488, fat 24g, protein 40g, carbs 30g, fiber 3g, sugars 7g, sodium 182mg

252. Beef Zoodle Stew

Cooking time: 1 h 25 mins | Servings: 6

INGREDIENTS:

- 1 pound beef stew meat
- 4 large zucchinis , spiralize
- 4 cup beef broth
- 2 celery stalks , diced
- 3 carrots , peeled and diced
- ½ red onion, diced
- 1 (14-ounce) can tomatoes , diced
- 1 cloves garlic, diced fine
- 1 to 2 bay leaves
- 2 tbsp Worcestershire sauce
- 2 tbsp olive oil
- 1 tsp thyme
- ¼ tsp red pepper flakes
- Salt and ground black pepper, to taste

DIRECTIONS:

1. Heat oil in a large saucepan over medium heat. Add beef and cook until brown on all sides. Remove from pan and set aside.
2. Add the garlic to the pan and cook 30 seconds. Then stir in onion and red pepper flakes. Cook 1 minute and add the celery and carrots. Sweat the vegetables for 2 mins, stirring occasionally.
3. Add the beef back to the pan with the Worcestershire, thyme, and stir. Season with salt and pepper to taste. Add the broth, tomatoes, and bay leaves and bring to a boil.
4. Reduce heat , cover and let simmer 40 mins. Remove the cover and cook 35 mins more or until stew thickens.
5. Divide the zucchini noodles evenly among four bowls. Ladle stew evenly over zucchini and let set for a few mins to cook the zucchini. Serve.

NUTRITION: calories 226, fat 6g, protein 29g, carbs 13g, fiber 3g, sugars 8g, sodium 320mg

253. Traditional Mexican Beef Stew

Cooking time: 1 h 30 mins | Servings: 6

INGREDIENTS:

- 1½ pound beef round steak, cut into ½-inch pieces
- 2 cups tomatoes, diced
- 1 cup carrots, sliced
- 1 cup onion, diced
- ¼ cup sweet red pepper, diced
- 1 jalapeno, seeded and diced
- 2 tbsp cilantro, diced
- 1¾ cup low sodium beef broth
- 2 clove garlic , diced
- 2 tbsp flour
- 1 tbsp vegetable oil
- 1½ tsps chili powder
- ½ tsp salt

DIRECTIONS:

1. Heat the oil in a large pot over medium-high heat. Add the steak and cook until brown on all sides.
2. Add the broth, carrots, onion, red pepper, jalapeno, garlic, and seasonings and bring to a low boil. Reduce heat to low, cover and simmer 45 mins, stirring occasionally.
3. Add the tomatoes and continue cooking 15 mins.
4. Stir the flour and water together in a measuring up until smooth. Add to stew with the cilantro and continue cooking another 20 to 30 mins or until stew has thickened. Serve.

NUTRITION: calories 313, fat 13g, protein 39g, carbs 9g, fiber 2g, sugars 4g, sodium 306mg

254. African Holiday Stew

Cooking time: 1 h 40 mins | Servings: 6

INGREDIENTS:

- 3½ pounds chicken, whole pieces with bones in
- 6 Roma tomatoes
- 2 scallions, diced white and green parts
- 1 onion, sliced thin
- 1 cup carrots , sliced
- 2 cups water
- ⅛ cup vegetable oil
- 2 tbsp parsley
- 1 cloves garlic , diced fine
- 1 tbsp paprika
- 1½ tsps thyme
- ¼ tsp curry powder
- 1 bay leaf
- Salt and pepper , to taste

DIRECTIONS:

1. Season chicken with salt and pepper on both sides.
2. Place the tomatoes, onion, and scallions in a food processor and pulse until puréed.
3. In a large soup pot, heat the oil over medium heat. Add chicken and brown on both sides.
4. Pour the tomato mixture over the chicken and add the remaining ingredients. Bring to a low boil.
5. Reduce heat to low, cover , and simmer 60 to 90 mins until the chicken is cooked through and the carrots are tender. Discard bay leaf before serving. Serve as it is or over cauliflower rice.

NUTRITION: calories 481, fat 13g, protein 78g, carbs 9g, fiber 2g, sugars 5g, sodium 235mg

255. Hearty Bell Pepper Stew

Cooking time: 4 hours | Servings: 4

INGREDIENTS:

- ½ pound hot Italian sausage
- ½ pound lean ground sirloin
- 2 cups tomatoes , diced
- 2 cups green pepper , diced
- 2 cups onion , diced
- ½ cup cauliflower , grated
- 2 cup beef broth
- ½ cup tomato sauce
- 2 tbsp olive oil
- 4 cloves garlic, diced fine
- 1 tsp basil
- ½ tsp oregano

DIRECTIONS:

1. Heat the oil in a large skillet over medium-high heat. Add in both kinds of meat and cook, breaking it up with a spoon, until no longer pink on the outside. Remove the meat with a slotted spoon and place in crock pot.
2. Add the green pepper, onion and garlic to the skillet. Cook, stirring frequently , about 5 mins. Remove the vegetables with a slotted spoon and add to the meat mixture.

3. Add in the broth, tomatoes , tomato sauce and seasonings. Cover and cook on high 2 to 3 hours.
4. Add the cauliflower and cook another 60 mins or until cauliflower is tender.

NUTRITION: calories 313, fat 20g, protein 19g, carbs 14g, fiber 2g, sugars 8g, sodium 952mg

256. Tasty Seafood Stew

Cooking time: 40 mins | Servings: 4

INGREDIENTS:

- 6 live blue crabs
- 1 pound medium shrimp, peeled, deveined and tails removed
- ½ pound jumbo lump crabmeat
- 3 scallions , diced
- 2 stalks celery, diced
- 1yellow onions, diced
- 1 green bell pepper, diced
- 1/3 cup parsley, diced fine
- 1 tbsp lemon juice
- 4 cup vegetable broth
- 3 cloves garlic, diced fine
- ½ cup olive oil
- ½ cup whole wheat flour
- 1 tbsp Worcestershire sauce
- 2 bay leaves
- Salt and pepper, to taste

DIRECTIONS:

1. Prepare crabs, working with one at a time. Remove and discard legs. Remove and save the claws. Discard the underside , the triangular section , and pull the body away from the shell. Remove gills and organs and rinse thoroughly. Place clean crabs in a bowl , cover and refrigerate till ready to use.
2. Heat oil in a large stock pot over medium-high heat. Whisk in flour and cook , stirring constantly , until you have a dark roux. Add vegetables and cook , stirring frequently , until vegetables are soft , about 10 to 12 mins.
3. Add the cleaned crabs, broth, Worcestershire and spices and bring to a boil. Reduce heat, cover and simmer 15 to 20 mins.
4. Add remaining seafood and cook until shrimp turn pink , 3 to 5 mins. Stir in parsley , lemon juice and scallions. Serve.

NUTRITION: calories 441, fat 19g, protein 54g, carbs 17g, fiber 1g, sugars 3g, sodium 1371mg

CHAPTER 7 Meatless Mains

257. Lemony Spinach-Tofu Bake

Cooking time: 30 mins | Servings: 2

INGREDIENTS:

- 1cup frozen spinach, thawed and drained
- 1 cup (about 8 oz) crumbled firm tofu
- ½ cup chopped red bell pepper
- ¼ cup chopped onion
- 2 tbsp lemon juice
- 1 garlic clove , minced
- 1 tsp dried marjoram
- ½ tsp red pepper flakes
- ½ cup chopped walnuts
- olive oil cooking spray

DIRECTIONS:

1. Preheat the oven to 375°F.
2. Spray 2 mini loaf pans with cooking spray. Set aside.
3. In a medium bowl, mix together the spinach, tofu, bell pepper, onion, lemon juice, marjoram, and red pepper flakes.
4. Over the bottom of each prepared pan , sprinkle about 2 tbsp of walnuts in a thin layer.
5. Add half of the spinach-tofu mixture to each pan.
6. Top each with about 2 tbsp of the remaining walnuts.
7. Place the pans in the preheated oven. Bake for 30 mins , or until set.
8. Remove the loaves from the pans and serve immediately.

NUTRITION: calories 204 , fat 11g, protein 15g, carbs 13g, sugars 4g, fiber 4g, sodium 128mg

258. Grilled Vegetables on White Bean Hummus

Cooking time: 30 mins | Servings: 2

INGREDIENTS:

- 1 (8-ounce) can white beans, drained and rinsed
- 2 medium zucchini, sliced
- 1 red bell pepper, seeded and quartered
- 2 portobello mushroom caps, quartered
- 2 tsps olive oil , divided
- 1 garlic clove , minced
- ½ cup vegetable broth
- 3 cups baby spinach , divided
- Salt and pepper , to taste
- 2 lemon wedges , divided , for garnish

DIRECTIONS:

1. Preheat the grill. Use a stove-top grill pan or broiler if a grill is not available.
2. Lightly brush the zucchini, red bell pepper , and mushrooms with 1½ tsps of olive oil. Arrange them in a barbecue grill pan. Place the pan on the preheated grill. Cook the vegetables for 5 to 8 mins , or until lightly browned. Turn the vegetables. Brush with the remaining 1½ tsps of olive oil. Cook for 5 to 8 mins more, or until tender.
3. To a small pan set over high heat , add the white beans , garlic , and vegetable broth. Bring to a boil. Reduce the heat to low. Simmer for 10 mins , uncovered. Using a potato

masher , roughly mash the beans , adding a little more broth if they seem too dry.

4. Place 2 cups of spinach on each serving plate.
5. Top each with half of the bean mash and half of the grilled vegetables. Season with salt and pepper.
6. Place 1 lemon wedge on each plate and serve.

NUTRITION: calories 244, fat 8g, protein 13g, carbs 35g, sugars 9g, fiber 6g, sodium 241mg

259. Sweet Potato and Chickpea Bowl

Cooking time: 15 mins | Servings: 2

INGREDIENTS:

Bowl:

- 1 small sweet potato , peeled and finely diced
- 2 cups baby kale
- 1 tsp olive oil
- 1 cup from 1 (15-ounce) can chickpeas , drained and rinsed

Sauce:

- 2 tbsp Greek yogurt
- 1 tbsp tahini
- 1 garlic clove , minced
- Pinch salt

DIRECTIONS:

Make the Sauce

1. In a small bowl, whisk together the yogurt and tahini.
2. Stir in the hemp seeds, garlic , and salt. Season with pepper. Add 2 to 3 tbsp water to create a creamy yet pourable consistency. Set aside.

Make the Bowl

3. Preheat the oven to 425°F. Line a baking sheet with parchment paper.
4. Arrange the sweet potato on the prepared baking sheet and drizzle with the olive oil. Toss. Roast for 10 to 15 mins, stirring once, until tender and browned.
5. In each of 2 bowls, arrange ½ cup of chickpeas , 1 cup of kale , and half of the cooked sweet potato. Drizzle with half the creamy tahini sauce and serve.

NUTRITION: calories 322, fat 14g, protein 17g, carbs 36g, sugars 7g, fiber 8g, sodium 305mg

260. Black Bean Enchilada Skillet

Cooking time: 15 mins | Servings: 6

INGREDIENTS:

- 1 (15-ounce) can black beans, drained and rinsed
- 1 (10-ounce) can enchilada sauce
- ½ onion , chopped
- ½ red bell pepper, seeded and chopped
- ½ green bell pepper, seeded and chopped
- 2 zucchini , chopped
- 2 garlic cloves, minced
- 1 tsp ground cumin
- ¼ tsp salt and pepper
- ½ cup shredded cheddar cheese, divided
- 2 (6-inch) corn tortillas , cut into strips
- 1 tbsp olive oil
- chopped fresh cilantro , for garnish

DIRECTIONS:

1. Heat the broiler to high.
2. In a large oven-safe skillet , heat the oil over medium-high heat.
3. Add the onion, red bell pepper , green bell pepper , zucchini , and garlic to the skillet , and cook for 3 to 5 mins until the onion softens.
4. Add the black beans, enchilada sauce , cumin , salt , pepper , ¼ cup of cheese , and tortilla strips , and mix together. Top with the remaining ¼

cup of cheese.

5. Put the skillet under the broiler and broil for 5 to 8 mins until the cheese is melted and bubbly. Garnish with cilantro and serve.

NUTRITION: calories 171, fat 7g, protein 8g, carbs 21g, sugars 3g, fiber 7g, sodium 565mg

261. Mushroom Cutlets with Creamy Sauce

Cooking time: 20 mins | Servings: 4

INGREDIENTS:

Cutlets:

- 2 eggs
- 2 cups chopped mushrooms
- 1 cup quick oats
- 2 scallions, chopped
- ¼ cup shredded cheddar cheese
- ½ tsp salt and pepper

Sauce:

- ¼ cup shredded cheddar cheese
- 1 tbsp olive oil
- 2 tbsp whole-wheat flour
- 1½ cups unsweetened almond milk
- ¼ tsp salt
- Worcestershire sauce

DIRECTIONS:

Make the Sauce

1. In a medium saucepan, heat the oil over medium heat. Add the flour and stir constantly for about 2 mins until browned.
2. Slowly whisk in the almond milk and bring to a boil. Reduce the heat to low and simmer for 6 to 8 mins until the sauce thickens.
3. Season with the salt and Worcestershire sauce. Add the cheese and stir until melted. Turn off the heat and cover to keep warm while you make the cutlets.

Make the Cutlets

4. In a large mixing bowl, beat the eggs. Add the mushrooms, oats, scallions, cheese, salt, and pepper. Stir to combine.
5. Using your hands , form the mixture into 8 patties , each about ½ inch thick.
6. In a large skillet, heat the oil over medium-high heat. Cook the patties , in batches if necessary , for 3 mins per side until crisp and brown.
7. Serve the cutlets warm with sauce drizzled over the top.

NUTRITION: calories 261, fat 17g, protein 11g, carbs 18g, sugars 2g, fiber 3g, sodium 559mg

262. French Ratatouille

Cooking time: 30 mins | Servings: 4

INGREDIENTS:

- 2 cups diced eggplant
- 2 cups diced zucchini
- 1 cup diced onion
- 1 cup chopped green bell pepper
- 4 tbsp olive oil , divided
- 1 (15-ounce) can diced tomatoes
- 1 tsp oregano
- ½ tsp garlic powder
- Salt and pepper , to taste

DIRECTIONS:

1. Heat a large saucepan over medium heat. When hot , heat 2 tbsp of oil , then add the eggplant and the zucchini. Cook for 10 mins, stirring occasionally. Watch to prevent burning because the eggplant will absorb the oil. Add the remaining 2 tbsp of oil as necessary.
2. Add the onion and bell pepper, and cook for 5 mins.
3. Add the diced tomatoes with their juices , oregano , and garlic powder , and cook for 15 mins. Season with salt and pepper.

NUTRITION: calories 190, fat 14g, protein 3g, carbs 15g, sugars 8g, fiber 4g, sodium 28mg

263. Zucchini Boats

Cooking time: 15 mins | Servings: 4

INGREDIENTS:

- 1 cup canned chickpeas , drained and rinsed
- 1 cup no-sugar-added spaghetti sauce
- 2 zucchini
- ¼ cup shredded Parmesan cheese
- 1 tsp oregano

DIRECTIONS:

1. Preheat the oven to 425°F.
2. In a medium bowl, mix the chickpeas and spaghetti sauce together.
3. Cut the zucchini in half lengthwise, and scrape a spoon gently down the length of each half to remove the seeds.
4. Fill each zucchini half with the chickpea sauce, and top with one-quarter of the Parmesan cheese and oregano.
5. Place the zucchini halves on a baking sheet and roast in the oven for 15 mins.

NUTRITION: calories 139, fat 4g, protein 8g, carbs 20g, sugars 6g, fiber 5g, sodium 344mg

264. Tofu and Bean Chili

Cooking time: 30 mins | Servings: 4

INGREDIENTS:

- 6 oz extra-firm tofu
- 1 (15-ounce) can red kidney beans, drained and rinsed , divided
- 2 (15-ounce) cans diced tomatoes
- 1cup vegetable broth
- ½ tsp chili powder
- ½ tsp ground cumin
- ½ tsp garlic powder
- ½ tsp dried oregano
- ¼ tsp onion powder
- ¼ tsp salt

DIRECTIONS:

1. In a small bowl, mash 1/3 of the beans with a fork.
2. Put the mashed beans, the remaining whole beans , and the diced tomatoes with their juices in a large stockpot.
3. Add the broth, chili powder , cumin , garlic powder, dried oregano, onion powder, and salt. Simmer over medium-high heat for 15 mins.
4. Press the tofu between 3 or 4 layers of paper towels to squeeze out any excess moisture.
5. Crumble the tofu into the stockpot and stir. Simmer for another 10 to 15 mins.

NUTRITION: calories 203, fat 3g, protein 15g, carbs 29g, sugars 10g, fiber 5g, sodium 249mg

265. Cauliflower Steaks

Cooking time: 20 mins | Servings: 4

INGREDIENTS:

Cauliflower:

- 1 head cauliflower
- Avocado oil cooking spray
- ½ tsp garlic powder
- 3 cups arugula

Dressing:

- 1tbsp honey mustard
- 1tbsp olive oil
- 1 tsp lemon juice

DIRECTIONS:

Make the Cauliflower

1. Preheat the oven to 425°F.
2. Remove the leaves from the cauliflower head and cut it in half lengthwise.

3. Cut 1½-inch-thick steaks from each half.
4. Spray both sides of each steak with cooking spray, and season both sides with garlic powder.
5. Place the cauliflower steaks on a baking sheet, cover with foil, and roast for 10 mins.
6. Remove the baking sheet from the oven and gently pull back the foil to avoid the steam. Flip the steaks, then roast uncovered for 10 mins more.
7. Divide the cauliflower steaks into four equal portions. Top each portion with one-quarter of the arugula and dressing.

Make the Dressing

8. In a small bowl, whisk together the honey mustard, olive oil, and lemon juice.

NUTRITION: calories 115, fat 6g, protein 5g, carbs 14g, sugars 6g, fiber 4g, sodium 97mg

266. Mushroom Pesto Flatbread

Cooking time: 15 mins | Servings: 2

INGREDIENTS:

- 2 whole-wheat flatbreads
- ¼ cup shredded mozzarella cheese
- ½ cup sliced mushrooms
- ½ red onion, sliced
- ¼ cup pesto sauce
- 1 tsp olive oil
- Salt and black pepper, to taste

DIRECTIONS:

1. Preheat the oven to 350°F.
2. In a small skillet, heat the oil over medium heat. Add the mushrooms and onion , and season with salt and pepper. Sauté for 3 to 5 mins until the onion and mushrooms begin to soften.
3. Spread 2 tbsp of pesto on each flatbread.
4. Divide the mushroom-onion mixture between the two flatbreads. Top each with 2 tbsp of cheese.
5. Place the flatbreads on a baking sheet , and bake for 10 to 12 mins until the cheese is melted and bubbly. Serve warm.

NUTRITION: calories 347, fat 23g, protein 14g, carbs 28g, sugars 4g, fiber 7g, sodium 791mg

267. Stuffed Squash with Cheese and Artichokes

Cooking time: 45 mins | Servings: 4

INGREDIENTS:

- 1 small spaghetti squash , halved and seeded
- ½ cup low-fat: cottage cheese
- ¼ cup shredded mozzarella cheese , divided
- 1 garlic clove , minced
- 1 cup artichoke hearts , chopped
- 1 cup thinly sliced kale
- ¼ tsp salt

DIRECTIONS:

1. Preheat the oven to 400°F. Line a baking sheet with parchment paper.
2. Place the cut squash halves on the prepared baking sheet cut-side down , and roast for 30 to 40 mins , depending on the size and thickness of the squash , until they are fork-tender. Set aside to cool slightly.
3. In a large bowl, mix the cottage cheese , 2 tbsp of mozzarella cheese , garlic , artichoke hearts , kale , salt.
4. Preheat the broiler to high.
5. Using a fork, break apart the flesh of the spaghetti squash into strands, being careful to leave the skin intact. Add the strands to the cheese and vegetable mixture. Toss gently to combine.

6. Divide the mixture between the two hollowed-out squash halves and top with the remaining 2 tbsp of cheese.
7. Broil for 5 to 7 mins until browned and heated through.
8. Cut each piece of stuffed squash in half to serve.

NUTRITION: calories 142, fat 4g, protein 9g, carbs 19g, sugars 10g, fiber 4g, sodium 312mg

268. Kale and Mushroom Bread Pudding

Cooking time: 8 mins | Servings: 2

INGREDIENTS:

- 1 large egg
- 1 slice sourdough bread (about 1 ounce), cut into 1-inch cubes
- ½ cup 2% milk
- ½ tsp nutmeg
- ½ tsp salt
- 1 tbsp avocado oil
- ¼ cup chopped onion
- 2 oz (57 g) mushrooms , sliced (about 3 creminis)
- 1 cup chopped kale, stems and ribs removed (from 2 stems)
- Nonstick cooking spray
- ¼ cup grated Gruyère cheese
- 1 tbsp shredded Parmesan

DIRECTIONS:

1. In a 2-cup measuring cup with a spout , whisk together the egg , milk , nutmeg , and salt. Add the bread and submerge it in the liquid.
2. Set the electric pressure cooker to the Sauté setting. When the pot is hot , pour in the avocado oil.
3. Add the onion, mushrooms, and thyme to the pot and sauté for 3 to 5 mins or until the onion begins to soften. Stir in the kale and cook for about 2 mins or until it wilts. Hit Cancel.
4. Spray the ramekins with cooking spray. Divide the mushroom mixture between the ramekins. Top each with 2 tbsp Gruyère. Pour half of the egg mixture into each ramekin and stir. Make sure the bread stays submerged. Cover with foil.
5. Pour 1 cup of water into the electric pressure cooker and insert a wire rack or trivet. Place the ramekins on the rack.
6. Close and lock the lid of the pressure cooker. Set the valve to sealing.
7. Cook on high pressure for 8 mins.
8. When the cooking is complete, hit Cancel. Allow the pressure to release naturally for 10 mins, then quick release any remaining pressure.
9. Using tongs or the handles of the rack , transfer the ramekins to a cutting board. Carefully lift the foil and sprinkle the Parmesan on top. Replace the foil for about 5 mins or until the cheese melts.
10. Remove the foil and serve immediately.

NUTRITION: calories 295, fat 17g, protein 13g, carbs 23g, sugars 7g, fiber 3g, sodium 313mg

269. Chickpea Coconut Curry

Cooking time: 15 mins | Servings: 4

INGREDIENTS:

- 2 cups fresh or frozen cauliflower florets
- 1 cup almond milk
- 1 (15-ounce) can coconut milk
- 1 (15-ounce) can chickpeas , drained and rinsed
- 1 tbsp curry powder
- ¼ tsp ground ginger
- ¼ tsp garlic powder
- ⅛ tsp onion powder
- ¼ tsp salt

DIRECTIONS:

1. In a large stockpot, combine the cauliflower , almond milk , coconut milk , chickpeas , curry , ginger , garlic powder , and onion powder. Stir and cover.
2. Cook over medium-high heat for 10 mins.
3. Reduce the heat to low , stir , and cook for 5 mins more , uncovered. Season with up to ¼ tsp salt.

NUTRITION: calories 410, fat 30g, protein 10g, carbs 30g, sugars 6g, fiber 9g, sodium 118mg

270. Apple Pita Pockets

Cooking time: 0 mins | Servings: 2

INGREDIENTS:

- 1 apple , cored and chopped
- ¼ cup butter
- ½ tsp cinnamon
- 1 whole-wheat pita , halved

DIRECTIONS:

1. In a medium bowl , stir together the apple , almond butter , and cinnamon.
2. Spread with a spoon into the pita pocket halves.

NUTRITION: calories 313, fat 20g, protein 8g, carbs 31g, sugars 6g, fiber 7g, sodium 174mg

271. Beans and Brown Rice

Cooking time: 15 mins | Servings: 8

INGREDIENTS:

- 2 cups cooked brown rice
- ½ sweet onion , chopped
- 1 tsp minced garlic
- 1 (15-ounce) can red beans , rinsed and drained
- 2 tsps olive oil
- 2 tomatoes , chopped
- 1 tsp chopped fresh thyme
- salt and pepper , to taste

DIRECTIONS:

1. Place a large skillet over medium-high heat and add the olive oil.
2. Sauté onion and garlic until softened , about 3 mins.
3. Stir in beans, tomatoes , and thyme.
4. Cook until heated through, about 10 mins. Season with salt and pepper.
5. Serve over the warm brown rice.

NUTRITION: calories 199, fat 2g, protein 9g, carbs 37g, sugars 2g, fiber 6g, sodium 37mg

272. Quinoa Veggie Skillet

Cooking time: 15 mins | Servings: 4

INGREDIENTS:

- 1 cup quinoa, well rinsed and drained
- 1 cup vegetable broth
- 1 tsp olive oil
- ½ sweet onion, chopped
- 2 tsps minced garlic
- ½ large green zucchini, halved lengthwise and cut into half disks
- 1 red bell pepper , seeded and cut into thin strips
- 1 cup fresh or frozen corn kernels
- 1 tsp chopped fresh basil
- salt and pepper , to taste

DIRECTIONS:

1. Place a medium saucepan over medium heat and add the vegetable broth. Bring the broth to a boil and add the quinoa. Cover and reduce the heat to low.
2. Cook until the quinoa has absorbed all the broth, about 15 mins. Remove from the heat and let it cool slightly.
3. While the quinoa is cooking, place a large skillet over medium-high heat and add the oil.
4. Sauté the onion and garlic until softened and translucent, about 3 mins.
5. Add the zucchini, bell pepper, and corn , and sauté until the vegetables

are tender-crisp , about 5 mins.

6. Remove the skillet from the heat. Add the cooked quinoa and the basil to the skillet , stirring to combine. Season with salt and pepper , and serve.

NUTRITION: calories 158, fat 3g, protein 7g, carbs 26g, sugars 3g, fiber 3g, sodium 298mg

273. Spinach Mini Quiches

Cooking time: 15 mins | Servings: 4

INGREDIENTS:

- 2 cups baby spinach
- 6 large eggs , beaten
- 1 onion , finely chopped
- ¼ cup whole milk
- 2 garlic cloves , minced
- 2 tbsp olive oil
- 1 tsp oregano
- ½ tsp salt
- ¼ tsp freshly ground black pepper
- 1 cup shredded Swiss cheese
- Nonstick cooking spray

DIRECTIONS:

1. Preheat the oven to 375°F. Spray a 6-cup muffin tin with nonstick cooking spray.
2. In a large skillet over medium-high heat, heat the olive oil until it shimmers. Add the onion and cook until soft, about 4 mins. Add the spinach and cook, stirring , until the spinach softens , about 1 minute. Add the garlic. Cook, stirring constantly , for 30 seconds. Remove from heat and let cool.
3. In a medium bowl, beat together the eggs , milk , salt , and pepper.
4. Fold the cooled vegetables and the cheese into the egg mixture. Spoon the mixture into the prepared muffin tins. Bake until the eggs are set , about 15 mins. Allow to rest for 5 mins before serving.

NUTRITION: calories 218, fat 17g, protein 14g, carbs 4g, sugars 3g, fiber 0g, sodium 237mg

274. Tempeh Wraps

Cooking time: 5 mins | Servings: 2

INGREDIENTS:

- 1 package tempeh , crumbled
- 1 head lettuce
- ½ red bell pepper , diced
- ½ onion , diced
- 1 tbsp garlic , diced fine
- 1 tbsp olive oil
- 1 tbsp low-sodium soy sauce
- 1 tsp ginger ,
- 1 tsp onion powder
- 1 tbsp plain yogurt
- 1 tsp lemon juice

DIRECTIONS:

1. Heat oil and garlic in a large skillet over medium heat.
2. Add onion , tempeh , and bell pepper and sauté for 3 mins.
3. Add soy sauce and spices and cook for another 2 mins.
4. Spoon mixture into lettuce leaves.
5. Serve with a sauce of yogurt and lemon juice.

NUTRITION: calories 131, fat 5g, protein 8g, carbs 14g, fiber 4g, sugars 2g, sodium 268mg

275. Tex Mex Vegetarian Bake

Cooking time: 35 mins | Servings: 4

INGREDIENTS:

- 1 cup cauliflower, grated
- 1 cup fat: free sour cream
- ½ cup cheddar cheese, grated
- ½ cup Mexican cheese blend , grated
- ½ cup red onion, diced
- 1 (11-ounce) can Mexicorn , drain
- 5 oz tomatoes and green chilies
- ½ cup black beans , rinsed
- ½ cup salsa

- ¼ tsp pepper
- Nonstick cooking spray

DIRECTIONS:

1. Heat oven to 350°F. Spray a 2½-quart baking dish with cooking spray.
2. In a large bowl, combine beans , corn , tomatoes , salsa , sour cream , cheddar cheese , pepper , and cauliflower. Transfer to baking dish. Sprinkle with onion.
3. Bake 30 mins. Sprinkle with Mexican blend cheese and bake another 5 to 10 mins, or until cheese is melted and casserole is heated through. Let rest 10 mins before serving.

NUTRITION: calories 267, fat 8g, protein 16g, carbs 33g, fiber 6g, sugars 8g, sodium 812mg

276. Party Casserole

Cooking time: 30 mins | Servings: 6

INGREDIENTS:

- ½ head cauliflower , grated
- 1 red bell pepper, diced fine
- 1 jalapeno pepper, seeded and diced fine
- ½ white onion, diced fine
- 1 cup cheddar cheese, grated
- 1 tsp cilantro , diced fine
- ½ cup salsa
- 1 tbsp water
- 1 tsp chili flakes
- Nonstick cooking spray

DIRECTIONS:

1. Heat oven to 350°F. Spray a 7x11x2-inch baking pan with cooking spray.
2. In a large skillet , over medium heat , cook onions and peppers until soft , about 5 mins. Add cilantro and chili flakes and stir.
3. Place the cauliflower and water in a glass bowl and microwave on high for 3 mins. Stir in 1 cup cheese and the salsa.
4. Stir the pepper mixture into the cauliflower and combine. Spread in prepared pan. Sprinkle the remaining cheese over the top and bake 30 to 35 mins.
5. Let rest 5 mins before cutting into 12 squares and serving.

NUTRITION: calories 75, fat 5g, protein 4g, carbs 4g, fiber 1g, sugars 2g, sodium 206mg

277. Roasted Cauliflower

Cooking time: 45 mins | Servings: 4

INGREDIENTS:

- 1 large head cauliflower, in florets
- 2 scallions , sliced
- 1 onion , diced fine
- 1 (15-ounce) can tomatoes , diced
- 3 cloves garlic , diced fine
- 3 tbsp olive oil , divided
- 1 tbsp balsamic vinegar
- 1 tsp salt and ground black pepper
- ½ tsp chili flakes

DIRECTIONS:

1. Heat oven to 400°F.
2. Place cauliflower on a large baking sheet and drizzle with 2 tbsp of oil. Sprinkle with salt and pepper , to taste. Use hands to rub oil and seasoning into florets then lay in single layer. Roast until fork tender.
3. Heat 1 tbsp oil in a large skillet over medium-low heat. Add onion and cook until soft.
4. Stir in tomatoes , with juice , vinegar , and the tsp of salt. Bring to a boil , reduce heat and simmer 20 to 25 mins. For a smooth sauce , use an immersion blender to process until smooth , or leave it chunky.
5. In a separate skillet , heat remaining oil over medium-low heat and sauté garlic 1 to 2 mins. Stir in tomato sauce and increase heat to medium. Cook , stirring frequently , 5 mins.

Add chili powder and cauliflower and toss to coat. Serve garnished with scallions.

NUTRITION: calories 108, fat 0g, protein 6g, carbs 23g, fiber 7g, sugars 12g, sodium 751mg

278. Chili Rellenos Casserole

Cooking time: 35 mins | Servings: 6

INGREDIENTS:

- 2 large eggs
- 2 (7ounce) cans whole green chilies , drain well
- ½ cup Monterey jack cheese, grated
- ½ cup cheddar cheese, grated
- ½ cup milk
- 1 (7ounce) can tomato sauce
- ½ tsp salt
- Nonstick cooking spray

DIRECTIONS:

1. Heat oven to 350°F .Spray a baking pan with cooking spray.
2. Slice each chili down one long side and lay flat.
3. Arrange half the chilies in the prepared baking pan , skin side down , in single layer.
4. Sprinkle with the pepper cheese and top with remaining chilies , skin side up.
5. In a small bowl, beat eggs , salt , tomato and milk. Pour over chilies. Top with cheddar cheese.
6. Bake 35 mins, or until top is golden brown. Let rest 10 mins before serving.

NUTRITION: calories 296, fat 13g, protein 13g, carbs 36g, fiber 14g, sugars 21g, sodium 463mg

279. Simply Eggplant Parmesan

Cooking time: 2 hours | Servings: 4

INGREDIENTS:

- 1 large eggplant , peeled and cut into 1-inch cubes
- 2 zucchini , cut into 1-inch pieces
- 1 onion , cut into thin wedges
- 1½ cups spaghetti sauce
- $^{2}/_{3}$ cup Parmesan cheese , grated

DIRECTIONS:

1. Place the vegetables , spaghetti sauce and $^{1}/_{3}$ cup Parmesan in the crock pot. Stir to combine. Cover and cook on high for 2 to 2 ½ hours , or on low 4 to 5 hours.
2. Sprinkle remaining Parmesan on top before serving.

NUTRITION: calories 82, fat 2g, protein 5g, carbs 12g, fiber 5g, sugars 7g, sodium 456mg

280. Collard Greens and Tomato

Cooking time: 20 mins | Servings: 4

INGREDIENTS:

- 1 large bunch collard greens including stems , roughly chopped
- 1 cup vegetable broth
- ½ onion , thinly sliced
- 2 garlic cloves , thinly sliced
- 2 tomatoes , chopped
- 1 tsp ground cumin
- ½ tsp freshly ground black pepper

DIRECTIONS:

1. Add ½ cup of vegetable broth to a Dutch oven over medium heat and bring to a simmer.
2. Stir in the onion and garlic and cook for about 4 mins until tender.
3. Add the remaining broth, tomato, greens, cumin, and pepper, and gently stir to combine.
4. Reduce the heat to low and simmer uncovered for 15 mins. Serve warm.

NUTRITION: calories 68, fat 2g, protein 4g, carbs 13g, fiber 7g, sugars 2g, sodium 67mg

281. Mushroom and Pesto Flatbreads

Cooking time: 13 to 17 mins | Servings: 2

INGREDIENTS:

- 2 whole-wheat flatbreads
- 1 shredded mozzarella cheese
- ¼ cup pesto sauce
- 1 tsp olive oil
- 1 red onion , sliced
- ½ cup sliced mushrooms
- Salt and pepper, to taste

DIRECTIONS:

1. Preheat the oven to 350°F.
2. Heat the olive oil in a small skillet over medium heat. Add the onion slices and mushrooms to the skillet , and sauté for 3 to 5 mins , stirring occasionally , or until they start to soften. Season with salt and pepper.
3. Meanwhile, spoon 2 tbsp of pesto sauce onto each flatbread and spread it all over. Evenly divide the mushroom mixture between two flatbreads, then scatter each top with 2 tbsp of shredded cheese.
4. Transfer the flatbreads to a baking sheet and bake until the cheese melts and bubbles, about 10 to 12 mins.
5. Let the flatbreads cool for 5 mins and serve warm.

NUTRITION: calories 346, fat 22g, protein 14g, carbs 27g, fiber 7g, sugars 4g, sodium 790mg

282. Italian Pasta with Sauce

Cooking time: 35 mins | Servings: 6

INGREDIENTS:

- 8 oz cooked whole-wheat spaghetti
- 2 (28-ounce) cans diced tomatoes
- 1 tbsp olive oil
- 2 tsps minced garlic
- 1 sweet onion , chopped
- 1 tbsp chopped fresh oregano
- 2 tbsp chopped fresh basil
- ½ tsp red pepper flakes
- ½ cup quartered , pitted black olives

DIRECTIONS:

1. Heat the olive oil in a large saucepan over medium-high heat.
2. Add the garlic and onion to the saucepan and sauté for about 3 mins ,stirring occasionally, or until softened.
3. Toss in the tomatoes , oregano , basil , and pepper flakes and stir to combine. Allow the sauce to boil , stirring often to prevent from sticking to the bottom of the pan.
4. Reduce the heat to low and bring the sauce to a simmer , stirring occasionally , about 20 mins.
5. Add the olives and mix well.
6. Remove from the heat and spoon the sauce over the spaghetti. Toss well and serve warm.

NUTRITION: calories 199, fat 4g, protein 7g, carbs 34g, fiber 3g, sugars 8g, sodium 89mg

283. Cauliflower and Mushroom Risotto

Cooking time: 30 mins | Servings: 2

INGREDIENTS:

- 1 medium head cauliflower , grated
- 1 cup mushrooms , sliced
- ½ yellow onion , diced fine
- 2 cup vegetable broth
- 1 tsp garlic , diced fine
- 2 tsps white wine vinegar
- Salt and ground black pepper , to taste
- Olive oil cooking spray

DIRECTIONS:

1. Heat oven to 350°F. Line a baking sheet with foil.
2. Place the mushrooms on the prepared pan and spray with cooking

spray. Sprinkle with salt and toss to coat. Bake 10 to 12 mins, or until golden brown and the mushrooms start to crisp.

3. Spray a large skillet with cooking spray and place over medium-high heat. Add onion and cook, stirring frequently , until translucent , about 3 to 4 mins. Add garlic and cook 2 mins , until golden.
4. Add the cauliflower and cook 1 minute , stirring.
5. Place the broth in a saucepan and bring to a simmer. Add to the skillet , ¼ cup at a time , mixing well after each addition.
6. Stir in vinegar. Reduce heat to low and let simmer , 4 to 5 mins , or until most of the liquid has evaporated.
7. Spoon cauliflower mixture onto plates , or in bowls , and top with mushrooms. Serve.

NUTRITION: calories 135, fat 0g, protein 10g, carbs 22g, fiber 2g, sugars 5g, sodium 1105mg

284. BBQ Tofu Veggie Skewers

Cooking time: 15 mins | Servings: 4

INGREDIENTS:

- 1 block tofu
- 2 small zucchini, sliced
- 1 red bell pepper, cut into 1-inch cubes
- 1 yellow bell pepper, cut into 1-inch cubes
- 1 red onion , cut into 1-inch cubes
- 1 cup cherry tomatoes
- 2 tbsp lite soy sauce
- 2 tsps barbecue sauce
- 2 tsps sesame seeds
- Salt and ground black pepper , to taste
- Nonstick cooking spray

DIRECTIONS:

1. Press tofu to extract liquid, for about half an hour. Then, cut tofu into cubes and marinate in soy sauce for at least 15 mins.
2. Heat the grill to medium-high heat. Spray the grill rack with cooking spray.
3. Assemble skewers with tofu alternating with vegetables.
4. Grill for 2 to 3 mins per side until vegetables start to soften, and tofu is golden brown. At the very end of cooking time, season with salt and pepper and brush with barbecue sauce. Serve garnished with sesame seeds.

NUTRITION: calories 65, fat 2g, protein 5g, carbs 10g, fiber 3g, sugars 6g, sodium 237mg

285. Stuffed Sweet Potato

Cooking time: 20 mins | Servings: 2

INGREDIENTS:

- 1 medium sweet potato
- ¼ cup Greek yogurt
- ½ cup chopped red bell pepper
- ¼ cup chopped red onion
- ½ tsp chili powder
- ½ tsp paprika
- ½ tsp ground cumin
- 1 tsp olive oil
- Pinch salt and pepper
- ½ cup fresh, or frozen, edamame
- 2 tbsp shredded cheddar cheese , divided
- ½ small avocado , sliced

DIRECTIONS:

1. Poke the sweet potato with a fork. Place in the microwave. Cook for 6 to 8 mins on high, or until soft and cooked through.
2. In a small bowl, blend together the yogurt , chili powder , paprika , and cumin.
3. In a small pot set over medium heat

, heat the olive oil. Add the bell pepper , onion , salt , and pepper. Cook for about 5 mins , or until the onions have caramelized slightly.

4. Add the edamame. Stir to combine. Cook for 5 mins more , or until heated through.
5. Slice the potato in half lengthwise.
6. Top each half with half of the edamame mixture , about 2 tbsp of cheddar cheese and a dollop of the yogurt mixture.
7. Finish with half of the avocado slices and serve.

NUTRITION: calories 259, fat 11g, protein 15g, carbs 33g, sugars 7g, fiber 9g, sodium 417mg

286. Veggie and Olives Nachos

Cooking time: 10 mins | Servings: 2

INGREDIENTS:

- 2 (4-inch) whole-wheat pita rounds, quartered
- ½ cup quartered grape tomatoes
- ½ cup diced cucumber
- ¼ cup diced red bell pepper
- 2 tbsp sliced olives
- 4 tbsp purchased or homemade hummus , divided

DIRECTIONS:

1. Preheat the oven to 375°F.
2. On a baking sheet, spread the pita pieces in a single layer. Place the sheet in the preheated oven. Bake for 8 to 10 mins , or until toasted.
3. In a medium bowl , combine the grape tomatoes , cucumber , bell pepper , and olives.
4. Divide the toasted pita between 2 plates.
5. Drop some hummus onto the pita. Spoon the vegetable mixture on top.
6. Serve immediately!

NUTRITION: calories 282, fat 19g, protein 7g, carbs 30g, sugars 3g, fiber 5g, sodium 208mg

287. Portobello Mushroom Pizza

Cooking time: 25 mins | Servings: 2

INGREDIENTS:

- 2 large portobello mushroom caps
- 1 cup shredded nonfat: mozzarella cheese , divided
- 1 medium tomato, sliced , divided
- 2 tsps black olives
- 1 tbsp olive oil
- 1 tsp dried oregano
- ½ tsp red pepper flakes
- Salt and pepper , to taste
- 3 tbsp chopped fresh basil , divided

DIRECTIONS:

1. Preheat the oven to 375°F.
2. On a baking sheet, place the mushrooms. Put the sheet in the preheated oven. Bake for 5 mins. Remove from the oven.
3. Drizzle the mushrooms with the olive oil.
4. Sprinkle with the oregano and red pepper flakes. Season with salt and pepper.
5. Spread ½ cup of mozzarella cheese in each mushroom cap.
6. Top each with half of the tomato slices , 1½ tsps of the black olives , and about 2 tbsp of basil.
7. Top each with ¼ cup of the remaining mozzarella cheese.
8. Return to the oven. Bake for 20 mins , or until the cheese melts and is golden.

NUTRITION: calories 152, fat 8g, protein 11g, carbs 9g, sugars 4g, fiber 2g, sodium 348mg

288. Cauliflower and Cheese

Cooking time: 30 mins | Servings: 2

INGREDIENTS:

Cauliflower Crust:

- 1 small cauliflower head, cut into florets (about 3 cups)
- 1 large egg , lighten beaten
- ½ cup shredded nonfat: cheddar cheese
- olive oil , for greasing
- ½ tsp salt and pepper
- 1 tbsp nutritional yeast

Sandwiches:

- Olive oil cooking spray
- 1/3 cup nonfat: shredded cheddar cheese

DIRECTIONS:

Make the Cauliflower Crust

1. Preheat the oven to 450°F.
2. Place a rack in the middle of the oven.
3. Line a baking sheet with parchment paper. Grease with the olive oil. Set aside.
4. In a food processor , process the cauliflower florets until it resembles rice. You should have about 3 cups.
5. Transfer to a microwave-safe dish. Microwave on high for about 8 mins , or until cooked.
6. In a kitchen towel , add the cauliflower rice in the center. Twist the towel around the cauliflower to squeeze out as much moisture as possible. You should get about 1 cup of liquid. The cauliflower rice must be very dry to create the dough. Transfer to a large mixing bowl.
7. Mix in the egg , cheddar cheese , salt , pepper , and nutritional yeast.
8. Spread the mixture onto the prepared baking sheet. Shape into 4 squares. Place the sheet in the preheated oven. Bake for about 16 mins , or until golden.
9. Remove from the oven. Cool for 10 mins. Peel the squares from the parchment , being careful not to break.

Make the Sandwiches

10. Spray a large skillet with cooking spray. Place it over medium heat.
11. Lightly coat one side of each slice of "bread" with cooking spray.
12. In the skillet , place 2 "bread" slices , sprayed-side down.
13. Sprinkle half of the cheddar cheese on each.
14. Top each sandwich with 1 of the 2 remaining "bread" slices , sprayed-side up. Reduce the heat to low.
15. Cook for 2 to 4 mins , or until golden brown. Gently flip. Cook for 2 to 4 mins more , until golden brown on the other side.
16. Serve immediately and enjoy!

NUTRITION: calories 157, fat 2g, protein 21g, carbs 10g, sugars 3g, fiber 3g, sodium 365mg

289. Marinara Spaghetti Squash

Cooking time: 45 mins | Servings: 2

INGREDIENTS:

"Spaghetti":

- 1 medium spaghetti squash , halved lengthwise , seeds removed

Marinara:

- 1 portobello mushroom cap , coarsely chopped
- 1 tsp olive oil
- 1 small onion , chopped
- 1 garlic clove , minced
- 1 (8-ounce) can diced tomatoes
- 1 tsp Italian seasoning
- ½ cup shredded nonfat: mozzarella

cheese , divided
- Salt and pepper , to taste

DIRECTIONS:

Make the "Spaghetti"

1. Preheat the oven to 350°F.
2. In a large baking dish , place the squash halves cut-side down. With a fork , prick the skin all over. Place the dish into the preheated oven. Bake for 30 to 40 mins , or until tender.

Make the Marinara

3. In a medium skillet set over medium-high heat , heat the olive oil.
4. Add the onion , mushroom , and garlic. Sauté for about 5 mins , or until tender.
5. Stir in the tomatoes and Italian seasoning. Bring to a boil. Reduce the heat to low. Simmer for about 5 mins , uncovered , stirring frequently , or until it is the desired consistency.

To serve

6. Using a fork , carefully rake the stringy pulp from the squash , separating into spaghetti-like strands , and fluff. Divide the strands between 2 plates.
7. Top each plate with half of the marinara.
8. Sprinkle each with ¼ cup of mozzarella cheese. Season with salt and pepper.
9. Enjoy immediately!

NUTRITION: calories 233, fat 2g, protein 14g, carbs 41g, sugars 16g, fiber 8g, sodium 389mg

290. Eggplant Lasagna

Cooking time: 50 mins | Servings: 2

INGREDIENTS:

- 2 eggplant slices , ¼-inch thick , cut lengthwise
- 1 large egg white
- ½ cup ricotta cheese
- ¼ cup shredded mozzarella cheese
- 1 garlic clove , minced
- ¼ tsp salt
- ½ cup chopped fresh mushrooms
- ½ cup frozen spinach
- 1 cup diced tomatoes , with juice
- 1 tbsp chopped fresh basil
- olive oil cooking spray
- 2 sheets whole-wheat oven-ready lasagna noodles

DIRECTIONS:

1. Preheat the oven to 425°F.
2. Spray both sides of the eggplant slices with cooking spray. Place on a baking sheet and into the preheated oven. Bake for 10 mins. Carefully turn the slices over. Bake for 10 mins more , or until browned and softened.
3. In a medium bowl , blend together the egg white , ricotta cheese , basil , garlic , and salt. Mix well. Set aside.
4. Spray a nonstick skillet with cooking spray. Place it over medium-high heat.
5. Add the mushrooms and spinach. Cook for about 4 mins , stirring occasionally , or until softened.
6. Add the vegetables to the ricotta mixture. Stir to combine. Set aside.
7. In a small bowl , stir together the tomatoes and Italian seasoning. Set aside.
8. Spray a large loaf pan with cooking spray.
9. Pour ¼ cup of the seasoned tomatoes evenly over the bottom of the pan. Top with 1 lasagna sheet. Spread half of the ricotta-vegetable mixture on top. Cover with another ¼ cup of the tomatoes. Top with 1 eggplant slice.
10. Repeat another layer with ¼ cup of

tomatoes , 1 lasagna sheet , the remaining half of the ricotta-vegetable mixture , the remaining ¼ cup of tomatoes , and the remaining 1 eggplant slice.

11. Spread the mozzarella cheese over the top.
12. Place the pan in the preheated oven. Bake for 20 to 25 mins , or until the cheese starts to brown.
13. Serve!

NUTRITION: calories 215, fat 3g, protein 16g, carbs 31g, sugars 7g, fiber 7g, sodium 326mg

291. Mock and Cheese

Cooking time: 45 mins | Servings: 2

INGREDIENTS:

- 2 cups cauliflower florets
- 2 tsps olive oil
- 1 tbsp coconut flour
- ½ cup nonfat: milk
- 1 garlic clove , minced
- ½ cup shredded nonfat: cheddar cheese
- ¼ cup nutritional yeast
- 1 large egg yolk
- 2 tbsp toasted wheat germ , divided
- olive oil cooking spray

DIRECTIONS:

1. Preheat the oven to 350°F.
2. Spray 2 (8-ounce) ramekins with cooking spray. Set aside.
3. Bring a medium pot of salted water to a boil over high heat.
4. Add the cauliflower. Boil for 5 mins , or until just tender. Drain , reserving ¼ cup of the cooking liquid. Set aside.
5. In the same pot set over medium heat , heat the olive oil.
6. Whisk in the coconut flour. Cook for 1 minute , stirring constantly.
7. Whisk in the milk , garlic , and reserved cooking liquid. Cook for 7 to 10 mins , or until thickened , whisking constantly. Remove from the heat.
8. Stir in the cheddar cheese , yeast , and egg yolk. Continue stirring until the cheese melts.
9. Fold in the cauliflower.
10. Evenly divide the cauliflower mixture between the ramekins.
11. Sprinkle each serving with about 2 tbsp of the wheat germ. Spray the wheat germ with cooking spray.
12. Place the ramekins on a baking sheet. Carefully transfer the sheet to the preheated oven. Bake for 30 mins , or until the casseroles are hot and bubbly and the wheat germ is crisp and brown.

NUTRITION: calories 338 , fat 10g, protein 31g, carbs 39g, sugars 7g, fiber 11g, sodium 354mg

CHAPTER 8 Sides

292. Spaghetti Squash

Cooking time: 15 mins | Servings: 2

INGREDIENTS:

- 1 (1-pound) spaghetti squash, halved lengthwise and seeded
- ¼ cup water
- 3 tsps olive oil, divided, plus additional as needed
- 1 small red onion, sliced
- 1 small zucchini, cut into ½-inch slices
- 1 medium tomato , diced
- ¼ tsp salt and pepper
- 1 tsp dried oregano
- Fresh basil , or parsley , for garnish

DIRECTIONS:

1. In a large glass baking dish , place the squash halves cut-side down. Add the water. Cover with plastic wrap. Microwave on high for 8 to 10 mins , or until tender. Set aside.
2. While the squash cooks , place a large skillet over medium-high heat. Add 1½ tsps of olive oil.
3. Add the red onion. Cook for 3 mins , or until translucent.
4. Add the zucchini. Cook for 4 to 5 mins more | or until the zucchini browns.
5. Add the tomato , salt , oregano , and pepper. Reduce the heat to low. Gently simmer for 10 mins.
6. With a fork , scrape the cooked squash strands into a bowl. Add the remaining 1½ tsps of olive oil. Toss to coat.
7. Mound the squash onto a serving platter. Spoon the vegetable mixture around the squash. Drizzle with additional olive oil, if desired.
8. Garnish with the basil or parsley.

NUTRITION: calories 195, fat 7g, protein 4g, carbs 32g, fiber 6g, sugars 14g, sodium 359mg

293. Roasted Peppers and Eggplants

Cooking time: 20 mins | Servings: 2

INGREDIENTS:

- 1 small eggplant, halved and sliced
- 1 red bell pepper, cut into thick strips
- 1 yellow bell pepper, cut into thick strips
- 1 red onion, sliced
- 2 garlic cloves, quartered
- 1 tbsp olive oil
- Salt and pepper, to taste
- ½ cup chopped fresh basil
- Olive oil cooking spray

DIRECTIONS:

1. Preheat the oven to 350°F.
2. Coat a nonstick baking dish with cooking spray.
3. To the prepared dish, add the eggplant, red bell pepper, yellow bell pepper, onion, and garlic. Drizzle with the olive oil. Toss to coat well. Spray any uncoated surfaces with cooking spray.
4. Place the dish in the preheated oven. Bake for 20 mins, turning once halfway through cooking.
5. Transfer the vegetables to a serving dish. Season with salt and pepper.
6. Garnish with the basil and serve.

NUTRITION: calories 160, fat 7g, protein 4g, carbs 23g, sugars 10g, fiber 10g, sodium 11mg

294. Sautéed Spinach with Parmesan

Cooking time: 5 mins | Servings: 2

INGREDIENTS:

- 2 (5-ounce) bags spinach
- 2 tsps balsamic vinegar
- 1 tbsp olive oil
- 2 tbsp sliced almonds
- 1 garlic cloves, minced
- ⅛ tsp salt
- 2 tbsp Parmesan cheese
- ground black pepper, to taste

DIRECTIONS:

1. In a large nonstick skillet or Dutch oven set over medium-high heat, heat the olive oil.
2. Add the almonds and garlic. Cook for 30 seconds, stirring, or until fragrant.
3. Add the spinach. Cook for about 2 mins, stirring, until just wilted. Remove the pan from the heat.
4. Stir in the balsamic vinegar and salt.
5. Sprinkle with the soy Parmesan cheese. Season with pepper and serve immediately.

NUTRITION: calories 148, fat 9g, protein 8g, carbs 8g, sugars 1g, fiber 3g, sodium 243mg

295. Braised Carrots and Kale

Cooking Time: 10 mins | Servings: 2

INGREDIENTS:

- 3 medium carrots, sliced thinly
- 5 cloves of garlic, minced
- 10 oz of kale, chopped
- ½ cup water
- 1 tbsp coconut oil
- 1 onion, sliced thinly
- salt and pepper to taste
- A dash of red pepper flakes

DIRECTIONS:

1. Heat the oil in a skillet over medium flame and sauté the onion and garlic until fragrant. Toss in the carrots and stir for 1 minute. Add the kale and water. Season it with salt and pepper to taste.
2. Close the lid and allow simmering for 5 mins.
3. Sprinkle with red pepper flakes.
4. Serve.

NUTRITION: calories 161, fat 8g, carbs 20g, protein 8g, fiber 6g, sodium 63mg, potassium 900mg

296. Butternut Squash Hummus

Cooking Time: 15 mins | Servings: 8

INGREDIENTS:

- 2 pounds butternut squash, seeded and peeled
- 1 tbsp olive oil
- ¼ cup tahini
- 2 tbsps lemon juice
- 2 cloves of garlic, minced
- Salt and pepper to taste

DIRECTIONS:

1. Heat the oven to 300°F.
2. Coat the butternut squash with olive oil.
3. Place in a baking dish and bake for 15 mins in the oven.
4. Once the squash is cooked, place in a food processor together with the rest of the ingredients.
5. Pulse it until smooth.
6. Place in individual containers.
7. Put a label and store in the fridge.
8. Allow to warm at room temperature before heating in the microwave oven.
9. Serve with carrots or celery sticks.

NUTRITION: calories 109, fat 6g, carbs 15g, protein 2g, fiber 4g, sodium 14mg, potassium 379mg

297. Zucchini mini cakes

Cooking Time: 20 mins | Servings: 4

INGREDIENTS:

- 1 shredded medium zucchini
- ground black pepper
- 1 finely diced red onion
- 1 egg white
- Homemade horseradish sauce
- ¾ cup salt-free bread crumbs

DIRECTIONS:

1. Preheat oven to 400°F. Spray a baking sheet lightly with oil and set aside.
2. Press shredded zucchini gently between paper towels to remove excess liquid.
3. In a large bowl, combine zucchini, onion, egg white, bread crumbs, seasoning, and black pepper. Mix well.
4. Shape mixture into patties and place on the prepared baking sheet.
5. Place baking sheet on middle rack in oven and bake for 10 mins. Gently flip patties and return to oven to bake for another 10 mins.
6. Remove from oven and serve immediately.

NUTRITION: calories 94, fat 1g, carbs 19g, protein 4g, fiber 4g, sodium 68mg, potassium 135mg

298. Chickpeas Veggie Burger

Cooking Time: 20 mins | Servings: 4

INGREDIENTS:

- 1 (15-ounce) can chickpeas, drained and rinsed
- ½ cup frozen spinach, thawed
- ⅓1/3 cup rolled oats
- 1 tsp garlic powder
- 1 tsp onion powder

DIRECTIONS:

1. Preheat oven to 400°F. Grease a sheet or line one with parchment paper and set aside.
2. In a mixing bowl, add half of the beans and mash with a fork until fairly smooth. Set aside.
3. Add the remaining half of the beans, spinach, oats, and spices to a food processor or blender and blend until puréed. Add the mixture to the bowl of mashed beans and stir until well combined.
4. Divide mixture into 4 equal portions and shape into patties. Bake for 7 to 10 mins. Carefully turn over and bake for another 7 to 10 mins or until crusty on the outside.
5. Place on a whole grain bun with your favorite toppings.

NUTRITION: calories 118, fat 2g, carbs 21g, protein 7g, fiber 6g, sodium 200mg, potassium 185mg

299. Quinoa and Fruits Salad

Cooking Time: 20 mins | Servings: 5

INGREDIENTS:

- 3 ½ oz quinoa
- 3 peaches, diced
- 1 and ½ oz toasted hazelnuts, chopped
- handful of mint, chopped
- handful of parsley, chopped
- 2 tbsps olive oil
- zest of 1 lemon
- juice of 1 lemon

DIRECTIONS:

1. Take medium sized saucepan and add quinoa
2. Add 1 and ¼ cups of water and bring it to a boil over medium-high heat

3. Lower down the heat to low and simmer for 20 mins
4. Drain any excess liquid
5. Add fruits, herbs, Hazelnuts to the quinoa
6. Allow it to cool and season
7. Take a bowl and add olive oil, lemon zest and lemon juice
8. Pour the mixture over the salad and serve

NUTRITION: calories 203, fat 2g, carbs 51g, protein 2g, fiber 6g, sodium 150mg, potassium 121mg

300. Boiles Sweet Potatoes

Cooking Time: 25 mins | Servings: 4

INGREDIENTS:

- 2 large, sweet potatoes, peeled and cut into 1-inch cubes
- 2 tbsps olive oil
- 2 tbsps butter
- 1 red onion, chopped
- ¼ cup half-and-half
- 1 tbsp honey
- ¼ tsp salt
- ⅛ tsp freshly ground black pepper

DIRECTIONS:

1. In a large saucepan, fill the pot with water to about an inch above the potatoes. Add the sweet potato cubes and bring to a boil. Boil for 10 mins.
2. Drain the sweet potatoes, discarding the water.
3. In the same saucepan, fill the pot to the same level again. Add the sweet potato cubes and bring to a boil. Boil for 10 to 15 mins, or until the potatoes are tender.
4. Meanwhile, in a large skillet, heat the olive oil and butter. Add the red onion and cook for 3 to 5 mins, stirring, until the onion is very tender.
5. Drain the sweet potatoes once more, discarding the water again. Add the sweet potatoes to the skillet along with the half-and-half, honey, salt, and pepper.
6. Mash the potatoes, using an immersion blender or a potato masher, until the desired consistency. Serve.

NUTRITION: calories 246, fat 18g, carbs 20g, protein 2g, fiber 6g, sodium 235mg, potassium 201mg

301. Caramelized Onions

Cooking Time: 20 mins | Servings: 4

INGREDIENTS:

- 1 yellow onion, chopped
- 2 tbsps butter
- 1 tbsp olive oil
- 1 bunch kale, rinsed and torn into pieces
- 2 tbsps water
- 1 tbsp freshly squeezed lemon juice
- 1 tsp maple syrup
- Salt and pepper

DIRECTIONS:

1. In a heavy saucepan, combine the onion, butter, and olive oil over medium heat. Cook for about 3 mins, until the onion starts to become translucent, stirring frequently.
2. Reduce the heat to low and continue cooking for 10 to 15 mins longer, stirring frequently, until the onion starts to brown.
3. Increase the heat to medium and add the kale and water. Cover the pan and cook for about 2 mins, shaking the pan occasionally, until the kale starts to soften.
4. Add the lemon juice and maple syrup, and season with salt and pepper. Cook for 3 to 4 mins longer, stirring frequently until the kale is tender. Serve.

NUTRITION: calories 115, fat 10g, carbs 6g, protein 2g, fiber 2g, sodium 112mg, potassium 224mg

302. Roasted White Bean Dip

Cooking Time: 50 mins | Servings: 2

INGREDIENTS:

- 2 onions, cut into 8 wedges each
- 2 garlic heads, whole
- ¼ cup olive oil, divided
- 1 (15-ounce) can no-salt-added cannellini beans, drained and rinsed
- 2 tbsps freshly squeezed lemon juice
- 1 tsp dried marjoram leaves
- ⅛ tsp salt and pepper

DIRECTIONS:

1. Preheat the oven to 375°F.
2. On a rimmed baking sheet, place the onions.
3. Cut the top inch off each garlic head, just enough to expose the cloves, and discard the top. Place the garlic, with the exposed cloves facing up, on the baking sheet. Drizzle 1 tbsp of olive oil directly into the garlic heads, then wrap each head in aluminum foil and place back on the baking sheet. Drizzle the onions with another 1 tbsp of olive oil.
4. Roast the vegetables for 45 to 55 mins, stirring the onions once during cooking, until the onions are golden brown, and the garlic is brown and soft.
5. Remove the foil from the garlic and let the garlic and onions cool for 30 mins.
6. In a blender or food processor, combine the cannellini beans, lemon juice, marjoram, salt, and pepper.
7. Add the onions. Remove the garlic cloves from the head by squeezing the head so the cloves pop out and add to the blender. Blend or process the mixture, drizzling in the remaining 2 tbsps of olive oil, until it is mostly smooth, with some texture.
8. Serve immediately or cover and chill for a few hours before serving.

NUTRITION: calories 166, fat 10g, carbs 17g, protein 4g, fiber 4g, sodium 74mg, potassium 241mg

303. Rosemary Endives

Cooking Time: 20 mins | Servings: 4

INGREDIENTS:

- 2 halved endives
- 2 tbsp olive oil
- 1 tsp. dried rosemary
- ¼ tsp. black pepper
- ½ tsp. turmeric powder

DIRECTIONS:

1. In a baking pan, combine the endives with the oil and the other ingredients, toss gently, introduce in the oven and bake at 400°F for 20 mins.
2. Divide between plates and serve.

NUTRITION: calories 66, fat 7.8g, carbs 1.6g, protein 0.2g, fiber 2g, sodium 55mg, potassium 184mg

304. Sage Carrots

Cooking Time: 30 mins | Servings: 4

INGREDIENTS:

- 1 lb. peeled and roughly cubed carrots
- 2 tsps. sweet paprika
- 1 tbsp chopped sage
- 2 tbsp olive oil
- ¼ tsp. black pepper
- 1 chopped red onion

DIRECTIONS:

1. In a baking pan, combine the carrots with the oil and the other ingredients, toss and bake at 380°F for 30 mins.
2. Divide between plates and serve.

NUTRITION: calories 200, fat 8.8g, carbs 7.6g, protein 4.2g, fiber 2g, sodium 56mg, potassium 155mg

305. Braised Cabbage

Cooking Time: 20 mins | Servings: 4

INGREDIENTS:

- 3 cups of chopped green cabbage
- 1 cup of low- Sodium vegetable broth
- 1½ tsp. of olive oil
- 2 minced garlic cloves
- 1 thinly sliced onion
- Freshly ground black pepper, to taste

DIRECTIONS:

1. In a large skillet, heat oil on medium-high heat.
2. Add garlic and sauté for about 1 minute.
3. Add onion and sauté for about 4–5 mins.
4. Add cabbage and sauté for about 3–4 mins.
5. Stir in broth and black pepper and immediately reduce the heat to low.
6. Cook, covered for about 20 mins.

NUTRITION: calories 45, fat 1.8g, carbs 6g, protein 1.2g, fiber 2g, sodium 46mg, potassium 136mg

306. Sweet Zucchini Bowl

Cooking Time: 20 mins | Servings: 4

INGREDIENTS:

- 1 onion, chopped
- 3 zucchini, cut into medium chunks
- 2 tbsps coconut milk
- 2 garlic cloves, minced
- 4 cups chicken stock
- 2 tbsps coconut oil

DIRECTIONS:

1. Take a pot and place it over medium heat
2. Add oil and let it heat up
3. Add zucchini, garlic, onion, and stir
4. Cook for 5 mins
5. Add stock, salt, pepper, and stir
6. Bring to a boil and lower down the heat
7. Simmer for 20 mins.
8. Remove heat and add coconut milk
9. Use an immersion blender until smooth
10. Ladle into soup bowls and serve

NUTRITION: calories 160, carbs 4g, protein 7g, fat 20g, phosphorus 116mg, potassium 445mg, sodium 92mg

307. Cabbage Quiche

Cooking Time: 40 mins | Servings: 6

INGREDIENTS:

- 3 large eggs, beaten
- 3 large egg whites, beaten
- Olive oil cooking spray
- 2 tbsps of olive oil
- 3 cups of coleslaw blend with carrots
- ½ cup of half-and-half
- 1 tsp of dried dill weed
- ⅛ tsp of salt
- ⅛ tsp of freshly ground black pepper
- 1 cup of grated Swiss cheese

DIRECTIONS:

1. Preheat the oven to 350°F. Spray pie plate (9-inch) with cooking spray and set aside.
2. In a skillet, put an oil and put it in medium heat. Add the coleslaw mix and cook for 4 to 6 mins, stirring, until the cabbage is tender. Transfer the vegetables from the pan to a medium bowl to cool.
3. Meanwhile, in another medium bowl, combine the eggs and egg whites, half-and-half, dill, salt, and pepper and beat to combine.
4. Stir the cabbage mixture into the egg mixture and pour into the prepared pie plate.
5. Sprinkle with the cheese.
6. Bake for 30 to 35 mins, or until the mixture is puffed, set, and light

golden brown. Let stand for 5 mins, then slice to serve.

NUTRITION: calories 203, carbs 5g, protein 35g, fat 14g, phosphorus 169mg, potassium 155mg, sodium 321mg

308. Lemony Asparagus

Cooking Time: 15 mins | Servings: 4

INGREDIENTS:

- 20 medium asparagus spears, rinsed and trimmed
- 1 fresh lemon, rinsed (for peel and juice)
- 2 tbsps reduced-fat mayonnaise
- 1 tbsp dried parsley
- 1/8 tsp ground black pepper

DIRECTIONS:

1. Place 1 inch of water in a 4-quart pot with a lid. Place a steamer basket inside the pot, and add asparagus.
2. Cover and bring to a boil over high heat. Reduce heat to medium. Cook for 5–10 mins, until asparagus is easily pierced with a sharp knife. Do not overcook.
3. While the asparagus cooks, grate the lemon zest into a small bowl. Cut the lemon in half and squeeze the juice into the bowl. Use the back of a spoon to press out extra juice and remove pits. Add mayonnaise, parsley, pepper, and salt. Stir well. Set aside.
4. When the asparagus is tender, remove the pot from the heat. Place asparagus spears in a serving bowl. Drizzle the lemon sauce evenly over the asparagus (about 1-1/2 tsps per portion) and serve.

NUTRITION: calories 39, fat 4g, carbs 9g, protein 1g, fiber 2g, sodium 99mg, potassium 183mg

309. Eggs and Beans

Cooking Time: 35 mins | Servings: 3

INGREDIENTS:

- 5 beaten eggs
- 1 tsp. chili powder
- 2 chopped garlic cloves
- ½ cup milk
- ½ cup tomato sauce
- 1 cup cooked white beans

DIRECTIONS:

1. Add milk and eggs to a bowl and mix well
2. Add the rest of the ingredients and mix well
3. Add a cup of water to the pot
4. Transfer the bowl to your pot and lock up the lid
5. Cook on HIGH pressure for 18 mins
6. Release the pressure naturally over 10 mins
7. Serve with warm bread

NUTRITION: calories 206, fat 4g, carbs 29g, protein 1g, fiber 4g, sodium 113mg, potassium 263mg

310. Oven-Fried Yucca

Cooking Time: 35 mins | Servings: 6

INGREDIENTS:

- 1 lb fresh yucca (cassava), cut into 3-inch sections and peeled (or 1 lb peeled frozen yucca)
- nonstick cooking oil spray

DIRECTIONS:

1. In a kettle, combine the yucca with enough cold water to cover it by 1 inch. Bring the water to a boil, and slowly simmer the yucca for 20 to 30 mins, or until it is tender.

2. Preheat oven to 350° F.

3. Transfer the yucca with a slotted spoon to a cutting board, let it cool, and cut it lengthwise into 3/4-inch-wide wedges, discarding the thin woody core.

4. Spray cookie sheet with the nonstick cooking oil spray. Spread yucca wedges on cookie sheet, and spray wedges with cooking oil spray. Cover with foil paper and bake for 8 mins. Uncover and return to oven to bake for an additional 7 mins.

NUTRITION: calories 91, fat 1g, carbs 19g, protein 11g, fiber 4g, sodium 128mg, potassium 189mg

311. Roasted Onion Dip

Cooking Time: 35 mins | Servings: 1

INGREDIENTS:

- 1 red onion, chopped
- 2 tbsps olive oil
- 1 (8-ounce) package cream cheese, at room temperature
- 2 tbsps mayonnaise (made with avocado oil or olive oil)
- 1 tbsp freshly squeezed lemon juice
- ½ tsp dried thyme leaves

DIRECTIONS:

1. Preheat the oven to 400°F.
2. On a rimmed baking sheet, combine the onion and olive oil and toss to coat.
3. Roast for 30 to 35 mins, stirring occasionally until the onions are soft and golden brown. Don't let them burn. Transfer to a plate and set aside.
4. In a medium bowl, beat the cream cheese, mayonnaise, lemon juice, and thyme leaves. Stir in the onions.
5. You can serve the dip at this point or cover and refrigerate it up to 8 hours before serving.

NUTRITION: calories 212, fat 21g, carbs 4g, protein 3g, fiber 0g, sodium 149mg, potassium 82mg

312. Crab Dip

Cooking Time: 0 mins | Servings: 1

INGREDIENTS:

- 1 cup mascarpone cheese
- 2 tbsps freshly squeezed lemon juice
- ½ cup lump crab meat, drained
- 1 cup grated carrots
- 4 scallions, both green and white parts, chopped

DIRECTIONS:

1. In a medium bowl, beat the mascarpone and lemon juice until smooth.
2. Look over the crab, removing any bits of cartilage and discarding.
3. Stir the crab, carrots, and scallions into the mascarpone mixture. Serve immediately or cover and chill for 4 to 6 hours before serving.

NUTRITION: calories 194, fat 18g, carbs 4g, protein 5g, fiber 2g, sodium 146mg, potassium 184mg

313. Glazed Snap Peas

Cooking Time: 5 mins | Servings: 2

INGREDIENTS:

- 1 cup snap peas
- 2 tsp Erythritol
- 1 tsp butter, melted
- ¾ tsp ground nutmeg
- ¼ tsp salt
- 1 cup water, for cooking

DIRECTIONS:

1. Pour water into the pan. Add snap peas and bring them to boil.
2. Boil the snap peas for 5 mins over the medium heat.
3. Then drain water and chill the snap peas.
4. Meanwhile, whisk together ground nutmeg, melted butter, salt, and Erythritol.
5. Preheat the mixture in the microwave oven for 5 seconds.

6. Pour the sweet butter liquid over the snap peas and shake them well.
7. The side dish should be served only warm.

NUTRITION: calories 80, fat 3g, carbs 11g, protein 4g, fiber 2g, sodium 8mg, potassium 4mg

314. Cauliflower Hash Brown

Cooking Time: 20 mins | Servings: 6

INGREDIENTS:

- 4 eggs, beaten
- ½ cup coconut milk
- ½ tsp dry mustard
- Salt and pepper to taste
- 1 large head cauliflower, shredded

DIRECTIONS:

1. Place all ingredients in a mixing bowl and mix until well combined. Place a nonstick fry pan and heat over medium flame.
2. Add a large dollop of cauliflower mixture in the skillet.
3. Fry one side for 3 mins, flip and cook the other side for a minute, like a pancake. Repeat process to remaining ingredients.
4. Serve and enjoy.

NUTRITION: calories 102, fat 8g, carbs 4g, protein 5g, fiber 1g, sodium 63mg, potassium 251mg

315. Baked Eggplant Slices

Cooking Time: 15 mins | Servings: 3

INGREDIENTS:

- 1 large eggplant, trimmed
- 1 tbsp butter, softened
- 1 tsp minced garlic
- 1 tsp salt

DIRECTIONS:

1. Slice the eggplant and sprinkle it with salt. Mix up well and leave for 10 mins to make the vegetable "give" bitter juice.
2. After this, dry the eggplant with a paper towel.
3. In the shallow bowl, mix minced garlic and softened butter.
4. Brush every eggplant slice with the garlic mixture.
5. Line the baking tray with baking paper. Preheat the oven to 355°F.
6. Place the sliced eggplants in the tray to make 1 layer and transfer it to the oven.
7. Bake the eggplants for 15 mins. The cooked eggplants will be tender but not soft!

NUTRITION: calories 81, fat 4g, carbs 11.4g, protein 2g, fiber 1g, sodium 63mg, potassium 211mg

316. Veggie Garam Masala

Cooking Time: 18 mins | Servings: 4

INGREDIENTS:

- 2 cups green beans, chopped
- 1 cup white mushroom, chopped
- ¾ cup tomatoes, crushed
- 1 tsp minced garlic
- 1 tsp minced ginger
- 1 tsp chili flakes
- 1 tbsp garam masala
- 1 tbsp olive oil

DIRECTIONS:

1. Line the tray with parchment and preheat the oven to 360°F.
2. Place the green beans and mushrooms in the tray.
3. Sprinkle the vegetables with crushed tomatoes, minced garlic and ginger, chili flakes, garam masala, olive oil, and salt.
4. Mix up well and transfer in the oven.
5. Cook vegetable masala for 18 mins.

NUTRITION: calories 60, fat 30.8g, carbs 6.4g, protein 2g, fiber 2g, sodium 63mg, potassium 251mg

317. Mushroom Tacos

Cooking Time: 15 mins | Servings: 6

INGREDIENTS:

- 6 leaves of collard greens
- 2 cups mushrooms, chopped
- 1 white onion, diced
- 1 tbsp taco seasoning
- 1 tbsp coconut oil
- ½ tsp salt
- ¼ cup fresh parsley
- 1 tbsp mayonnaise

DIRECTIONS:

1. Put the coconut oil in the skillet and melt it.
2. Add chopped mushrooms and diced onion. Mix the ingredients.
3. Close the lid and cook them for 10 mins.
4. After this, sprinkle the vegetables with Taco seasoning, salt, and add fresh parsley.
5. Mix the mixture and cook for 5 mins more.
6. Then add mayonnaise and stir well.
7. Chill the mushroom mixture a little.
8. Fill the collard green leaves with the mushroom mixture and fold up them.

NUTRITION: calories 52, fat 3.8g, carbs 5.4g, protein 1.2g, fiber 1.2g, sodium 63mg, potassium 211mg

318. Baby Spinach Salad

Cooking Time: 5 mins | Servings: 2

INGREDIENTS:

- 1 bag baby spinach, washed and dried
- 1 red bell pepper, cut in slices
- 1 cup cherry tomatoes, cut in halves
- 1 small red onion, finely chopped
- 1 cup black olives, pitted

For dressing

- 1 tsp dried oregano
- 1 large garlic clove
- 3 tbsps red wine vinegar
- 4 tbsps olive oil
- Sunflower seeds and pepper to taste

DIRECTIONS:

1. Prepare the dressing by blending in garlic, olive oil, vinegar in a food processor
2. Take a large salad bowl and add spinach leaves, toss well with the dressing
3. Add remaining Ingredients: and toss again, season with sunflower seeds and pepper and enjoy

NUTRITION: calories 135, fat 1.8g, carbs 12.4g, protein 25g, fiber 2g, sodium 63mg, potassium 251mg

319. Sweet Potato Puree

Cooking Time: 15 mins | Servings: 6

INGREDIENTS:

- 2 pounds sweet potatoes, peeled
- 1 ½ cups of water
- 5 dates, pitted and chopped

DIRECTIONS:

1. Place water and potatoes in a pot. Close the lid and allow boiling for 15 mins until the potatoes are soft.
2. Drain the potatoes and place in a food processor together with the dates.
3. Pulse it until smooth.
4. Serve and enjoy.

NUTRITION: calories 172, fat 0.2g, carbs 41g, protein 3g, fiber 5g, sodium 10mg, potassium 776mg

320. Vegan Chili

Cooking Time: 20 mins| Servings: 4

INGREDIENTS:

- 1 cup cremini mushrooms, chopped
- 1 zucchini, chopped
- 1 bell pepper, diced
- 1/3 cup crushed tomatoes
- 1 oz celery stalk, chopped
- 1 tsp chili powder
- 1 tsp salt
- ½ tsp chili flakes
- ½ cup water
- 1 tbsp olive oil
- ½ tsp diced garlic
- ½ tsp ground black pepper
- 1 tsp cocoa powder
- 2 oz Cheddar cheese, grated

DIRECTIONS:

1. Pour olive oil into the pan and preheat it.
2. Add chopped mushrooms and roast them for 5 mins. Stir them from time to time.
3. After this, add chopped zucchini and bell pepper.
4. Sprinkle the vegetables with the chili powder, salt, chili flakes, diced garlic, and ground black pepper.
5. Stir the vegetables and cook them for 5 more mins.
6. After this, add crushed tomatoes. Mix well.
7. Bring the mixture to boil and add water and cocoa powder.
8. Then add celery stalk.
9. Mix up the chili well and close the lid.
10. Cook the chili for 10 mins over the medium-low heat.
11. Then transfer the cooked vegan chili to the bowls and top with the grated cheese.

NUTRITION: calories 127, fat 8.2g, carbs 41g, protein 5g, fiber 2.5g, sodium 50mg, potassium 576mg

321. Spinach and Chickpeas Salad

Cooking Time: 0 mins | Servings: 4

INGREDIENTS:

- 16 oz canned chickpeas, drained and rinsed
- 2 cups baby spinach leaves
- ½ tbsp lime juice
- 2 tbsps olive oil
- 1 tsp cumin, ground
- A pinch of salt and black pepper
- ½ tsp chili flakes

DIRECTIONS:

In a bowl, mix the chickpeas with the spinach and the rest of the ingredients, toss, and serve cold.

NUTRITION: calories 240, fat 9g, carbs 12g, protein 12g, fiber 1.2g, sodium 63mg, potassium 111mg

322. Classical Greek Salad

Cooking Time: 5 mins | Servings: 6

INGREDIENTS:

- 2 cucumbers, diced
- 2 tomatoes, sliced
- 1 green lettuce, cut into thin strips
- 2 red bell peppers, cut
- ½ cup black olives pitted
- 3 and ½ oz feta cheese, cut
- 1 red onion, sliced
- 2 tbsps olive oil
- 2 tbsps lemon juice
- Sunflower seeds and pepper to taste

DIRECTIONS:

1. Dice cucumbers and slice up the tomatoes
2. Tear the lettuce and cut it up into thin strips
3. De-seed and cut the peppers into strips
4. Take a salad bowl and mix in all the listed vegetables, add olives and feta cheese (cut into cubes)
5. Take a small cup and mix in olive oil and lemon juice, season with sunflower seeds and pepper. Pour

mixture into the salad and toss well, enjoy!

NUTRITION: calories 155, fat 1.2g, carbs 15g, protein 22g, fiber 2.5g, sodium 250mg, potassium 386mg

323. Vegan Tortilla

Cooking Time: 40 mins | Servings: 5

INGREDIENTS:

- 1 zucchini, diced
- 1 onion, chopped
- 2 carrots, chopped
- Pinch of pepper
- 1 tsp of Parsley
- 3 small potatoes
- 1 tbsp of olive oil
- 3 tbsp of chickpea flour

DIRECTIONS:

1. Peel potatoes, onions, and carrots. Wash the zucchini and cut all the vegetables into as small as possible (in brunoise).
2. In a pan, fry all the vegetables with a little oil until they are very soft. Add pepper, and a few sprigs of chopped parsley and leave over medium heat.
3. We undo the chickpea flour in a little water. It has to be a texture like a beaten egg, so we will be adding the water little by little until it is almost liquid. We add it to the pan of the vegetables and, without stopping to stir, until it is fully integrated. There will be a paste that can be worked with your hands.
4. When the mixture has cooled a little, and we can work by hand, we flour our hands and make balls as twice the size of a meatball. Then we flatten them a bit to give them a hamburger shape, and we put them on the griddle with a drop of oil on both sides.
5. Ready to serve.

NUTRITION: calories 196, fat 9.8g, carbs 25.4g, protein 7g, fiber 1.2g, sodium 73mg, potassium 153mg

324. Curried Okra

Cooking Time: 12 mins | Servings: 4

INGREDIENTS:

- 1 lb. small to medium okra pods, trimmed
- ¼ tsp curry powder
- ½ tsp kosher salt
- 1 tsp finely chopped serrano chile
- 1 tsp ground coriander
- 1 tbsp olive oil
- ¾ tsp brown mustard seeds

DIRECTIONS:

1. On medium high fire, place a large and heavy skillet and cook mustard seeds until fragrant, around 30 seconds.
2. Add canola oil. Add okra, curry powder, salt, chile, and coriander. Sauté it in a minute while stirring every once
3. Cover and cook low fire for at least 8 mins. Stir occasionally.
4. Uncover, increase fire to medium high and cook until okra is lightly browned, around 2 mins more.
5. Serve and enjoy.

NUTRITION: calories 78, fat 6g, carbs 6g, protein 2g, fiber 3g, sodium 553mg, potassium 187mg

325. Cauliflower and Herbs Tortilla

Cooking Time: 25 mins | Servings: 4

INGREDIENTS:

- 2 cups asparagus, chopped and trimmed
- 1 ½ cups white onion, chopped
- 2 cups cauliflower florets, chopped
- ½ tsp minced garlic
- ¼ tsp ground nutmeg

- ¼ tsp dried thyme leaves
- 2 tbsps parsley, chopped
- 2 tsps olive oil
- 1 cup liquid egg substitute

DIRECTIONS:

1. Take a heatproof bowl, add cauliflower florets and asparagus, drizzle with water, cover the bowl with plastic wrap, pierce some holes in it, and microwave for 5 mins, or until tender-crisp.
2. Meanwhile, take a medium-sized skillet pan, place it over medium heat, add oil, and when hot, add onion and cook for 7 mins until golden brown.
3. Stir in garlic, cook for 1 minute until fragrant, switch heat to medium-low level, add steamed cauliflower-asparagus mixture in the pan, sprinkle with nutmeg, black pepper, salt, thyme, and parsley, and pour in egg substitute.
4. Continue cooking for 10 to 15 mins, or until the tortilla has set and the bottom is nicely browned, and when done, slide the tortilla onto a dish by running the knife along the edges.

NUTRITION: calories 102, fat 3g, carbs 6g, protein 9g, fiber 4g, sodium 353mg, potassium 113mg

326. Broccoli with Pine Nuts

Cooking time: 5 mins | Servings: 2

INGREDIENTS:

- 1 bunch broccoli rabe
- 1 cup broccoli florets
- 3 cups water
- 1 tbsp olive oil
- 2 medium garlic cloves, minced
- 1 tbsp freshly squeezed lemon juice
- Salt and pepper, to taste
- 2 tbsp pine nuts

DIRECTIONS:

1. Rinse the broccoli rabe well in cold water to remove any dirt particles. Tear into stalks. Set aside.
2. In a saucepan set over high heat, bring the water to a boil.
3. Place a colander in the sink. Add the broccoli rabe pieces and broccoli florets. Pour the boiling water over them to scald. Drain well. Set aside.
4. In a sauté pan or skillet set over medium heat, heat the olive oil.
5. Add the garlic. Sauté for 1 minute, or until browned.
6. Add the broccoli rabe and broccoli florets. Toss to coat with the garlic. Cook for about 3 mins, or until heated through.
7. Drizzle the vegetables with the lemon juice. Season with salt and pepper.
8. Top with the pine nuts and serve.

NUTRITION: calories 157, fat 14g, protein 4g, carbs 6g, sugars 1g, fiber 1g, sodium 10mg

327. Green Beans and Peppers

Cooking time: 15 mins | Servings: 2

INGREDIENTS:

- 8 oz fresh green beans, broken into 2-inch pieces
- 4 sun-dried tomatoes (not packed in oil), halved
- 1 medium red bell pepper, cut into ¼-inch strips
- 1 tsp olive oil
- Salt and pepper, to taste

DIRECTIONS:

1. In a 1-quart saucepan set over high heat, add the green beans to 1 inch of water. Bring to a boil. Boil for 5 mins, uncovered.
2. Add the sun-dried tomatoes. Cover and boil 5 to 7 mins more, or until the beans are crisp-tender, and the tomatoes have softened. Drain. Transfer to a serving bowl.

3. Add the red bell pepper and olive oil. Season with salt and pepper. Toss to coat.
4. Serve warm.

NUTRITION: calories 90, fat 2g, protein 4g, carbs 16g, sugars 9g, fiber 5g, sodium 220mg

328. Asparagus with Sweet Peppers

Cooking time: 15 mins | Servings: 2

INGREDIENTS:

- 1/3 pound fresh asparagus, trimmed
- 2 tsps olive oil mixed with 1 tsp warm water
- 1 red bell pepper, seeded and julienned
- 1 tbsp grated orange zest
- Salt and pepper, to taste
- 1 tsp granulated stevia, divided

DIRECTIONS:

1. Preheat the broiler to high.
2. In a steamer or large pot of boiling water, cook the asparagus for about 7 mins, or until barely tender. Drain. Set aside.
3. In a small skillet set over medium-high heat, heat the olive oil and water.
4. Add the bell pepper. Cook for about 5 mins, stirring frequently, until slightly softened. Remove from the heat.
5. Stir in the orange zest. Season with salt and pepper.
6. Evenly divided the asparagus between 2 gratin dishes. Spoon half of the red bell pepper and sauce over each. Sprinkle each with ½ tsp of stevia. Place the dished under the preheated broiler. Broil for 2 to 3 mins, or until lightly browned.
7. Serve immediately.

NUTRITION: calories 47, fat 2g, protein 1g, carbs 5g, sugars 2g, fiber 2g, sodium 10mg

329. Mashed Cauliflower

Cooking time: 0 mins, Servings: 2

INGREDIENTS:

- 2 cups cooked cauliflower florets
- 1 tbsp plain nonfat: Greek yogurt
- ½ tsp olive oil
- Salt and pepper, to taste

DIRECTIONS:

1. To a food processor, add the cauliflower, yogurt, and olive oil. Process until smooth.
2. Season with salt and pepper before serving.

NUTRITION: calories 39, fat 1g, protein 2g, carbs 4g, sugars 2g, fiber 0g, sodium 29mg

330. Sweet-and-Sour Slaw

Cooking time: 0 mins | Servings: 2

INGREDIENTS:

- 2 cups angel hair cabbage
- 1 apple, cored and diced
- 2 tbsp apple cider vinegar
- 1 tbsp granulated stevia
- ½ cup shredded carrot
- 1 medium scallion, sliced
- 1 tbsp sliced almonds

DIRECTIONS:

1. In a medium bowl, stir together the vinegar and stevia.
2. In a large bowl, mix together the cabbage, apple, carrot, and scallions.
3. Pour the sweetened vinegar over the vegetable mixture. Toss to combine.
4. Garnish with the sliced almonds and serve.

NUTRITION: calories 100, fat 4g, protein 3g, carbs 16g, sugars 9g, fiber 5g, sodium 59mg

331. Zucchini and Pine Nuts Ribbons

Cooking time: 1 min | Servings: 2

INGREDIENTS:

- 2 zucchini, thinly sliced lengthwise into ribbons
- 1 tbsp ricotta cheese
- 1 tbsp pine nuts
- 1 tbsp fresh tarragon
- 1½ tsps olive oil
- 1 tsp chili flakes

DIRECTIONS:

1. Bring a large pot of water to a boil.
2. Add the zucchini. Cook for 30 to 60 seconds, or until crisp-tender. Drain. Transfer the zucchini to a serving bowl.
3. Add the ricotta cheese, pine nuts, tarragon, olive oil, and red pepper flakes. Gently toss until the zucchini is coated.
4. Serve and enjoy!

NUTRITION: calories 102, fat 7g, protein 4g, carbs 7g, sugars 5g, fiber 2g, sodium 34mg

332. Broiled Tomatoes with Cheese

Cooking time: 10 mins | Servings: 2

INGREDIENTS:

- 2 large ripe tomatoes, halved widthwise
- ¼ cup ricotta cheese, divided
- 1 tsp dried basil, divided
- Salt and pepper, to taste

DIRECTIONS:

1. Preheat the broiler.
2. Top each tomato half with 1 tbsp of ricotta cheese. Sprinkle with ⅛ tsp of basil. Season with salt and pepper.
3. On a broiler rack, place the tomatoes cut-side up. Place the rack into the preheated oven. Broil for 7 to 10 mins.
4. Serve!

NUTRITION: calories 53, fat 0g, protein 5g, carbs 9g, sugars 6g, fiber 2g, sodium 75mg

333. Braised Kale with Ginger

Cooking time: 25 mins | Servings: 2

INGREDIENTS:

- 6 cups (2 bunches) chopped kale, stemmed
- ¼ cup water, plus additional as needed
- 2 tbsp balsamic vinegar
- 1 garlic clove, minced
- 2 tsps chopped fresh ginger
- 1 tbsp sesame seeds

DIRECTIONS:

1. In a saucepan set over medium heat, whisk together the balsamic vinegar, garlic, and ginger. Cook for 5 mins.
2. Add the kale. Stir to combine. Cook for 10 to 15 mins, or until wilted.
3. Add the water. Cover and simmer for 2 mins, adding more water as needed to keep the kale from sticking. Uncover and cook for 1 to 2 mins more, or until any remaining liquid evaporates.
4. Sprinkle with the sesame seeds and serve.

NUTRITION: calories 135, fat 5g, protein 7g, carbs 20g, sugars 6g, fiber 4g, sodium 46mg

334. Garlic Fettuccine

Cooking time: 30 mins | Servings: 5

INGREDIENTS:

- 6 oz whole-wheat fettuccine pasta
- 2 tbsp olive oil
- 10 plum tomatoes, seeded and diced
- 3 cloves garlic, minced
- ¼ tsp salt and black pepper
- 1 tsp capers
- 2 tsps pitted black olives, chopped
- Freshly chopped parsley, for garnish

DIRECTIONS:

1. In a large saucepan over medium heat, heat the oil. Add the tomatoes, garlic, salt, pepper, capers, and olives. Let simmer over low heat for 30 mins, stirring occasionally.
2. Prepare the fettuccine according to package directions (without adding salt) and drain. Transfer the fettucine to a serving bowl and spoon the sauce on top. Garnish with parsley to serve.

NUTRITION: calories 210, fat 7g, protein 7g, carbs 31g, sugars 4g, fiber 5g, sodium 160mg

335. Linguine with Pesto

Cooking time: 6 mins | Servings: 4

INGREDIENTS:

- 6 oz whole-wheat linguine
- 3 cups fresh basil, stems removed
- 3 garlic cloves, chopped
- ¼ cup olive oil
- 1 cup pine nuts, toasted
- ¼ cup Parmesan cheese
- Freshly ground black pepper

DIRECTIONS:

1. Wash and dry the basil. Place the basil in a blender or food processor with the garlic, olive oil, pine nuts, cheese, and pepper, and process until smooth.
2. Transfer the cooked linguine to a serving bowl. Add the pesto, and toss thoroughly to serve.

NUTRITION: calories 130, fat 10g, protein 3g, carbs 9g, sugars 1g, fiber 2g, sodium 10mg

336. Pasta with Peppers

Cooking time: 20 mins | Servings: 3

INGREDIENTS:

- ½ pound cooked whole-wheat pasta
- 1 (15-ounce) can tomato purée
- ½ red bell pepper, cut into thin strips
- ½ green bell pepper, cut into thin strips
- ½ yellow bell pepper, cut into thin strips
- 2 tbsp chopped fresh sage
- 2 tbsp chicken broth
- 1 garlic clove, minced
- 1 chopped onion

DIRECTIONS:

1. In a large skillet over medium heat, heat the broth. Add the garlic and onion, and sauté for 5 to 8 mins. Add the peppers, and sauté for another 7 mins.
2. Add the sage and tomato purée. Lower the heat to a simmer, and cook for 15 mins.
3. Add the cooked pasta and let stand for 5 mins. Serve.

NUTRITION: calories 120, fat 1g, protein 5g, carbs 24g, sugars 5g, fiber 4g, sodium 50mg

337. Vegetable Clam Sauce Shells

Cooking time: 10 mins | Servings: 3

INGREDIENTS:

- ½ pound cooked whole-wheat shells
- 2 small tomatoes, chopped
- 2 scallions, chopped
- ¼ pound fresh mushrooms, sliced
- 2 tbsp olive oil
- 4 cloves garlic, crushed
- 4 celery stalks, chopped
- 2 tbsp chopped fresh parsley

- 1 (7-ounce) can clams, undrained
- 1/3 cup dry white wine
- 2 tbsp fresh lemon juice
- Freshly ground black pepper

DIRECTIONS:

1. In a large skillet over medium heat, heat the oil. Sauté the garlic until lightly browned. Add the celery, scallions, mushrooms, and parsley; sauté until the vegetables are just tender (about 5 mins).
2. Add the clams with their juice, tomatoes, wine, lemon juice, and pepper; stir well. Let simmer, uncovered, for 4 to 5 mins.
3. Place the cooked pasta on a serving platter. Remove the sauce from the heat and spoon over the pasta and serve.

NUTRITION: calories 180, fat 4g, protein 8g, carbs 28g, sugars 3g, fiber 4g, sodium 75mg

338. Fettuccine with Peppers and Broccoli

Cooking time: 20 mins | Servings: 3

INGREDIENTS:

- 6 oz whole-wheat fettuccine
- 3 cups fresh broccoli florets, washed
- 2 tbsp olive oil
- 2 medium garlic cloves, minced
- 2 large red bell peppers, halved, seeded, and cut into ½-inch strips
- 3 tbsp Parmesan

DIRECTIONS:

1. In a large skillet over medium heat, heat the olive oil. Add the garlic, and sauté for 1 minute. Add the peppers and continue sautéing for 3 to 5 mins or until the peppers are just tender, stirring occasionally. Remove from the heat, and set aside.
2. Prepare the fettucine according to package directions (without adding salt) and drain.
3. Add the broccoli to a large pot of boiling water, and then turn off the heat. After 1 minute, rinse the broccoli under cold running water to stop the cooking process; drain. (This method of blanching helps the broccoli to retain its bright green color and crispness.)
4. In a large bowl, toss the fettucine with the peppers, and arrange the broccoli on top. Sprinkle with the Parmesan cheese, and serve.

NUTRITION: calories 320, fat 10g, protein 15g, carbs 47g, sugars 9g, fiber 12g, sodium 95mg

339. Veggie Lo Mein

Cooking time: 10 mins | Servings: 4

INGREDIENTS:

- ½ pound cooked whole-wheat vermicelli
- 1 cup plus 2 tbsp low-sodium chicken broth
- 2 garlic cloves, minced
- ¼ cup minced scallions
- 2 tsps grated fresh ginger
- 2 carrots, peeled and cut into ¼-inch slices
- 2 celery stalks, cut on the diagonal into ¼-inch slices
- ½ cup sliced mushrooms
- 1 cup broccoli florets
- 2 tbsp dry sherry
- 1 tbsp light soy sauce
- 1 tsp sesame oil

DIRECTIONS:

1. In a large skillet or wok, heat 2 tbsp of the broth. Add the garlic, scallions, and ginger, and sauté for 30 seconds.
2. Add the carrots, celery, and mushrooms, and sauté for 5 mins. Add the broccoli and ½ cup of the broth, cover, and steam for 5 mins.

3. In a small bowl, combine the remaining ½ cup of broth with the sherry, soy sauce, and sesame oil. Mix well.
4. Remove the cover and add the cornstarch mixture. Cook for 1 minute more until the mixture thickens. Toss in the cooked noodles and mix well. Serve.

NUTRITION: calories 80, fat 1g, protein 4g, carbs 13g, sugars 2g, fiber 2g, sodium 120mg

340. Asian Stir-Fried Rice

Cooking time: 20 mins | Servings: 4

INGREDIENTS:

- 2 cups cooked brown rice, cold
- 2 egg whites
- ½ cup sliced scallions
- ¼ cup chopped onion
- 1 cup sliced carrot
- 1 green bell pepper, diced
- 2 tbsp peanut oil
- 1 tbsp grated fresh ginger
- ½ cup sliced mushrooms
- 1 tbsp light soy sauce

DIRECTIONS:

1. In a large skillet, heat the oil. Sauté the onion, carrot, green pepper, and ginger for 5 to 6 mins.
2. Stir in the rice, mushrooms, and soy sauce, and stir-fry for 8 to 10 mins.
3. Stir in the egg whites and continue to stir-fry for another 3 mins. Top with the sliced scallions to serve.

NUTRITION: calories 220, fat 8g, protein 6g, carbs 32g, sugars 4g, fiber 4g, sodium 200mg

341. Rainbow Rice Casserole

Cooking time: 20 mins | Servings: 4
INGREDIENTS:

- 2 cups cooked brown (or white) rice
- 2 cups zucchini, thinly sliced
- 2 chopped scallions
- 1 cup corn kernels
- 1 tbsp olive oil
- 1 can chopped tomatoes, undrained
- 1 tbsp chopped parsley
- 1 tsp oregano

DIRECTIONS:

1. In a large skillet, heat the oil. Add the zucchini and scallions, and sauté for 5 mins.
2. Add the remaining ingredients, cover, reduce heat, and simmer for 10 to 15 mins or until the vegetables are heated through. Season with salt, if desired, and pepper. Transfer to a bowl and serve.

NUTRITION: calories 110, fat 2g, protein 3g, carbs 21g, sugars 4g, fiber 2g, sodium 20mg

342. Brown Rice with Spinach

Cooking time: 15 mins | Servings: 4

INGREDIENTS:

- 2 cups brown rice
- 1 medium onion, diced
- 1 cup sliced mushrooms
- 1½ cups water
- 1 tbsp olive oil
- 2 garlic cloves, minced
- 1 tbsp lemon juice
- ½ tsp dried oregano
- 3 cups fresh spinach, stems trimmed, washed, patted dry, and coarsely chopped
- 1/3 cup crumbled fat-free feta cheese
- ⅛ tsp freshly ground black pepper

DIRECTIONS:

1. In a medium saucepan over medium heat, combine the rice and water. Bring to a boil, cover, reduce heat, and simmer for 15 mins. Transfer to a serving bowl.
2. In a skillet, heat the oil. Sauté the onion, mushrooms, and garlic for 5 to 7 mins. Stir in the lemon juice and

oregano. Add the spinach, cheese, and pepper, tossing until the spinach is slightly wilted.

3. Toss with rice and serve.

NUTRITION: calories 170, fat 4g, protein 6g, carbs 28g, sugars 2g, fiber 3g, sodium 115mg

343. Curried Rice with Broccoli

Cooking time: 35 mins, Servings: 4

INGREDIENTS:

- 2 cups uncooked brown basmati rice, soaked in water 20 mins and drained before cooking
- 8 broccoli florets
- 1 onion, chopped
- 1cup water
- 1cup low-sodium chicken broth
- 2 red bell peppers, minced
- 1 tsp curry powder
- 1 tsp ground turmeric
- 1 tsp ground ginger
- 2 garlic cloves, minced
- ¼ cup sliced almonds, toasted

DIRECTIONS:

1. In a medium saucepan, combine the onion, water, and chicken broth. Bring to a boil, and add the rice, peppers, curry powder, turmeric, ginger, and garlic. Cover, placing a paper towel in between the pot and the lid, and reduce the heat. Simmer for 25 mins.
2. Add the broccoli and continue to simmer 5 to 7 mins more until rice is tender and water is absorbed. Taste and add salt, if desired. Transfer to a serving bowl, and garnish with almonds to serve.

NUTRITION: calories 130, fat 2g, protein 4g, carbs 25g, sugars 6g, fiber 3g, sodium 25mg

344. Zucchini Pasta with Mango-Kiwi Sauce

Cooking Time: 0 mins | Servings: 2

INGREDIENTS:

- 2 cup zucchini, spiralized
- ¼ cup roasted cashew
- 1 tsp dried herbs – optional
- ½ cup raw kale leaves, shredded
- 2 small dried figs
- 3 dates
- 4 medium kiwis
- 2 big mangos, peeled and seed discarded

DIRECTIONS:

1. On a salad bowl, place kale then topped with zucchini noodles and sprinkle with dried herbs. Set aside.
2. In a food processor, grind to a powder the cashews. Add figs, dates, kiwis and mangoes then puree to a smooth consistency.
3. Pour over zucchini pasta, serve and enjoy.

NUTRITION: calories 370, fat 9g, carbs 76g, protein 6g, fiber 9g, sodium 8mg, potassium 868mg

345. Beans Burger

Cooking Time: 15 mins | Servings: 4

INGREDIENTS:

- 1 cup of canned white beans, drained and rinsed
- 1 cup of cooked brown rice
- 1 tsp of garlic powder
- 2 tsps of dried thyme
- ½ tsp of ground chipotle pepper
- ½ sweet onion, finely chopped
- ½ cup of fresh or frozen corn
- ½ cup of red bell pepper, finely chopped
- Juice of 1 lemon
- ⅓ cup of whole wheat flour
- 1 large egg
- Freshly ground black pepper
- 2 tsps of olive oil

DIRECTIONS:

1. In a large bowl, mash the beans with a potato masher, leaving a few whole beans as desired. Add the rice, garlic powder, thyme, chipotle pepper, onion, corn, bell pepper, lemon, flour, and egg, and mix well to blend. Season with pepper.
2. Using your hands, form the mixture into four patties. Set your oil on in a skillet on medium heat. Cook the burgers for 5 mins, until browned on one side, flip, and cook the other side for an additional 5 mins.

NUTRITION: calories 305, fat 3g, carbs 57g, protein 9g, fiber 4g, sodium 281mg, potassium 515mg, phosphorus 181 mg

346. Barley Veggie Bowl

Cooking Time: 30 mins | Servings: 4

INGREDIENTS:

- 2 small Asian eggplants, diced
- 2 small zucchini, diced
- ½ red bell pepper, chopped
- ½ sweet onion, cut into wedges
- 2 tbsps of olive oil, divided
- Freshly ground black pepper
- 1 cup of barley
- Juice of 1 lemon
- 3 garlic cloves, minced
- ¼ cup of basil leaves, roughly chopped
- ¼ cup of crumbled feta cheese
- 2 cups of arugula or mixed baby salad greens

DIRECTIONS:

1. Preheat the oven to 425°F. In a medium bowl, toss your onion, bell pepper, zucchini, and eggplant with 1 tbsp of olive oil and transfer to a baking tray in a single layer. Season with pepper.
2. Roast the vegetables for about 25 mins, stirring once or twice, until they are browned and tender. Set aside. Meanwhile, in a medium pot, add the barley and 2 cups of water.
3. Bring to a boil, reduce the heat to simmer, cover, and cook for 20 mins. Turn off the heat and let rest for 10 mins. Fluff with a fork and drain any remaining water.
4. In a small bowl, whisk the lemon juice, garlic, and remaining tbsp of olive oil. Toss the vegetables with the barley, and then mix with the lemon-garlic dressing. Right before serving, stir in the basil, feta cheese, and salad greens.

NUTRITION: calories 292, fat 10g, carbs 44g, protein 9g, fiber 4g, sodium 119mg, potassium 543mg, phosphorus 201 mg

347. Roasted Eggplant with Feta Dip

Cooking Time: 30 mins | Servings: 6

INGREDIENTS:

- 1 lb. 1 medium eggplant
- ½ cup red onion, finely chopped
- ½ cup Greek feta cheese, crumbled
- ¼ cup olive oil
- Pinch of sugar
- ¼ tsp salt
- ¼ tsp cayenne pepper or to taste
- 1 tbsp parsley, chopped
- 2 tbsp fresh basil, chopped
- 1 small chili pepper, seeded and minced, optional
- 2 tbsp lemon juice

DIRECTIONS:

1. Preheat broiler and position rack 6 inches away from heat source.
2. Pierce the eggplant with a knife or fork. Then with a foil, line a baking pan and place the eggplant and broil. Make sure to turn eggplant every five mins or until the skin is charred and eggplant is soft which takes around

14 to 18 mins of broiling. Once done, remove from heat and let cool.

3. In a medium bowl , add lemon. Then cut eggplant in half , lengthwise , and scrape the flesh and place in the bowl with lemon. Add oil and mix until well combined. Then add salt , cayenne , parsley , basil , chili pepper , bell pepper , onion and feta. Toss until well combined and add sugar to taste if wanted.

NUTRITION: calories 139, fat 12g, carbs 7g, protein 3g, fiber 3g, sodium 178mg, potassium 249mg

348. Vegetable Potpie

Cooking Time: 30 mins | Servings: 8

INGREDIENTS:

- 1 recipe pastry for double crust pie
- 1 cup fresh green beans, trimmed and snapped into ½ inch pieces
- 2 cups cauliflower florets
- 2 stalks celery, sliced ¼ inch wide
- 2 potatoes, peeled and diced
- 2 large carrots, diced
- 1 clove garlic, minced
- 8 oz mushroom
- 2 tbsp cornstarch
- 1 tsp ground black pepper
- 1 tsp kosher salt
- 3 cups vegetable broth
- 1 onion, chopped
- 2 tbsp olive oil

DIRECTIONS:

1. In a large saucepan , sauté garlic in oil until lightly browned , add onions and continue sautéing until soft and translucent.
2. Add celery , potatoes and carrots and sauté for 3 mins.
3. Add vegetable broth , green beans and cauliflower and bring to a boil. Slow fire and simmer until vegetables are slightly tender. Season it with pepper and salt.
4. Mix ¼ cup water and cornstarch in a small bowl. Stir until mixture is smooth and has no lumps. Then pour into the vegetable pot while mixing constantly.
5. Continue mixing until soup thickens , around 3 mins. Remove from fire.
6. Meanwhile , roll out pastry dough and place on an oven safe 11x7 baking dish. Pour the vegetable filling and then cover with another pastry dough. Seal and flute the edges of the dough and prick the top dough with fork on several places.
7. Bake the dish in a preheated oven of 425°F for 30 mins or until crust has turned a golden brown.

NUTRITION: calories 202, fat 10g, carbs 26g, protein 4g, fiber 3g, sodium 466mg, potassium 483mg

349. Marsala Roasted Carrots

Cooking Time: 40 mins | Servings: 8

INGREDIENTS:

- 2 lbs. julienned carrots
- pepper and salt to taste
- 2 tbsp balsamic vinegar
- 2 tbsp olive oil
- ½ cup marsala

DIRECTIONS:

1. Peel the carrots and place on baking sheet.
2. Add vinegar, olive oil and marsala. Toss to coat.
3. Roast carrots in oven for 30 mins at 425°F, while occasionally stirring.
4. Carrots are cooked once tender and lightly browned. Remove from oven and season it with pepper,| salt and fresh parsley.

NUTRITION: calories 62, fat 2g, carbs 11g, protein 1g, fiber 4g, sodium 101mg, potassium 333mg

350. Cajun Asparagus

Cooking Time: 10 mins | Servings: 3

INGREDIENTS:

- 1 tsp cajun seasoning
- 1-pound asparagus
- 1 tsp olive oil

DIRECTIONS:

1. Snap the asparagus and make sure that you use the tender part of the vegetable.
2. Place a large skillet on stovetop and heat on high for a minute.
3. Then grease skillet with cooking spray and spread asparagus in one layer.
4. Cover skillet and continue cooking on high for 5 to eight mins.
5. Halfway through cooking time, stir skillet and then cover and continue to cook.
6. Once done cooking , transfer to plates , serve , and enjoy!

NUTRITION: calories 47, fat 2g, carbs 6g, protein 3g, fiber 3g, sodium 73mg, potassium 315mg

CHAPTER 9 Fish and Seafood

351. Cajun-Spiced Tilapia

Cooking time: 5 mins | Servings: 2

INGREDIENTS:

- 8 oz tilapia fillets
- ½ tsp Chinese five-spice powder
- 2 tbsp reduced-sodium soy sauce
- 1 tbsp granulated stevia
- 2 tsps olive oil
- 1 cup sugar snap peas
- 2 scallions, thinly sliced

DIRECTIONS:

1. Sprinkle both sides of the fillets with the Chinese five-spice powder.
2. In a small bowl, stir together the soy sauce and stevia. Set aside.
3. In a large nonstick skillet set over medium-high heat, heat the olive oil.
4. Add the tilapia. Cook for about 2 mins, or until the outer edges are opaque. Reduce the heat to medium. Turn the fish over. Stir the soy mixture and pour into the skillet.
5. Add the sugar snap peas. Bring the sauce to a boil. Cook for about 2 mins, or until the fish is cooked through, the sauce thickens, and the peas are bright green.
6. Add scallions. Remove from the heat.
7. Serve the fish and the sugar snap peas drizzled with the pan sauce.

NUTRITION: calories 202, fat 7g, protein 26g, carbs 7g, sugars 3g, fiber 0g, sodium 619mg

352. Open-Faced Tuna Melts

Cooking time: 5 mins | Servings: 3

INGREDIENTS:

- 3 English muffins, 100% whole-wheat
- 2 (5-ounce) cans tuna, drained
- 2 tbsp plain Greek yogurt
- ½ tsp freshly ground black pepper
- ¾ cup shredded cheddar cheese

DIRECTIONS:

1. If your broiler is in the top of your oven, place the oven rack in the center position. Turn the broiler on high.
2. Split the English muffins, if necessary, and toast them in the toaster.
3. Meanwhile, in a medium bowl, mix the tuna, yogurt, and pepper.
4. Place the muffin halves on a baking sheet, and spoon one-sixth of the tuna mixture and 2 tbsp of cheddar cheese on top of each half. Broil for 2 mins or until the cheese melts.

NUTRITION: calories 392, fat 13g, protein 40g, carbs 28g, sugars 6g, fiber 5g, sodium 474mg

353. Grilled Cod

Cooking Time: 10 mins| Servings: 4

INGREDIENTS:

- 2 (8 ounce) fillets cod, cut in half
- 1 tbsp oregano
- ½ tsp lemon pepper
- ¼ tsp ground black pepper
- 2 tbsps olive oil
- 1 lemon, juiced
- 2 tbsps chopped green onion (white part only)

DIRECTIONS:

1. Season both sides of cod with oregano, lemon pepper, and black

pepper. Set fish aside on a plate. Heat butter in a small saucepan over medium heat , stir in lemon juice and green onion , and cook until onion is softened , about 3 mins.

2. Place cod onto oiled grates and grill until fish is browned and flakes easily, about 3 mins per side; baste with olive oil mixture frequently while grilling. Allow cod to rest off the heat for about 5 mins before serving.

NUTRITION: calories 92, fat 7.4g, sodium 19mg, carbs 2.5g, fiber 1g, protein 5.4g, potassium 50mg, phosphorus 36 mg

354. Cod and Green Bean Curry

Cooking Time: 60 mins| Servings: 4

INGREDIENTS:

- 1/2-pound green beans, trimmed and cut into bite-sized pieces
- 1 white onion, sliced
- 2 cloves garlic, minced
- 1 tbsp olive oil, or more as needed
- *Curry Mixture:*
- 2 tbsps water, or more as needed
- 2 tsps curry powder
- 2 tsps ground ginger
- 1 1/2 (6 ounce) cod fillets

DIRECTIONS:

1. Preheat the oven to 400 °F.
2. Combine green beans, onion , and garlic in a large glass baking dish. Toss with olive oil to coat; season with the pepper.
3. Bake in the preheated oven, stirring occasionally , until edges of onion are slightly charred and green beans start to look dry , about 40 mins. In the meantime , mix water , curry powder , and ginger together.
4. Remove dish and stir the vegetables; stir in curry mixture. Increase oven temperature to 450°F.
5. Lay cod over the bottom of the dish and coat with vegetables. Continue baking until fish is opaque, 25 to 30 mins depending on thickness.

NUTRITION: calories 64, fat 3.8g, sodium 5mg, carbs 7.7g, fiber 2.9g, protein 1.6g, potassium 180mg, phosphorus 101 mg

355. Calamari Salad

Cooking Time: 0 mins| Servings: 2

INGREDIENTS:

- 1 peeled and sliced cucumber
- lettuce leaves
- 3 ½ oz. washed, cleaned and sliced calamari fillets
- fresh parsley, chopped
- 1 peeled, boiled and sliced potato
- 1 tbsp sour cream
- 1 peeled, cored and sliced apple

DIRECTIONS:

1. Place the calamari into boiling salted water and cook for 5 min.
2. Arrange lettuce leaves on the bottom of a salad bowl. Mix the apple and vegetable strips with the calamari. Dress with sour cream, place on the lettuce leaves, and garnish with the parsley.

NUTRITION: calories 468, fat 8g, sodium 49mg, carbs 5.4g, fiber 1.3g, protein 17g, potassium 142mg, phosphorus 151 mg

356. Salmon and Veggie Soup

Cooking Time: 22 mins| Servings: 4

INGREDIENTS:

- 4 oz salmon, skinless and boneless, cubed
- 2 tbsps olive oil
- 1 leek, chopped
- 1 red onion, chopped
- 2 carrots, chopped
- 4 cups low stock vegetable stock
- ½ cup coconut cream
- 1 tbsp dill, chopped

DIRECTIONS:

1. Take a pan and place it over medium heat, add leek, onion, stir and cook for 7 mins
2. Add pepper, carrots, stock and stir
3. Boil for 10 mins
4. Add salmon, cream, dill and stir
5. Boil for 5-6 mins
6. Ladle into bowls and serve

NUTRITION: calories 200, fat 3g, sodium 37mg, carbs 51.4g, fiber 1.3g, protein 3.1g, potassium 142mg, phosphorus 151 mg

357. White Fish Soup

Cooking Time: 20 mins| Servings: 4

INGREDIENTS:

- 1 1/2 pounds cod, cut into 3/4-inch cubes
- 2 tbsps olive oil
- 1 onion, finely diced
- 1 green bell pepper, chopped
- 1 rib celery, thinly sliced
- 3 cups chicken broth, or more to taste
- 1/4 cup chopped fresh parsley
- 1 dash red pepper flakes

DIRECTIONS:

1. Heat oil in a soup pot over medium heat.
2. Add onion , bell pepper , and celery and cook until wilted , about 5 mins.
3. Add broth and bring to a simmer, about 5 mins.
4. Cook 15 to 20 mins.
5. Add cod, parsley, and red pepper flakes and simmer until fish flakes easily with a fork, 8 to 10 mins more.
6. Season with black pepper.

NUTRITION: calories 117, fat 7.2g, sodium 37mg, carbs 5.4g, fiber 1.3g, protein 8.1g, potassium 122mg, phosphorus 111 mg

358. Onion Dijon Crusted Catfish

Cooking Time: 25 mins | Servings: 4

INGREDIENTS:

- 4 (6 ounce) fillets catfish fillets
- 1 onion, finely chopped
- 1/4 cup honey Dijon mustard
- Dried parsley flakes

DIRECTIONS:

1. Preheat the oven to 350°F.
2. In a small bowl mix together the onion and mustard. Season the catfish fillets with pepper. Place on a baking tray and coat with the onion and honey. Sprinkle parsley flakes over the top.
3. Bake for 20 mins in the preheated oven, then turn the oven to broil. Broil until golden, 3 to 5 mins.

NUTRITION: calories 215, fat 6.1g, sodium 86mg, carbs 10.4g, fiber 0.6g, protein 31.6g, potassium 46mg, phosphorus 30 mg

359. Herb Baked Tuna

Cooking Time: 20 mins| Servings: 4

INGREDIENTS:

- 4 (6 ounce) tuna fillets
- 2 tbsps dried parsley
- 3/4 tsp paprika
- ½ tsp dried thyme
- ½ tsp dried oregano
- ½ tsp dried basil
- ½ tsp ground black pepper
- 2 tbsps lemon juice
- 1 tbsp olive oil
- 1/4 tsp garlic powder

DIRECTIONS:

1. Preheat oven to 350° F.
2. Arrange tuna fillets in a 9x13-inch baking dish. Combine parsley, paprika, thyme, oregano, basil, and black pepper in a small bowl; sprinkle herb mixture over fish. Mix lemon

juice, olive oil, and garlic powder in another bowl; drizzle olive oil mixture over fish.

3. Bake in preheated oven until fish is easily flaked with a fork, about 20 mins.

NUTRITION: calories 139, fat 12.5g, sodium 3mg, carbs 1g, fiber 0.5g, protein 6.2g, potassium 39mg, phosphorus 20 mg

360. Cilantro Lime Salmon

Cooking Time: 20 mins| Servings: 4

INGREDIENTS:

- 5 (5 ounce) fillets salmon
- ¼ cup olive oil
- ¼ cup chopped fresh cilantro
- ½ tsp chopped garlic
- ½ lemon, juiced
- ½ lime, juiced

DIRECTIONS:

1. Heat the olive oil in a skillet over medium heat.
2. Stir cilantro and garlic into the oil; cook about 1 minute.
3. Season salmon fillets with black pepper; lay gently into the oil mixture.
4. Place a cover on the skillet. Cook fillets 10 mins, turn, and continue cooking until the fish flakes easily with a fork and is lightly browned, about 10 mins more.
5. Squeeze lemon juice and lime juice over the fillets to serve.

NUTRITION: calories 249, fat 18g, sodium 48mg, carbs 1.7g, fiber 0.5g, protein 20.7g, potassium 26mg, phosphorus 20 mg

361. Tuna and Potato Salad

Cooking Time: 20 mins| Servings: 4

INGREDIENTS:

- 1 lb baby potatoes, scrubbed, boiled
- 1 cup tuna chunks, drained
- 1 cup cherry tomatoes, halved
- 1 cup medium onion, thinly sliced
- 8 pitted black olives
- 2 medium hard-boiled eggs, sliced
- 1 head romaine lettuce
- ¼ cup olive oil
- 2 tbsps lemon juice
- 1 tbsp Dijon mustard
- 1 tsp dill weed, chopped

DIRECTIONS:

1. Take a small glass bowl and mix in your olive oil, lemon juice, Dijon mustard and dill
2. Add in the tuna, baby potatoes, cherry tomatoes, red onion, green beans, black olives and toss everything nicely
3. Arrange your lettuce leaves on a beautiful serving dish to make the base of your salad
4. Top them up with your salad mixture and place the egg slices
5. Drizzle it with the previously prepared dressing
6. Serve hot

NUTRITION: calories 142, fat 2.5g, sodium 3mg, carbs 16g, fiber 0.5g, protein 20g, potassium 79mg, phosphorus 45 mg

362. Oven-Fried Catfish

Cooking Time: 35 mins| Servings: 4

INGREDIENTS:

- 1 egg white
- ½ cup of whole wheat flour
- ¼ cup of cornmeal
- ¼ cup of panko bread crumbs
- 1 tsp of salt-free Cajun seasoning
- 1 pound of catfish fillets

DIRECTIONS:

1. Heat oven to 450°F.
2. Use cooking spray to spray a non-stick baking sheet.

3. Using a bowl, beat the egg white until very soft peaks are formed. Don't over-beat.
4. Use a sheet of wax paper and place the flour over it.
5. Use a different sheet of wax paper to combine and mix the cornmeal, panko, and the Cajun seasoning.
6. Cut the catfish fillet into four pieces, then dip the fish in the flour, shaking off the excess.
7. Dip coated fish in the egg white, rolling into the cornmeal mixture.
8. Place the fish on the baking pan. Repeat with the remaining fish fillets.
9. Use cooking spray to spray over the fish fillets. Bake for about 10 to 12 mins or until the sides of the fillets become browned and crisp.

NUTRITION: calories 249, fat 18g, sodium 48mg, carbs 19g, fiber 1.5g, protein 22.7g, potassium 401mg, phosphorus 262 mg

363. Asian Ginger tuna

Cooking Time: 20 mins| Servings: 4

INGREDIENTS:

- 1 1/4 pounds thin tuna fillets
- 1 cup water
- 1 tbsp minced fresh ginger root
- 1 tbsp minced garlic
- 2 tbsps soy sauce
- 6 large white mushrooms, sliced
- 1/4 cup sliced green onion
- 1 tbsp chopped fresh cilantro (optional)

DIRECTIONS:

1. Put water, ginger, and garlic in a wide pot with a lid.
2. Bring the water to a boil, reduce heat to medium-low, and simmer 3 to 5 mins.
3. Stir soy sauce into the water mixture; add tuna fillets.
4. Place cover on the pot, bring water to a boil, and let cook for 3 mins more.
5. Add mushrooms, cover, and cook until the fish loses pinkness and begins to flake, about 3 mins more.
6. Sprinkle green onion over the fillets, cover, and cook for 30 seconds.
7. Garnish with cilantro to serve.

NUTRITION: calories 109, fat 7.9g, sodium 454mg, carbs 3.1g, fiber 0.6g, protein 7g, potassium 158mg, phosphorus 120 mg

364. Cheesy Tuna Chowder

Cooking Time: 20 mins| Servings: 4

INGREDIENTS:

- 1 1/2 pounds tuna fillets, cut into 1-inch pieces
- 1 1/2 cups shredded Cheddar cheese
- 2 tbsps olive oil
- 1/2 small onion, chopped
- 1 cup water
- 1/2 cup chopped celery
- 1 cup sliced baby carrots
- 3 cups soy milk, divided
- 1/3 cup whole wheat flour
- 1/2 tsp ground black pepper

DIRECTIONS:

1. In a Dutch oven over medium heat, heat olive oil and sauté the onion until tender. Pour in water. Mix in celery, carrots, cook 10 mins, stirring occasionally, until vegetables are tender.
2. In a small bowl, whisk together 1 1/2 cups milk and whole wheat flour. Mix into the Dutch oven.
3. Mix remaining milk, and pepper into the Dutch oven. Stirring occasionally, continue cooking the mixture about 10 mins, until thickened.
4. Stir tuna into the mixture, and cook 5 mins, or until fish is easily flaked with

a fork. Mix in Cheddar cheese, and cook another 5 mins, until melted.

NUTRITION: calories 228, fat 15.5g, sodium 206mg, carbs 11g, fiber 1g, protein 11.6g, potassium 163mg, phosphorus 150 mg

365. Fish with Mushrooms

Cooking Time: 16 mins| Servings: 4

INGREDIENTS:

- 1-pound cod fillet
- 2 tbsps butter
- ¼ cup white onion, chopped
- 1 cup fresh mushrooms
- 1 tsp dried thyme

DIRECTIONS:

1. Put the fish in a baking pan.
2. Preheat your oven to 450° F.
3. Melt the butter and cook onion and mushroom for 1 minute.
4. Spread mushroom mixture on top of the fish.
5. Season with thyme.
6. Bake in the oven for 15 mins.

NUTRITION: calories 156, protein 21g, carbs 3 g, fat 7 g, sodium 110 mg, potassium 561 mg, phosphorus 225 mg, fiber 0.5 g

366. Salmon with Spicy Honey

Cooking time: 8 mins| Servings: 2

INGREDIENTS:

- 16-ounce salmon fillet
- 3 tbsp honey
- 3/4 tsp lemon peel
- 3 bowls arugula salad
- 1/2 tsp black pepper
- 1/2 tsp garlic powder
- 2 tsp olive oil
- 1 tsp hot water

DIRECTIONS:

1. Prepare a small bowl with some hot water and put in honey, grated lemon peel, ground pepper, and garlic powder.
2. Spread the mixture over salmon fillets.
3. Warm some olive oil at a medium heat and add spiced salmon fillet and cook for 4 mins.
4. Turn the fillets on one side then on the other side.
5. Continue to cook for other 4 mins at a reduced heat and try to check when the salmon fillets flake easily.
6. Put some arugula on each plate and add the salmon fillets on top, adding some aromatic herbs or some dill. Serve!

NUTRITION: calories 320, protein 23 g, sodium 65 mg, potassium 450 mg, phosphorus 250 mg

367. Salmon with Maple Glaze

Cooking Time: 2 hours| Servings: 4

INGREDIENTS:

- 1-pound salmon fillets
- 1 tbsp green onion, chopped
- 1 tbsp low Sodium soy sauce
- 2 garlic cloves, pressed
- 2 tbsp fresh cilantro
- 3 tbsp lemon juice (or juice of 1 lemon)
- 3 tbsp maple syrup

DIRECTIONS:

1. Combine all ingredients except for salmon.
2. Put salmon on platter and then pour marinade over fillets. Let it marinate 2 hours or more.
3. Preheat broiler.
4. Remove salmon from marinade.
5. Place salmon on bottom rack and broil for 10 mins. Do not turn over.

6. Serve hot/cold with a wedge of lemon.

NUTRITION: calories 220, carbs 12g, protein 24g, fat 8g, phosphorus 374mg, potassium 440mg, sodium 621mg

368. Dijon Mustard and Marinated Shrimp

Cooking Time: 80 mins| Servings: 8

INGREDIENTS:

- 1-pound uncooked shrimp, peeled and deveined
- 1 bay leaf
- 3 whole cloves
- ½ cup rice vinegar
- 1 cup water
- ½ tsp hot sauce
- 2 tbsps. capers
- 2 tbsps. Dijon mustard
- ½ cup fresh lime juice, plus lime zest as garnish
- 1 medium red onion, chopped

DIRECTIONS:

1. Mix hot sauce, mustard, capers, lime juice and onion in a shallow baking dish and set aside.
2. Bring it to a boil in a large saucepan bay leaf, cloves, vinegar and water.
3. Once boiling, add shrimps and cook for a minute while stirring continuously.
4. Drain shrimps and pour shrimps into onion mixture.
5. For an hour, refrigerate while covered the shrimps.
6. Then serve shrimps cold and garnished with lime zest.

NUTRITION: calories 123, carbs 3g, protein 12g, fat: 1g, phosphorus 119mg, potassium 87mg, sodium 568mg

369. Fish and Veggie Stew

Cooking Time: 10 mins| Servings: 4

INGREDIENTS:

- 2 lbs fish
- 1 diced large onion
- 2 small tomatoes
- 3 stalks scallion
- 1 cup Vegetables
- ¾ cup fish stock
- 2 slices hot pepper
- ¼ cup oil

DIRECTIONS:

1. Scale, clean and prepare fish for frying
2. Allow oil to cool, strain nearly all of it from frying pan, put aside Sauté seasonings and vegetables in frying pan
3. Add water or stock to frying pan with sautéed vegetables and simmer until all flavors blend
4. Add fish, cover and cook for five mins.

NUTRITION: calories 352, carbs 15g, protein 36g, fat 3g, phosphorus 182mg, potassium 407mg, sodium 82mg

370. Baked Cod Crusted with Herbs

Cooking Time: 10 mins| Servings: 4

INGREDIENTS:

- 4 pieces of 4-ounce cod fillets
- ¼ cup honey
- ½ cup panko
- ½ tsp pepper
- 1 tbsp olive oil
- 1 tbsp lemon juice
- 1 tsp dried basil
- 1 tsp dried parsley
- 1 tsp rosemary

DIRECTIONS:

1. With olive oil, grease a 9 x 13-inch baking pan and preheat oven to 375°F.
2. In a zip top bag mix panko, rosemary, pepper, parsley and basil.

3. Evenly spread cod fillets in prepped dish and drizzle with lemon juice.
4. Then brush the fillets with honey on all sides. Discard remaining honey if any.
5. Then evenly divide the panko mixture on top of cod fillets.
6. Pop in the oven and bake for ten mins or until fish is cooked.
7. Serve and enjoy.

NUTRITION: calories 113, carbs 21g, protein 5g, fat 2g, phosphorus 89mg, potassium 115mg, sodium 139mg

371. Salmon Meal

Cooking Time: 20 mins| Servings: 6

INGREDIENTS:

- 4 (6-ounce) (1-inch thick) skinless salmon fillets
- Freshly ground black pepper, to taste
- 2 cups of finely chopped zucchini, chopped finely
- 1 cup of halved cherry tomatoes
- 1 tbsp. of olive oil
- 1 tbsp. of fresh lemon juice

DIRECTIONS:

1. Preheat the oven to 425°F. Grease an 11x7-inch baking sheet.
2. Place the salmon fillets in the prepared baking sheet in a single layer and sprinkle with black pepper generously.
3. In a bowl, mix the remaining ingredients.
4. Place the mixture over salmon fillets evenly.
5. Bake for about 22 mins.
6. Remove from the oven and keep aside to cool slightly.
7. Cut the salmon into small chunks and mix with the veggie mixture.

NUTRITION: calories 233, carbs 2.1g, protein 22.5g, fat 14g, phosphorus 89mg, potassium 175mg, sodium 71mg

372. Tangy Orange Shrimp

Cooking Time: 15 mins| Servings: 4

INGREDIENTS:

- 12 oz (26/30 count) of shrimp, peeled and deveined, tails left on
- 1 cup of broccoli florets
- ½ cup of freshly squeezed orange juice
- ½ tsp of cornstarch
- ¼ tsp of freshly grated orange zest
- 1 tsp of olive oil
- 1 tsp of unsalted butter
- ½ cup of orange segments
- ground black pepper

DIRECTIONS:

1. In a small bowl, whisk together the orange juice, cornstarch, and orange zest and set aside.
2. In a large skillet over medium-high heat, heat the olive oil.
3. Add the shrimp and sauté until just cooked through and opaque, about 5 mins. Transfer the cooked shrimp to a plate. Add the broccoli and sauté until tender, about 4 mins. Transfer to the plate with the shrimp.
4. Pour the orange juice mixture into the skillet, and whisk until the sauce has thickened and is glossy about 3 mins.
5. Whisk in the butter, and add the orange segments, shrimp, and broccoli to the skillet.
6. Toss to combine and season with pepper. Serve immediately.

NUTRITION: calories 140, fat 3g, sodium 132mg, carbs 8g, fiber 1g, phosphorus 196mg potassium 329mg, protein 18g

373. Shrimp Italian Pasta

Cooking Time: 15 mins| Servings: 6

INGREDIENTS:

- 1¼ cup sliced asparagus
- 12 oz whole wheat penne
- 1 cup green peas
- 2 tsp olive oil
- 1 tbsp minced garlic
- 1/8 tsp crushed red pepper
- 1 lb. shrimp
- ½ cup sliced green onion
- 2 tsp lemon juice
- 1 tbsp chopped parsley
- 1/3 cup grated parmesan cheese

DIRECTIONS:

1. Set a large saucepan over high heat, and allow to come to a boil.
2. Once boiling, add asparagus then cook until fork tender (about 4 mins) Carefully remove the asparagus from the hot water using a slotted spoon then add your pasta to the same pot.
3. Cook until done based on the instructions on the package. When the pasta was 2 mins out add peas
4. When fully cooked, drain, and add to a large bowl with the asparagus
5. Set a skillet with olive oil over medium heat, then add red pepper, and garlic, then cook, while stirring for about a minute
6. Add shrimp and cook until it becomes opaque (about 4 mins), stirring
7. Add your remaining ingredients to the skillet on top of shrimp and toss to coat.

NUTRITION: calories 440, fat 18g, sodium 96mg, carbs 2g, fiber 1g, phosphorus 199mg, potassium 215mg, protein 31g

374. Salmon and Cauliflower

Cooking Time: 20 mins| Servings: 4

INGREDIENTS:

- 4 boneless salmon fillets
- 2 tbsp coconut aminos
- 1 sliced big red onion
- ¼ cup coconut sugar
- 1 head separated cauliflower florets
- 2 tbsp olive oil

DIRECTIONS:

1. In a smaller bowl, mix sugar with coconut aminos and whisk.
2. Heat up a pan with half the oil over medium-high heat, add cauliflower and onion, stir and cook for 10 mins.
3. Put the salmon inside baking dish, drizzle the remainder inside oil, add coconut aminos, toss somewhat, season with black pepper, introduce within the oven and bake at 400°F for 10 mins.
4. Divide the salmon along using the cauliflower mix between plates and serve.

NUTRITION: calories 227, fat 3g, sodium 96mg, carbs 12g, fiber 1g, phosphorus 151mg, potassium 242g, protein 9g

375. Shrimp and Greens

Cooking Time: 15 mins| Servings: 4

INGREDIENTS:

- 12 oz (26/30 count) of shrimp, peeled, deveined, tails removed
- 1 tbsp of olive oil
- 2 tsps of minced garlic
- 2 cups of fresh spinach
- ½ cup of halved cherry tomatoes
- ½ tsp of ground nutmeg

DIRECTIONS:

1. In a large skillet over medium-high heat, heat the olive oil.
2. Add the shrimp and sauté until opaque and pink, about 6 mins.
3. With a slotted spoon, remove the shrimp to a plate.
4. In the skillet, sauté the garlic until softened, about 3 mins.

5. Stir in the spinach and tomatoes, and sauté until the spinach has wilted and the tomatoes are cooked, about 5 mins.
6. Stir in the shrimp, sprinkle in the nutmeg, and toss to combine.
7. Season with pepper, and serve.

NUTRITION: calories 127, fat 8g, sodium 96mg, carbs 2g, fiber 1g, phosphorus 178mg, potassium 287mg, protein 18g

376. Seared Herbed Scallops

Cooking Time: 5 mins| Servings: 4

INGREDIENTS:

- 12 oz of sea scallops, rinsed and patted dry
- 1 tbsp of olive oil
- Freshly ground black pepper
- 2 tbsps of freshly squeezed lemon juice
- 1 tsp of chopped fresh parsley
- 1 tsp of chopped fresh thyme
- 1 tsp of chopped fresh chives

DIRECTIONS:

1. In a large skillet over medium-high heat, heat the olive oil.
2. Lightly season the scallops with pepper. Add them to the skillet.
3. Sear the scallops, turning once, until just cooked through and browned, about 4 mins total.
4. Stir in the lemon juice, parsley, thyme, and chives.
5. Turn the scallops to coat in the herb sauce.
6. Serve hot.

NUTRITION: calories 131, fat 5g, sodium 136mg, carbs 2g, fiber 0g, phosphorus 176mg, potassium 268mg, protein 14g

377. Almond-Crusted Sole

Cooking Time: 15 mins| Servings: 4

INGREDIENTS:

- 4 (3-ounce) sole fillets, patted dry
- Freshly ground black pepper
- 3 tbsps of almond flour
- 1 tbsp of chopped fresh parsley
- 1 tsp of chopped fresh thyme
- 1 tsp of olive oil

DIRECTIONS:

1. Preheat the oven to 350°F.
2. Line a baking sheet with parchment paper.
3. Lightly season the sole fillets with pepper.
4. In a shallow bowl, mix together the almond flour, parsley, and thyme until blended.
5. Lightly brush the fish with the olive oil, and dredge in the almond flour mixture.
6. Place the sole fillets on the prepared baking sheet, and bake until the fish is opaque, about 15 mins.
7. Serve immediately.

NUTRITION: calories 113, fat 3g, sodium 70mg, carbs 1g, fiber 0g, phosphorus 168mg, potassium 327mg, protein 17g

378. Breaded Baked Sole

Cooking Time: 10 mins| Servings: 4

INGREDIENTS:

- 4 (2-ounce) sole fillets, skinless, patted dry
- ¼ cup of bread crumbs
- 1 tbsp of unsalted butter, at room temperature
- 2 tsps of chopped fresh parsley
- 2 tsps of chopped fresh thyme
- 2 tsps of freshly grated lemon zest
- Freshly ground black pepper

DIRECTIONS:

1. Preheat the oven to 400°F.

2. In a small bowl, stir together the bread crumbs, butter, parsley, thyme, and lemon zest.
3. Lightly season the fish fillets with pepper, and place them on a baking sheet.
4. Divide the bread crumb mixture evenly among the fillets, pressing it down lightly to adhere.
5. Bake until the fish is just cooked through and the bread crumbs are golden, about 10 mins.

NUTRITION: calories 103, fat 3g, sodium 96mg, carbs 5g, fiber 0g, phosphorus 116mg, potassium 200mg, protein 8g

379. Roasted Tilapia with Garlic Butter

Cooking Time: 10 mins| Servings: 4

INGREDIENTS:

- 4 (3-ounce) tilapia fillets, patted dry
- ¼ cup of melted unsalted butter
- 1 shallot, minced
- 1 tsp of minced garlic
- Juice and zest of ½ lemon
- 2 tbsps of chopped fresh parsley
- 1 tbsp of whole wheat flour
- 1 tbsp of olive oil
- ground black pepper

DIRECTIONS:

1. Preheat the oven to 400°F.
2. In a small bowl, stir together the butter, shallot, garlic, lemon juice, lemon zest, parsley, and flour and set aside.
3. In a large ovenproof skillet over medium-high heat, heat the oil. Season the fillets with pepper and set them in the skillet. Brown the fish, turning once, about 4 mins total.
4. Pour the butter mixture over the fish, and place the skillet, uncovered, in the oven. Roast the fish until just cooked through and opaque in the center, about 4 mins.
5. Serve immediately with a spoonful of sauce from the skillet.
6. Substitution tip: Onion or scallion can be substituted for the shallot in the sauce. Shallot has a lighter, sweeter flavor.

NUTRITION: calories 219, fat 16g, sodium 45mg, carbs 2g, fiber 0g, phosphorus 149mg, potassium 252mg, protein 17g

380. Pesto-Crusted Tilapia

Cooking Time: 15 mins| Servings: 4

INGREDIENTS:

- 4 (3-ounce) tilapia fillets, patted dry
- olive oil, for the baking sheet
- ½ cup of bread crumbs
- 1 tbsp of grated parmesan cheese
- 1 tbsp of basil pesto (here)

DIRECTIONS:

1. Preheat the oven to 400°F.
2. Lightly coat a 9-by-9-inch baking sheet with olive oil, and set it aside.
3. In a small bowl, add the bread crumbs, Parmesan cheese, and pesto and stir until blended.
4. Place the fish in the baking sheet, and spoon the pesto mixture over the fish, so each piece is evenly coated.
5. Bake until just cooked through, about 15 mins.
6. Serve hot.
7. Cooking tip: If you have a barbecue, this recipe is perfect for cooking outdoors on a balmy summer evening. Turn one side of your barbecue on high and leave the other side off. Place the fish in a foil package instead of a baking sheet, on the cool side of the barbecue, for about 25 mins.

NUTRITION: calories 159, fat 5g, sodium 162mg, carbs 10g, fiber 1g, phosphorus 164mg, potassium 272mg, protein 19g

381. Lime Baked Haddock

Cooking Time: 10 mins| Servings: 4

INGREDIENTS:

- 4 (3-ounce) haddock fillets, patted dry
- freshly ground black pepper
- olive oil cooking spray
- 3 limes, thinly sliced
- 1 tbsp of olive oil
- 3 tbsps of crushed almonds
- 2 tsps of chopped fresh dill

DIRECTIONS:

1. Preheat the oven to 400°F.
2. Lightly season the fish with pepper.
3. Lightly coat a 9-by-9-inch baking sheet with cooking spray.
4. Lay the lime slices in the bottom of the baking sheet and arrange the fish fillets on top.
5. Brush the fish with the olive oil and sprinkle them with the almonds.
6. Bake the fish until just cooked through, and the almonds are golden, about 10 mins.
7. Serve with the chopped dill.

NUTRITION: calories 124, fat 6g, sodium 59mg, carbs 1g, fiber 0g, phosphorus 176mg, potassium 283mg, protein 17g

382. Fish Tacos with Vegetable Slaw

Cooking Time: 0 minute| Servings: 4

INGREDIENTS:

For the slaw:

- 2 cups of finely shredded red cabbage
- 1 carrot, shredded
- 3 radishes, grated
- 2 tbsps of apple cider vinegar
- Juice of 1 lime
- 1 tsp of honey
- 1 tsp of chopped fresh cilantro

For the tacos:

- 4 (6-inch) flour tortillas
- 8 oz of halibut fillet, cooked

DIRECTIONS:

1. To make the slaw:
2. In a medium bowl, toss together the cabbage, carrot, radishes, vinegar, lime juice, honey, and cilantro until well mixed.
3. Place the bowl in the refrigerator for 1 hour to let the flavors mellow.
4. To make the tacos:
5. Place the tortillas on a clean work surface. Divide the fish evenly among them, then top with the slaw.
6. Fold the tortillas over the fish and serve.

NUTRITION: calories 131, fat 3g, sodium 57mg, carbs 13g, fiber 2g, phosphorus 144mg, potassium 307mg, protein 12g

383. Dill Relish on White Sea Bass

Cooking Time: 60 mins| Servings: 4

INGREDIENTS:

- 4 pieces of 4-ounce white sea bass fillets
- 1 tsp lemon juice
- 1 tsp Dijon mustard
- 1 lemon, quartered
- 1 ½ tsps. chopped fresh dill
- 1 tsp pickled baby capers, drained
- 1 ½ tbsps. chopped white onion

DIRECTIONS:

1. Preheat oven to 375°F.
2. Mix lemon juice, mustard, dill, capers and onions in a small bowl.
3. Prepare four aluminum foil squares and place 1 fillet per foil.

4. Squeeze a lemon wedge per fish.
5. Evenly divide into 4 the dill spread and drizzle over fillet.
6. Close the foil over the fish securely and pop in the oven.
7. Bake for 9 to 12 mins or until fish is cooked through.
8. Remove from foil and transfer to a serving platter, serve and enjoy.

NUTRITION: calories 71, carbs 11g, protein 7g, fat 1g, phosphorus 91mg, potassium 237mg, sodium 94mg

384. Tilapia with Lemon Garlic Sauce

Cooking Time: 30 mins| Servings: 4

INGREDIENTS:

- 4 tilapia fillets
- 1 tsp dried parsley flakes
- 1 clove garlic (finely chopped)
- 1 tbsp butter (melted)
- 3 tbsps. fresh lemon juice

DIRECTIONS:

1. First, spray baking dish with non-stick cooking spray then preheat oven at 375°.
2. In cool water, rinse tilapia fillets and using paper towels pat dry the fillets.
3. Place tilapia fillets in the baking dish then pour butter and lemon juice and top off with pepper, parsley and garlic.
4. Bake tilapia in the preheated oven for 30 mins and wait until fish is white.

NUTRITION: calories 168, carbs 4g, protein 24g, fat 5g, phosphorus 207mg, potassium 431mg, sodium 85mg

385. Spinach with White Beans and Shrimps

Cooking Time: 15 mins| Servings: 4

INGREDIENTS:

- 1-pound large shrimp (peeled and deveined)
- 1 ½ oz crumbled reduce-fat feta cheese
- 5 cups baby spinach
- 15 oz can no salt added cannellini beans (rinsed and drained)
- ½ cup low Sodium, fat-free chicken broth
- 2 tbsps. balsamic vinegar
- 2 tsps. chopped fresh sage
- 4 cloves garlic (minced)
- 1 medium onion (chopped)
- 2 tbsps. olive oil

DIRECTIONS:

1. Heat 1 tsp oil. Heat it over medium-high.
2. Then for about 2 to 3 mins, cook the shrimps using the heated skillet then place them on a plate. Heat on the same skillet the sage, garlic, and onions then cook for about 4 mins. Add and stir in vinegar for 30 seconds.
3. For about 2 mins, add chicken broth. Then, add spinach and beans and cook for an additional 2 to 3 mins.
4. Remove skillet then add and stir in cooked shrimps topped with feta cheese.
5. Serve and divide into 4 bowls. Enjoy!

NUTRITION: calories 343, carbs 21g, protein 22g, fat 11g, phosphorus 400mg, potassium 599mg, sodium 766mg

386. Bagel with Salmon and Egg

Cooking Time: 10 mins| Servings: 1

INGREDIENTS:

- ½ bagel
- 1 tbsp cream cheese
- 1 tbsp scallions
- ½ tsp fresh dill
- 2 fresh basil leaves
- 1 slice tomato
- arugula

- 1 large egg
- 1 ounce cooked salmon

DIRECTIONS:

1. Start by slicing the bagel through the center horizontally. Take one half of the bagel and toast it in an oven or a toaster.
2. Finely chop the dill, basil leaves, and scallions. Set aside.
3. Add in the cream cheese. Toss in the chopped dill, basil, and scallions. Mix well to combine. Take the toasted bagel and spread the herbs and cream cheese mixture evenly over it.
4. Place the tomato slice and arugula on top. Set aside.
5. Take a small mixing bowl and then beat the egg.
6. Take a non-stick saucepan and grease it using cooking spray. Stir after pouring the beaten egg into the pan and. Cook for about 1 minute over medium heat. Keep stirring to make a perfect scrambled egg.
7. Take the cooked salmon and place it in the same pan as the egg. This will help you heat the salmon and cook the egg at the same time.
8. Place the scrambled egg over the tomato slice and top it with the salmon.

NUTRITION: protein 19g, fat 14g, carbs 29g, calories 218, potassium 338mg, sodium 378mg, phosphorus 270 mg, fiber 2.6 g

387. Salmon Stuffed Pasta

Cooking time: 35 mins| Servings: 24

INGREDIENTS:

- 24 jumbo pasta shells, boiled
- 1 cup coffee creamer
- *Filling:*
- 2 eggs, beaten
- 2 cups creamed cottage cheese
- ¼ cup chopped onion
- 1 red bell pepper, diced
- 2 tsps dried parsley
- ½ tsp lemon peel
- 1 can salmon, drained
- *Dill Sauce:*
- 1 ½ tsp butter
- 1 ½ tsp whole wheat flour
- 1/8 tsp pepper
- 1 tbsp lemon juice
- 1 ½ cup coffee creamer
- 2 tsps dried dill weed

DIRECTIONS:

1. Beat the cream cheese with the egg and all the other filling ingredients in a bowl.
2. Divide the filling in the pasta shells and place the shells in a 9x13 baking dish.
3. Pour the coffee creamer around the stuffed shells then cover with a foil.
4. Bake the shells for 30 mins at 350° F.
5. Meanwhile, whisk all the ingredients for dill sauce in a saucepan.
6. Stir for 5 mins until it thickens.
7. Pour this sauce over the baked pasta shells.
8. Serve warm.

NUTRITION: calories 268, fat 4.8g, sodium 86mg, protein 11.5g, calcium 27mg, phosphorus 314mg, potassium 181mg

388. Cod and Green Bean risotto

Cooking time: 25 mins| Servings: 4

INGREDIENTS:

- 4 oz. cod fillet
- 1 finely diced white onion
- 1 cup white rice
- 2 lemon wedges
- 1 cup boiling water
- ¼ tsp black pepper
- 1 cup low Sodium chicken broth
- 1 tbsp olive oil
- ½ cup green beans

DIRECTIONS:

1. Heat the oil in a large pan on medium heat.
2. Sauté the chopped onion for 5 mins until soft before adding in the rice and stirring for 1-2 mins.
3. Combine the broth with boiling water.
4. Add half of the liquid to the pan and stir slowly.
5. Slowly add the rest of the liquid whilst continuously stirring for up to 20-30 mins.
6. Stir in the green beans to the risotto.
7. Place the fish on top of the rice, cover, and steam for 10 mins.
8. Ensure the water does not dry out and keep topping up until the rice is cooked thoroughly.
9. Use your fork to break up the fish fillets and stir into the rice.
10. Sprinkle with freshly ground pepper and a squeeze of fresh lemon to serve
11. Garnish with the lemon wedges and serve.

NUTRITION: calories 221, carbs 29g, fat 8.5g, sodium 398mg, phosphorus 241mg, potassium 347mg

389. Citrus Glazed Salmon

Cooking time: 17 mins| Servings: 4

INGREDIENTS:

- 24 oz. salmon filet
- 2 garlic cloves, crushed
- 1 1/2 tbsps lemon juice
- 2 tbsps olive oil
- 1 tbsp butter
- 1 tbsp Dijon mustard
- 2 dashes cayenne pepper
- 1 tsp dried basil leaves
- 1 tsp dried dill

DIRECTIONS:

1. Place a 1-quart saucepan over moderate heat and add the oil, butter, garlic, lemon juice, mustard, cayenne pepper, dill, and basil to the pan.
2. Stir this mixture for 5 mins after it has boiled.
3. Prepare and preheat a charcoal grill over moderate heat.
4. Place the fish on a foil sheet and fold the edges to make a foil tray.
5. Pour the prepared sauce over the fish.
6. Place the fish in the foil in the preheated grill and cook for 12 mins.
7. Slice and serve.

NUTRITION: calories 401, fat 20.5g, sodium 256mg, carbs 0.5g, calcium 549mg, phosphorus 214mg, potassium 446mg

390. Broiled Salmon Fillets

Cooking time: 13 mins| Servings: 4

INGREDIENTS:

- 4 salmon fillets, skinless
- 1 tbsp ginger root, grated
- 1 clove garlic, minced
- ¼ cup maple syrup
- 1 tbsp hot pepper sauce

DIRECTIONS:

1. Grease a pan with cooking spray and place it over moderate heat.
2. Add the ginger and garlic and sauté for 3 mins then transfer to a bowl.
3. Add the hot pepper sauce and maple syrup to the ginger-garlic.
4. Mix well and keep this mixture aside.
5. Place the salmon fillet in a suitable baking tray, greased with cooking oil.
6. Brush the maple sauce over the fillets liberally
7. Broil them for 10 mins at the oven at broiler settings.
8. Serve warm.

NUTRITION: calories 289, fat 11.1g, sodium 80mg, carbs 13.6g, phosphorus 230 mg, potassium 331mg

391. Grilled Lemony Cod

Cooking time: 10 mins| Servings: 4

INGREDIENTS:

- 1 lb. cod fillets
- 1 tsp salt-free lemon pepper seasoning
- 1/4 cup lemon juice

DIRECTIONS:

1. Rub the cod fillets with lemon pepper seasoning and lemon juice.
2. Grease a baking tray with cooking spray and place the salmon in the baking tray.
3. Bake the fish for 10 mins at 350°F in a preheated oven.
4. Serve warm.

NUTRITION: calories 155, fat 7.1g, sodium 53mg, protein 22.2g, phosphorus 237mg, potassium 461mg

392. Marinated Salmon Steak

Cooking Time: 10 mins| Servings: 4

INGREDIENTS:

- 4 (4 ounce) salmon steaks ¼ cup lime juice
- ¼ cup soy sauce
- 2 tbsps olive oil
- 1 tbsp lemon juice
- 2 tbsps chopped fresh parsley
- 1 clove garlic, minced
- ½ tsp chopped fresh oregano
- ½ tsp ground black pepper

DIRECTIONS:

1. In a large non-reactive dish, mix together the lime juice, soy sauce, olive oil, lemon juice, parsley, garlic, oregano, and pepper. Place the salmon steaks in the marinade and turn to coat. Cover, and refrigerate for at least 30 mins.
2. Preheat grill for high heat.
3. Lightly oil grill grate. Cook the salmon steaks for 5 to 6 mins, then salmon and baste with the marinade. Cook for an additional 5 mins, or to desired doneness. Discard any remaining marinade.

NUTRITION: calories 108, fat 8.4g, sodium 910mg, carbs 3.6g, fiber 0.4g, protein 5.4g, potassium 172mg, phosphorus 165 mg

393. Tuna with honey Glaze

Cooking Time: 10 mins| Servings: 4

INGREDIENTS:

- 1/4 cup honey
- 2 tbsps Dijon mustard
- 4 (6 ounce) boneless tuna fillets
- Ground black pepper to taste

DIRECTIONS:

1. Preheat the oven's broiler and set the oven rack at about 6 inches from the heat source; prepare the rack of a broiler pan with cooking spray.
2. Season the tuna with pepper and arrange onto the prepared broiler pan. Whisk together the honey and Dijon mustard in a small bowl; spoon mixture evenly onto top of salmon fillets.
3. Cook under the preheated broiler until the fish flakes easily with a fork, 10 to 15 mins.

NUTRITION: calories 160, fat 8.1g, sodium 90mg, carbs 17.9g, fiber 0.3g, protein 5.7g, potassium 22mg, phosphorus 16 mg

394. Stuffed Mushrooms

Cooking Time: 10 mins| Servings: 4

INGREDIENTS:

- 12 large fresh mushrooms, stems removed

- ½ pound crabmeat, flaked
- 2 cups olive oil
- 2 cloves garlic, peeled and minced
- garlic powder to taste
- crushed red pepper to taste

DIRECTIONS:

1. Arrange mushroom caps on a medium baking sheet, bottoms up. Chop and reserve mushroom stems.
2. Preheat oven to 350° F.
3. In a medium saucepan over medium heat, heat oil. Mix in garlic and cook until tender, about 5 mins.
4. In a medium bowl, mix together reserved mushroom stems, and crab meat. Liberally stuff mushrooms with the mixture. Drizzle with the garlic. Season with garlic powder and crushed red pepper.
5. Bake uncovered in the preheated oven 10 to 12 mins, or until stuffing is lightly browned.

NUTRITION: calories 312, fat 33.8g, carbs 3.8g, fiber 0.3g, protein 2.2g, potassium 93mg, phosphorus 86 mg

395. Crispy Fish Fillets

Cooking Time: 10 mins| Servings: 4

INGREDIENTS:

- 1 egg
- 4 (6 ounce) fish fillets
- 2 tbsps prepared yellow mustard
- 1/4 cup oil for frying
- ½ cup graham crakes

DIRECTIONS:

1. In a shallow dish, whisk together the egg, mustard, set aside. Place the graham crakes in another shallow dish.
2. Heat oil in a large heavy skillet over medium-high heat.
3. Dip fish fillets in the egg mixture. Dredge the fillets in the graham crakes, making sure to completely coat the fish. For extra crispy, dip into egg and graham crakes again.
4. Fry fish fillets in oil for 3 to 4 mins on each side, or until golden brown.

NUTRITION: calories 194, fat 17.8g, sodium 225mg, carbs 4.4g, fiber 0.4g, protein 5g, potassium 98mg, phosphorus 76 mg

396. Simple Soup

Cooking Time: 15 mins| Servings: 4

INGREDIENTS:

- 2 tsps tuna
- 4 cups water
- 1 (8 ounce) package silken tofu, diced
- 2 green onions, sliced diagonally into 1/2-inch pieces

DIRECTIONS:

1. In a medium saucepan over medium-high heat, combine tuna and water; bring to a boil.
2. Reduce heat to medium, Stir in tofu.
3. Separate the layers of the green onions and add them to the soup.
4. Simmer gently for 2 to 3 mins before serving.

NUTRITION: calories 77, fat 3.3g, carbs 1.9g, fiber 0.3g, protein 9.7g, potassium 104mg, phosphorus 88mg

397. Lime-Marinated Salmon

Cooking Time: 15 mins| Servings: 4

INGREDIENTS:

- 2 (4 ounce) salmon fillets
- ¼ cup olive oil
- 1 clove garlic, minced
- 1/8 tsp ground black pepper
- 1/2 tsp cayenne pepper
- 2 tbsps lime juice

- 1/8 tsp grated lime zest

DIRECTIONS:

1. Preheat an outdoor grill for medium heat, and lightly oil the grate.

- Whisk the olive oil, minced garlic, black pepper, cayenne pepper, lime juice, and grated lime zest together in a bowl to make the marinade.

2. Place the salmon fillets in the marinade and turn to coat; allow to marinate at least 15 mins.
3. Cook on the preheated grill until the fish flakes easily with a fork and is lightly browned, 3 to 4 mins per side.
4. Garnish with the twists of lime zest to serve.

NUTRITION: calories 126, fat 9.7g, sodium 20mg, carbs 2.7g, fiber 0.3g, protein 8.5g, potassium 206mg, phosphorus 108mg

398. Tuna with Pineapple

Cooking Time: 15 mins| Servings: 4

INGREDIENTS:

- 3 (4 ounce) fillets tuna
- 2 tbsps olive oil
- 1 tbsp minced fresh garlic
- 1 tbsp chopped onion
- 1/2 red bell pepper, diced
- 1 cup pineapple - peeled, seeded and cubed
- 1 tsp corn-starch
- 1 tbsp water
- 2 tbsps lime juice
- 1 tbsp lime juice
- 1 tbsp melted butter

DIRECTIONS:

1. Preheat the oven's broiler and set the oven rack about 6 inches from the heat source.
2. Heat olive oil in a saucepan over medium heat. Stir in the garlic and onion; cook and stir until the onion begins to soften, about 2 mins. Add the red bell pepper and pineapple. Continue cooking a few more mins until the bell pepper begins to soften. Stir together the corn-starch, water, and 2 tbsps of lime juice. Stir into the pineapple sauce until thickened, stirring constantly. Keep the sauce warm over very low heat.
3. Stir 1 tbsp of lime juice together with the melted butter, and brush on the tuna fillets. Place onto a broiler pan.
4. Cook under the preheated broiler for 4 mins, then turn the fish over, and continue cooking for 4 mins more. Season to taste with salt and serve with the pineapple sauce.

NUTRITION: calories 98, fat 7.1g, sodium 2mg, carbs 10.1g, fiber 1g, protein 0.6g, potassium 111mg, phosphorus 101mg

399. Tangy Glazed Black Cod

Cooking Time: 15 mins| Servings: 4

INGREDIENTS:

- 3 tbsps fresh lime juice
- 2 tbsps honey
- 2 tbsps vinegar
- 1 tbsp soy sauce
- 1 (1 pound) fillet black cod, bones removed

DIRECTIONS:

1. Preheat oven to 425°F. Spray the bottom of a Dutch oven or covered casserole dish with cooking spray.
2. Combine lime juice, honey, vinegar, and soy sauce in a saucepan over medium heat; cook and stir until sauce is thickened, about 5 mins.
3. Place cod in the prepared Dutch oven. Pour sauce over fish Cover dish with an oven-safe lid.
4. Bake in the preheated oven until fish flakes easily with a fork, about 10 mins.

NUTRITION: calories 44, fat 0g, sodium 127mg, carbs 11.8g, fiber 0.2g, protein 0.5g, potassium 58mg, phosphorus 40mg

400. Spicy Lime and Basil Grilled Fish

Cooking Time: 30 mins| Servings: 4

INGREDIENTS:

- 2 pounds salmon fillets, each cut into thirds
- 6 tbsps butter, melted
- 1 lime, juiced
- 1 tbsp dried basil
- 1 tsp red pepper flakes
- 1 onion, sliced crosswise 1/8-inch thick

DIRECTIONS:

1. Preheat grill for medium heat and lightly oil the grate.
2. Lay 4 8x10-inch pieces of aluminum foil onto a flat work surface and spray with cooking spray.
3. Arrange equal amounts of the salmon into the center of each foil square.
4. Stir butter, lime juice, basil, and red pepper flakes together in a small bowl; drizzle evenly over each portion of fish. Top each portion with onion slices.
5. Bring opposing ends of the foil together and roll together to form a seam. Roll ends toward fish to seal packets.
6. Cook packets on the preheated grill until fish flakes easily with a fork, 5 to 7 mins per side.

NUTRITION: calories 151, fat 13.4g, sodium 95mg, carbs 3.1g, fiber 0.8g, protein 6g, potassium 158mg

401. Shrimp Paella

Cooking time:10 mins| Servings:2

INGREDIENTS:

- 6 oz. frozen cooked shrimp
- 1 cup cooked brown rice
- 1 chopped red onion
- 1 tsp. paprika
- 1 chopped garlic clove
- 1 tbsp. olive oil
- 1 deseeded and sliced chili pepper
- 1 tbsp. oregano

DIRECTIONS:

1. Heat the olive oil in a large pan on medium-high heat.
2. Add the onion and garlic and sauté for 2-3 mins until soft.
3. Now add the shrimp and sauté for a further 5 mins or until hot through.
4. Now add the herbs, spices, chili and rice with 1/2 cup boiling water.
5. Stir until everything is warm and the water has been absorbed.
6. Plate up and serve.

NUTRITION: calories 221, protein 17g, carbs 31g, fat 8g, sodium 235 mg, potassium 176 mg, phosphorus 189 mg

402. Shrimp Scampi

Cooking Time: 8 mins| Servings: 3

INGREDIENTS:

- 4 oz of dry linguini
- ½ pound of cleaned and peeled shrimp
- 1 tbsp of olive oil
- 1 minced garlic clove
- ¼ cup of dry white wine
- 1 tbsp of lemon juice
- ½ tsp of basil
- 1 tbsp of chopped fresh parsley

DIRECTIONS:

1. Heat the oil in a large non-stick skillet; then add the garlic and the shrimp and cook while stirring for about 4 mins
2. Add the wine, the lemon juice, the basil and the parsley

3. Cook for about 5 mins longer; then boil the linguini in unsalted water for a few mins
4. Drain the linguini; then top it with the shrimp
5. Serve and enjoy your lunch!

NUTRITION: calories 340, fat 26g, carbs 11.3g, fiber 2.1g, potassium 189mg, sodium 85mg, phosphorus 167mg, protein 15g

403. Salmon & Pesto Salad

Cooking time:15 mins| Servings:2

INGREDIENTS:

For the pesto:

- 1 minced garlic clove
- ½ cup fresh arugula
- ¼ cup olive oi l
- ½ cup fresh basil
- 1 tsp. black pepper

For the salmon:

- 4 oz. skinless salmon fillet
- 1 tbsp. coconut oil

For the salad:

- ½ juiced lemon
- 2 sliced radishes
- ½ cup iceberg lettuce
- 1 tsp. black pepper

DIRECTIONS:

1. Prepare the pesto by blending all the ingredients for the pesto in a food processor or by grinding with a pestle and mortar. Set aside.
2. Add a skillet to the stove on medium-high heat and melt the coconut oil.
3. Add the salmon to the pan.
4. Cook for 7-8 mins and turn over.
5. Cook for a further 3-4 mins or until cooked through.
6. Remove fillets from the skillet and allow to rest.
7. Mix the lettuce and the radishes and squeeze over the juice of ½ lemon.
8. Flake the salmon with a fork and mix through the salad.
9. Toss to coat and sprinkle with a little black pepper to serve.

NUTRITION: calories 221, protein 13 g, carbs 1 g, fat 34 g, sodium 80 mg, potassium 119 mg, phosphorus 158 mg

404. Baked Fennel & Garlic Sea Bass

Cooking time:15 mins| Servings:2

INGREDIENTS:

- 6 oz. sea bass fillets
- 1 lemon
- ½ sliced fennel bulb
- 1 tsp. black pepper
- 2 garlic cloves

DIRECTIONS:

1. Preheat the oven to 375°F.
2. Sprinkle black pepper over the Sea Bass.
3. Slice the fennel bulb and garlic cloves.
4. Add 1 salmon fillet and half the fennel and garlic to one sheet of baking paper or tin foil.
5. Squeeze in ½ lemon juices.
6. Repeat for the other fillet.
7. Fold and add to the oven for 12-15 mins or until fish is thoroughly cooked through.
8. Meanwhile, add boiling water to your couscous, cover and allow to steam.
9. Serve with your choice of rice or salad.

NUTRITION: calories 221, protein 14 g, carbs 3 g, fat 2 g, sodium 119 mg, potassium 398 mg, phosphorus 149 mg

405. Lemon Cilantro & Tuna and Rice

Cooking time:0 mins| Servings:2

INGREDIENTS:

- 3 oz. canned tuna
- ½ cup arugula
- 1 tbsp olive oil
- 1 cup cooked brown rice
- 1 tsp. black pepper
- ¼ finely diced red onion
- 1 juiced lemon
- 2 tbsps chopped fresh cilantro

DIRECTIONS:

1. Mix the olive oil, pepper, cilantro and red onion in a bowl.
2. Stir in the tuna, cover and leave in the fridge for as long as possible (if you can) or serve immediately.
3. When ready to eat, serve up with the cooked rice and arugula!

NUTRITION: calories 221, protein 11 g, carbs 26 g, fat 7 g, sodium 143 mg, potassium197 mg, phosphorus 182 mg

406. Red Cod Risotto

Cooking time: 40 mins | Servings:2

INGREDIENTS:

- 4 oz. cod fillet
- 1 finely diced white onion
- 1 cup brown rice
- 1 cup boiling water
- ¼ tsp. black pepper
- 1 cup low sodium chicken broth
- 1 tbsp olive oil
- ½ cup tomatoes

DIRECTIONS:

1. Heat the oil in a large pan on medium heat.
2. Sauté the chopped onion for 5 mins until soft before adding in the rice and stirring for 1-2 mins.
3. Combine the broth with boiling water.
4. Add half of the liquid to the pan and stir slowly.
5. Slowly add the rest of the liquid whilst continuously stirring for up to 20-30 mins.
6. Stir in the tomatoes to the risotto.
7. Place the fish on top of the rice, cover and steam for 10 mins.
8. Ensure the water does not dry out and keep topping up until the rice is cooked thoroughly.
9. Use your fork to break up the fish fillets and stir into the rice.
10. Sprinkle with freshly ground pepper to serve.

NUTRITION: calories 221, protein 12 g, carbs 29 g, fat 8 g, sodium 398 mg, potassium 347 mg, phosphorus 241 mg

407. Sardine Fish Cakes

Cooking Time: 10 mins| Servings:4

INGREDIENTS:

- 11 oz sardines, canned, drained
- 1/3 cup shallot, chopped
- 1 tsp chili flakes
- ½ tsp salt
- 2 tbsp wheat flour, whole grain
- 1 egg, beaten
- 1 tbsp chives, chopped
- 1 tsp olive oil
- 1 tsp butter

DIRECTIONS:

1. Put the butter in the skillet and melt it.
2. Add shallot and cook it until translucent.
3. After this, transfer the shallot in the mixing bowl.
4. Add sardines, chili flakes, salt, flour, egg, chives, and mix up until smooth with the help of the fork.

5. Make the medium size cakes and place them in the skillet.
6. Add olive oil.
7. Roast the fish cakes for 3 mins from each side over the medium heat.
8. Dry the cooked fish cakes with the paper towel if needed and transfer in the serving plates.

NUTRITION: calories 221, fat 12.2, fiber 0.1, carbs 5.4, protein 21.3

408. Cajun Catfish

Cooking Time: 10 mins| Servings:4

INGREDIENTS:

- 16 oz catfish steaks (4 oz each fish steak)
- 1 tbsp Cajun spices
- 1 egg, beaten
- 1 tbsp sunflower oil

DIRECTIONS:

1. Pour sunflower oil in the skillet and preheat it until shimmering.
2. Meanwhile, dip every catfish steak in the beaten egg and coat in Cajun spices.
3. Place the fish steaks in the hot oil and roast them for 4 mins from each side.
4. The cooked catfish steaks should have a light brown crust.

NUTRITION: calories 263, fat 16.7, fiber 0, carbs 0.1, protein 26.3

409. 4-Ingredients Salmon Fillet

Cooking Time: 25 mins| Servings:1

INGREDIENTS:

- 4 oz salmon fillet
- ½ tsp salt
- 1 tsp sesame oil
- ½ tsp sage

DIRECTIONS:

1. Rub the fillet with salt and sage.
2. Place the fish in the tray and sprinkle it with sesame oil.
3. Cook the fish for 25 mins at 365°F.
4. Flip the fish carefully onto another side after 12 mins of cooking.

NUTRITION: calories 191, fat 11.6, fiber 0.1, carbs 0.2, protein 22

410. Tuna and Shallot

Cooking Time: 15 mins| Servings: 4

INGREDIENTS:

- 4 tuna fillets, boneless and skinless
- 1 tbsp olive oil
- 2 shallots, chopped
- 2 tbsps lime juice
- Pinch of pepper
- 1 tsp sweet paprika
- ½ cup low sodium fish stock

DIRECTIONS:

1. Take a pan and place it over medium heat, add shallots and Sauté for 3 mins
2. Add fish, cook for 4 mins
3. Add remaining ingredients, cook for 3 mins

NUTRITION: calories 121, fat 8.2, fiber 1, carbs 8, protein 7, potassium 181mg, sodium 84mg, phosphorus 137mg

411. Brazilian Fish Stew

Cooking Time: 25 mins| Servings: 4

INGREDIENTS:

- 2 lbs tilapia fillets, cut into bits
- 4 tbsps lime juice
- 1 and ½ tbsp cumin, ground
- 1 and ½ tbsp paprika
- 2 and ½ tsps garlic, minced
- 1 and ½ tsp pepper
- 1 large onion, chopped
- 3 large bell pepper, cut into strips
- 1 can (14 oz) tomato, drained
- 1 can (14 oz) coconut milk
- handful of cilantro, chopped
- 4 tbsps lime juice

DIRECTIONS:

1. Take a large sized bowl and add lime juice, cumin, paprika, garlic, pepper and mix well
2. Add tilapia and coat it up
3. Cover and allow it to marinate for 20 mins
4. Set your pot to HIGH and add olive oil
5. Add onions and cook for 3 mins until tender
6. Add pepper strips, tilapia, and tomatoes to a skillet
7. Pour coconut milk and cover, simmer for 20 mins
8. Add cilantro during the final few mins

NUTRITION: calories 132, fat 11, fiber 4, carbs 9, protein 8, potassium 172mg, sodium 74mg, phosphorus 117mg

412. Spanish Cod in Sauce

Cooking Time: 5.5 hours| Servings:2

INGREDIENTS:

- 7 oz Spanish cod fillet
- 1 tsp tomato paste
- 1 tsp garlic, diced
- 1 white onion, sliced
- 1 jalapeno pepper, chopped
- 1/3 cup chicken stock
- 1 tsp paprika

DIRECTIONS:

1. Pour chicken stock in the saucepan.
2. Add tomato paste and mix up the liquid until homogenous.
3. Add garlic, onion, jalapeno pepper, paprika, and salt.
4. Bring the liquid to boil and then simmer it.
5. Chop the cod fillet and add it in the tomato liquid.
6. Close the lid and simmer the fish for 10 mins over the low heat.
7. Serve the fish in the bowls with tomato sauce.

NUTRITION: calories 113, fat 1.2, fiber 1.9, carbs 7.2, protein 18.9

413. Fish Shakshuka

Cooking Time: 15 mins| Servings:5

INGREDIENTS:

- 5 eggs
- 1 cup tomatoes, chopped
- 3 bell peppers, chopped
- 1 tbsp butter
- 1 tsp tomato paste
- 1 tsp chili pepper
- 1 tsp salt
- 1 tbsp fresh dill
- 5 oz cod fillet, chopped
- 1 tbsp scallions, chopped

DIRECTIONS:

1. Melt butter in the skillet and add chili pepper, bell peppers, and tomatoes.
2. Sprinkle the vegetables with scallions, dill, salt, and chili pepper. Simmer them for 5 mins.
3. After this, add chopped cod fillet and mix up well.
4. Close the lid and simmer the ingredients for 5 mins over the medium heat.
5. Then crack the eggs over fish and close the lid.
6. Cook shakshuka with the closed lid for 5 mins.

NUTRITION: calories 143, fat 7.3, fiber 1.6, carbs 7.9, protein 12.8

414. Ginger Shrimp

Cooking Time: 12 mins| Servings: 4

INGREDIENTS:

- 1 pound of medium shrimp, shelled and deveined
- 2 tbsps of olive oil
- 1 tbsp of minced peeled fresh ginger
- 2 cups of snow peas
- 1½ cups of frozen baby peas

- 3 tbsps of water
- 2 tbsps of low-Sodium soy sauce

DIRECTIONS:

1. Using a large wok, heat the olive oil over medium heat.
2. Add the ginger and stir-fry for 1 to 2 mins, until the ginger is fragrant.
3. Add the snow peas and stir-fry for 2 to 3 mins, until they are tender-crisp.
4. Add the baby peas and the water and stir. Cover the wok and steam for 2 to 3 mins or until the vegetables are tender.
5. Stir in the shrimp and stir-fry for 3 to 4 mins, or until the shrimp have curled and turned pink.
6. Add the soy sauce and pepper; stir and serve.

NUTRITION: calories 237, fat 7.3, fiber 4.6, carbs 12.9, protein 32.8 potassium 504mg phosphorus 350 mg

415. Monk-fish Curry

Cooking Time: 20 mins| Servings: 2

INGREDIENTS:

- 4 oz. Monkfish fillet
- 1 garlic clove
- 3 finely chopped green onions
- 1 tsp grated ginger
- 1 cup water
- 2 tsps chopped fresh basil
- 1 cup cooked rice noodles
- 1 tbsp coconut oil
- ½ sliced red chili
- ½ finely sliced stick lemongrass
- 2 tbsps chopped shallots

DIRECTIONS:

1. Slice the Monkfish into bite-size pieces.
2. Using a pestle and mortar or food processor, crush the basil, garlic, ginger, chili, and lemongrass to form a paste.
3. Heat the oil in a large wok or pan over medium-high heat and add the shallots.
4. Now add the water to the pan and bring to a boil.
5. Add the Monkfish, lower the heat and cover to simmer for 10 mins or until cooked through.
6. Enjoy with rice noodles and scatter with green onions to serve.

NUTRITION: calories 249, fat 8.3g, sodium 32mg, carbs 37g, fiber 1.1g, protein 12.3g, potassium 398mg

416. Steamed Fish with Garlic

Cooking Time: 45 mins| Servings: 4

INGREDIENTS:

- 2 (6 ounce) fillets cod fillets
- 3 tbsps olive oil
- 1 onion, chopped
- 4 cloves garlic, minced
- 3 pinches dried rosemary
- black pepper to taste
- 1 lemon, halved

DIRECTIONS:

1. Preheat oven to 350°F.
2. Place cod fillets on an 18x18-inch piece of aluminum foil; top with oil. Sprinkle onion, garlic, rosemary, and pepper over oil and cod. Squeeze juice from ½ lemon evenly on top.
3. Lift up bottom and top ends of the aluminum foil towards the center; fold together to 1 inch above the cod. Flatten short ends of the aluminum foil; fold over to within 1 inch of the sides of the cod. Place foil package on a baking sheet.
4. Bake in the preheated oven until haddock flakes easily with a fish, about 45 mins. Let sit, about 5 mins. Open ends of the packet carefully;

squeeze juice from the remaining 1/2 lemon on top.

NUTRITION: calories 171, fat 11.3g, sodium 308mg, carbs 5g, fiber 1.1g, protein 14.3g, potassium 76mg

417. Baked Haddock

Cooking Time: 45 mins| Servings: 4

INGREDIENTS:

- 4 haddock fillets
- 3/4 cup soy milk
- 3/4 cup graham crackers crumbs
- 1/4 cup grated Parmesan cheese
- 1/4 tsp ground dried dill weeds
- 1/4 cup butter, melted

DIRECTIONS:

1. Preheat oven to 500°F.
2. In a small bowl, combine the soy milk. In a separate bowl, mix together the graham crackers crumbs, Parmesan cheese, and dill. Dip the haddock fillets in the milk, then press into the crumb mixture to coat. Place haddock fillets in a glass baking dish, and drizzle with melted butter.
3. Bake on the top rack of the preheated oven until the fish flakes easily, about 15 mins

NUTRITION: calories 281, fat 17.6g, sodium 283mg, carbs 16g, fiber 1.3g, protein 14.5g, potassium 201mg, phosphorus 167mg

418. Sauté Fillets

Cooking Time: 5 mins| Servings: 4

INGREDIENTS:

- 1 lb. sliced haddock
- 1 tbsp olive oil
- 1/3 cup whole wheat flour
- freshly ground pepper

DIRECTIONS:

1. Combine flour, salt and pepper in a shallow dish; thoroughly dredge fillets
2. Heat oil in a large nonstick skillet over medium-high heat.
3. Add the fish, working in batches if necessary, and cook until lightly browned and just opaque in the center, 3 to 4 mins per side.
4. Serve immediately.

NUTRITION: calories 111, fat 12g, sodium 200mg, carbs 15g, fiber 1g, protein 13g, potassium 87mg

419. Lemon Scallops

Cooking Time: 5 mins| Servings: 4

INGREDIENTS:

- 1 and ¼ lbs dried scallops
- 1 tbsp olive oil
- 2 tbsps whole wheat flour
- ¼ tsp sunflower seeds
- 4-5 garlic cloves, minced
- 1 scallion, chopped
- 1 pinch of ground sage
- 1 lemon juice
- 2 tbsps parsley, chopped

DIRECTIONS:

1. Take a non-stick skillet and place it over medium-high heat
2. Add oil and allow the oil to heat up
3. Take a medium sized bowl and add scallops alongside sunflower seeds and flour
4. Place the scallops in the skillet and add scallions, garlic, and sage
5. Saute for 3-4 mins until they show an opaque texture
6. Stir in lemon juice and parsley
7. Remove heat and serve hot!

NUTRITION: calories 121, fat 8g, sodium 108mg, carbs 8g, fiber 1.1g, protein 7.3g, potassium 79mg

420. Tuna Casserole

Cooking time: 40 mins| Servings: 4

INGREDIENTS:

- 1 (10-ounce) package zucchini noodles
- 2 (5-ounce) cans chunk-light tuna, drained
- avocado oil cooking spray
- 1 yellow onion, diced
- 2 tbsp whole-wheat flour
- 2 cups chicken broth
- ½ cup unsweetened almond milk
- 1 cup fresh or frozen broccoli florets
- 1 cup shredded cheddar cheese

DIRECTIONS:

1. Preheat the oven to 375°F.
2. Heat a medium skillet over medium heat. When hot, coat the cooking surface with cooking spray. Put the onion into the skillet and cook for 3 mins.
3. Add the flour and stir. Cook for 2 mins, stirring once.
4. Add the broth slowly, then the almond milk, stirring constantly.
5. Increase the heat to high. Once the mixture comes to a boil, add the broccoli and noodles. Reduce the heat to medium and cook for 5 to 7 mins. The mixture will thicken.
6. Add the tuna and stir.
7. Transfer the mixture to an 8-by-8-inch casserole dish and top with the cheese.
8. Cover with foil and bake for 20 mins.
9. Uncover and broil for 2 mins.

NUTRITION: calories 269, fat 12g, protein 29g, carbs 11g, sugars 3g, fiber 3g, sodium 351mg

421. Lemon Pepper Salmon

Cooking time: 20 mins| Servings: 4

INGREDIENTS:

- 1 pound salmon fillet
- ½ tsp freshly ground black pepper
- ½ tsp salt
- Zest and juice of ½ lemon
- ¼ tsp dried thyme
- Nonstick cooking spray

DIRECTIONS:

1. Preheat the oven to 425°F. Spray a baking sheet with nonstick cooking spray.
2. In a small bowl, combine the pepper, salt, lemon zest and juice, and thyme. Stir to combine.
3. Place the salmon on the prepared baking sheet, skin-side down. Spread the seasoning mixture evenly over the fillet.
4. Bake for 15 to 20 mins, depending on the thickness of the fillet, until the flesh flakes easily.

NUTRITION: calories 163, fat 7g, protein 23g, carbs 1g, sugars 0g, fiber 0g, sodium 167mg

422. Tilapia with Mango Salsa

Preparation time: 15 mins, Cooking time: 10 mins| Servings: 2

INGREDIENTS:

Tilapia:

- ½ pound boneless tilapia fillets
- 1 tbsp paprika
- 1 tsp onion powder
- ½ tsp salt and black pepper
- ½ tsp dried thyme
- ½ tsp garlic powder
- 2 tsps olive oil
- 1 lime, cut into wedges, for serving

Salsa:

- 1 cup chopped mango
- 2 tbsp chopped red onion
- 2 tbsp chopped fresh cilantro
- 2 tbsp freshly squeezed lime juice
- ½ jalapeño pepper, seeded and minced
- Pinch salt

DIRECTIONS:

Make the Salsa

1. In a medium bowl, toss together the mango, onion, cilantro, lime juice, jalapeño, and salt. Set aside.

Make the Tilapia

2. In a small bowl, mix the onion powder, pepper, thyme, garlic powder, and salt. Rub the mixture on both sides of the tilapia fillets.
3. In a large skillet, heat the oil over medium heat, and cook the fish for 3 to 5 mins on each side until the outer coating is crisp and the fish is cooked through.
4. Spoon half of the salsa over each fillet and serve with lime wedges on the side.

NUTRITION: calories 240, fat 8g, protein 25g, carbs 22g, sugars 13g, fiber 4g, sodium 417mg

423. Honey Roasted Salmon

Cooking time: 20 mins| Servings: 4

INGREDIENTS:

- 1 pound salmon fillet
- 2 tbsp whole-grain mustard
- 1 tbsp honey
- 2 garlic cloves, minced
- ¼ tsp salt
- ¼ tsp freshly ground black pepper
- Nonstick cooking spray

DIRECTIONS:

1. Preheat the oven to 425°F. Spray a baking sheet with nonstick cooking spray.
2. In a small bowl, whisk together the mustard, honey, garlic, salt, and pepper.
3. Place the salmon fillet on the prepared baking sheet, skin-side down. Spoon the sauce onto the salmon and spread evenly.
4. Roast for 15 to 20 mins, depending on the thickness of the fillet, until the flesh flakes easily.

NUTRITION: calories 186, fat 7g, protein 23g, carbs 6g, sugars 4g, fiber 0g, sodium 312mg

424. Halibut with Green Beans

Cooking time: 15 mins| Servings: 4

INGREDIENTS:

- 4 (4-ounce) halibut fillets
- ½ pound green beans, trimmed
- 2 red bell peppers, seeded and cut into strips
- 1 onion, sliced
- Zest and juice of 2 lemons
- 2 garlic cloves, minced
- 2 tbsp olive oil
- 1 tsp dried dill
- 1 tsp dried oregano
- ½ tsp salt
- ¼ tsp freshly ground black pepper

DIRECTIONS:

1. Preheat the oven to 400°F. Line a baking sheet with parchment paper.
2. In a large bowl, toss the green beans, bell peppers, onion, lemon zest and juice, garlic, olive oil, dill, and oregano.
3. Use a slotted spoon to transfer the vegetables to the prepared baking sheet in a single layer, leaving the juice behind in the bowl.
4. Gently place the halibut fillets in the bowl, and coat in the juice. Transfer the fillets to the baking sheet, nestled between the vegetables, and drizzle them with any juice left in the bowl. Sprinkle the vegetables and halibut with the salt and pepper.
5. Bake for 15 to 20 mins until the vegetables are just tender and the fish flakes apart easily.

NUTRITION: calories 234, fat 9g, protein 24g, carbs 16g, sugars 8g, fiber 5g, sodium 349mg

425. Salmon with Brussels Sprouts

Cooking time: 20 mins| Servings: 4

INGREDIENTS:

- 4 (4-ounce) skinless salmon fillets
- 16 Brussels sprouts, halved lengthwise
- ½ tsp garlic powder
- ½ tsp salt and freshly ground black pepper
- 2 tsps freshly squeezed lemon juice
- Avocado oil cooking spray

DIRECTIONS:

1. Heat a large skillet over medium-low heat. When hot, coat the cooking surface with cooking spray, and put the Brussels sprouts cut-side down in the skillet. Cover and cook for 5 mins.
2. Meanwhile, season both sides of the salmon with the garlic powder, pepper, and salt.
3. Flip the Brussels sprouts and move them to one side of the skillet. Add the salmon and cook, uncovered, for 4 to 6 mins.
4. Check the Brussels sprouts. When they are tender, remove them from the skillet and set them aside.
5. Flip the salmon fillets. Cook for 4 to 6 more mins, or until the salmon is opaque and flakes easily with a fork. Remove the salmon from the skillet, and let it rest for 5 mins.
6. Divide the Brussels sprouts into four equal portions and add 1 salmon fillet to each portion. Sprinkle the lemon juice on top and serve.

NUTRITION: calories 193, fat 7g, protein 25g, carbs 10g, sugars 2g, fiber 4g, sodium 222mg

426. Simply Sole Piccata

Cooking time: 20 mins| Servings: 4

INGREDIENTS:

- 4 (5-ounce) sole fillets, patted dry
- 1 tsp olive oil
- 2 tbsp butter
- 1 tsp minced garlic
- 2 tbsp whole wheat flour
- 2 cups chicken broth
- Juice and zest of ½ lemon
- 2 tbsp capers

DIRECTIONS:

1. Place a large skillet over medium-high heat and add the olive oil.
2. Pat the sole fillets dry with paper towels then pan-sear them until the fish flakes easily when tested with a fork, about 4 mins on each side. Transfer the fish to a plate and set it aside.
3. Return the skillet to the stove and add the butter.
4. Sauté the garlic until translucent, about 3 mins.
5. Whisk in the flour to make a thick paste and cook, stirring constantly, until the mixture is golden brown, about 2 mins.
6. Whisk in the chicken broth, lemon juice, and lemon zest.
7. Cook until the sauce has thickened, about 4 mins.
8. Stir in the capers and serve the sauce over the fish.

NUTRITION: calories 271, fat 13g, protein 30g, carbs 7g, sugars 2g, fiber 0g, sodium 413mg

427. Crusted Halibut

Cooking time: 20 mins| Servings: 4

INGREDIENTS:

- 4 (5-ounce) halibut fillets

- ½ cup coarsely ground unsalted pistachios
- 1 tbsp chopped fresh parsley
- 1 tsp chopped fresh thyme
- 1 tsp chopped fresh basil
- Pinch sea salt and pepper
- Olive oil, for brushing

DIRECTIONS:

1. Preheat the oven to 350°F.
2. Line a baking sheet with parchment paper.
3. Pat the halibut fillets dry with a paper towel and place them on the baking sheet.
4. Brush the halibut generously with olive oil.
5. In a small bowl, stir together the pistachios, parsley, thyme, basil, salt, and pepper.
6. Spoon the nut and herb mixture evenly on the fish, spreading it out so the tops of the fillets are covered.
7. Bake the halibut until it flakes when pressed with a fork, about 20 mins.
8. Serve immediately.

NUTRITION: calories 262, fat 11g, protein 32g, carbs 4g, sugars 1g, fiber 2g, sodium 77mg

428. Curried Tuna Salad Wraps

Cooking time: 0 mins| Servings: 2

INGREDIENTS

- 2 (2.6-ounce) package tuna packed in water, drained
- 2 large butter lettuce leaves
- 1/3 cup mayonnaise
- 1 tbsp lemon juice
- 1 tsp curry powder
- 1 tsp reduced-sodium soy sauce
- ½ tsp sriracha (or to taste)
- ½ cup canned water chestnuts, drained and chopped

DIRECTIONS:

1. In a medium bowl, whisk together the mayonnaise, lemon juice, curry powder, soy sauce, and sriracha.
2. Add the water chestnuts and tuna. Stir to combine.
3. Serve wrapped in the lettuce leaves.

NUTRITION: calories 271, fat 14g, protein 19g, carbs 18g, sugars 1g, fiber 3g, sodium 627mg

429. Veggie-Stuffed Trout

Cooking time: 25 mins| Servings: 2

INGREDIENTS:

- 2 (8-ounce) whole trout fillets, dressed
- ½ red bell pepper, seeded and thinly sliced
- 1 onion, thinly sliced
- 2 or 3 shiitake mushrooms, sliced
- 1 tbsp olive oil
- ¼ tsp salt
- ⅛ tsp freshly ground black pepper
- 1 poblano pepper, seeded and thinly sliced
- 1 lemon, sliced
- Nonstick cooking spray

DIRECTIONS:

1. Preheat the oven to 425°F. Spray a baking sheet with nonstick cooking spray.
2. Rub both trout, inside and out, with the olive oil, then season with the salt and pepper.
3. In a large bowl, combine the bell pepper, onion, mushrooms, and poblano pepper. Stuff half of this mixture into the cavity of each fish. Top the mixture with 2 or 3 lemon slices inside each fish.
4. Arrange the fish on the prepared baking sheet side by side and roast for 25 mins until the fish is cooked through and the vegetables are tender.

NUTRITION: calories 452, fat 22g, protein 49g, carbs 14g, sugars 2g, fiber 3g, sodium 357mg

430. Lemony Cod with Asparagus

Cooking time: 15 mins| Servings: 4

INGREDIENTS:

- ½ cup uncooked brown rice or quinoa
- 4 (4-ounce) cod fillets
- 20 asparagus spears
- ¼ tsp salt and black pepper
- ¼ tsp garlic powder
- 1 tbsp unsalted butter
- 1 tbsp freshly squeezed lemon juice

DIRECTIONS:

1. Cook the rice according to the package instructions.
2. Meanwhile, season both sides of the cod fillets with the salt, pepper, and garlic powder.
3. Cut the bottom 1½ inches from the asparagus.
4. Heat a large skillet over medium-low heat. When hot, melt the butter in the skillet, then arrange the cod and asparagus in a single layer.
5. Cover and cook for 8 mins.
6. Divide the rice, fish, and asparagus into four equal portions. Drizzle with the lemon juice to finish.

NUTRITION: calories 230, fat 8g, protein 22g, carbs 20g, sugars 2g, fiber 5g, sodium 274mg

431. Cajun Catfish

Cooking time: 15 mins| Servings: 4

INGREDIENTS:

- 4 (8-ounce) catfish fillets
- 2 tbsp olive oil
- 2 tsps garlic salt
- 2 tsps thyme
- 2 tsps paprika
- ½ tsp red hot sauce
- ¼ tsp black pepper
- Nonstick cooking spray

DIRECTIONS:

1. Heat oven to 450°F. Spray a baking dish with cooking spray.
2. In a small bowl whisk together everything but catfish. Brush both sides of fillets, using all the spice mix.
3. Bake 10 to 13 mins or until fish flakes easily with a fork. Serve.

NUTRITION: calories 367, fat 24g, protein 35g, carbs 0g, fiber 0g, sugars 0g, sodium 70mg

432. BBQ Tuna Steaks

Cooking time: 10 mins| Servings: 4

INGREDIENTS:

- 4 (6-ounce) tuna steaks
- 4 tbsp fresh basil, diced
- 4 tsps olive oil
- ½ tsp salt
- ¼ tsp pepper
- Nonstick cooking spray

DIRECTIONS:

1. Heat grill to medium heat. Spray rack with cooking spray.
2. Drizzle both sides of the tuna with oil. Sprinkle with basil, salt and pepper.
3. Place on grill and cook 5 mins per side, tuna should be slightly pink in the center. Serve.

NUTRITION: calories 344, fat 14g, protein 51g, carbs 0g, fiber 0g, sugars 0g, sodium 367mg

433. Rosemary Trout

Cooking time: 7 to 8 mins| Servings: 2

INGREDIENTS:

- 8 oz trout fillets, about ¼ inch thick; rinsed and patted dry
- ½ tsp olive oil
- ⅛ tsp salt and pepper
- 4 fresh rosemary sprigs

- 1 tsp fresh lemon juice

DIRECTIONS:

1. Preheat the oven to 350°F.
2. Put the rosemary sprigs in a small baking pan in a single row. Spread the fillets on the top of the rosemary sprigs.
3. Brush both sides of each piece of fish with the olive oil. Sprinkle with the salt, pepper, and lemon juice.
4. Bake in the preheated oven for 7 to 8 mins, or until the fish is opaque and flakes easily.
5. Divide the fillets between two plates and serve hot.

NUTRITION: calories 180, fat 9g, protein 23g, carbs 0g, fiber 0g, sugars 0g, sodium 210mg

434. Lemony White Fish Fillets

Preparation time: 10mins, Cooking time: 10 mins| Servings: 4

INGREDIENTS:

- 4 (6-ounce) lean white fish fillets, rinsed and patted dry
- ½ tsp lemon zest
- ¼ cup olive oil
- ¼ tsp dried dill
- 1 medium lemon, halved
- 1 tbsp parsley, finely chopped
- paprika, to taste
- Cooking spray

DIRECTIONS:

1. Preheat the oven to 400°F. Line a baking sheet with aluminum foil and spray with cooking spray.
2. Place the fillets on the foil and scatter with the paprika. Season as desired with salt and pepper.
3. Bake in the preheated oven for 10 mins, or until the flesh flakes easily with a fork.
4. Meanwhile, stir together the parsley, lemon zest, olive oil, and dill in a small bowl.
5. Remove the fish from the oven to four plates. Squeeze the lemon juice over the fish and serve topped with the parsley mixture.

NUTRITION: calories 283, fat 17g, protein 33g, carbs 1g, fiber 0g, sugars 0g, sodium 74mg

435. Greek Scampi

Cooking time: 5 mins| Servings: 2

INGREDIENTS:

- ½ pound shrimp, peeled, deveined, and thoroughly rinsed
- 1 garlic cloves, minced
- 2 tbsp olive oil
- 1 cup diced tomatoes
- ½ cup nonfat: ricotta cheese
- 8 black olives
- Juice of ½ lemon
- 1 tbsp chopped fresh dill, or ¾ tsp dried
- Salt and pepper, to taste

DIRECTIONS:

1. In a large skillet set over medium heat, sauté the garlic in the olive oil for 30 seconds.
2. Add the shrimp. Cook for 1 minute.
3. Add the tomatoes, ricotta cheese, olives, lemon juice, and dill. Reduce the heat to low. Simmer for 5 to 10 mins, stirring so the shrimp cook on both sides. When the shrimp are pink and the tomatoes and ricotta have made a sauce, the dish is ready.
4. Sprinkle with salt and pepper.
5. Serve immediately.

NUTRITION: calories 350, fat 20g, protein 30g, carbs 11g, sugars 6g, fiber 1g, sodium 558mg

436. Scallops with Asparagus

Cooking time: 15 mins| Servings: 4

INGREDIENTS:

- 1 pound asparagus, trimmed and cut into 2-inch segments
- 1 pound sea scallops
- 1 tbsp butter
- ¼ cup dry white wine
- Juice of 1 lemon
- 2 garlic cloves, minced
- 4 tsps olive oil, divided
- ¼ tsp freshly ground black pepper

DIRECTIONS:

1. In a large skillet, heat 1½ tsps of oil over medium heat.
2. Add the asparagus and sauté for 5 to 6 mins until just tender, stirring regularly. Remove from the skillet and cover with aluminum foil to keep warm.
3. Add the remaining 1½ tsps of oil and the butter to the skillet. When the butter is melted and sizzling, place the scallops in a single layer in the skillet. Cook for about 3 mins on one side until nicely browned. Use tongs to gently loosen and flip the scallops, and cook on the other side for another 3 mins until browned and cooked through. Remove and cover with foil to keep warm.
4. In the same skillet, combine the wine, lemon juice, garlic, and pepper. Bring to a simmer for 1 to 2 mins, stirring to mix in any browned pieces left in the pan.
5. Return the asparagus and the cooked scallops to the skillet to coat with the sauce. Serve warm.

NUTRITION: calories 252, fat 7g, protein 26g, carbs 15g, sugars 3g, fiber 2g, sodium 493mg

437. Shrimp Burgers with Mango

Cooking time: 30 mins| Servings: 4

INGREDIENTS:

Burgers:

- 1 pound shrimp, peeled and deveined
- 2 eggs
- ½ red bell pepper, seeded and coarsely chopped
- ¼ cup chopped scallions, both white and green parts
- 2 tbsp fresh chopped cilantro
- 1 garlic clove
- 1 tbsp olive oil
- 3 cups mixed salad greens

Salsa:

- 1 cup diced mango
- 1 avocado, diced
- 1 scallion, both white and green parts, finely chopped
- 1 tbsp chopped fresh cilantro
- Juice of 1 lime

DIRECTIONS:

Make the Salsa

1. In a small bowl, toss the mango, avocado, scallion, and cilantro. Sprinkle with the lime juice and pepper. Mix gently to combine and set aside.

Make the Burgers

2. In the bowl of a food processor, add half the shrimp and process until coarsely puréed. Add the egg, bell pepper, scallions, cilantro, and garlic, and process until uniformly chopped. Transfer to a large mixing bowl.
3. Chop the remaining half pound of shrimp into small pieces. Add to the puréed mixture and stir well to combine. Form the mixture into 4 patties of equal size. Arrange on a plate, cover, and refrigerate for 30 mins.
4. In a large skillet, heat the olive oil over medium heat. Cook the burgers

for 3 mins on each side until browned and cooked through.

5. On each of 4 plates, arrange 1 cup of salad greens, and top with a scoop of salsa and a shrimp burger.

NUTRITION: calories 229, fat 11g, protein 19g, carbs 14g, sugars 7g, fiber 4g, sodium 200mg

438. Cajun Shrimp Casserole

Cooking time: 30 mins| Servings: 6

INGREDIENTS:

- 1 pound shrimp, peeled and deveined
- 1 cup quinoa
- 1 cup water
- 1½ tsps Cajun seasoning, divided
- 3 tomatoes, diced
- 1 tbsp plus 2 tsps olive oil, divided
- ½ onion, diced
- 1 jalapeño pepper, seeded and minced
- 2 garlic cloves, minced
- ¼ tsp freshly ground black pepper
- ½ cup shredded pepper jack cheese

DIRECTIONS:

1. In a pot, combine the quinoa and water. Bring to a boil, reduce the heat, cover, and simmer on low for 10 to 15 mins until all the water is absorbed. Fluff with a fork.
2. Preheat the oven to 350ºF .
3. In a large mixing bowl, toss the shrimp and ¾ tsp of Cajun seasoning.
4. In another bowl, toss the remaining ¾ tsp of Cajun seasoning with the tomatoes and 1½ tsps of olive oil.
5. In a large, oven-safe skillet, heat 1 tbsp of olive oil over medium heat. Add the shrimp and cook for 3 mins per side until they are opaque and firm. Remove from the skillet and set aside.
6. In the same skillet, heat the remaining ½ tsp of olive oil over medium-high heat. Add the onion, jalapeño, and garlic, and cook 5 mins.
7. Add the seasoned tomatoes, tomato paste, cooked quinoa, and pepper. Stir well to combine.
8. Return the shrimp to the skillet, placing them in a single layer on top of the quinoa. Sprinkle the cheese over the top.
9. Transfer the skillet to the oven and bake for 15 mins. Turn the broiler on high, and broil for 2 mins to brown the cheese. Serve.

NUTRITION: calories 255, fat 12g, protein 18g, carbs 15g, sugars 1g, fiber 2g, sodium 469mg

439. Original Cioppino

Cooking time: 20 mins| Servings: 4

INGREDIENTS:

- 8 oz cod, pin bones removed, cut into 1-inch pieces
- 8 oz shrimp, peeled and deveined
- 1 (14-ounce) can tomato sauce
- 2 tbsp olive oil
- 1 onion, finely chopped
- 1 garlic clove, minced
- ½ cup dry white wine
- 1 tbsp Italian seasoning
- ½ tsp sea salt

DIRECTIONS:

1. In a large skillet over medium-high heat, heat the olive oil until it shimmers. Add the onion and cook, stirring occasionally, for 3 mins. Add the garlic and cook, stirring constantly, for 30 seconds. Add the wine and cook, stirring, for 1 minute.
2. Add the tomato sauce. Bring to a simmer. Stir in the cod, shrimp, Italian seasoning and salt. Simmer until the fish is just opaque, about 5 mins.

NUTRITION: calories 243, fat 8g, protein 23g, carbs 11g, sugars 7g, fiber 2g, sodium 271mg

440. Orange Scallops

Cooking time: 10 mins| Servings: 4

INGREDIENTS:

- 2 pounds scallops
- ¼ cup freshly squeezed orange juice
- 2 tbsp olive oil
- 1 tbsp minced garlic
- 1 tsp orange zest
- 1 tsp chopped fresh thyme, for garnish
- salt and black pepper, to taste

DIRECTIONS:

1. Clean the scallops and pat them dry with paper towels, then season them lightly with salt and pepper.
2. Place a large skillet over medium-high heat and add the olive oil.
3. Sauté the garlic until it is softened and translucent, about 3 mins.
4. Add the scallops to the skillet and cook until they are lightly seared and just cooked through, turning once, about 4 mins per side.
5. Transfer the scallops to a plate, cover to keep warm, and set them aside.
6. Add the orange juice and zest to the skillet and stir to scrape up any cooked bits.
7. Spoon the sauce over the scallops and serve, garnished with the thyme.

NUTRITION: calories 267, fat 8g, protein 38g, carbs 8g, sugars 1g, fiber 0g, sodium 361mg

441. Shrimp with Feta

Cooking time: 30 mins| Servings: 4

INGREDIENTS:

- 1½ pounds shrimp, peeled, deveined, tails removed
- 4 tomatoes, coarsely chopped
- ½ cup feta cheese, crumbled
- ½ cup chopped sun-dried tomatoes
- 1 tsp minced garlic
- 2 tsps olive oil
- 1 tsp chopped fresh oregano
- Freshly ground black pepper, to taste
- 1 tbsp freshly squeezed lemon juice

DIRECTIONS:

1. Heat the oven to 450°F.
2. In a medium bowl, toss the tomatoes, sun-dried tomatoes, garlic, oil, and oregano until well combined.
3. Season the mixture lightly with pepper.
4. Transfer the tomato mixture to a 9-by-13-inch glass baking dish.
5. Bake until softened, about 15 mins.
6. Stir the shrimp and lemon juice into the hot tomato mixture and top evenly with the feta.
7. Bake until the shrimp are cooked through, about 15 mins more.

NUTRITION: calories 306, fat 11g, protein 39g, carbs 12g, sugars 5g, fiber 3g, sodium 502mg

442. Jambalaya

Cooking time: 40 mins| Servings: 6

INGREDIENTS:

- 1 pound raw shrimp, peel and devein
- 14 oz sausage, cut into 1-inch pieces
- ½ cauliflower, riced
- 2 stalks celery, diced
- ½ white onion, diced
- ½ red bell pepper, diced
- 3 tbsp margarine
- 2 cups low sodium chicken broth
- ½ can tomatoes and green chilies
- 3 cloves garlic, diced fine
- 2 tsps garlic powder
- 1½ tsps onion powder
- 1 tsp oregano
- 1 tsp basil

- ½ tsps cayenne pepper

DIRECTIONS:

1. Place large stock pot over medium-high heat.
2. In a small bowl, stir together garlic powder, onion powder, oregano, basil, and cayenne until combined.
3. Add 2 tbsp margarine to the stock pot and let melt.
4. Add the riced cauliflower with 2 tsps of the spice mixture. Cook, stirring frequently, about 5 mins. Transfer to a bowl.
5. Add the remaining margarine to the stock pot and melt. Then add the sausage and cook 5 mins, stirring to brown all sides.
6. Add onion, celery, and pepper and stir to combine. Cook about 3 mins until vegetables start to get soft.
7. Add the garlic and cook, stirring, 1 minute. Add the cauliflower and combine then add half the spice mixture and tomatoes, simmer 2 to 3 mins.
8. Pour in the broth and bring to a boil, cook 8 to 10 mins.
9. Season shrimp with remaining spice mixture and add to the pot, cook 3 to 4 mins just until shrimp turn pink. Serve.

NUTRITION: calories 429, fat 27g, protein 33g, carbs 13g, fiber 3g, sugars 4g, sodium 753mg

443. Traditional Paella

Cooking time: 35 mins| Servings: 6

INGREDIENTS:

- 1 pound chicken thighs, skinless and boneless
- 1 pound medium shrimp, raw, peel and devein
- 1 dozen mussels, cleaned
- 2 chorizo sausages, cut into pieces
- 1 medium head cauliflower, grated
- 1 yellow onion, diced fine
- 1 green bell pepper, sliced into strips
- 1 cup frozen peas
- 1 (15-ounce) can tomatoes, diced, drain well
- 2 tbsp olive oil
- 2 tsps garlic, diced fine
- 2 tsps salt
- 1 tsp saffron
- ¼ tsp paprika
- Nonstick cooking spray

DIRECTIONS:

1. Heat the oven to broil. Spray a baking dish with cooking spray.
2. Sprinkle salt and pepper on both sides of the chicken and place in baking dish. Bake, about 4 mins per side, until no longer pink in the middle. Let cool completely.
3. Heat 1 tbsp of the oil in a medium skillet over medium heat. Add onion, pepper, and garlic. Cook, about 4 to 5 mins, stirring frequently, until peppers start to get soft. Transfer to a bowl.
4. Add chorizo to the skillet and cook 2 mins, stirring frequently. Drain off the fat: and add to the vegetables.
5. Once the chicken has cooled, cut into small pieces and add it to the vegetables.
6. In a large saucepot, over medium heat, add the remaining oil. Once it is hot, add the cauliflower and seasonings. Cook 8 to 10 mins, until cauliflower is almost tender, stirring frequently.
7. Add the mussels and shrimp and cook until mussels open and shrimp start to turn pink.
8. Add the mixture in the bowl with the tomatoes and peas and stir to combine everything together. Cook another 5 mins until everything is

heated through and all of the mussels have opened. Serve.

NUTRITION: calories 424, fat 18g, protein 46g, carbs 21g, fiber 6g, sugars 9g, sodium 1371mg

444. Seafood Enchiladas

Cooking time: 1 hour| Servings: 6

INGREDIENTS:

- 1¼ pounds medium shrimp, raw, peel and devein
- 8 oz fresh halibut, cod, tilapia, or sea bass
- 2 poblano peppers, stemmed, seeded, and diced
- 1 red bell pepper, diced
- 1 onion, diced
- 1 cup light sour cream
- ¾ cup skim milk
- ½ cup reduced fat cream cheese, soft
- ½ cup green onions, sliced thin
- 6 (6-inch) low-carb whole wheat flour tortillas
- 4 cups water
- 2 cloves garlic, diced fine
- 2 tbsp flour
- 2 tsps olive oil
- ¼ tsp salt and pepper
- Nonstick cooking spray

DIRECTIONS:

1. Rinse shrimp and fish then pat dry with paper towels.
2. Heat oven to 350°F. Spry a 3-quart rectangular baking dish with cooking spray.
3. Add water to a large saucepan and bring to boiling over medium-high heat. Add shrimp and cook until shrimp turn pink, 1 to 3 mins. Drain, rinse with cold water, and chop.
4. Place a steamer insert into a deep skillet with a tight fitting lid. Add water to just below the insert and bring to a boil. Place fish in the insert, cover and steam 4 to 6 mins, or until fish flakes easily with a fork.
5. Flake the fish into bite-size pieces and set aside.
6. Heat oil in a large nonstick skillet over medium heat. Add bell pepper, poblanos, and onion. Cook 5 to 10 mins, or until vegetables are tender. Stir in garlic and 1 minute more. Remove from heat and add shrimp and fish.
7. Wrap tortillas in foil, making sure it's tight, and place in the oven until heated through, about 10 mins.
8. In a medium bowl, beat cream cheese until smooth. Beat in sour cream, ¼ tsp salt and pepper. Slowly beat in the milk until smooth. Stir ½ cup sauce into the fish and shrimp mixture.
9. To assemble, spoon shrimp mixture on one side of the tortillas and roll up. Place, seam side down, in prepare baking dish. Pour remaining sauce over the top.
10. Cover with foil, and bake 35 mins, or until heated through. Let rest 5 mins before serving. Garnish with chopped green onions.

NUTRITION: calories 459, fat 17g, protein 34g, carbs 38g, fiber 21g, sugars 4g, sodium 470mg

445. Steamed Mussels

Cooking time: 10 mins| Servings: 4

INGREDIENTS:

- 2 pounds mussels, cleaned
- 2 plum tomatoes, peeled, seeded and diced
- 1 cup onion, diced
- 2 tbsp fresh parsley, diced
- ¼ cup dry white wine
- 2 cloves garlic, diced fine
- 2 tbsp olive oil
- 2 tbsp fresh breadcrumbs

- ¼ tsp crushed red pepper flakes

DIRECTIONS:

1. Heat oil in a large sauce pot over medium heat. Add the onions and cook until soft, about 2 to 3 mins. Add garlic and cook 1 minute more.
2. Stir in wine, tomatoes, and pepper flakes. Bring to a boil, stirring occasionally. Add the mussels and cook 3 to 4 mins, or until all the mussels have opened. Discard any mussels that do not open.
3. Once mussels open, transfer them to a serving bowl. Add bread crumbs to the sauce and continue to cook, stirring frequently, until mixture thickens. Stir in parsley and pour evenly over mussels. Serve.

NUTRITION: calories 341, fat 16g, protein 29g, carbs 18g, fiber 2g, sugars 4g, sodium 682mg

446. Breaded Scallop Patties

Cooking time: 10 to 14 mins| Servings: 4

INGREDIENTS:

- 4 cups frozen chopped scallops, thawed
- 4 medium egg whites
- 1 cup chickpea crumbs
- ½ cup fat-free milk
- ½ tsp ground cumin
- ¼ tsp freshly ground black pepper
- 1 small onion, finely chopped
- 1 garlic clove, minced
- 2 celery stalks, finely chopped
- Juice of 2 limes

DIRECTIONS:

1. Preheat the oven to 350°F.
2. Whisk together the egg whites, chickpea crumbs, milk, cumin, and black pepper in a large bowl until well combined.
3. Stir in the scallops, onion, garlic, and celery. Shape the mixture into golf ball-sized balls and flatten them into patties with your hands.
4. Arrange the patties on a rimmed baking sheet, spacing them 1 inch apart.
5. Bake in the preheated oven for 10 to 14 mins until golden brown. Flip the patties halfway through the cooking time.
6. Serve drizzled with the lime juice.

NUTRITION: calories 338, fat 0g, protein 50g, carbs 24g, fiber 6g, sugars 4g, sodium 465mg

447. Panko-Crusted Coconut Shrimp

Cooking time: 6 to 8 mins| Servings: 4

INGREDIENTS:

- 1 pound large raw shrimp, peeled, deveined, and patted dry
- 2 egg whites
- 1 tbsp water
- ½ cup whole-wheat panko bread crumbs
- ¼ cup coconut flakes
- ½ tsp turmeric
- ½ tsp ground cumin
- ⅛ tsp salt
- Nonstick cooking spray

DIRECTIONS:

1. Preheat the air fry to 400°F.
2. In a shallow dish, beat the egg whites and water until slightly foamy. Set aside.
3. In a separate shallow dish, mix the bread crumbs, coconut flakes, turmeric, cumin, and salt, and stir until well combined.
4. Dredge the shrimp in the egg mixture, shaking off any excess, then coat them in the crumb-coconut

mixture.

5. Spritz the air fryer basket with nonstick cooking spray and arrange the coated shrimp in the basket.
6. Air fry for 6 to 8 mins, flipping the shrimp once during cooking, or until the shrimp are golden brown and cooked through.
7. Let the shrimp cool for 5 mins before serving.

NUTRITION: calories 181, fat 4g, protein 27g, carbs 9g, fiber 2g, sugars 1g, sodium 227mg

CHAPTER 10 Poultry

448. Chicken Grilled Cheese

Cooking time: 15 mins | Servings: 4

INGREDIENTS:

- 2 cups shredded rotisserie chicken
- 1 tbsp butter
- 1 small yellow onion
- 4 slices 100% whole-wheat bread
- 4 slices provolone or Swiss cheese
- 3 cups fresh spinach
- Avocado oil cooking spray

DIRECTIONS:

1. Cut the onion into ½-inch rounds. Leave them intact; do not separate.
2. Heat a medium or large skillet over medium-low heat. When hot, coat the cooking surface with cooking spray. Place the onions in the skillet. Cover and cook for 7 to 10 mins, or until the onions are translucent. Remove from the skillet.
3. Meanwhile, shred the chicken, and butter one side of each slice of bread. Tear each slice of cheese into 3 strips.
4. Place 2 or 3 strips of cheese on the nonbuttered side of each piece of bread, then place the buttered side down on the skillet.
5. Layer one-quarter of the onion, spinach, and shredded chicken on top of each slice of bread.
6. Toast for 2 to 3 mins over medium-low heat.

NUTRITION: calories 318, fat 13g, protein 27g, carbs 23g, sugars 3g, fiber 4g, sodium 496mg

449. Braised Chicken with Apple Slaw

Preparation time: 20 mins | Cooking time: 20 mins | Servings: 8

INGREDIENTS:

Chicken:

- 2 bone-in skin-on chicken breasts (about 2 pounds)
- 1 cup brown ale
- 1 tsp white wheat flour
- salt and freshly ground black pepper to taste

Slaw:

- ¼ head purple or red cabbage, thinly sliced
- 2 cups seedless green grapes, halved
- 1 apple , cut into matchstick-size slices
- ¼ cup cider vinegar
- 2 tbsp olive oil
- 1 tbsp honey
- 1 tbsp coarse-grain mustard
- salt and black pepper to taste

DIRECTIONS:

Make the Chicken

1. In a 2-cup measuring cup or small bowl | whisk together the ale and flour. Pour into the electric pressure cooker.
2. Sprinkle the chicken breasts with salt and pepper. Place them in the electric pressure cooker | meat-side down.
3. Close and lock the lid of the pressure cooker. Set the valve to sealing.
4. Cook on high pressure for 20 mins. While the chicken is cooking, make the slaw.
5. When the cooking is complete, hit Cancel. Allow the pressure to release naturally for 5 mins, then quick release any remaining pressure.

6. Once the pin drops, unlock and remove the lid.
7. Using tongs, remove the chicken breasts to a cutting board. Hit Sauté/More and bring the liquid in the pot to a boil, scraping up any brown bits on the bottom of the pot. Cook, stirring occasionally, for about 5 mins or until the sauce has reduced in volume by about a third. Hit Cancel and whisk in the mustard.
8. When the chicken is cool enough to handle, remove the skin, shred the meat, and return it to the pot. Let the chicken soak in the sauce for at least 5 mins.
9. Serve the chicken topped with the slaw.

Make the Slaw

9. In a small jar with a screw-top lid, combine the vinegar, olive oil, honey, and mustard. Shake well, then season with salt and pepper, and shake again.
10. In a large bowl, toss together the cabbage, grapes, and apple. Add the dressing and mix well. Let the mixture sit at room temperature while the chicken cooks.

NUTRITION: (½ cup chicken, plus ½ cup slaw) calories 203, fat 9g, protein 13g, carbs 16g, sugars 12g, fiber 2g, sodium 80mg

450. One-Pan Chicken Meal

Cooking time: 35 mins | Servings: 4

INGREDIENTS:

- 4 (4-ounce) boneless | skinless chicken breasts
- 3 tbsp olive oil
- 1 tbsp apple cider vinegar
- ¼ tsp garlic powder
- 3 tbsp Italian seasoning
- 1 cup cubed sweet potatoes
- 16 Brussels sprouts, halved lengthwise

DIRECTIONS:

1. Preheat the oven to 400°F.
2. In a large bowl, whisk together the oil, vinegar, garlic powder, and Italian seasoning.
3. Add the chicken, sweet potatoes, and Brussels sprouts, and coat thoroughly with the marinade.
4. Remove the ingredients from the marinade and arrange them on a baking sheet in a single layer. Roast for 15 mins.
5. Remove the baking sheet from the oven, flip the chicken over, and bake for another 15 to 20 mins.

NUTRITION: calories 342, fat 16g, protein 30g, carbs 23g, sugars 8g, fiber 9g, sodium 186mg

451. Coconut Lime Chicken

Cooking time: 15 mins | Servings: 4

INGREDIENTS:

- 4 (4-ounce) boneless | skinless chicken breasts
- 1 tbsp coconut oil
- 1 red bell pepper, cut into ¼-inch-thick slices
- 16 asparagus spears, bottom ends trimmed
- 1 cup coconut milk
- ½ tsp salt
- 2 tbsp freshly squeezed lime juice
- ½ tsp garlic powder
- ¼ cup chopped fresh cilantro

DIRECTIONS:

1. In a large skillet, heat the oil over medium-low heat. When hot, add the chicken.
2. Season the chicken with the salt. Cook for 5 mins, then flip.
3. Push the chicken to the side of the skillet, and add the bell pepper and

asparagus. Cook, covered, for 5 mins.

4. Meanwhile, in a small bowl, whisk together the coconut milk, lime juice and garlic powder.
5. Add the coconut milk mixture to the skillet, and boil over high heat for 2 to 3 mins.
6. Top with the cilantro.

NUTRITION: calories 321, fat 19g, protein 30g, carbs 11g, sugars 6g, fiber 4g, sodium 378mg

452. Slow Chicken Curry

Cooking time: 4 hours | Servings: 4

INGREDIENTS:

- 1lb skinless chicken breasts
- 1 medium onion, thinly sliced
- 1 15 ounce can chickpeas, drained and rinsed well
- 2 medium sweet potatoes, peeled and diced
- ½ cup light coconut milk
- ½ cup chicken stock (see recipe)
- 1 15ounce can Sodium-free tomato sauce
- 2 tbsp curry powder
- 1 tsp low-Sodium salt
- ½ cayenne powder
- 1 cup green peas
- 2 tbsp lemon juice

DIRECTIONS:

1. Place the chicken breasts, onion, chickpeas, and sweet potatoes into a 4 to 6-quart slow cooker.
2. Mix the coconut milk, chicken stock, tomato sauce, curry powder, salt, and cayenne together and pour into the slow cooker, stirring to coat well.
3. Cover and cook on low for 8 hours or high for 4 hours.
4. Stir in the peas and lemon juice 5 mins before serving.

NUTRITION: Calories 302, Fat 5g, Carbs 43g, Protein 24g, Fiber 9g, Potassium 573mg

453. Apple & Cinnamon Spiced Pork loin

Cooking time: 6 h | Servings: 6

INGREDIENTS:

- 1 2-3lb boneless pork loin roast
- ½ tsp low-Sodium salt
- ¼ tsp pepper
- 1 tbsp canola oil
- 3 medium apples, peeled and sliced
- ¼ cup honey
- 1 small red onion, halved and sliced
- 1 tbsp ground cinnamon

DIRECTIONS:

1. Season the pork with salt and pepper.
2. Heat the oil in a skillet and brown the pork on all sides.
3. Arrange half the apples in the base of a 4 to 6-quart slow cooker.
4. Top with the honey and remaining apples.
5. Sprinkle with cinnamon and cover.
6. Cover and cook on low for 6-8 hours until the meat is tender.

NUTRITION: calories 290, fat 10g, carbs 19g, protein 29g, fiber 2g, potassium 789mg, sodium 22mg

454. Lemon & herb turkey breasts

Cooking time: 3 1/2 hours | Servings: 12

INGREDIENTS:

- 1 can (14-1/2 oz) chicken broth
- 1/2 cup lemon juice
- 1/4 cup packed brown sugar
- 1/4 cup fresh sage
- 1/4 cup fresh thyme leaves
- 1/4 cup lime juice
- 1/4 cup cider vinegar
- 1/4 cup olive oil

- 1 envelope low-Sodium onion soup mix
- 2 tbsp dijon mustard
- 1 tbsp fresh marjoram, minced
- 1 tsp paprika
- 1 tsp garlic powder
- 1 tsp pepper
- ½ tsp low-Sodium salt
- 2 2lb boneless skinless turkey breast halves

DIRECTIONS:

1. Make a marinade by blending all the ingredients in a blender.
2. Pour over the turkey and leave overnight.
3. Place the turkey and marinade in a 4 to 6-quart slow cooker and cover.
4. Cover and cook on high for 3-1/2 to 4-1/2 hours or until a thermometer reads 165°F.

NUTRITION: calories 219, fat 5g, carbs 3g, protein 36g, fiber 0g, potassium 576mg, sodium 484mg

455. Orange Grilled Chicken

Cooking time: 50 mins | Servings: 4

INGREDIENTS

- 4 pieces of 6-ounce boneless, skinless chicken breasts
- ¼ cup fresh lime juice
- ¼ cup minced red onion
- 1 avocado
- 1 cup low-Fat yogurt
- 1 small red onion, sliced thinly
- 1 tbsp honey
- 2 oranges, peeled and cut
- 2 tbsps chopped cilantro

DIRECTIONS:

1. In a large bowl mix honey, cilantro, minced red onion, and yogurt.
2. Submerge chicken into mixture and marinate for at least 30 mins.
3. Grease grate and preheat grill to medium-high fire.
4. Remove chicken from marinade and season with pepper and salt.
5. Grill for 6 mins per side or until chicken is cooked and juices run clear.
6. Meanwhile, peel the avocado and discard the seed. Chop avocados and place it in a bowl. Quickly add lime juice and toss avocado to coat well with juice.
7. Add cilantro, thinly sliced onions, and oranges into the bowl of avocado, mix well.
8. Serve grilled chicken and avocado dressing on the side.

NUTRITION: calories 209, fat 10g, carbs 26g, protein 9g, fiber 2g, potassium 548mg, sodium 122mg phosphorus 157 mg

456. Roasted Citrus Chicken

Cooking time: 6 hours | Servings: 8

INGREDIENTS

- ½ large chicken breast for 1 chicken thigh
- 1 tbsp olive oil
- 2 cloves garlic, minced
- 1 tsp Italian seasoning
- ½ tsp black pepper
- 8 chicken thighs
- 2 cups chicken broth, reduced Sodium
- 3 tbsps lemon juice

DIRECTIONS:

1. Warm oil in a huge skillet.
2. Include garlic and seasonings.
3. Include chicken bosoms and dark-colored all sides.
4. Spot chicken in the moderate cooker and include the chicken soup.
5. Cook on LOW heat for 6 to 8 hours

6. Include lemon juice toward the part of the bargain time.

NUTRITION: calories 265, Fat 19g, carbs 1g, protein 21g, fiber 2g, potassium 711mg, sodium 22mg

457. Chicken Vegetable Curry

Cooking Time: 9 hours | Servings: 5

INGREDIENTS:

- 2 to 3 boneless chicken breasts
- ¼ Cup of chopped green onions
- 1 can of 4 oz of diced green chili peppers
- 2 tsps of minced garlic
- 1 and 1/2 tsps of curry powder
- 1 tsp of chili Powder
- 1 tsp of cumin
- ½ tsp of cinnamon
- 1 tsp of lime juice
- 1 and 1/2 cups water
- 1 can or 7 oz of coconut milk
- 2 Cups of white cooked rice
- Chopped cilantro, for garnish

DIRECTIONS:

1. Combine the green onion with the chicken, the green chili peppers, the garlic, the curry powder, the chili powder, the cumin, the cinnamon, the lime juice, and the water in the bottom of a 6-qt slow cooker
2. Cover the slow cooker with a lid and cook your ingredients on Low for about 7 to 9 hours
3. After the cooking time ends up; shred the chicken with the help of a fork
4. Add in the coconut milk and cook on High for about 15 mins
5. Top the chicken with cilantro; then serve your dish with rice
6. Enjoy your lunch!

NUTRITION: calories 254, fat 18g, carbs 6g, fiber 1.6g, potassium 370mg, sodium 240mg phosphorus: 114mg, protein 17g

458. Chicken Paella

Cooking Time: 10 mins | Servings: 8

INGREDIENTS:

- ½ pound of skinned, boned and cut into pieces, chicken breasts
- 1/4 cup of water
- 1 can of 10-1/2 oz of low-sodium chicken broth
- ½ pound of peeled and cleaned medium-size shrimp
- ½ cup of frozen green pepper
- 1/3 cup of chopped red bell
- 1/3 cup of thinly sliced green onion
- 2 minced garlic cloves
- 1/4 tsp of pepper
- 1 dash of ground saffron
- 1 cup of uncooked instant brown rice

DIRECTIONS:

1. Combine the first 3 ingredients in medium casserole and cover it with a lid; then microwave it for about 4 mins
2. Stir in the shrimp and the following 6 ingredients; then cover and microwave the shrimp on a high heat for about 3 and ½ mins
3. Stir in the rice; then cover and set aside for about 5 mins
4. Serve and enjoy your paella!

NUTRITION: calories 236, Fat 11g, carbs 6g, fiber 1.2g, potassium 178mg, sodium 83mg, phosphorus 144mg, protein 28g

459. Chicken Rigatoni

Cooking time: 15 mins | Servings: 4

INGREDIENTS:

- 6 oz whole-wheat rigatoni (or any other pasta)
- 1 pound boneless, skinless chicken breasts, cut into pieces, and cooked
- 2 tomatoes, chopped
- ½ medium onion, chopped
- 1 large red bell pepper, julienned

- 1 large yellow bell pepper, julienned
- 2 garlic cloves, minced
- ¼ cup olive oil
- ½ cup low-sodium chicken broth
- ¼ cup minced fresh parsley
- 2 tbsp finely chopped fresh basil

DIRECTIONS:

1. Cook the rigatoni according to package directions: (without adding salt), drain, and set aside.
2. In a large skillet over medium heat, heat the oil. Add the onion, peppers, and garlic, and sauté for 6 mins.
3. Add the tomatoes, chicken broth, parsley, and salt and pepper if desired. Add the lemon juice. Add the chicken to the skillet and cook the chicken in the sauce over low heat just until the chicken is warmed in the sauce.
4. Arrange the cooked rigatoni on a serving platter. Spoon the chicken and pepper sauce over the rigatoni and serve.

NUTRITION: calories 380, Fat 11g, protein 31g, carbs 41g, sugars 6g, fiber 7g, sodium 80mg

460. Easy Chicken Fajitas

Cooking time: 15 mins | Servings: 4

INGREDIENTS:

- Cooking spray
- 4 cups frozen bell pepper strips
- 2 cups onion, sliced
- 1 tsp ground cumin
- 1 tsp chili powder
- 2 (10-ounce) cans no-salt diced tomatoes and green chilies (Ro-Tel brand)
- 8 (6-inch) whole-wheat flour tortillas, warmed

DIRECTIONS:

1. Spray a large skillet with cooking spray. Preheat skillet to medium-high heat. Add the bell peppers and onions and cook for 7 mins or until tender, stirring occasionally. Remove from skillet and set aside
2. Add chicken to skillet. Sprinkle with cumin and chili powder. Cook for 4 mins until no longer pink and an instant-read thermometer registers 165°F
3. Return peppers and onions to skillet; add drained tomatoes and green chilies. Cook for 2 mins more or until hot

NUTRITION: calories 424, Fat 8.8 g, carbs 51g, protein 33 g, sodium 54 mg

461. Chicken Asian style

Cooking time: 8 hours | Servings: 8

INGREDIENTS:

- 6 boneless chicken breasts
- 2 tbsps olive oil
- 1 cup low-Sodium chicken broth
- 3 tbsps reduced-Sodium soy sauce
- ¼ tsp crushed red pepper flakes
- 1 garlic clove, crushed
- 1 can (8oz) water chestnuts, sliced and rinsed (optional)
- ½ cup sliced green onions
- 1 cup chopped red or green bell pepper
- 1 cup chopped celery
- ¼ cup cornstarch
- ⅓ cup water
- 3 cups cooked white rice
- ½ large chicken breast for 1 chicken thigh

DIRECTIONS:

1. Include all fixings into the moderate cooker.
2. Cook on LOW for 8 hours
3. Serve over cooked white rice.

NUTRITION: calories 220,fat 7.8 g, carbs 19g, protein 24 g, sodium 54 mg

462. Crispy Chicken Rolls

Cooking time: 15 mins | Servings: 12

INGREDIENTS:

- 2 cups cooked and finely chopped chicken
- 4 oz blue cheese
- vegetable oil
- 12 egg roll wrappers
- ½ cup tomato sauce
- 2 chopped green onions
- ½ tsp erythritol
- 2 finely chopped celery stalks

DIRECTIONS:

1. Mix in a bowl the chicken meat with blue cheese, green onions, celery, tomato sauce and sweetener and stir well
2. Refrigerate for 2 hours
3. Arrange the egg wrappers on a working surface, divide chicken mix on them, roll and seal edges
4. Put in a pot vegetable oil and heat up to over medium-high heat
5. Include egg rolls and cook until they are golden, flip and cook on the other side as well
6. Place on a platter and serve them

NUTRITION: calories 224, fat 7.8 g, carbs 6g, protein 10 g, sodium 54 mg

463. Mango Chicken Stir-Fry

Cooking time: 15 mins | Servings: 4

INGREDIENTS:

- nonstick cooking spray
- 1 lb boneless, skinless chicken breasts, cut into bite-size chunks
- 1/4 cup pineapple juice
- 3 tbsps low-Sodium soy sauce
- 1/4 tsp ground ginger
- 1 red bell pepper, cut into bite-size strips
- 2 mangos, pitted and cut into bite-size strips
- 1/4 cup toasted, slivered almonds ground black pepper to taste
- 2 cups cooked brown rice

DIRECTIONS:

1. Spray a large wok or skillet with nonstick cooking spray.
2. Sauté chicken over medium-high heat until cooked through, about 10 mins.
3. In a sall bowl, stir together pineapple juice, soy sauce, and ginger. Add sauce and bell pepper to the skillet.
4. Cook and stir for about 5 mins until peppers are crisp-tender.
5. Add the mango and almonds to the wok or skillet and cook until hot. Season with ground black pepper to taste.
6. Serve each cup of stir-fry over 1/2 cup of brown rice.

NUTRITION: calories 387, fat 8.8 g, carbs 45g, protein 37 g, sodium 41 mg

464. Tuscany Meatballs

Cooking time: 15 mins | Servings: 16

INGREDIENTS:

- 1/4 cup almond flour
- 1 lb ground turkey meat
- 2 tbsp olive oil
- 2 tbsp egg
- 2 tbsp chopped basil
- ½ tsp garlic powder
- ½ cup shredded mozzarella cheese
- 2 tbsp chopped sundried tomatoes

DIRECTIONS:

1. Get a bowl and mix turkey with egg, almond flour, garlic powder, sundried tomatoes, mozzarella and basil and stir properly
2. In the mixture carve out the shape of 12 meatballs
3. Heat a pot containing the oil to over medium-high heat

4. Put the meatballs into the oil and cook
5. Set them for 2 mins on each side on a platter and serve

NUTRITION: calories 80, fat 8.8 g, carbs 5g, protein 7 g, sodium 38 mg

465. Chicken Fried Rice

Cooking time: 8 mins | Servings: 2

INGREDIENTS:

- 4 oz cubed chicken breast
- 4 oz shrimp
- 2 tbsp oil
- 2 minced garlic cloves
- 1 cup mix vegetables-frozen
- 12 oz overnight rice
- 1 tbsp fish sauce
- 1 tbsp soy sauce
- ¼ tsp oyster sauce
- ¼ tsp white pepper
- 2 eggs

DIRECTIONS:

1. In a pan, add oil and garlic, cook, until the aroma of the garlic becomes present
2. Add shrimp, chicken, and vegetables
3. Put in in rice and stir to combine with veggies
4. Add soy sauce, fish sauce, oyster sauce, salt, and pepper and stir the rice for a few mins
5. Use a spatula to make a gap in the center of the rice
6. Dispense eggs in the center and let it sit for 30 sec

NUTRITION: calories 307, fat 5.8 g, carbs 55g, protein 15 g, sodium 88 mg

466. Turkey Club burger

Cooking time: 15 mins | Servings: 4

INGREDIENTS:

- 12 oz 99 percent Fat-free ground turkey
- 1/2 cup scallions (green onions), rinsed and sliced
- 1/4 tsp ground black pepper
- 1 large egg
- 1 tbsp olive oil

For spread

- 2 tbsps light mayonnaise
- 1 tbsp Dijon mustard
- For toppings
- 4 oz spinach or arugula, rinsed and dried
- 4 oz portabella mushroom, rinsed, grilled or broiled, and sliced (optional)
- 4 whole-wheat hamburger buns

DIRECTIONS:

1. Preheat oven broiler on high temperature (with the rack 3 inches from heat source) or grill on medium-high heat.
2. To prepare burgers, combine ground turkey, scallions, pepper, and egg, and mix well. Form into 1/2- to 3/4-inch thick patties, and coat each lightly with olive oil.
3. Broil or grill burgers for about 7–9 mins on each side (to a minimum internal temperature of 160 °F).
4. Combine mayonnaise and mustard to make a spread.
5. Assemble 3/4 tbsp spread, 1 ounce spinach or arugula, several slices of grilled portabella mushroom (optional), and one burger on each bun.

NUTRITION: calories 299, fat 11.8 g, carbs 26g, protein 29 g, sodium 54 mg

467. Chicken Enchiladas

Cooking time: 40 mins | Servings: 4

INGREDIENTS:

- 1 cup cooked, chopped chicken breast

- nonstick cooking spray
- 1 large onion, peeled and chopped
- 1 green bell pepper, seeded and chopped
- 1 large zucchini, chopped
- 3/4 cup red enchilada sauce
- 2 (8-ounce) cans no salt added tomato sauce
- 8 (6-inch) corn tortillas
- 2/3 cup shredded reduced Fat: Monterey Jack cheese

DIRECTIONS:

1. Preheat oven to 375°F.
2. Spray large skillet with nonstick cooking spray. Sauté onion for 5 mins , stirring occasionally. Add bell pepper and zucchini; cook for 5 mins more. Stir in chicken; set aside.
3. Meanwhile, combine enchilada sauce and tomato sauce in a small bowl; add 1/2 cup to vegetable and chicken mixture.
4. Soften tortillas on the stovetop or in the microwave. Dip each tortilla in sauce and place equal amounts of vegetable and chicken mixture on one side. Roll up and place in a 13x9-inch baking pan. Pour remaining sauce over the top.
5. Cover loosely with foil and bake for 20 to 25 mins. Remove cover and sprinkle cheese over top; bake for 5 mins more. Serve while hot.

NUTRITION: calories 311, fat 5.8 g, carbs 42g, protein 25 g, sodium 71 mg

468. Cheesy Wings

Cooking time: 25 mins | Servings: 6

INGREDIENTS:

- 6 lb chicken wings cut in halves
- ½ tsp Italian seasoning
- a pinch crushed red pepper flakes
- 2 tbsp ghee
- 1 tsp garlic powder
- ½ cup grated parmesan cheese
- 1 egg

DIRECTIONS:

1. Place the chicken wings on a lined baking sheet
2. Preheat your oven to 425°F and introduce the chicken wings and bake for 17 mins
3. On the other hand; mix ghee with cheese, egg, salt, pepper, pepper flakes, garlic powder and Italian seasoning in your blender and blend until it is smooth
4. Remove the chicken wings from the oven, flip them, turn oven to broil and broil them for about 5 mins more
5. Remove the chicken pieces out of the oven again and pour the sauce over them, toss to coat thoroughly and cook for 1 min more
6. Serve them as a quick appetizer.

NUTRITION: calories 135, fat 7.8 g, carbs 5g, protein 14 g, sodium 68mg

469. Chicken Salad balsamic

Cooking time: 15 mins | Servings: 6

INGREDIENTS:

- 3 cup diced cold, cooked chicken
- 1 cup diced apple
- ½ cup diced celery
- 2 green onions, chopped
- ½ cup chopped walnuts
- 3 tbsps. balsamic vinegar
- 5 tbsps. olive oil
- salt and pepper to taste

DIRECTIONS:

1. Toss together the celery, chicken, onion, walnuts, and apple in a big bowl.
2. Whisk the oil together with the vinegar in a small bowl. Pour the dressing over the salad. Then add pepper and salt to taste. Combine the ingredients thoroughly. Leave the

mixture for 10-15 mins. Toss once more and chill.

NUTRITION: calories 336, fat 26.8 g, carbs 6g, protein 19g, sodium 58 mg

470. Chicken and Veggie Soup

Cooking time: 6 hours | Servings: 8

INGREDIENTS:

- 4 cups cooked and chopped chicken
- 7 cups reduced-Sodium chicken broth
- 1-pound frozen white corn
- 1 medium onion diced
- 4 cloves garlic minced
- 2 carrots peeled and diced
- 2 celery stalks chopped
- 2 tsps oregano
- 2 tsp curry powder
- ½ tsp black pepper

DIRECTIONS:

1. Warm oil in a skillet and dark-colored chicken on all sides.
2. Add chicken to a slow cooker with the remainder of the fixings aside from cornstarch and water.
3. Spread and cook on LOW for 6 to 8hours
4. Following 6-8 hours | independently blend cornstarch and cold water until smooth. Gradually include into the moderate cooker.

NUTRITION: calories 220, fat 7.8 g, carbs 19g, protein 24 g, sodium 54 mg

471. Chicken and Broccoli

Cooking time: 10 mins | Servings: 4

INGREDIENTS:

- 2 tbsp sesame oil (or olive oil) | divided
- 4 cups cubed chicken
- 2 cups cubed carrots
- 1 cup broccoli florets
- 3 tbsp balsamic vinegar, divided
- 2 tsps ground ginger

DIRECTIONS:

1. Heat ½ tbsp of olive oil in a wok or large sauté pan over medium heat. Add the cubed chicken and cook until lightly browned and cooked through (about 5 to 7 mins). transfer chicken to a bowl, cover, and set aside
2. add 1½ tbsp of olive oil to the pan, along with the garlic and carrots. cook until the carrots begin to soften (about 3 to 4 mins). add the thawed broccoli florets and water chestnuts along with 1 tbsp of balsamic vinegar and cook for 3 to 4 mins
3. add the remaining balsamic vinegar and ground ginger. add the cooked chicken and stir until well combined

NUTRITION: calories 195, fat 9.8 g, carbs 15g, protein 14 g, sodium 48mg

472. Tagine with Meatballs

Cooking time: 45 mins | Servings: 4

INGREDIENTS:

For Dumplings

- 3 cup of minced meat
- 1 egg
- 2 tbsp parsley very finely chopped
- 1/2 onion very finely cut
- 1 shredded garlic clove

For the Sauce

- 1/2 onion | finely chopped
- 6 tbsp of oil
- 1 cube of chicken broth
- Pepper and cinnamon
- 4 cup of zucchini cut to taste slightly salted and fries
- 3 cup of boiling water

DIRECTIONS:

1. Put all the ingredients of the meatballs in a salad bowl.
2. Knead everything with your hand | and make balls of a size of a walnut.
3. In a small pot, heat the oil.
4. Add the onion, pepper, cinnamon and fry for 5 mins over low heat.

5. Wet with boiling water, immerse your meatballs and crumble your bouillon cube.
6. Let it cook for 40 mins
7. Remove the meatballs and brown them in a pan with 2 tbsp of oil.
8. Reduce the sauce | turn off the heat | and put the meatballs back on.
9. When serving | heat the zucchini in the pan.

NUTRITION: calories 207, fat 19g, carbs 12g, protein 14g, sodium 55 mg, phosphorus 27 mg, potassium 206mg

473. Parmesan Roasted Cauliflower

Cooking time: 25 mins | Servings: 4

INGREDIENTS:

- 4 cups cauliflower florets
- ½ cup grated Parmesan cheese
- 2 tbsps olive oil
- 4 garlic cloves | minced
- ½ tsp dried thyme leaves
- ¼ tsp freshly ground black pepper

DIRECTIONS

1. Preheat the oven to 400°F.
2. On a baking sheet, combine the cauliflower, Parmesan cheese, olive oil, garlic, thyme, pepper, and salt and toss to coat.
3. Roast for 25 to 30 mins, stirring once during cooking time, until the cauliflower has light golden-brown edges and is tender. Serve.

NUTRITION: calories 144, fat 11.7 g, carbs 4.8g, protein 7.3g, sodium 332 mg, phosphorus 130 mg

474. Cabbage Apple Stir-Fry

Cooking time: 10 mins | Servings: 4

INGREDIENTS:

- 2 tbsps olive oil
- 3 cups chopped red cabbage
- 2 tbsps water
- 1 Granny Smith apple, chopped
- 3 scallions, both white and green parts chopped
- 1 tbsp freshly squeezed lemon juice
- 1 tsp caraway seeds

DIRECTIONS

1. In a big skillet or frying pan, heat the olive oil over medium-high temperature.
2. Add the cabbage and stir-fry for 2 mins. Add the water, cover and cook for 2 mins.
3. Uncover and stir in the apple and scallions and sprinkle with the lemon juice, caraway seeds and salt. Stir-fry for 4 to 6 mins longer, or until the cabbage is crisp-tender. Serve.

NUTRITION: calories 107, fat 7.7 g, carbs 10.8g, protein 17.3 g, sodium 55 mg, phosphorus 27 mg, potassium 206mg

475. Mozzarella Salad

Cooking time: 10 mins | Servings: 2

INGREDIENTS:

- 1 avocado, pitted, halved
- 1/3 cup Mozzarella balls, cherry size
- 1 cup fresh basil
- 1 tbsp walnuts
- ¼ tsp garlic, minced
- ¾ tsp salt
- ¾ tsp ground black pepper
- 4 tbsps olive oil
- 1 oz Parmesan, grated
- 1/3 cup cherry tomatoes

DIRECTIONS:

1. To make pesto sauce, blend salt, minced garlic, walnuts, fresh basil, ground black pepper, and olive oil.
2. When the mixture is smooth, add grated cheese and pulse it for 3 seconds more.
3. Then scoop ½ flesh from the avocado halves.
4. In the mixing bowl, mix mozzarella balls and cherry tomatoes.

5. Add pesto sauce and shake it well.
6. Preheat the oven to 360°F.
7. Fill the avocado halves with the cherry tomato mixture and bake for 10 mins.

NUTRITION: calories 526, fat 11.7 g, carbs 11.8g, protein 7.3g, sodium 332 mg, phosphorus 110 mg

476. Celery and Fennel Salad with berries

Cooking time: 0 | Servings: 6

INGREDIENTS:

- 2 cups sliced celery
- ½ cup chopped fennel
- ½ cup dried cranberries
- ¼ cup olive oil
- 2 tbsps freshly squeezed lemon juice
- 1 tbsp Dijon mustard
- 2 tbsps minced celery leaves

DIRECTIONS:

4. In a serving bowl, whisk the olive oil, lemon juice, and mustard.
5. Add the celery, fennel, and cranberries to the dressing and toss to coat. Sprinkle with the celery leaves and serve.

NUTRITION: calories 130, fat 9.8 g, carbs 12g, protein 1 g, potassium 107 mg, sodium 88 mg

477. Red Cabbage Burgers

Cooking time: 15 mins | Servings: 3

INGREDIENTS:

- 1 cup red cabbage
- 3 tbsps almond flour
- 1 tbsp cream cheese
- 1 oz scallions | chopped
- ½ tsp salt
- ½ tsp chili powder
- ½ cup fresh cilantro

DIRECTIONS:

1. Chop red cabbage roughly and transfer in the blender.
2. Add fresh cilantro and blend the mixture until very smooth.
3. After this, transfer it to the bowl.
4. Add cream cheese, scallions, salt, chili powder, and almond flour.
5. Stir the mixture well.
6. Make 3 big burgers from the cabbage mixture or 6 small burgers.
7. Line the baking tray with baking paper.
8. Place the burgers in the tray.
9. Bake the cilantro burgers for 15 mins at 360°F.
10. Flip the burgers onto another side after 8 mins of cooking.

NUTRITION: calories 182, fat 15.7 g, carbs 8.8g, protein 6.3g, sodium 182 mg, phosphorus 170 mg

478. Easy Noodles

Cooking time: 7 mins | Servings: 6

INGREDIENTS:

- 1-pound jicama, peeled
- 2 tbsps butter
- 1 tsp chili flakes
- 1 tsp salt
- ¾ cup of water

DIRECTIONS:

1. Spiralize jicama with the help of a spiralizer and place in jicama spirals in the saucepan.
2. Add butter, chili flakes, and salt.
3. Then add water and preheat the ingredients until the butter is melted.
4. Mix it well.
5. Close the lid and cook noodles for 4 mins over the medium heat.
6. Stir the jicama noodles well before transferring them to the serving plates.

NUTRITION: calories 62, fat 3.7g, carbs 6.8g, protein 0.6g, sodium 195 mg, phosphorus 199 mg

479. Chow Mein

Cooking time: 10 mins | Servings: 6

INGREDIENTS:

- 7 oz kelp noodles
- 5 oz broccoli florets
- 1 tbsp tahini sauce
- ¼ tsp minced ginger
- 1 tsp Sriracha
- ½ tsp garlic powder
- 1 cup of water

DIRECTIONS:

1. Pour water into the saucepan and bring it to boil.
2. Add broccoli and boil it for 4 mins over the high heat.
3. Then drain water into the bowl and chill it till it comes to the room temperature.
4. Soak the kelp noodles in the "broccoli water".
5. Meanwhile, place tahini sauce, sriracha, minced ginger, and garlic in the saucepan.
6. Bring the mixture to boil. Add oil if needed.
7. Then add broccoli and soaked noodles.
8. Add 3 tbsps of "broccoli water".
9. Mix the noodles and bring to boil.
10. Switch off the heat and transfer the Chow Mein into the serving bowls.

NUTRITION: calories 18, fat 0.8 g, carbs 3g, protein 0.9g, potassium 149 mg, sodium 98 mg

480. Lemony Roasted Chicken

Cooking time: 1 hour + 30 mins| Servings: 8

INGREDIENTS

- 1 3-lb whole chicken ½ tsp ground black pepper
- ½ tsp mustard powder
- ½ tsp salt
- 1 tsp garlic powder
- 2 lemons
- 2 tbsps. olive oil
- 2 tsps. Italian seasoning

DIRECTIONS:

1. In a small bowl, mix black pepper, garlic powder, mustard powder, and salt.
2. Rinse chicken well and slice off giblets.
3. In a greased 9 x 13 baking dish, place chicken on it. Add 1½ tsp of seasoning made earlier inside the chicken and rub the remaining seasoning around the chicken.
4. In a small bowl, mix olive oil and juice from 2 lemons. Drizzle over chicken.
5. Bake chicken in an oven preheated at 350°F until juices run clear, for around 1½ hour. Occasionally, baste the chicken with its juices.

NUTRITION: calories 190, fat: 7.8 g, carbs 2g, protein 37 g, potassium 439 mg, sodium 328 mg

481. Chicken and Apples Mix

Cooking Time: 40 mins | Servings: 4

INGREDIENTS:

- ½ cup chicken stock
- 1 red onion, sliced
- ½ cup tomato sauce
- 2 green apples, cored and chopped
- 1-pound breast, skinless, boneless and cubed
- 1 tsp thyme, chopped
- 1 and ½ tbsps olive oil
- 1 tbsp chives, chopped

DIRECTIONS:

1. In a roasting pan, combine the chicken with the tomato sauce, apples and the rest of the ingredients except the chives, introduce the pan in the oven and bake at 425°F for 40 mins.

2. Divide the mix between plates, sprinkle the chives on top and serve.

NUTRITION: calories 292, fat: 16.1, fiber 9.4, carbs 15.4, protein 16.4

482. Walnut Turkey and Peaches

Cooking Time: 1 hour | Servings: 4

INGREDIENTS:

- 2 turkey breasts, skinless, boneless and sliced
- ¼ cup chicken stock
- 1 tbsp walnuts, chopped
- 1 red onion, chopped
- Salt and black pepper to the taste
- 2 tbsps olive oil
- 4 peaches, pitted and cut into quarters
- 1 tbsp cilantro, chopped

DIRECTIONS:

1. In a roasting pan greased with the oil, combine the turkey and the onion and the rest of the ingredients except the cilantro, introduce in the oven and bake at 390°F for 1 hour.
2. Divide the mix between plates, sprinkle the cilantro on top and serve.

NUTRITION: calories 500, fat: 14, fiber 3, carbs 15, protein 10

483. Chicken Curry

Cooking time: 18 mins | Servings: 3-4

INGREDIENTS

- 1-pound lean ground chicken
- 3 tbsps essential olive oil
- 2 bay leaves
- 2 onions, ground to some paste
- ½ tbsp garlic paste
- ½ tbsp ginger paste
- 2 tomatoes, chopped finely
- 1 tbsp ground cumin
- 1 tbsp ground coriander
- 1 tsp ground turmeric
- 1 tsp red chili powder
- Salt, to taste
- 2 cups frozen peas
- 1½ cups water
- 1-2 tsps garam masala powder

DIRECTIONS:

1. In a deep skillet, heat oil on medium heat.
2. Add bay leaves and sauté for approximately half a minute.
3. Add onion paste and sauté for approximately 3-4 mins.
4. Add garlic and ginger paste and sauté for around 1-1½ mins.
5. Add tomatoes and spices, and cook, stirring occasionally for about 3-4 mins.
6. Stir in chicken and cook for about 4-5 mins.
7. Stir in peas and water and bring to a boil on high heat.
8. Reduce the heat to low and simmer approximately 5-8 mins or till desired doneness.
9. Stir in garam masala and remove from heat.

NUTRITION: calories 450, fat 10 g, carbs 19g, protein 38 g, potassium 239 mg, sodium 228 mg

484. Chicken Couscous

Cooking time: 30 mins | Servings: 4

INGREDIENTS:

- 1 lb skinless chicken legs, split (about 4 whole legs)
- 1 tbsp Moroccan spice blend
- 1 cup carrots, rinsed, peeled, and diced
- 1 tbsp olive oil
- 1 cup onion, diced
- 1/4 cup lemon juice
- 2 cups low-Sodium chicken broth
- 1/2 cup ripe black olives, sliced
- 1 tbsp chili sauce (optional)

For couscous

- 1 cup low-Sodium chicken broth
- 1 cup couscous (try whole-wheat couscous)
- 1 tbsp fresh mint, rinsed, dried, and shredded thin (or 1 tsp dried)

DIRECTIONS:

1. Heat olive oil in a large sauté pan. Add chicken legs, and brown on all sides, about 2–3 mins per side. Remove chicken from pan and put on a plate with a cover to hold warm.
2. Add spice blend to sauté pan and toast gently.
3. Add carrots and onion to sauté pan, and cook for about 3–4 mins or until the onions have turned clear, but not brown.
4. Add lemon juice, chicken broth, and olives to sauté pan, and bring to a boil over high heat. Add chicken legs, and return to a boil. Cover and gently simmer for about 10–15 mins (to a minimum internal temperature of 165 °F).
5. Meanwhile, prepare the couscous by bringing chicken broth to a boil in a saucepan. Add couscous and remove from the heat. Cover and let stand for 10 mins.
6. Fluff couscous with a fork, and gently mix in the mint.
7. When chicken is cooked, add salt. Serve two chicken legs over 1/2 cup couscous topped with 1/2 cup sauce in a serving bowl. Add chili sauce to taste.

NUTRITION: calories 333, fat 12.8 g, carbs 36g, protein 37g, potassium 239 mg, sodium 158 mg

485. Roasted Turkey

Cooking time: 45 mins | Servings: 6

INGREDIENTS:

- 1 whole turkey
- 2 tsp garlic paste
- 1 tsp ginger powder
- 2 tbsp soya sauce
- 1 tsp cayenne pepper
- 3 tbsp lemon juice
- 2 tbsp red wine vinegar
- ½ tsp mustard powder
- 1 tsp cinnamon powder
- 2 tbsp sesame seeds oil

DIRECTIONS:

1. In a bowl add garlic paste, ginger powder, cayenne pepper, black pepper, cinnamon powder, mustard powder, lemon juice, oil, vinegar, soya sauce and salt, mix well
2. Now pour this marinate over turkey and rub with hands all over it
3. Cover and leave to marinade for 15-20 mins
4. Preheat oven at 355° F
5. Spread aluminum foil in baking tray and place turkey on it
6. Bake for 40-45 mins or till nicely golden.

NUTRITION: calories 244, fat 7 g, carbs 3g, protein 44 g, potassium 199mg, sodium 208 mg

486. Smokey Turkey Chili

Cooking time: 45 mins | Servings: 8

INGREDIENTS:

- 12-ounce lean ground turkey
- 1/2 red onion, chopped
- 2 cloves garlic, crushed and chopped
- ½ tsp of smoked paprika
- ½ tsp of chili powder
- ½ tsp of dried thyme
- ¼ cup reduced-Sodium beef stock
- ½ cup of water
- 1½ cups baby spinach leaves, washed
- 3 wheat tortillas

DIRECTIONS:

1. Brown the ground beef in a dry skillet over medium-high heat.
2. Add in the red onion and garlic.
3. Sauté the onion until it goes clear.
4. Transfer the contents of the skillet to the slow cooker.
5. Add the remaining ingredients and simmer on low for 30–45 mins.
6. Stir through the spinach for the last few mins to wilt.
7. Slice tortillas and gently toast under the broiler until slightly crispy.
8. Serve on top of the turkey chili.

NUTRITION: calories 93, fat 5.8 g, carbs 3g, protein 8 g, potassium 142.5 mg, sodium 84 mg

487. Homemade Turkey Soup

Cooking time: 1 hour | Servings: 4

INGREDIENTS

- 6 lbs turkey breast. It should have some meat (at least 2 cups) remaining on it to make a good, rich soup.
- 2 medium onions
- 3 stalks of celery
- 1 tsp dried thyme
- 1/2 tsp dried rosemary and sage
- 1 tsp dried basil
- 1/2 tsp dried tarragon
- 1/2 lb Italian pastina or pasta

DIRECTIONS

1. Place turkey breast in a large 6-quart pot. Cover with water, at least 3/4 full.
2. Peel onions, cut in large pieces, and add to pot. Wash celery stalks, slice, and add to pot also.
3. Simmer covered for about 1 hour.
4. Remove carcass from pot. Divide soup into smaller, shallower containers for quick cooling in the refrigerator.
5. While soup is cooling, remove remaining meat from turkey carcass. Cut into pieces.
6. Add turkey meat to skimmed soup along with herbs and spices.
7. Bring to a boil and add pastina. Continue cooking on low boil for about 20 mins until pastina is done. Serve at once or refrigerate for later reheating.

NUTRITION: calories 226, fat 5g, carbs 3g, protein 9g, potassium 131mg, sodium 79mg

488. Tropical Chicken salad

Cooking time: 0 mins | Servings: 4

INGREDIENTS

- 1 1/2 cup of shredded cooked chicken
- 1/2 cup of diced celery
- 1 cup of peeled and diced apples
- 1 cup of drained unsweetened pineapple chunks
- 1/2 cup of seedless grapes
- 1 cup of diced pears
- 1/2 tsp. of sugar
- 2 tbsp. of lemon juice
- 1/2 cup of mayonnaise
- Dash hot sauce
- 1 tsp. of pepper
- Paprika for garnish

DIRECTIONS:

1. Mix sugar, juice, mayo, hot sauce, and pepper.
2. In a large bowl, mix together the rest of the ingredients.
3. Add dressing to fruit and chicken and combine well.
4. Serve on a bed of lettuce and sprinkle with paprika.

NUTRITION: calories 443, fat: 17.3 g, carbs 7.5g, protein 33.8 g, sodium 245 mg

489. Chicken Meatballs

Cooking time: 25 mins | Servings: 3-4

INGREDIENTS

- 1-pound lean ground chicken
- 1 tbsp onion paste
- 1 tsp fresh ginger paste
- 1 tsp garlic paste
- 1 green chili | chopped finely
- 1 tbsp fresh cilantro leaves, chopped
- 1 tsp ground coriander
- ½ tsp cumin seeds
- ½ tsp red chili powder
- ½ tsp ground turmeric
- Salt, to taste

For Curry:

- 3 tbsps olive oil
- ½ tsp cumin seeds
- 1 (1-inch) cinnamon stick
- 3 whole cloves
- 3 whole green cardamoms
- 1 whole black cardamom
- 2 onions, chopped
- 1 tsp fresh ginger, minced
- 1 tsp garlic, minced
- 4 whole tomatoes, chopped finely
- 2 tsps ground coriander
- 1 tsp garam masala powder
- ½ tsp ground nutmeg
- ½ tsp red chili powder
- ½ tsp ground turmeric
- Salt, to taste
- 1 cup water
- Chopped fresh cilantro, for garnishing

DIRECTIONS:

1. For meatballs in a substantial bowl, add all ingredients and mix till well combined.
2. Make small equal-sized meatballs from the mixture.
3. In a big deep skillet, heat oil on medium heat.
4. Add meatballs and fry for approximately 3-5 mins or till browned from all sides.
5. Transfer the meatballs into a bowl.
6. In the same skillet, add cumin seeds, cinnamon stick, cloves, green cardamom, and black cardamom and sauté, approximately for 1 minute.
7. Add onions and sauté for around 4-5 mins.
8. Add ginger and garlic paste and sauté approximately for 1 minute.
9. Add tomato and spices and cook, crushing with the back of the spoon for approximately 2-3 mins.
10. Add water and meatballs and let it boil.
11. Reduce heat to low.
12. Simmer for approximately 10 mins.
13. Serve hot with all the garnishing of cilantro.

NUTRITION: calories 421, carbs 18g ,phosphorus 126mg, potassium 128mg, sodium 120mg, protein 16g

490. Asian chicken Satay

Cooking time: 10 mins | Servings: 6

INGREDIENTS:

- 2 limes juice
- 2 tbsps brown sugar
- 1 tbsp minced garlic
- 2 tsps ground cumin
- 12 boneless, skinless chicken breast, cut into strips

DIRECTIONS:

1. In a bowl, stir together the cumin, garlic, brown sugar, and lime juice.
2. Add the chicken strips to the bowl and marinate in the refrigerator for 1 hour.
3. Heat the barbecue to medium-high.
4. Remove the chicken from the marinade and thread each strip onto wooden skewers that have been soaked in the water.
5. Grill the chicken for about 4 mins per side or until the meat is cooked through but still juicy.

NUTRITION: calories 78,carbs 4g, phosphorus 116mg, potassium 108mg, sodium 100mg, protein 12g

491. Chicken Creole style

Cooking time: 20 mins | Servings: 6

INGREDIENTS:

- nonstick cooking spray
- 1 lb boneless, skinless chicken breasts, cut into large chunks
- 1 large onion, chopped
- 1 (14-1/2-ounce) can diced tomatoes
- 1/3 cup tomato paste
- 2 stalks celery, chopped
- 1-1/2 tsps garlic powder
- 1 tsp onion powder
- 1/4 tsp red pepper flakes
- 1/8 tsp ground black pepper
- 1-1/2 cups broccoli florets

DIRECTIONS

1. Spray a large skillet with nonstick cooking spray and heat over medium heat.
2. Add chicken and onion; cook, stirring frequently, for 10 mins.
3. Stir in all remaining Ingredients: except broccoli and cook for 5 mins, stirring occasionally.
4. Stir in broccoli, cook for 5 mins more. Serve while hot.

NUTRITION: calories 140, fat 3g, sodium 132mg, carbs 11g, fiber 1g, phosphorus 196mg, potassium 289mg, protein 18g

492. Turkey burger with jalapeno peppers

Cooking time: 10 mins | Servings: 4

INGREDIENTS:

- 1 pound turkey meat (ground)
- 1 cup zucchini, shredded
- ½ cup onion, minced
- 1 jalapeño pepper, seeded and minced
- 1 egg
- 1 tsp extra-spicy blend
- Fresh poblano peppers (seeded and sliced in half lengthwise)
- 1 tsp mustard

DIRECTIONS:

1. Start by taking a mixing bowl and adding in the turkey meat, zucchini, onion, jalapeño pepper, egg, and extra-spicy blend. Mix well to combine.
2. Divide the mixture into 4 equal portions. Form burger patties out of the same.
3. Prepare an electric griddle or an outdoor grill. Place the burger patties on the grill and cook until the top is blistered and tender. Place the sliced poblano peppers on the grill alongside the patties. Grilling the patties should take about 5 mins on each side.
4. Once done, place the patties onto the buns and top them with grilled peppers.

NUTRITION: protein 25g, carbs 5g, fat: 10g, calories 125 mg, sodium 128 mg, potassium 475 mg, phosphorus 280mg, fiber1.6 g

493. Gnocchi and chicken dumplings

Cooking time: 40 mins, Servings: 10

INGREDIENTS:

- 2 pounds chicken breast
- 1 pound gnocchi
- ¼ cup olive oil
- 6 cups chicken stock (reduced-Sodium)
- ½ cup fresh celery, diced finely
- ½ cup fresh onions, diced finely
- ½ cup fresh carrots, diced finely
- ¼ cup fresh parsley, chopped
- 1 tsp Italian seasoning

DIRECTIONS:

1. Start by placing the stock over a high flame. Add in the oil and let it heat through.
2. Add the chicken to the hot oil and shallow-fry until all sides turn golden brown.
3. Toss in the carrots, onions, and celery and cook for about 5 mins. Pour in the chicken stock and let it cool on a high flame for about 30 mins.
4. Reduce the flame and add in the italian seasoning. Stir well.
5. Toss in the store-bought gnocchi and let it cook for about 15 mins. Keep stirring.
6. Once done, transfer into a serving bowl. Add parsley and serve hot!

NUTRITION: protein 28g, carbs 38g, fat 10g, calories 58, sodium 121 mg

494. Turkey Sausage

Cooking time: 10 mins | Servings: 2

INGREDIENTS

- 1 pound 7% fat ground turkey
- 1/4 tsp salt
- 1/8 tsp garlic powder
- 1/8 tsp onion powder
- 1 tsp fennel seed

DIRECTIONS:

Press the fennel seed and in a small cup put together turkey with fennel seed, garlic, and onion powder, and salt.

NUTRITION calories 306, fat 22 g, carbs 6g, protein 19g, sodium 58 mg

495. Chicken Salad Wrap

Cooking time: 10 mins | Servings: 4

INGREDIENTS:

- 3-4 oz chicken breasts
- 2 whole chipotle peppers
- 1/4 cup white wine vinegar
- 1/4 cup low-calorie mayonnaise
- 2 diced stalks celery
- 2 carrots, cut into matchsticks
- 1 small yellow onion, diced (about 1/2 cup)
- 1/2 cup thinly sliced rutabaga or another root vegetable
- 4 oz spinach, cut into strips
- 2 whole-grain tortillas (12-inch diameter)

DIRECTIONS:

1. Set the oven or a grill to heat at 375°F. Bake the chicken for 10 mins per side.
2. Blend chipotle peppers with mayonnaise and wine vinegar in the blender.
3. Dice the baked chicken into cubes or small chunks.
4. Mix the chipotle mixture with all the ingredients except tortillas and spinach.
5. Spread 2 oz of spinach over tortilla and scoop the stuffing on top.
6. Wrap the tortilla and cut it into the half.

NUTRITION calories 300, fat 17.8 g, carbs 9g, protein 37 g, potassium 105 mg, sodium 70 mg

496. Chicken Salad with Apples | Grapes

Cooking time: 25 mins | Servings: 12

INGREDIENTS

- 4 cooked chicken breasts , shredded
- 2 granny smith apples, cut into small chunks
- 2cupchopped walnuts, or to taste
- 1/2 red onion , chopped
- 3 stalks celery , chopped
- 3 tbsps. Lemon juice
- 1/2cup vanilla yogurt
- 5 tbsps. Creamy salad dressing
- 5 tbsps. Mayonnaise
- 25 seedless red grapes , halved

DIRECTIONS:

1. In a big bowl, toss together the shredded chicken, lemon juice , apple chunks, celery, red onion, and walnuts.
2. Get another bowl and whisk together the dressing, vanilla yogurt, and mayonnaise. Pour over the chicken mixture. Toss to coat. Fold the grapes carefully into the salad.

NUTRITION: calories 307, fat 22g, carbs 10.8g , protein 17.3 g , sodium 128 mg

497. Chicken Spanish Style

Cooking time: 5 mins | Servings: 5

INGREDIENTS:

- 3-1/2 cups chicken breasts , cooked , skin and bone removed , and diced
- 1 cup onions , chopped
- 3/4 cup green peppers
- 2 tsps vegetable oil
- 1 8 oz can tomato sauce
- 1 tsp parsley , chopped
- 1/2 tsp black pepper
- 1-1/4 tsps garlic , minced
- 5 cups cooked brown rice (cooked in unsalted water)

DIRECTIONS:

In a large skillet , sauté onions and green peppers in oil for 5 mins on medium heat.

Add tomato sauce and spices. Heat through.

NUTRITION: calories 428 , fat 7.8 g , carbs 52g , protein 35 g

498. Smoky Chicken

Cooking time: 21 mins | Servings: 6

INGREDIENTS:

- 1 (3½-pound) whole chicken , rinsed and patted dry , giblets removed
- 1 cup chicken bone broth
- 2 large carrots , each cut into 4 pieces
- 2 celery stalks , each cut into 4 pieces
- 2 tbsp olive oil
- 1 tbsp salt and pepper
- 1½ tsps smoked paprika
- ¼ tsp cayenne pepper
- 1 large lemon , halved
- 6 garlic cloves , peeled and crushed
- 1 large onion , cut into 8 wedges , divided

DIRECTIONS:

1. In a small bowl , combine the olive oil , salt , paprika , pepper , and cayenne.
2. Place the chicken on a cutting board and rub the olive oil mixture under the skin and all over the outside. Stuff the cavity with the lemon halves , garlic cloves , and 3 to 4 wedges of onion.
3. Pour the broth into the electric pressure cooker. Add the remaining onion wedges , carrots , and celery. Insert a wire rack or trivet on top of the vegetables.
4. Place the chicken , breast-side up , on the rack.
5. Close and lock the lid of the pressure cooker. Set the valve to sealing.
6. Cook on high pressure for 21 mins.
7. When the cooking is complete , hit Cancel and allow the pressure to release naturally for 15 mins , then quick release any remaining pressure.
8. Once the pin drops , unlock and remove the lid.
9. Carefully remove the chicken to a clean cutting board. Remove the skin and cut the chicken into pieces or shred/chop the meat and serve.

NUTRITION: calories 215 , fat 9g , protein 25g , carbs 5g , sugars 2g , fiber 1g , sodium 847mg

499. Chicken Noodles

Cooking time: 15 mins | Servings: 4

INGREDIENTS:

- 8 oz noodles
- 2 boneless, skinless chicken breasts, halved lengthwise
- 1 large cucumber, seeded and diced
- 1 scallion, cut into 1-inch segments
- ¼ cup tahini
- 1 tbsp rice vinegar
- 1 tbsp soy sauce or tamari
- 1 tsp toasted sesame oil
- 1 (1-inch) piece fresh ginger, finely grated
- 1/3 cup water
- 1 tbsp sesame seeds

DIRECTIONS:

1. Preheat the broiler to high.
2. Bring a large pot of water to a boil. Add the noodles and cook until tender, according to the package directions. Drain and rinse the noodles in cool water.
3. On a baking sheet, arrange the chicken in a single layer. Broil for 5 to 7 mins on each side, depending on the thickness, until the chicken is cooked through and its juices run clear. Use two forks to shred the chicken.
4. In a small bowl, combine the tahini, rice vinegar, soy sauce, sesame oil, ginger, and water. Whisk to combine.
5. In a large bowl, toss the shredded chicken, noodles, cucumber, and scallions. Pour the tahini sauce over the noodles and toss to combine. Served sprinkled with the sesame seeds.

NUTRITION: calories 251, fat 8g, protein 16g, carbs 35g, sugars 2g, fiber 2g, sodium 482mg

500. Peppered Chicken with Kale

Cooking time: 15 mins | Servings: 4

INGREDIENTS:

- 4 (4-ounce) boneless, skinless chicken breasts
- 8 cups stemmed and roughly chopped kale, loosely packed (about 2 bunches)
- ¼ tsp salt
- 1 tbsp freshly ground black pepper
- 2 tbsp unsalted butter
- 1 tbsp olive oil
- ½ cup balsamic vinegar
- 16 cherry tomatoes, halved

DIRECTIONS:

1. Season both sides of the chicken breasts with the salt and pepper.
2. Heat a large skillet over medium heat. When hot, heat the butter and oil. Add the chicken and cook for 8 to 10 mins, flipping halfway through. When cooked all the way through, remove the chicken from the skillet and set aside.
3. Increase the heat to medium-high. Put the kale in the skillet and cook for 3 mins, stirring every minute.
4. Add the vinegar and the tomatoes and cook for another 3 to 5 mins.
5. Divide the kale and tomato mixture into four equal portions and top each portion with 1 chicken breast.

NUTRITION: calories 293, fat 11g, protein 31g, carbs 18g, sugars 4g, fiber 3g, sodium 328mg

501. Teriyaki Chicken with Broccoli

Cooking time: 20 mins | Servings: 4

INGREDIENTS:

Entrée:

- 4 (4-ounce) boneless | skinless chicken breasts | cut into bite-size cubes
- 1 (12-ounce) bag frozen broccoli
- 1 (12-ounce) bag frozen cauliflower rice
- 1 tbsp sesame oil

Sauce:

- ½ cup water
- 1 tbsp low-sodium soy sauce
- 2 tbsp honey
- 2 tbsp rice vinegar
- ¼ tsp garlic powder
- Pinch ground ginger
- 1 tbsp cornstarch

DIRECTIONS:

Make the Sauce

1. In a small saucepan, whisk together the water, soy sauce, honey, rice vinegar, garlic powder, and ginger. Add the cornstarch and whisk until it is fully incorporated.
2. Over medium heat, bring the teriyaki sauce to a boil. Let the sauce boil for 1 minute to thicken. Remove the sauce from the heat and set aside.

Make the Entrée

3. Heat a large skillet over medium-low heat. When hot, add the oil and the chicken. Cook for 5 to 7 mins, until the chicken is cooked through, stirring as needed.
4. Steam the broccoli and cauliflower rice in the microwave according to the package instructions.
5. Divide the cauliflower rice into four equal portions. Put one-quarter of the broccoli and chicken over each portion and top with the teriyaki sauce.

NUTRITION calories 247, fat 7g, protein 29g, carbs 20g, sugars 12g, fiber 5g, sodium 418mg

502. Coconut Chicken Curry

Cooking time: 35 mins | Servings: 4

INGREDIENTS:

- 3 (5-ounce) boneless, skinless chicken breasts, cut into 1-inch chunks
- 1 cup canned coconut milk
- 2 carrots, peeled and diced
- 1 sweet potato, diced
- 2 tsps olive oil
- 1 tbsp grated fresh ginger
- 1 tbsp minced garlic
- 2 tbsp curry powder
- 2 cups low-sodium chicken broth
- 2 tbsp chopped fresh cilantro

DIRECTIONS:

1. Place a large saucepan over medium-high heat and add the oil.
2. Sauté the chicken until lightly browned and almost cooked through, about 10 mins.
3. Add the ginger, garlic, and curry powder, and sauté until fragrant, about 3 mins.
4. Stir in the chicken broth, coconut milk, carrot, and sweet potato and bring the mixture to a boil.
5. Reduce the heat to low and simmer, stirring occasionally, until the vegetables and chicken are tender, about 20 mins.
6. Stir in the cilantro and serve.

NUTRITION: calories 327, fat 17g, protein 29g, carbs 15g, sugars 4g, fiber 1g, sodium 276mg

503. Chicken 'Cacciatore'

Cooking time 45 mins | Servings 6

INGREDIENTS:

- 6 chicken legs
- 8 oz brown mushrooms
- 1 (28-ounce) can whole tomatoes, drained
- 1 onion, sliced
- 1 red bell pepper, seeded and cut into strips
- 3 garlic cloves, minced
- 3 tsps olive oil, divided
- ½ cup dry red wine
- 1 thyme sprig
- 1 rosemary sprig
- ½ tsp salt
- ¼ tsp freshly ground black pepper

DIRECTIONS:

1. Preheat the oven to 350°F.
2. In a Dutch oven (or any oven-safe covered pot), heat 2 tsps of oil over medium-high heat. Sear the chicken on all sides until browned. Remove and set aside.
3. Heat the remaining 1 tsp of oil in the Dutch oven and sauté the mushrooms for 3 to 5 mins until they brown and begin to release their water. Add the onion, bell pepper, and garlic, and mix together with the mushrooms. Cook an additional 3 to 5 mins until the onion begins to soften.
4. Add the red wine and deglaze the pot. Bring to a simmer. Add the tomatoes, breaking them into pieces with a spoon. Add the thyme, rosemary, salt, and pepper to the pot and mix well.
5. Add the water, then nestle the cooked chicken, along with any juices that have accumulated, in the vegetables.
6. Transfer the pot to the oven. Cook for 30 mins until the chicken is cooked through and its juices run clear. Remove the thyme and rosemary sprigs and serve.

NUTRITION: calories 257, fat 11g, protein 28g, carbs 11g, sugars 6g, fiber 2g, sodium 398mg

504. Greek Stuffed Peppers

Cooking time 30 mins | Servings 4

INGREDIENTS:

- 4 (4-ounce) boneless, skinless chicken breasts
- 2 large red bell peppers
- 1 cup uncooked brown rice or quinoa
- 2 tsps olive oil, divided
- ¼ tsp garlic powder
- ¼ tsp onion powder
- ½ tsp dried thyme
- ½ tsp dried oregano
- ½ cup crumbled feta

DIRECTIONS:

1. Cut the bell peppers in half and remove the seeds.
2. In a large skillet, heat 1 tsp of olive oil over low heat. When hot, place the bell pepper halves cut-side up in the skillet. Cover and cook for 20 mins.
3. Cook the rice according to the package instructions.
4. Meanwhile, cut the chicken into 1-inch pieces.
5. In a medium skillet, heat the remaining 1 tsp of olive oil over medium-low heat. When hot, add the chicken.
6. Season the chicken with the garlic powder, onion powder, thyme, and oregano.
7. Cook for 5 mins, stirring occasionally, until cooked through.
8. In a large bowl, combine the cooked rice and chicken. Scoop one-quarter of the chicken and rice mixture into each pepper half, cover, and cook for 10 mins over low heat.
9. Top each pepper half with 2 tbsp of crumbled feta.

NUTRITION: calories 288, fat 10g, protein 32g, carbs 20g, sugars 4g, fiber 4g, sodium 267mg

505. Creole Chicken

Cooking time 25 mins | Servings 2

INGREDIENTS:

- 2 chicken breast halves, boneless and skinless
- 1 cup cauliflower rice, cooked
- $^1/_3$ cup green bell pepper, julienned
- ¼ cup celery, diced
- 1 onion, diced
- 7 oz stewed tomatoes, diced
- 1 tsp sunflower oil

- 1 tsp chili powder
- ½ tsp thyme

DIRECTIONS:

1. Heat oil in a small skillet over medium heat. Add chicken and cook 5 to 6 mins per side or cooked through. Transfer to plate and keep warm.
2. Add the pepper, celery, onion, tomatoes, and seasonings. Bring to a boil. Reduce heat, cover, and simmer 10 mins or until vegetables start to soften.
3. Add chicken back to pan to heat through. Serve over cauliflower rice.

NUTRITION: calories 361, fat 14g, protein 45g, carbs 14g, fiber 4g, sugars 8g, sodium 335mg

506. Cashew Chicken

Cooking time 10 mins | Servings 4

INGREDIENTS:

- 1 pound skinless boneless chicken breast, cut in cubes
- 2 tbsp green onion, diced
- ½ onion, sliced
- ½ tsp fresh ginger, peeled and grated
- 1 cup whole blanched cashews, toasted
- 1 clove garlic, diced fine
- 4 tbsp olive oil
- 2 tbsp soy sauce or tamari
- 2 tbsp water
- 2 tsps cornstarch
- 2 tsps dry sherry
- 1 tsp Splenda
- 1 tsp sesame seed oil

DIRECTIONS:

1. Place chicken in a large bowl and add cornstarch, sherry, and ginger. Stir until well mixed.
2. In a small bowl, whisk together soy sauce, Splenda, and water stirring until smooth.
3. Heat the oil in a wok or a large skillet over high heat. Add garlic and onion and cook, stirring until garlic sizzles, about 30 seconds.
4. Stir in chicken and cook, stirring frequently, until chicken is almost done, about 2 mins.
5. Reduce heat to medium and stir in sauce mixture. Continue cooking and stirring until everything is blended together. Add cashews and cook 30 seconds.
6. Drizzle with sesame oil, and cook another 30 seconds, stirring constantly. Serve immediately garnished with green onions.

NUTRITION: calories 484, fat 32g, protein 33g, carbs 19g, fiber 2g, sugars 6g, sodium 447mg

507. Citrus Chicken Thighs

Cooking time 30 mins | Servings 4

INGREDIENTS:

- 4 chicken thighs, bone-in, skinless
- 1 tbsp grated fresh ginger
- 2 tbsp olive oil
- 2 tbsp honey
- Juice and zest of 1 lemon
- 1 tbsp low-sodium soy sauce
- Pinch red pepper flakes, to taste
- Sea salt, to taste
- 1 tbsp chopped fresh cilantro

DIRECTIONS:

1. In a large bowl, combine the ginger and salt. Dunk the chicken thighs and toss to coat well.
2. Heat the olive oil in a nonstick skillet over medium-high heat until shimmering.
3. Add the chicken thighs and cook for 10 mins or until well browned. Flip halfway through the cooking time.
4. Meanwhile, combine the orange juice and zest, lemon juice and zest, soy

sauce, red pepper flakes, and honey. Stir to mix well.

5. Pour the mixture in the skillet. Reduce the heat to low, then cover and braise for 20 mins. Add tbsp of water if too dry.
6. Serve the chicken thighs garnished with cilantro.

NUTRITION: calories 114, fat 5g, protein 9g, carbs 9g, fiber 0g, sugars 9g, sodium 287mg

508. Chicken Pappardelle

Cooking time 15 mins | Servings 4

INGREDIENTS:

- ¾ pound chicken breast, sliced lengthwise into ⅛-inch strips
- 1 onion, sliced thin
- 6 cup spinach, chopped fine
- 3 cup low sodium chicken broth
- 1 cup fresh basil
- 2 quarts water
- ¼ cup Parmesan cheese, divided
- 6 cloves garlic, diced
- 1 tbsp walnuts, chopped
- ¼ tsp cinnamon
- ¼ tsp paprika
- ¼ tsp red pepper flakes
- Salt, to taste
- Olive oil cooking spray

DIRECTIONS:

1. Bring 2 quarts water to a simmer in a medium pot.
2. Lightly spray a medium skillet with cooking spray and place over medium-high heat. Add the garlic and cook until golden brown. Add the cinnamon, paprika, red pepper flakes, basil leaves, and onion. Cook until the onion has softened, about 2 mins.
3. Add the spinach and cook until it has wilted and softened, another 2 mins. Add the broth, bring to a simmer, cover, and cook until tender, about 5 mins.
4. Add a pinch of salt to the now-simmering water. Turn off the heat and add the chicken and stir so that all the strips are separated. Cook just until the strips have turned white; they will be half-cooked. Using a slotted spoon, transfer the strips to a plate to cool.
5. Check the spinach mixture; cook it until most of the broth has evaporated Stir in half the cheese and season with salt to taste. Add the chicken, toss to coat, and continue to cook until the chicken strips have cooked through, about 90 seconds. Spoon the mixture onto four plates, top with the remaining cheese and serve.

NUTRITION: calories 175, fat 5g, protein 24g, carbs 7g, fiber 2g, sugars 2g, sodium 309mg

509. Tropical Chicken

Cooking time 3 hours | Servings 6

INGREDIENTS:

- 6 chicken thighs, bone-in and skin-on
- 1 red bell pepper, diced
- 1 red onion, diced
- 8 oz can crushed pineapple
- 1 cup pineapple juice
- ½ cup low sodium chicken broth
- ¼ cup Splenda brown sugar
- ¼ cup water
- 3 tbsp light soy sauce
- 2 tbsp apple cider vinegar
- 2 tbsp honey
- 2 tbsp cornstarch
- 1 tsp garlic powder
- 1 tsp Sriracha
- ½ tsp ginger
- 2 tbsp fresh parsley, chopped
- 2 tbsp margarine

DIRECTIONS:

1. Season chicken with salt and pepper.

2. Melt butter in a large skillet over medium heat. Add chicken, skin side down, and sear both side until golden brown. Add chicken to the crock pot.
3. In a large bowl, combine pineapple juice, broth, Splenda, soy sauce, honey, vinegar, Sriracha, garlic powder, and ginger. Pour over chicken.
4. Top with pineapple. Cover and cook on high 2 hours. Baste the chicken occasionally.
5. Mix the cornstarch and water together until smooth. Stir into chicken and add the pepper and onion, cook another 60 mins, or until sauce has thickened. Serve garnished with parsley.

NUTRITION: calories 300, fat 13g, protein 17g, carbs 24g, fiber 1g, sugars 18g, sodium 280mg

510. Coconut-Encrusted Chicken

Cooking time 20 mins | Servings 4

INGREDIENTS:

- 4 chicken breasts, each cut lengthwise into 3 strips
- 2 tbsp unsweetened plain almond milk
- ½ cup coconut flour
- 3 eggs
- 1 cup unsweetened coconut flakes
- ½ tsp salt
- ¼ tsp freshly ground black pepper

DIRECTIONS:

1. Preheat the oven to 400°F.
2. On a clean work surface, rub the chicken with salt and black pepper.
3. Whisk together the eggs and almond milk in a bowl. Put the coconut flour in another bowl. Put the coconut flakes in a third bowl.
4. Dunk the chicken in the bowl of flour to coat, then dredge in the egg mixture, and then dip in coconut flakes. Shake the excess off.
5. Arrange the well coated chicken in a baking pan lined with parchment paper. Bake in the preheated oven for 16 mins. Flip the chicken halfway through the cooking time or until well browned.
6. Remove the chicken from the oven and serve in a plate.

NUTRITION: calories 218, fat 12g, protein 20g, carbs 8g, fiber 6g, sugars 2g, sodium 345mg

511. Turkey and Quinoa Casserole

Cooking time 35 mins |Servings 4

INGREDIENTS:

- ½ pound lean ground turkey
- 2 cups spinach leaves, finely sliced
- 1 (7-ounce) can fire-roasted tomatoes, drained
- 4 oz mozzarella cheese, thinly sliced
- ⅔ cup quinoa
- 1 cup water
- 2 tsps olive oil
- 1 chopped red onion
- 1 tsp salt
- 2 garlic cloves, minced
- ¼ cup sliced fresh basil
- ¼ cup chicken or vegetable broth
- 2 large ripe tomatoes, sliced
- Nonstick cooking spray

DIRECTIONS:

1. In a small pot, combine the quinoa and water. Bring to a boil, reduce the heat, cover, and simmer for 10 mins. Turn off the heat, and let the quinoa sit for 5 mins to absorb any remaining water.
2. Preheat the oven to 400°F. Spray a baking dish with nonstick cooking spray.

3. In a large skillet, heat the oil over medium heat. Add the turkey, onion, and salt. Cook until the turkey is cooked through and crumbled.
4. Add the tomatoes, spinach, garlic, and basil. Stir in the broth and cooked quinoa. Transfer the mixture to the prepared baking dish. Arrange the tomato and cheese slices on top.
5. Bake for 15 mins until the cheese is melted and the tomatoes are softened. Serve.

NUTRITION: calories 218, fat 9g, protein 18g, carbs 17g, sugars 3g, fiber 3g, sodium 340mg

512. Mushroom Stuffed Turkey

Cooking time 1 hour 5 mins | Servings 4

INGREDIENTS:

- 1 pound boneless, skinless turkey breast, butterflied
- 4 oz brown mushrooms, finely chopped
- 2 tbsp olive oil, divided
- 2 garlic cloves, minced
- ½ tsp salt, divided
- ¼ tsp freshly ground black pepper, divided
- 2 tbsp chopped fresh sage

DIRECTIONS:

1. Preheat the oven to 375°F.
2. In a large skillet, heat 1 tbsp of oil over medium heat. Add the mushrooms and cook for 4 to 5 mins, stirring regularly, until most of the liquid has evaporated from the pan. Add the garlic, ¼ tsp of salt, and ⅛ tsp of pepper, and continue to cook for an additional minute. Add the sage to the pan, cook for 1 minute, and remove the pan from the heat.
3. On a clean work surface, lay the turkey breast flat. Use a kitchen mallet to pound the breast to an even 1-inch thickness throughout.
4. Spread the mushroom-sage mixture on the turkey breast, leaving a 1-inch border around the edges. Roll the breast tightly into a log.
5. Using kitchen twine, tie the breast two or three times around to hold it together. Rub the remaining 1 tbsp of oil over the turkey breast. Season with the remaining ¼ tsp of salt and ⅛ tsp of pepper.
6. Transfer to a roasting pan and roast for 50 to 60 mins, until the juices run clear, the meat is cooked through, and the internal temperature reaches 180°F.
7. Let rest for 5 mins. Cut off the twine, slice, and serve.

NUTRITION: calories 232, fat 6g, protein 41g, carbs 2g, sugars 0g, fiber 0g, sodium 320mg

513. Herbed Whole Turkey Breast

Cooking time 30 mins |Servings 6

INGREDIENTS:

- 1 pound bone-in, skin-on whole turkey breast, rinsed and patted dry
- 2 tbsp olive oil
- 1tbsp poultry seasoning
- 2 tsps minced garlic
- 1 tsp lemon zest (from 1 small lemon)
- 1 tbsp salt
- 1½ tsps freshly ground black pepper

DIRECTIONS:

1. In a small bowl, whisk together the olive oil, poultry seasoning, garlic, lemon zest, salt, and pepper.
2. Rub the outside of the turkey and under the skin with the olive oil mixture.
3. Pour 1 cup of water into the electric pressure cooker and insert a wire rack or trivet.
4. Place the turkey on the rack, skin-side up.

5. Close and lock the lid of the pressure cooker. Set the valve to sealing.
6. Cook on high pressure for 30 mins.
7. When the cooking is complete, hit Cancel. Allow the pressure to release naturally for 20 mins, then quick release any remaining pressure.
8. Once the pin drops, unlock and remove the lid.
9. Carefully transfer the turkey to a cutting board. Remove the skin, slice and serve.

NUTRITION: calories 146, fat 9g, protein 16g, carbs 0g, sugars 0g, fiber 0g, sodium 413mg

514. Herb-Roasted Turkey and Veggies

Cooking time: 2 hours | Servings: 6

INGREDIENTS:

- 2 pounds boneless, skinless whole turkey breast
- 2 sweet potatoes, peeled and cut into 2-inch chunks
- 3 carrots, peeled and cut into 2-inch chunks
- 2 parsnips, peeled and cut into 2-inch chunks
- 2 onion, peeled and cut into eighths
- 2 tsps minced garlic
- 1 tbsp chopped parsley
- 1 tsp chopped thyme
- 1 tsp rosemary
- 3 tsps olive oil, divided
- Sea salt and freshly ground black pepper, to taste

DIRECTIONS

1. Preheat the oven to 350°F.
2. Line a large roasting pan with aluminum foil and set it aside.
3. In a small bowl, mix together the garlic, parsley, thyme, and rosemary.
4. Place the turkey breast in the roasting pan and rub it all over with 1 tsp of olive oil.
5. Rub the garlic-herb mixture all over the turkey and season lightly with salt and pepper.
6. Place the turkey in the oven and roast for 30 mins.
7. While the turkey is roasting, toss the sweet potatoes, carrots, parsnips, onion, and the remaining 2 tsps of olive oil in a large bowl.
8. Remove the turkey from the oven and arrange the vegetables around it.
9. Roast until the turkey is cooked through (170°F internal temperature) and the vegetables are lightly caramelized, about 1 ½ hours.

NUTRITION calories 273, fat 3g, protein 38g, carbs 20g, sugars 6g, fiber 4g, sodium 116mg

515. Roasted Duck Legs

Cooking time 1 h 30 mins | Servings 4

INGREDIENTS:

- 4 duck legs
- 3 plum tomatoes, diced
- 1 red chili, deseeded and sliced
- ½ small Savoy cabbage, quartered
- 2 tsps fresh ginger, grated
- 2 cloves garlic, sliced
- 2 tbsp soy sauce
- 2 tbsp honey

DIRECTIONS:

1. Heat oven to 350°F.
2. Place the duck in a large skillet over low heat and cook until brown on all sides and most of the fat is rendered, about 10 mins. Transfer duck to a deep baking dish. Drain off all but 2 tbsp of the fat.
3. Add ginger, garlic, and chili to the skillet and cook 2 mins until soft. Add

soy sauce, tomatoes and 2 tbsp water and bring to a boil.

4. Rub the duck with the five spice seasoning. Pour the sauce over the duck and drizzle with the honey. Cover with foil and bake 1 hour. Add the cabbage for the last 10 mins.

NUTRITION: calories 212, fat 5g, protein 25g, carbs 19g, fiber 3g, sugars 14g, sodium 365mg

516. Mexican Turkey Sliders

Cooking time 6 mins | Servings 6

INGREDIENTS:

- 1 pound lean ground turkey
- 6 mini whole-wheat hamburger buns
- 6 tomato slices
- 3½ slices pepper Jack cheese, cut in half
- 1 mashed avocado
- 1 tbsp chili powder
- ½ tsp garlic powder
- ¼ tsp ground black pepper

DIRECTIONS:

1. Preheat the grill to high heat.
2. Combine the ground turkey, chili powder, garlic powder, and black pepper in a large bowl. Stir to mix well.
3. Divide and shape the mixture into 7 patties, then arrange the patties on the preheated grill grates.
4. Grill for 6 mins or until well browned. Flip the patties halfway through.
5. Assemble the patties with buns, tomato slices, cheese slices, and mashed avocado to make the sliders, then serve immediately.

NUTRITION: calories 225, fat 9g, protein 17g, carbs 21g, fiber 4g, sugars 6g, sodium 230mg

517. Turkey Zoodles with Spaghetti Sauce

Cooking time 20 mins | Servings 4

INGREDIENTS:

- 1 (10-ounce) package zucchini noodles, rinsed and patted dry
- 2 tbsp olive oil, divided
- ½ pound 93% lean ground turkey
- ½ tsp dried oregano
- 1 cup low-sodium spaghetti sauce
- ½ cup cheddar cheese, shredded

DIRECTIONS:

1. Preheat the broiler to high.
2. Warm 1 tbsp olive oil over in an oven-safe skillet over medium heat.
3. Add the zucchini noodles to the skillet and cook for 3 mins until soft. Stir the zucchini noodles frequently.
4. Drizzle the remaining olive oil over, then add the ground turkey and oregano to the skillet. Cook for 8 mins until the turkey is well browned.
5. Pour the spaghetti sauce over the turkey and stir to coat well.
6. Spread the cheddar on top, then broil in the preheated broiler for 5 mins until the cheese is melted and frothy.
7. Remove them from the broiler and serve warm.

NUTRITION: calories 337, fat 20g, protein 28g, carbs 20g, fiber 3g, sugars 4g, sodium 214mg

518. Turkey Tacos

Cooking time 20 mins, Servings 4

INGREDIENTS:

- ½ pound ground turkey
- 3 tbsp olive oil
- 1 onion, chopped

- 1 green bell pepper, seeded and chopped
- ½ tsp sea salt
- 1 small head cauliflower, grated
- 1 cup corn kernels
- ½ cup prepared salsa
- ½ cup shredded pepper Jack cheese

DIRECTIONS:

1. In a large nonstick skillet over medium-high heat, heat the olive oil until it shimmers.
2. Add the turkey. Cook, crumbling with a spoon, until browned, about 5 mins.
3. Add the onion, bell pepper, and salt. Cook, stirring occasionally, until the vegetables soften, 4 to 5 mins.
4. Add the cauliflower, corn, and salsa. Cook, stirring, until the cauliflower rice softens, about 3 mins more.
5. Sprinkle with the cheese. Reduce heat to low, cover, and allow the cheese to melt, 2 or 3 mins.

NUTRITION calories 449, fat 30g, protein 30g, carbs 17g, fiber 4g, sugars 8g, sodium 650mg

519. Quick Turkey Potpie

Cooking time 20 mins, Servings 2

INGREDIENTS:

- ½ pound extra-lean ground turkey breast
- 2 tbsp olive oil, divided
- Salt and pepper, to taste
- 1 small onion, diced
- 1 small carrot, diced
- ½ cup frozen peas
- 1 tsp dried thyme
- 2 tbsp coconut flour
- 2 tbsp plain nonfat Greek yogurt
- 1 cup nonfat milk
- 2 slices sprouted whole-grain bread

DIRECTIONS:

1. In a small skillet set over medium heat, heat 1 tbsp of olive oil.
2. Crumble the turkey in the skillet. Season with salt and pepper. Cook for 5 to 7 mins, or until no pink color remains. Transfer to a bowl. Set aside.
3. Add the remaining 1 tbsp of olive oil to the pan. Reduce the heat to low.
4. Add the onion and carrot. Sauté for 5 mins, or until the vegetables have softened but are not browned.
5. Add the peas. Increase the heat to medium.
6. Sprinkle in the thyme. Stir to combine.
7. Sprinkle the coconut flour over the vegetables. Stir to combine. Cook for 1 minute.
8. Add the yogurt and milk. Season with salt and pepper. Stir to combine. Bring to a simmer. Cook for about 2 mins, or until thickened.
9. Toast the bread. Slice each piece diagonally. Divide between 2 plates.
10. Top each piece with half of the chicken mixture.
11. Serve immediately!

NUTRITION: calories 461, fat 17g, protein 41g, carbs 38g, sugars 12g, fiber 11g, sodium 279mg

CHAPTER 11 Beef, Pork, and Lamb

520. Peppered Beef

Cooking time: 20 mins | Servings: 2

INGREDIENTS:

- 1 (½-pound, ½-inch-thick) boneless beef sirloin, halved
- 2 tsps coarsely ground black pepper ,divided
- ¼ cup tomato sauce
- 1 tbsp red wine vinegar
- 1 tsp dried basil
- 2 cups (1 bunch) chopped kale
- 1 cup chopped green beans
- ¾ cup chopped red bell pepper, or yellow bell pepper
- 1 chopped onion

DIRECTIONS:

1. Rub each side of the steak halves with ½ tsp of coarsely ground pepper.
2. Heat a 10-inch nonstick skillet over medium heat. Add the beef. Cook for 8 to 12 mins, turning once halfway through.
3. Add the tomato sauce, red wine vinegar, and basil. Stir to combine.
4. Add the kale, green beans, bell pepper, and onion. Stir to mix with the sauce. Reduce the heat to medium-low. Cook for about 5 mins, uncovered, or until the vegetables are tender and beef is cooked medium doneness (160°F).
5. Serve immediately and enjoy!

NUTRITION: calories 372, fat 17g, protein 35g, carbs 22g, sugars 4g, fiber 6g, sodium 349mg

521. Steak Fajita Bake

Cooking time 15 mins | Servings 4

INGREDIENTS:

- 8 oz sirloin steak, trimmed of visible fat
- 1 green bell pepper
- 1 yellow bell pepper
- 1 red bell pepper
- 1 small white onion
- 2 tbsp avocado oil
- ½ tsp ground cumin
- ¼ tsp chili powder
- ¼ tsp garlic powder
- 4 (6-inch) 100% whole-wheat tortillas

DIRECTIONS:

1. Preheat the oven to 400°F.
2. Cut the green bell pepper, yellow bell pepper, red bell pepper, onion, and steak into ½-inch-thick slices, and put them on a large baking sheet.
3. In a small bowl, combine the oil, cumin, chili powder, and garlic powder, then drizzle the mixture over the meat and vegetables to fully coat them.
4. Arrange the steak and vegetables in a single layer, and bake for 10 to 15 mins, or until the steak is cooked through.
5. Divide the steak and vegetables equally between the tortillas.

NUTRITION: calories 349, fat 18g, protein 19g, carbs 28g, sugars 5g, fiber 5g, sodium 197mg

522. Beef Veggie Fajita Bowls

Cooking time 15 mins | Servings 4

INGREDIENTS:

- 1 pound sirloin steak, cut into ¼-inch-thick strips

- 3 tbsp olive oil, divided
- 1 head cauliflower, riced
- 1 red bell pepper, seeded and sliced
- 1 onion, thinly sliced
- 2 garlic cloves, minced
- Juice of 2 limes
- 1 tsp chili powder

DIRECTIONS:

1. In a large skillet over medium-high heat, heat 2 tbsp of olive oil until it shimmers. Add the cauliflower. Cook, stirring occasionally, until it softens, about 3 mins. Set aside.
2. Wipe out the skillet with a paper towel. Add the remaining 2 tbsp of oil to the skillet and heat it on medium-high until it shimmers. Add the steak and cook, stirring occasionally, until it browns, about 3 mins. Use a slotted spoon to remove the steak from the oil in the pan and set aside.
3. Add the bell pepper and onion to the pan. Cook, stirring occasionally, until they start to brown, about 5 mins.
4. Add the garlic and cook, stirring constantly, for 30 seconds.
5. Return the beef along with any juices that have collected and the cauliflower to the pan. Add the lime juice and chili powder. Cook, stirring, until everything is warmed through, 2 to 3 mins.

NUTRITION: calories 310, fat 18g, protein 27g, carbs 13g, sugars 2g, fiber 3g, sodium 93mg

523. Beef with Peppercorn Sauce

Cooking time 1 h 40 mins | Servings 4

INGREDIENTS:

- 1½ pounds top rump beef roast
- 3 tsps olive oil, divided
- 2 shallots, minced
- 2 tsps minced garlic
- 1 tbsp green peppercorns
- 1 tbsp dry sherry
- 2 tbsp whole wheat flour
- 1 cup beef broth
- salt and pepper, to taste

DIRECTIONS:

1. Heat the oven to 300°F.
2. Season the roast with salt and pepper.
3. Place a large skillet over medium-high heat and add 2 tsps of olive oil.
4. Brown the beef on all sides, about 10 mins in total, and transfer the roast to a baking dish.
5. Roast until desired doneness, about 1½ hours for medium. When the roast has been in the oven for 1 hour, start the sauce.
6. In a medium saucepan over medium-high heat, sauté the shallots in the remaining 1 tsp of olive oil until translucent, about 4 mins.
7. Stir in the garlic and peppercorns and cook for another minute. Whisk in the sherry to deglaze the pan.
8. Whisk in the flour to form a thick paste, cooking for 1 minute and stirring constantly.
9. Pour in the beef broth and whisk until the sauce is thick and glossy, about 4 mins. Season the sauce with salt and pepper.
10. Serve the beef with a generous spoonful of sauce.

NUTRITION: calories 330, fat 18g, protein 36g, carbs 4g, sugars 1g, fiber 0g, sodium 207mg

524. Beef Burrito Bowl

Cooking time 15 mins | Servings 4

INGREDIENTS:

- 1 pound 93% lean ground beef
- 1 cup canned low-sodium black beans, drained and rinsed
- ¼ tsp ground cumin

- ¼ tsp chili powder
- ¼ tsp garlic powder
- ¼ tsp onion powder
- ½ tsp salt
- 1 head lettuce, shredded
- 2 medium tomatoes, chopped
- 1 cup shredded cheddar cheese or packaged cheese blend

DIRECTIONS:

1. Heat a large skillet over medium-low heat. Put the beef, beans, cumin, chili powder, garlic powder, onion powder, and salt into the skillet, and cook for 8 to 10 mins, until cooked through. Stir occasionally.
2. Divide the lettuce evenly between four bowls. Add one-quarter of the beef mixture to each bowl and top with one-quarter of the tomatoes and cheese.

NUTRITION: calories 351, fat 18g, protein 35g, carbs 14g, sugars 4g, fiber 6g, sodium 424mg

525. Marinated Steak

Cooking time 10 mins | Servings 4

INGREDIENTS:

- 1 pound flank steak, trimmed of visible fat
- ¼ cup whole coffee beans
- 2 tsps minced garlic
- 1 tsp chopped fresh rosemary
- 2 tsps chopped fresh thyme
- 2 tbsp apple cider vinegar
- 2 tbsp olive oil

DIRECTIONS:

1. Place the coffee beans, garlic, rosemary, thyme, and black pepper in a coffee grinder or food processor and pulse until coarsely ground.
2. Transfer the coffee mixture to a resealable plastic bag and add the vinegar and oil. Shake to combine.
3. Add the flank steak and squeeze the excess air out of the bag. Seal it. Marinate the steak in the refrigerator for at least 2 hours, occasionally turning the bag over.
4. Preheat the broiler. Line a baking sheet with aluminum foil.
5. Take the steak out of the bowl and discard the marinade.
6. Place the steak on the baking sheet and broil until it is done to your liking, about 5 mins per side for medium.
7. Let the steak rest for 10 mins before slicing it thinly on a bias.
8. Serve with a mixed green salad or your favorite side dish.

NUTRITION: calories 313, fat 20g, protein 31g, carbs 0g, sugars 0g, fiber 0g, sodium 79mg

526. Broccoli Beef Stir-Fry

Cooking time 15 mins | Servings 4

INGREDIENTS:

- 1 pound sirloin steak, cut into ¼-inch-thick strips
- 3 cups broccoli florets
- ¼ cup beef broth
- 2 tbsp olive oil
- 1 garlic clove, minced
- 1 tsp peeled and grated fresh ginger
- 2 tbsp soy sauce and tamari
- ½ tsp hot mustard

DIRECTIONS:

1. In a large skillet over medium-high heat, heat the olive oil until it shimmers. Add the beef. Cook, stirring, until it browns, 3 to 5 mins. With a slotted spoon, remove the beef from the oil and set it aside on a plate.
2. Add the broccoli to the oil. Cook, stirring, until it is crisp-tender, about 4 mins.
3. Add the garlic and ginger and cook, stirring constantly, for 30 seconds.

4. Return the beef to the pan, along with any juices that have collected.
5. In a small bowl, whisk together the soy sauce, broth, and mustard.
6. Add the soy sauce mixture to the skillet and cook, stirring, until everything warms through, about 3 mins.

NUTRITION: calories 227, fat 11g, protein 27g, carbs 5g, sugars 0g, fiber 1g, sodium 375mg

527. Beer Braised Brisket

Cooking time 8 hours | Servings 4

INGREDIENTS:

- 1 pound beef brisket
- ½ bottle of lite beer
- 1 onion, sliced thin
- 1 (15-ounce) can tomatoes, diced
- 2 cloves garlic, diced fine
- 1 tbsp plus 1 tsp oregano
- 1 tbsp salt and pepper

DIRECTIONS:

1. Place the onion on the bottom of the crock pot. Add brisket, fat side up. Add the tomatoes, undrained and beer. Sprinkle the garlic and seasonings on the top.
2. Cover and cook on low heat 8 hours, or until beef is fork tender.

NUTRITION: calories 450, fat 14g, protein 69g, carbs 4g, fiber 1g, sugars 2g, sodium 941mg

528. Bunless Sloppy Joes

Cooking time 40 mins | Servings 4

INGREDIENTS:

- 1 pound lean ground beef
- 6 small sweet potatoes
- 1 (15-ounce) can low-sodium tomato sauce
- 1 onion, finely chopped
- 2 carrot, finely chopped
- 2 tbsp tomato paste
- ¼ cup finely chopped mushrooms
- 1 finely chopped red bell pepper
- 2 garlic cloves, minced
- 2 tsps Worcestershire sauce
- 1 tbsp white wine vinegar

DIRECTIONS:

1. Preheat the oven to 400°F.
2. Place the sweet potatoes in a single layer in a baking dish. Bake for 25 to 40 mins, depending on the size, until they are soft and cooked through.
3. While the sweet potatoes are baking, in a large skillet, cook the beef over medium heat until it's browned, breaking it apart into small pieces as you stir.
4. Add the onion, carrot, mushrooms, bell pepper, and garlic, and sauté briefly for 1 minute.
5. Stir in the Worcestershire sauce, vinegar, tomato sauce, and tomato paste. Bring to a simmer, reduce the heat, and cook for 5 mins for the flavors to meld.
6. Scoop ½ cup of the meat mixture on top of each baked potato and serve.

NUTRITION: calories 372, fat 19g, protein 16g, carbs 34g, sugars 13g, fiber 6g, sodium 161mg

529. Sunday Pot Roast

Cooking time 1 h 45 mins | Servings 4

INGREDIENTS:

- 1 pound beef rump roast
- 2 cups beef broth
- ½ tsp salt, divided
- 2 tbsp avocado oil
- 1 large onion, coarsely chopped
- 3 carrots, each cut into 4 pieces
- 1 tbsp minced garlic
- 1 tsp freshly ground black pepper
- 1 tbsp dried parsley
- 2 tbsp whole wheat flour

DIRECTIONS:

1. Rub the roast all over with 1 tsp of the salt.
2. Set the electric pressure cooker to the Sauté setting. When the pot is hot, pour in the avocado oil.
3. Carefully place the roast in the pot and sear it for 6 to 9 mins on each side. (You want a dark caramelized crust.) Hit Cancel.
4. Transfer the roast from the pot to a plate.
5. In order, put the onion, carrots, and garlic in the pot. Place the roast on top of the vegetables along with any juices that accumulated on the plate.
6. In a medium bowl, whisk together the broth, remaining 1 tsp of salt, pepper, and parsley. Pour the broth mixture over the roast.
7. Close and lock the lid of the pressure cooker. Set the valve to sealing.
8. Cook on high pressure for 1 hour and 30 mins.
9. When the cooking is complete, hit Cancel and allow the pressure to release naturally.
10. Once the pin drops, unlock and remove the lid.
11. Using large slotted spoons, transfer the roast and vegetables to a serving platter while you make the gravy.
12. Using a large spoon or fat separator, remove the fat from the juices in the pot. Set the electric pressure cooker to the Sauté setting and bring the liquid to a boil.
13. In a small bowl, whisk together the flour and 4 tbsp of water to make a slurry. Pour the slurry into the pot, whisking occasionally, until the gravy is the thickness you like. Season with salt and pepper, if necessary.
14. Serve the meat and carrots with the gravy.

NUTRITION: calories 245, fat 10g, protein 33g, carbs 6g, sugars 2g, fiber 1g, sodium 397mg

530. Classic Stroganoff

Cooking time 20 mins | Servings 4

INGREDIENTS:

- 1 pound beef tenderloin tips, boneless, sliced into 2-inch strips
- 4 oz cooked egg noodles
- 2 tsps olive oil
- 1cup white button mushrooms, sliced
- 1onion, minced
- 1 tbsp whole wheat flour
- ¼ cup dry white wine
- ¼ cup beef broth
- 1 tsp Dijon mustard
- ½ cup fat-free sour cream
- ¼ tsp salt and black pepper

DIRECTIONS:

1. Put the cooked egg noodles on a large plate.
2. Heat the olive oil in a nonstick skillet over high heat until shimmering.
3. Add the beef and sauté for 3 mins or until lightly browned. Remove the beef from the skillet and set on the plate with noodles.
4. Add the mushrooms and onion to the skillet and sauté for 5 mins or until tender and the onion browns.
5. Add the flour and cook for a minute. Add the white wine and cook for 2 more mins.
6. Add the beef broth and Dijon mustard. Bring to a boil. Keep stirring. Reduce the heat to low and simmer for another 5 mins.
7. Add the beef back to the skillet and simmer for an additional 3 mins. Add the remaining ingredients and simmer for 1 minute.

8. Pour them over the egg noodles and beef and serve immediately.

NUTRITION. calories 275, fat 7g, protein 23g, carbs 29g, fiber 4g, sugars 3g, sodium 250mg

531. Gingered-Pork Stir-Fry

Cooking time 20 mins | Servings 2

INGREDIENTS:

- ¼ pound lean pork, thinly sliced
- 2 tbsp olive oil
- 1 garlic clove, minced
- 1 (½-inch) piece fresh ginger, peeled, thinly sliced
- 2 tsps soy sauce or tamari
- 1 tsp granulated stevia
- 1 tsp sesame oil
- 1 cup snow peas
- 1 medium red bell pepper, sliced
- 4 whole fresh mushrooms, sliced
- 1 scallion, chopped
- 1 tbsp Chinese rice wine
- 2 tbsp chopped cashews, divided

DIRECTIONS:

1. In a large skillet or wok set over medium-high heat, heat the olive oil.
2. Add the garlic and ginger. Sauté for 1 to 2 mins, or until fragrant.
3. Add the pork, soy sauce, and stevia. Cook for 10 mins, stirring occasionally.
4. Stir in the sesame oil, snow peas, bell pepper, mushrooms, scallions, and rice wine. Reduce the heat to low. Simmer for 4 to 8 mins, or until the pork is tender.
5. Divide between 2 serving plates, sprinkle each serving with 1 tbsp of cashews and enjoy!

NUTRITION: calories 426, fat 28g, protein 30g, carbs 15g, sugars 4g, fiber 3g, sodium 308mg

532. Pork Tenderloin Roast with Glaze

Cooking time 20 mins | Servings 4

INGREDIENTS:

- 1 pound boneless pork tenderloin, trimmed of fat
- 1 tsp chopped rosemary
- 1 tsp chopped thyme
- ¼ tsp salt and pepper
- 1 tsp olive oil
- 1 tbsp honey
- 2 tbsp white wine vinegar
- 1 tbsp minced fresh ginger
- 1 cup diced mango

DIRECTIONS:

1. Preheat the oven to 400°F.
2. Season the tenderloin with the rosemary, thyme, ⅛ tsp of salt, and ⅛ tsp of pepper.
3. Heat the olive oil in an oven-safe skillet over medium-high heat, and sear the tenderloin until browned on all sides, about 5 mins total.
4. Transfer the skillet to the oven and roast for 12 to 15 mins until the pork is cooked through, the juices run clear, and the internal temperature reaches 145°F. Transfer to a cutting board to rest for 5 mins.
5. In a small bowl, combine the honey, vinegar, cooking wine, and ginger. In to the same skillet, pour the honey mixture and simmer for 1 minute. Add the mango and toss to coat. Transfer to a blender and purée until smooth. Season with the remaining ⅛ tsp of salt and ⅛ tsp of pepper.
6. Slice the pork into rounds and serve with the mango sauce.

NUTRITION: calories 182, fat 4g, protein 24g, carbs 12g, sugars 10g, fiber 1g, sodium 240mg

533. Roasted Pork Loin

Cooking time 40 mins | Servings 4

INGREDIENTS:

- 1 pound pork loin
- 1 tbsp olive oil, divided
- 1 tbsp honey
- ¼ tsp freshly ground black pepper
- ½ tsp dried rosemary
- 2 small gold potatoes, chopped into 2-inch cubes
- 3 carrots, chopped into ½-inch rounds

DIRECTIONS:

1. Preheat the oven to 350°F.
2. Rub the pork loin with ½ tbsp of oil and the honey. Season with the pepper and rosemary.
3. In a medium bowl, toss the potatoes and carrots in the remaining ½ tbsp of oil.
4. Place the pork and the vegetables on a baking sheet in a single layer. Cook for 40 mins.
5. Remove the baking sheet from the oven and let the pork rest for at least 10 mins before slicing. Divide the pork and vegetables into four equal portions.

NUTRITION: calories 343, fat 10g, protein 26g, carbs 26g, sugars 6g, fiber 4g, sodium 109mg

534. Cajun Smothered Pork Chops

Cooking time 25 mins | Servings 4

INGREDIENTS:

- 4 pork chops, thick-cut
- 1 onion, diced fine
- 1 cup mushrooms, sliced
- 1 cup sour cream
- 2 tbsp margarine
- ½ cup low sodium chicken broth
- ¼ cup water
- 2 cloves garlic, diced fine
- 1 tbsp Cajun seasoning
- 2 bay leaves
- Salt and pepper, to taste

DIRECTIONS:

1. Melt margarine in a large skillet over medium heat. Sprinkle chops with salt and pepper and cook until nicely browned, about 5 mins per side. Transfer to a plate.
2. Add onions and mushrooms and cook until soft, about 5 mins. Add garlic and cook one minute more.
3. Add broth and water and stir to incorporate brown bits on bottom of the pan. Add a dash of salt and the bay leaves. Add pork chops back to sauce. Bring to a simmer, cover, and reduce heat. Cook 5 to 8 mins, or until chops are cooked through.
4. Transfer chops to a plate and keep warm. Bring sauce to a boil and cook until it has reduced by half, stirring occasionally.
5. Reduce heat to low and whisk in sour cream, and Cajun seasoning. Cook, stirring frequently, 3 mins. Add chops back to the sauce and heat through. Serve.

NUTRITION: calories 325, fat 18g, protein 24g, carbs 13g, fiber 1g, sugars 5g, sodium 383mg

535. Chipotle Chili Pork Chops

Cooking time 20 mins | Servings 4

INGREDIENTS:

- 4 (5-ounce) pork chops, about 1 inch thick
- Juice and zest of 1 lime
- 2 tbsp olive oil
- 1 tbsp chipotle chili powder
- 1 tsps minced garlic
- 1 tsp ground cinnamon
- Pinch sea salt
- Lime wedges, for garnish

DIRECTIONS:

1. Combine the lime juice and zest, oil, chipotle chili powder, garlic, cinnamon, and salt in a resealable plastic bag. Add the pork chops. Remove as much air as possible and seal the bag.
2. Marinate the chops in the refrigerator for at least 4 hours, and up to 24 hours, turning them several times.
3. Preheat the oven to 400°F and set a rack on a baking sheet. Let the chops rest at room temperature for 15 mins, then arrange them on the rack and discard the remaining marinade.
4. Roast the chops until cooked through, turning once, about 10 mins per side.
5. Serve with lime wedges.

NUTRITION: calories 204, fat 9g, protein 30g, carbs 1g, sugars 1g, fiber 0g, sodium 317mg

536. Pork Chops with Red Cabbage

Cooking time 30 mins | Servings 4

INGREDIENTS:

- 4 (4-ounce) pork chops, about 1 inch thick
- 2 onions, thinly sliced
- 1 apple, peeled, cored, and sliced
- ½ red cabbage, finely shredded
- 2 tbsp apple cider vinegar
- 2 tbsp granulated sweetener
- Sea salt and freshly ground black pepper, to taste
- 2 tbsp olive oil
- 1 tsp chopped fresh thyme

DIRECTIONS:

1. In a small bowl, whisk together the vinegar and sweetener. Set it aside.
2. Season the pork with salt and pepper.
3. Place a large skillet over medium-high heat and add the olive oil.
4. Cook the pork chops until no longer pink, turning once, about 8 mins per side.
5. Transfer the chops to a plate and set aside.
6. Add the cabbage and onion to the skillet and sauté until the vegetables have softened, about 5 mins.
7. Add the vinegar mixture and the apple slices to the skillet and bring the mixture to a boil.
8. Reduce the heat to low and simmer, covered, for 5 additional mins.
9. Return the pork chops to the skillet, along with any accumulated juices and thyme, cover, and cook for 5 more mins.

NUTRITION: calories 223, fat 8g, protein 26g, carbs 12g, sugars 8g, fiber 3g, sodium 292mg

537. Curried Pork Skewers

Cooking time 15 mins | Servings 4

INGREDIENTS:

- 1 pound boneless pork tenderloin, cut into bite-size pieces
- 1 red bell pepper, seeded and cut into 2-inch squares
- 1 green bell pepper, seeded and cut into 2-inch squares
- 1 red onion, quartered and split into segments
- ¼ cup Greek yogurt
- 1 tbsp curry powder
- 1 tsp garlic powder
- 1 tsp ground turmeric
- Zest and juice of 1 lime
- ¼ tsp salt

DIRECTIONS

1. In a large bowl, mix the yogurt, curry powder, garlic powder, turmeric, lime zest, lime juice, salt, and pepper.
2. Add the pieces of pork tenderloin to the bowl and stir to coat. Refrigerate

for at least 1 hour or as long as 6 hours.

3. Preheat a grill or broiler to medium.
4. Thread the pork pieces, bell peppers, and onions onto skewers.
5. Grill or broil for 12 to 15 mins, flipping every 3 or 4 mins, until the pork is cooked through. Serve.

NUTRITION: calories 175, fat 3g, protein 27g, carbs 10g, sugars 4g, fiber 3g, sodium 188mg

538. Mustard Glazed Pork Chops

Cooking time 25 mins | Servings 4

INGREDIENTS:

- 4 bone-in, thin-cut pork chops
- ¼ cup Dijon mustard
- 2 tbsp pure maple syrup
- 2 tbsp rice vinegar

DIRECTIONS:

1. Preheat the oven to 400°F.
2. In a small saucepan, combine the mustard, maple syrup, and rice vinegar. Stir to mix and bring to a simmer over medium heat. Cook for about 2 mins until just slightly thickened.
3. In a baking dish, place the pork chops and spoon the sauce over them, flipping to coat.
4. Bake, uncovered, for 18 to 22 mins until the juices run clear.

NUTRITION: calories 257, fat 7g, protein 39g, carbs 7g, sugars 4g, fiber 0g, sodium 466mg

539. Lamb Kofta Meatballs with Cucumber Salad

Cooking time 15 mins | Servings 4

INGREDIENTS:

- 1 pound ground lamb
- ¼ cup red wine vinegar
- 2 cucumbers, peeled and chopped
- 1 red onion, finely chopped
- 2 tsps ground coriander
- 1 tsp ground cumin
- 2 garlic cloves, minced
- 1 tbsp fresh mint, chopped
- 1 tsp sea salt, divided

DIRECTIONS:

1. Preheat the oven to 375°F. Line a rimmed baking sheet with parchment paper.
2. In a medium bowl, whisk together the vinegar, red pepper flakes, and ½ tsp of salt. Add the cucumbers and onion and toss to combine. Set aside.
3. In a large bowl, mix the lamb, coriander, cumin, garlic, mint, and remaining ½ tsp of salt. Form the mixture into 1-inch meatballs and place them on the prepared baking sheet.
4. Bake until the lamb reaches 140°F internally, about 15 mins.
5. Serve with the salad on the side.

NUTRITION: calories 345, fat 27g, protein 20g, carbs 7g, sugars 3g, fiber 1g, sodium 362mg

540. Rosemary Lamb Chops

Cooking time 10 mins | Servings 4

INGREDIENTS:

- 1½ pounds lamb chops (4 small chops)
- 1 shallot, peeled and cut in quarters
- 1 tbsp tomato paste
- ½ cup beef broth
- 1 tsp salt
- 1 tsp rosemary
- 2 tbsp avocado oil

DIRECTIONS:

1. Place the lamb chops on a cutting board. Press the salt and rosemary leaves into both sides of the chops. Let rest at room temperature for 15 to 30 mins.

2. Set the electric pressure cooker to Sauté/More setting. When hot, add the avocado oil.
3. Brown the lamb chops, about 2 mins per side. (If they don't all fit in a single layer, brown them in batches.)
4. Transfer the chops to a plate. In the pot, combine the shallot, tomato paste, and broth. Cook for about a minute, scraping up the brown bits from the bottom. Hit Cancel.
5. Add the chops and any accumulated juices back to the pot.
6. Close and lock the lid of the pressure cooker. Set the valve to sealing.
7. Cook on high pressure for 2 mins.
8. When the cooking is complete, hit Cancel and quick release the pressure.
9. Once the pin drops, unlock and remove the lid.
10. Place the lamb chops on plates and serve immediately.

NUTRITION: (1 lamb chop) calories 233, fat 18g, protein 15g, carbs 1g, sugars 1g, fiber 0g, sodium 450mg

541. Lamb Burgers with Mushrooms

Cooking time 15 mins | Servings 4

INGREDIENTS:

- 7 oz grass-fed ground lamb
- 7 oz brown mushrooms, finely chopped
- ¼ tsp salt and pepper
- ¼ cup crumbled goat cheese
- 2 tbsp minced fresh basil

DIRECTIONS:

1. In a large mixing bowl, combine the lamb, mushrooms, salt, and pepper, and mix well.
2. In a small bowl, mix the goat cheese and basil.
3. Form the lamb mixture into 4 patties, reserving about ½ cup of the mixture in the bowl. In each patty, make an indentation in the center and fill with 1 tbsp of the goat cheese mixture. Use the reserved meat mixture to close the burgers. Press the meat firmly to hold together.
4. Heat the barbecue or a large skillet over medium-high heat. Add the burgers and cook for 5 to 7 mins on each side, until cooked through. Serve.

NUTRITION: calories 173, fat 13g, protein 11g, carbs 3g, sugars 1g, fiber 0g, sodium 154mg

542. Lime Lamb Cutlets

Cooking time 10 mins | Servings 4

INGREDIENTS:

- 12 lamb cutlets (about 1½ pounds)
- 2 tbsp lime zest
- 2 tbsp chopped parsley
- 3 tbsp olive oil
- ¼ cup lime juice
- Pinch sea salt and pepper

DIRECTIONS:

1. In a medium bowl, whisk together the oil, lime juice, zest, parsley, salt, and pepper.
2. Transfer the marinade to a resealable plastic bag.
3. Add the cutlets to the bag and remove as much air as possible before sealing.
4. Marinate the lamb in the refrigerator for about 4 hours, turning the bag several times.
5. Preheat the oven to broil.
6. Remove the chops from the bag and arrange them on an aluminum foil-lined baking sheet. Discard the marinade.

7. Broil the chops for 4 mins per side for medium doneness.
8. Let the chops rest for 5 mins before serving.

NUTRITION: calories 413, fat 29g, protein 31g, carbs 1g, sugars 0g, fiber 0g, sodium 100mg

543. Lamb and Pomegranate Salad

Cooking time 30 mins | Servings 8

INGREDIENTS:

- 1 (4-pound) lamb leg, deboned, butterflied, and fat trimmed
- 2 tbsp balsamic vinegar
- 2 tsps Dijon mustard
- ½ cup pomegranate seeds
- 1cup pomegranate juice
- 4 cups baby kale
- 4 cups fresh green beans, blanched
- ¼ cup toasted walnut halves
- 2 fennel bulbs, thinly sliced
- 4 tbsp olive oil, divided
- 1 tsp cumin
- 1 tbsp ground ginger
- 3 cloves garlic, chopped
- Salt and freshly ground black pepper, to taste

DIRECTIONS:

1. Mix the pomegranate juice, 1 tbsp of olive oil, cumin, ginger, garlic, salt, and black pepper in a large bowl. Stir to mix well.
2. Dunk the lamb leg in the mixture, press to coat well. Wrap the bowl in plastic and refrigerate to marinate for at least 8 hours.
3. Remove the bowl from the refrigerate and let sit for 20 mins. Pat the lamb dry with paper towels.
4. Preheat the grill to high heat.
5. Brush the grill grates with 1 tbsp of olive oil, then arrange the lamb on the grill grates.
6. Grill for 30 mins or until the internal temperature of the lamb reaches at least 145ºF. Flip the lamb halfway through the cooking time.
7. Remove the lamb from the grill and wrap with aluminum foil. Let stand for 15 mins.
8. Meanwhile, combine the vinegar, mustard, salt, black pepper, and remaining olive oil in a separate large bowl. Stir to mix well.
9. Add the remaining ingredients and lamb leg to the bowl and toss to combine well. Serve immediately.

NUTRITION: calories 380, fat 21g, protein 32g, carbs 16g, fiber 5g, sugars 6g, sodium 240mg

CHAPTER 12 Desserts

544. Peach Crumb Cobbler

Cooking time: 30 mins | Servings: 3

INGREDIENTS:

- 2 cups fresh peaches | sliced
- 1/3 cup graham cracker crumbs
- ½ tsp ground cinnamon
- ¼ tsp nutmeg
- 2 tsps canola oil

DIRECTIONS:

1. Preheat the oven to 350°F.
2. Place the sliced peaches in the bottom of an 8-x-8-x-2-inch baking pan.
3. In a small mixing bowl | combine the graham cracker crumbs | cinnamon | and nutmeg; mix well.
4. Gradually blend in the oil and sprinkle the mixture over the peaches. Bake uncovered at 350°F for 25 to 30 mins. Remove from the oven and let cool slightly before serving.

NUTRITION: calories 110, fat 4g, protein 2g, carbs 17g, sugars 12g, fiber 2g, sodium 55mg

545. Melon Pear Medley

Cooking time 10 mins | Servings 12

INGREDIENTS:

- 1 large orange
- 15 oz melon chunks
- 15 oz canned unsweetened pear halves, drained
- 15 oz canned unsweetened apricot halves, drained
- 6 whole cloves
- 2 cinnamon sticks

DIRECTIONS:

1. Peel the orange and reserve the rind. Divide the orange into sections and remove the membrane.
2. Drain the pineapple, reserve the juice, and set aside.
3. In a large bowl, combine the orange sections, pineapple, pears, and apricots. Toss, and set aside.
4. In a small saucepan over medium heat, combine the orange rind, pineapple juice, cloves, and cinnamon. Let simmer for 5 to 10 mins; then strain the juices and pour over the fruit.
5. Cover, and refrigerate for at least 2 to 3 hours. Toss before serving.

NUTRITION: calories 60, fat 0g, protein 1g, carbs 16g, sugars 13g, fiber 2g, sodium 0mg

546. Spiced Baked Apples

Cooking time 15 mins | Servings 4

INGREDIENTS:

- 3 apples, peeled, cored, and chopped
- 2 tbsp pure maple syrup
- ½ tsp cinnamon
- ½ tsp ground ginger
- ¼ cup chopped pecans

DIRECTIONS:

1. Preheat the oven to 350°F.
2. In a bowl, mix the apples, syrup, cinnamon, and ginger. Pour the mixture into a 9-inch square baking dish. Sprinkle the pecans over the top.
3. Bake until the apples are tender, about 15 mins.

NUTRITION: calories 122, fat 5g, protein 1g, carbs 21g, sugars 13g, fiber 3g, sodium 2mg

547. Maple Oatmeal Cookies

Cooking time 15 mins | Servings 16

INGREDIENTS:

- 1 large egg
- ¾ cup almond flour
- ¾ cup old-fashioned oats
- ¼ cup shredded unsweetened coconut
- 1 tsp baking powder
- 1 tsp ground cinnamon
- ¼ tsp salt
- ¼ cup unsweetened applesauce
- 2 tbsp pure maple syrup
- 2 tbsp coconut oil, melted

DIRECTIONS:

1. Preheat the oven to 350°F.
2. In a medium mixing bowl, combine the almond flour, oats, coconut, baking powder, cinnamon, and salt, and mix well.
3. In another medium bowl, combine the applesauce, egg, maple syrup, and coconut oil, and mix. Stir the wet mixture into the dry mixture.
4. Form the dough into balls a little bigger than a tbsp and place on a baking sheet, leaving at least 1 inch between them. Bake for 12 mins until the cookies are just browned. Remove from the oven and let cool for 5 mins.
5. Using a spatula, remove the cookies and cool on a rack.

NUTRITION: calories 76, fat 6g, protein 2g, carbs 5g, sugars 1g, fiber 1g, sodium 57mg

548. Peach and Almond Meal Fritters

Cooking time 15 mins | Servings 6

INGREDIENTS:

- 4 ripe pears, peeled
- 2 cups chopped peaches
- 2 eggs
- 2 medium egg whites
- ¾ cup almond meal
- ¼ tsp almond extract

DIRECTIONS:

1. In a large bowl, mash the pears and peaches together with a fork or potato masher.
2. Blend in the egg and egg whites.
3. Stir in the almond meal and almond extract.
4. Working in batches, place ¼-cup portions of the batter into the basket of an air fryer.
5. Set the air fryer to 390°F close and cook for 12 mins.
6. Once cooking is complete, transfer the fritters to a plate. Repeat until no batter remains.

NUTRITION: calories 164, fat 7g, protein 6g, carbs 22g, sugars 12g, fiber 4g, sodium 23mg

549. Tapioca Berry Parfaits

Cooking time 6 mins | Servings 4

INGREDIENTS:

- ½ cup small pearl tapioca, rinsed and still wet
- 1 cup unsweetened almond milk
- 1 tsp almond extract
- 1 tbsp pure maple syrup
- 2 cups berries
- ¼ cup slivered almonds

DIRECTIONS:

1. Pour the almond milk into the electric pressure cooker. Stir in the tapioca and almond extract.
2. Close and lock the lid of the pressure cooker. Set the valve to sealing.
3. Cook on High pressure for 6 mins.
4. When the cooking is complete, hit Cancel. Allow the pressure to release naturally for 10 mins, then

quick release any remaining pressure.

5. Once the pin drops, unlock and remove the lid. Remove the pot to a cooling rack.
6. Stir in the maple syrup and let the mixture cool for about an hour.
7. In small glasses, create several layers of tapioca, berries, and almonds. Refrigerate for 1 hour.
8. Serve chilled.

NUTRITION: calories 174, fat 5g, protein 3g, carbs 32g, sugars 11g, fiber 3g, sodium 77mg

550. Blackberry Yogurt Ice Pops

Cooking time 0 mins | Servings 4

INGREDIENTS:

- 12 oz plain Greek yogurt
- 1 cup blackberries
- Pinch nutmeg
- ¼ cup milk
- 2 (1-gram) packets stevia

DIRECTIONS:

1. In a blender, combine all the ingredients; blend until smooth.
2. Pour the mixture into 4 ice pop molds. Freeze for 6 hours before serving.

NUTRITION: calories 75, fat 6g, protein 9g, carbs 9g, sugars 5g, fiber 2g, sodium 7mg

551. Chocolate Almond Butter Fudge

Cooking time 0 mins | Servings 9 pieces

INGREDIENTS:

- 2 oz unsweetened baking chocolate
- ½ cup almond butter
- 1 can full-fat coconut milk, refrigerated overnight, thickened cream only
- 1 tsp vanilla extract
- 4 (1-gram) packets stevia (or to taste)

DIRECTIONS:

1. Line a 9-inch square baking pan with parchment paper.
2. In a small saucepan over medium-low heat, heat the chocolate and almond butter, stirring constantly, until both are melted. Cool slightly.
3. In a medium bowl, combine the melted chocolate mixture with the cream from the coconut milk, vanilla, and stevia. Blend until smooth. Taste and adjust sweetness as desired.
4. Pour the mixture into the prepared pan, spreading with a spatula to smooth. Refrigerate for 3 hours. Cut into squares.

NUTRITION: (1 piece) calories 200, fat 20g, protein 4g, carbs 6g, sugars 2g, fiber 2g, sodium 8mg

552. Pineapple Nice Cream

Cooking time 0 mins | Servings 6

INGREDIENTS:

- 2 ½ cups frozen pineapple
- 1 cup peanut butter (no added sugar, salt, or fat)
- ½ cup unsweetened almond milk

DIRECTIONS:

1. In a blender or food processor, combine the frozen pineapple and peanut butter and process.
2. Add the almond milk, and blend until smooth. The result should be a smooth paste.

NUTRITION: calories 301, fat 22g, protein 14g, carbs 15g, sugars 8g, fiber 4g, sodium 39mg

553. Grilled Peach and Yogurt Bowls

Cooking time 10 mins | Servings 4

INGREDIENTS:

- 3 peaches, halved and pitted
- ½ cup plain nonfat Greek yogurt
- 1 tsp pure vanilla extract
- ¼ cup unsweetened dried coconut flakes
- 2 tbsp unsalted pistachios, shelled and broken into pieces

DIRECTIONS:

1. Preheat the broiler to high. Arrange the rack in the closest position to the broiler.
2. In a shallow pan, arrange the peach halves, cut-side up. Broil for 6 to 8 mins until browned, tender, and hot.
3. In a small bowl, mix the yogurt and vanilla.
4. Spoon the yogurt into the cavity of each peach half.
5. Sprinkle 1 tbsp of coconut flakes and 1½ tsps of pistachios over each peach half. Serve warm.

NUTRITION: calories 102, fat 5g, protein 5g, carbs 11g, sugars 8g, fiber 2g, sodium 12mg

554. Creamy Strawberry Crepes

Cooking time 10 mins | Servings 4

INGREDIENTS:

- ½ cup old-fashioned oats
- 1 cup unsweetened plain almond milk
- 2 eggs
- 3 tsps honey, divided
- Nonstick cooking spray
- 2 oz low-fat cream cheese
- ¼ cup low-fat cottage cheese
- 2 cups sliced strawberries

DIRECTIONS:

1. In a blender jar, process the oats until they resemble flour. Add the almond milk, egg, and 1½ tsps honey, and process until smooth.
2. Heat a large skillet over medium heat. Spray with nonstick cooking spray to coat.
3. Add ¼ cup of oat batter to the pan and quickly swirl around to coat the bottom of the pan and let cook for 2 to 3 mins. When the edges begin to turn brown, flip the crepe with a spatula and cook until lightly browned and firm, about 1 minute. Transfer to a plate. Continue with the remaining batter, spraying the skillet with nonstick cooking spray before adding more batter. Set the cooked crepes aside, loosely covered with aluminum foil, while you make the filling.
4. Clean the blender jar, then combine the cream cheese, cottage cheese, and remaining 1½ tsps honey, and process until smooth.
5. Fill each crepe with 2 tbsp of the cream cheese mixture, topped with ¼ cup of strawberries. Serve.

NUTRITION: calories 149, fat 6g, protein 6g, carbs 20g, sugars 10g, fiber 3g, sodium 177mg

555. Flourless Orange Bundt Cake

Cooking time 30 mins, Servings 12

INGREDIENTS:

- 5 medium eggs, at room temperature
- Unsalted butter, for greasing the pan
- 1cup baking flour, plus more for dusting
- 1cup almond flour
- ½ tsp baking soda
- ½ tsp baking powder
- 1 cup coconut sugar
- Zest of 3 oranges
- Juice of 1 orange
- ½ cup olive oil

DIRECTIONS:

1. Preheat the oven to 325°F.

2. Grease two bundt pans with butter and dust with the baking flour.
3. In a medium bowl, whisk the baking flour, almond flour, baking soda, and baking powder together.
4. In a large bowl, whip the eggs with the coconut sugar until they double in size.
5. Add the orange zest and orange juice.
6. Add the dry ingredients to the wet ones, stirring to combine.
7. Add the olive oil, a little at a time, until incorporated.
8. Divide the batter between the two prepared bundt pans.
9. Transfer the bundt pans to the oven, and bake for 30 mins, or until browned and a toothpick inserted into the center comes out clean.
10. Remove the bundt pans from the oven and let cool for 15 mins.
11. Invert the bundt pans onto plates, and gently tap the cakes out of the pan.

NUTRITION: calories 179, fat 12g, protein 4g, carbs 15g, sugars 8g, fiber 1g, sodium 52mg

556. Avocado Chocolate Mousse

Cooking time 0 mins, Servings 4

INGREDIENTS:

- 2 avocados, mashed
- ¼ cup canned coconut milk
- 2 tbsp unsweetened cocoa powder
- 1 tbsp pure maple syrup
- ½ tsp vanilla extract

DIRECTIONS:

1. In a blender, combine all the ingredients, blend until smooth.
2. Pour the mixture into 4 small bowls and serve.

NUTRITION: calories 203, fat 17g, protein 2g, carbs 15g, sugars 6g, fiber 6g, sodium 11mg

557. Cottage Cheese Pancakes

Cooking time 20 mins | Servings 4

INGREDIENTS:

- 2 cups low-fat cottage cheese
- 4 egg whites
- 2 eggs
- 1 tbsp pure vanilla extract
- 1½ cups almond flour
- Nonstick cooking spray

DIRECTIONS:

1. Place the cottage cheese, egg whites, eggs, and vanilla in a blender and pulse to combine.
2. Add the almond flour to the blender and blend until smooth.
3. Place a large nonstick skillet over medium heat and lightly coat it with cooking spray.
4. Spoon ¼ cup of batter per pancake, 4 at a time, into the skillet. Cook the pancakes until the bottoms are firm and golden, about 4 mins.
5. Flip the pancakes over and cook the other side until they are cooked through, about 3 mins.
6. Remove the pancakes to a plate and repeat with the remaining batter.
7. Serve with fresh fruit.

NUTRITION: calories 344, fat 22g, protein 29g, carbs 11g, sugars 5g, fiber 4g, sodium 559mg

558. Frozen Chocolate Peanut Butter Bites

Cooking time 0 mins | Servings 32

INGREDIENTS:

- 1 cup coconut oil, melted
- ¼ cup cocoa powder
- ¼ cup honey

- ¼ cup natural peanut butter

DIRECTIONS:

1. Pour the melted coconut oil into a medium bowl. Whisk in the cocoa powder, honey, and peanut butter.
2. Transfer the mixture to ice cube trays in portions about 1½ tsp each.
3. Freeze for 2 hours or until ready to serve.

NUTRITION: calories 80, fat 8g, protein 1g, carbs 3g, sugars 2g, fiber 0g, sodium 20mg

559. Apple Crunch

Cooking time 2 mins | Servings 4

INGREDIENTS:

- 3 apples, peeled, cored, and sliced (about 1½ pounds)
- 2 tsp pure maple syrup
- 2 tsp apple pie spice or ground cinnamon
- ¼ cup unsweetened apple juice, apple cider, or water
- ¼ cup low-sugar granola

DIRECTIONS:

1. In the electric pressure cooker, combine the apples, maple syrup, apple pie spice, and apple juice.
2. Close and lock the lid of the pressure cooker. Set the valve to sealing.
3. Cook on high pressure for 2 mins.
4. When the cooking is complete, hit Cancel and quick release the pressure.
5. Once the pin drops, unlock and remove the lid.
6. Spoon the apples into 4 serving bowls and sprinkle each with 1 tbsp of granola.

NUTRITION: calories 103, fat 1g, protein 1g, carbs 26g, sugars 18g, fiber 4g, sodium 13mg

560. Goat Cheese-Stuffed Pears

Cooking time 2 mins | Servings 4

INGREDIENTS:

- 2 oz goat cheese, at room temperature
- 2 tsps pure maple syrup
- 3 ripe, firm pears, halved lengthwise and cored
- 2 tbsp chopped pistachios, toasted

DIRECTIONS:

1. Pour 1 cup of water into the electric pressure cooker and insert a wire rack or trivet.
2. In a small bowl, combine the goat cheese and maple syrup.
3. Spoon the goat cheese mixture into the cored pear halves. Place the pears on the rack inside the pot, cut-side up.
4. Close and lock the lid of the pressure cooker. Set the valve to sealing.
5. Cook on high pressure for 2 mins.
6. When the cooking is complete, hit Cancel and quick release the pressure.
7. Once the pin drops, unlock and remove the lid.
8. Using tongs, carefully transfer the pears to serving plates.
9. Sprinkle with pistachios and serve immediately.

NUTRITION: (½ pear) calories 120, fat 5g, protein 4g, carbs 17g, sugars 11g, fiber 3g, sodium 54mg

561. Gingerbread Soufflés

Cooking time 25 mins | Servings 8

INGREDIENTS:

- 4 eggs, separated
- 1 cup skim milk
- 1 cup fat free whipped topping
- 2 tbsp butter, soft

- ½ cup Splenda
- 1/3 cup molasses
- ¼ cup flour
- 2 tsps pumpkin pie spice
- 2 tsps vanilla
- 1 tsp ginger
- ¼ tsp salt
- ⅛ tsp cream of tartar
- Butter flavored cooking spray

DIRECTIONS:

1. Heat oven to 350°F. Spray 10 ramekins with cooking spray and sprinkle with Splenda to coat, shaking out excess. Place on a large baking sheet.
2. In a large saucepan, over medium heat, whisk together milk, Splenda, flour and salt until smooth. Bring to a boil, whisking constantly. Pour into a large bowl and whisk in molasses, butter, vanilla, and spices. Let cool 15 mins.
3. Once spiced mixture has cooled, whisk in egg yolks.
4. In a large bowl, beat egg whites and cream of tartar on high speed until stiff peaks form. Fold into spiced mixture, a third at a time, until blended completely. Spoon into ramekins.
5. Bake for 25 mins until puffed and set. Serve immediately with a dollop of whipped topping.

NUTRITION: calories 171, fat 5g, protein 4g, carbs 24g, fiber 0g, sugars 18g, sodium 289mg

562. Crispy Apple Chips

Cooking time 2 hours | Servings 4

INGREDIENTS:

- 2 medium apples, sliced
- 1 tsp ground cinnamon

DIRECTIONS:

1. Preheat the oven to 200°F. Line a baking sheet with parchment paper.
2. Arrange the apple slices on the prepared baking sheet, then sprinkle with cinnamon.
3. Bake in the preheated oven for 2 hours or until crispy. Flip the apple chips halfway through the cooking time.
4. Allow to cool for 10 mins and serve warm.

NUTRITION: calories 50, fat 0g, protein 0g, carbs 13g, fiber 2g, sugars 9g, sodium 0mg

563. Blackberry Soufflés

Cooking time 30 mins | Servings 4

INGREDIENTS:

- 12 oz blackberries
- 4 egg whites
- 1/3 cup Splenda
- 1 tbsp water
- 1 tbsp Swerve powdered sugar
- Nonstick cooking spray

DIRECTIONS:

1. Heat oven to 375°F. Spray 4 1-cup ramekins with cooking spray.
2. In a small saucepan, over medium-high heat, combine blackberries and 1 tbsp water, bring to a boil. Reduce heat and simmer until berries are soft. Add Splenda and stir over medium heat until Splenda dissolves, without boiling.
3. Bring back to boiling, reduce heat and simmer 5 mins. Remove from heat and cool 5 mins.
4. Place a fine meshed sieve over a small bowl and push the berry mixture through it using the back of a spoon. Discard the seeds. Cover and chill 15 mins.
5. In a large bowl, beat egg whites until soft peaks form. Gently fold in berry mixture. Spoon evenly into prepared ramekins and place them on a baking sheet.

6. Bake 12 mins, or until puffed and light brown. Dust with powdered Swerve and serve immediately.

NUTRITION: calories 142, fat 0g, protein 5g, carbs 26g, fiber 5g, sugars 20g, sodium 56mg

564. Carrot Cupcakes

Cooking time 35 mins | Servings 12

INGREDIENTS:

- 2 cup carrots, grated
- 1 cup low fat cream cheese, soft
- 2 eggs
- 2 tsps skim milk
- ½ cup coconut oil, melted
- ¼ cup coconut flour
- ¼ cup Splenda
- ¼ cup honey
- 2 tsps vanilla, divided
- 1 tsp baking powder
- 1 tsp cinnamon
- Nonstick cooking spray

DIRECTIONS:

1. Heat oven to 350°F. Lightly spray a muffin pan with cooking spray, or use paper liners.
2. In a large bowl, stir together the flour, baking powder, and cinnamon.
3. Add the carrots, eggs, oil, Splenda, and vanilla to a food processor. Process until are combined but carrots still have some large chunks remaining. Add to dry and stir to combine.
4. Pour evenly into prepared pan, filling cups ²/₃ full. Bake for 30 to 35 mins, or until cupcakes pass the toothpick test. Remove from oven and let cool.
5. In a medium bowl, beat cream cheese, honey, and vanilla on high speed until smooth. Add milk, one tsp at a time, beating after each addition, until frosting is creamy enough to spread easily.
6. Once cupcakes have cooled, spread each one with about 2 tbsp of frosting. Chill until ready to serve.

NUTRITION: calories 161, fat 10g, protein 4g, carbs 13g, fiber 1g, sugars 11g, sodium 96mg

565. Spicy Peaches

Cooking time 10 mins | Servings 2

INGREDIENTS:

- 1 cup canned peaches with juices
- ½ tsp cornstarch
- 1 tsp ground cloves
- 1 tsp ground cinnamon
- 1 tsp ground nutmeg
- Zest of ½ lemon
- ½ cup water

DIRECTIONS:

1. Drain peaches.
2. Combine cinnamon, cornstarch, nutmeg, ground cloves, and lemon zest in a pan on the stove.
3. Heat on a medium heat and add peaches.
4. Bring to a boil, reduce the heat and simmer for 10 mins.
5. Serve.

NUTRITION: calories 70, carbs 14g, sodium 3mg, protein 1g

566. Pumpkin Cheesecake bar

Cooking time 50 mins | Servings 4

INGREDIENTS:

- 2 ½ tbsps unsalted butter
- 4 oz cream cheese
- ½ cup whole wheat white flour
- 3 tbsps golden brown sugar
- ¼ cup granulated sugar
- ½ cup pureed pumpkin
- 2 egg whites
- 1 tsp ground cinnamon
- 1 tsp ground nutmeg
- 1 tsp vanilla extract

DIRECTIONS:

1. Preheat the oven to 350°F.
2. Mix flour and brown sugar in a bowl.
3. Mix in the butter to form breadcrumbs.
4. Place ¾ of this mixture in a dish.
5. Bake in the oven for 15 mins. Remove and cool.
6. Lightly whisk the egg and fold in the cream cheese, sugar, pumpkin, cinnamon, nutmeg and vanilla until smooth.
7. Pour this mixture over the oven-baked base and sprinkle with the rest of the breadcrumbs from earlier.
8. Bake in the oven for 30 to 35 mins more.
9. Cool, slice and serve.

NUTRITION: calories 248, fat 13g, carbs 33g, sodium 146mg, protein 4g

567. Blueberry Mini Muffins

Cooking time 35 mins | Servings 4

INGREDIENTS:

- 3 egg whites
- ¼ cup whole wheat white flour
- 1 tbsp Coconut flour
- 1 tsp baking soda
- 1 tbsp nutmeg
- 1 tsp vanilla extract
- 1 tsp stevia
- ¼ cup fresh blueberries

DIRECTIONS:

1. Preheat the oven to 325°F.
2. Mix all the ingredients in a bowl.
3. Divide the batter into 4 and spoon into a lightly oiled muffin tin.
4. Bake in the oven for 15 to 20 mins or until cooked through.
5. Cool and serve.

NUTRITION: calories 62, fat 0g, carbs 9g, phosphorus 103mg, potassium 65mg, sodium 62mg, protein 4g

568. Vanilla custard

Cooking time 30 mins | Servings 10

INGREDIENTS:

- 1 egg
- 1/8 tsp vanilla
- 1/8 tsp nutmeg
- ½ cup almond milk
- 2 tbsp stevia

DIRECTIONS:

1. Scald the milk then let it cool slightly.
2. Break the egg into a bowl and beat it with the nutmeg.
3. Add the scalded milk, the vanilla, and the sweetener to taste. Mix well.
4. Place the bowl in a baking pan filled with ½ deep of water.
5. Bake for 30 mins at 325°F. Serve.

NUTRITION: calories 167, fat 9g, carbs 11g, phosphorus 205mg, potassium 249mg, sodium 124mg, protein 10g

569. Coconut Cream Pie

Cooking time 10 mins | Servings 8

INGREDIENTS:

- 2 cup raw coconut, grated and divided
- 2 cans coconut milk, full fat and refrigerated for 24 hours
- ½ cup raw coconut, grated and toasted
- 2 tbsp margarine, melted
- 1 cup Splenda
- ½ cup macadamia nuts
- ¼ cup almond flour

DIRECTIONS:

1. Heat oven to 350°F.
2. Add the nuts to a food processor and pulse until finely ground. Add flour, ½ cup Splenda, and 1 cup grated

coconut. Pulse until are finely ground and resemble cracker crumbs.

3. Add the margarine and pulse until mixture starts to stick together. Press on the bottom and sides of a pie pan. Bake 10 mins or until golden brown. Cool
4. Turn the canned coconut upside down and open. Pour off the water and scoop the cream into a large bowl. Add remaining ½ cup Splenda and beat on high until stiff peaks form.
5. Fold in remaining 1 cup coconut and pour into crust. Cover and chill at least 2 hours. Sprinkle with toasted coconut, slice, and serve.

NUTRITION: calories 330, fat 23g, protein 4g, carbs 15g, fiber 11g, sugars 4g, sodium 24mg

570. Date and Almond Balls with Seeds

Cooking time 0 mins | Servings 36 Balls

INGREDIENTS:

- 1 pound pitted dates
- ½ pound blanched almonds
- ¼ cup water
- ¼ cup butter, at room temperature
- 1 tsp ground cardamom
- 1 tsp vanilla extract
- ½ tsp ground cinnamon
- 2 tbsp ground flaxseed
- 1 cup toasted sesame seeds

DIRECTIONS:

1. In a food processor, add the pitted dates, almonds, water, butter, cardamon, vanilla, and cinnamon, and pulse until the mixture has broken down into a smooth paste.
2. Scoop out the paste and form into 36 equal-sized balls with your hands.
3. Spread out the flaxseed and sesame seeds on a baking sheet. Roll the balls in the seed mixture until they are evenly coated on all sides.
4. Serve immediately or store in an airtight container in the fridge for 2 days.

NUTRITION: (1 ball) calories 113, fat 7g, protein 2g, carbs 12g, fiber 2g, sugars 7g, sodium 10mg

571. Apricot Soufflé

Cooking time 30 mins | Servings 6

INGREDIENTS:

- 4 egg whites
- 3 egg yolks, beaten
- 3 tbsp margarine
- ¾ cup sugar free apricot fruit spread
- $^1/_3$ cup dried apricots, diced fine
- ¼ cup warm water
- 2 tbsp flour
- ¼ tsp cream of tartar
- ⅛ tsp salt

DIRECTIONS:

1. Heat oven to 325°F.
2. In a medium saucepan, over medium heat, melt margarine. Stir in flour and cook, stirring, until bubbly.
3. Stir together the fruit spread and water in a small bowl and add it to the saucepan with the apricots. Cook, stirring, 3 mins or until mixture thickens.
4. Remove from heat and whisk in egg yolks. Let cool to room temperature, stirring occasionally.
5. In a medium bowl, beat egg whites, salt, and cream of tartar on high speed until stiff peaks form. Gently fold into cooled apricot mixture.
6. Spoon into a 1½–quart soufflé dish. Bake 30 mins, or until puffed and golden brown. Serve immediately.

NUTRITION: calories 116, fat 8g, protein 4g, carbs 7g, fiber 0g, sugars 1g, sodium 95mg

572. Mini Lime Tarts

Cooking time 10 mins | Servings 8

INGREDIENTS:

- 4 sheets phyllo dough
- ¾ cup skim milk
- ¾ cup fat-free whipped topping, thawed
- ½ cup egg substitute
- ½ cup fat free sour cream
- 6 tbsp fresh lime juice
- 2 tbsp cornstarch
- ½ cup Splenda
- Butter-flavored cooking spray

DIRECTIONS:

1. In a medium saucepan, combine milk, juice, and cornstarch. Cook, stirring, over medium heat 2 to 3 mins or until thickened. Remove from heat.
2. Add egg substitute and whisk 30 seconds to allow it to cook. Stir in sour cream and Splenda. Cover and chill until completely cool.
3. Heat oven to 350ºF. Spray 8 muffin cups with cooking spray.
4. Lay 1 sheet of the phyllo on a cutting board and lightly spray it with cooking spray. Repeat this with the remaining sheets so they are stacked on top of each other.
5. Cut the phyllo into 8 squares and gently place them in the prepared muffin cups, pressing firmly on the bottom and sides. Bake for 8 to 10 mins or until golden brown. Remove them from the pan and let cool.
6. To serve spoon the lime mixture evenly into the 8 cups and top with whipped topping. Garnish with fresh lime slices if desired.

NUTRITION: calories 83, fat 1g, protein 3g, carbs 13g, fiber 1g, sugars 10g, sodium 111mg

573. Bakery Squares

Cooking time 35 mins | Servings 6

INGREDIENTS:

- 8 oz cream cheese
- 1 cup whole wheat flour
- 6 tbsp margarine
- 14 oz condensed milk, skimmed
- ½ cup egg substitute
- 2 tsp vanilla extract
- ¼ cup cocoa powder
- ¾ cup stevia
- ¼ salt

DIRECTIONS:

- preheat the oven to 325°F and coat an 8-inches square baking tray with cooking spray.

2. now combine all the ingredients (except for cream cheese and milk) in a large mixing bowl; slice in margarine until brittle.
3. place aside 1/2 cup of the crumb mixture to use as a topping. cook for 9-minutes or until set.
4. inside a shallow mixing bowl, combine cream cheese, followed by condensed milk, then add egg substitute and vanilla extract. spill slowly over the crust.
5. cook for 20 minutes in the oven. top with 1/2 cup prepared mixture (already made in initial steps and preserved for topping), then bake for 15 minutes more, otherwise until set. allow cooling on a wire tray and serve.

NUTRITION: calories 113, fat 4g, protein 8g, carbs 27g, fiber 6g, sodium 214mg

574. Chocolate almond clusters

Cooking time 5 mins | Servings 6

INGREDIENTS:

- 1 cup minced almonds
- ¼ split almonds
- 2 chocolate bars – no sugar

DIRECTIONS:

1. line a baking tray using aluminum foil. cut the chocolate bars into small slices, then place inside a nonstick bowl.
2. microwave for 46-seconds. now transfer the bowl to a table-top and continue to stir until fully melted and smooth.
3. include the nuts into the melted chocolate, then whisk until well combined and all the pieces are covered.
4. using a teaspoon, drip a little spoonful of candy over the baking tray. if needed, top every cluster with almonds. chill for 22-minutes to allow the chocolate to harden. Serve

NUTRITION: calories 95, fat 8g, protein 2g, carbs 4g

575. Lemon squares

Cooking time 15 mins | Servings 6

INGREDIENTS:

- 12 oz condensed milk, half-skim
- 3 oz lemon gelatin, no-sugar
- 3 tbsp lemon juice
- 2 cup cracker crumbs, half skim
- 6 tbsp margarine
- ¾ cup stevia
- 1 cup boiling water

DIRECTIONS:

1. pour condensed milk inside a small size metal bowl, chill, covered, for at least 60 minutes. meanwhile, combine gelatin with stevia in hot water inside a large mixing bowl.
2. whisk in lemon juice, chill, cover for 60 minutes or until thickened.
3. combine crumbs with margarine inside a small bowl; place aside 3-tbsp for garnish. press the rest of the crumbs within the base of a 9-by-13-inches baking tray.
4. beat milk until smooth. now beat gelatin until little bubbles start to form. mix the milk within gelatin, then spill over the crust; garnish with reserved crumbs.
5. coat and refrigerate for 7-hours or until set. slice into squares. Serve!

NUTRITION: calories 120, fat 5g, protein 6g, carbs 16g, sodium 36mg

576. Peanut butter coconut balls

Cooking time 15 mins | Servings 6

INGREDIENTS:

- 2 cup rice cereal
- 1 cup peanut butter, half skim
- ½ cup granulated splenda
- ¾ coconut powder

DIRECTIONS:

1. line a baking tray with wax paper. inside a large mixing bowl, mix together rice cereal, followed by peanut butter, then add splenda until well combined.
2. spill coconut within a shallow bowl. shape mixture into balls with a teaspoon then tosses in coconut powder to cover.
3. put on the baking tray, then refrigerate for at least 60-minutes. transfer to an airtight box and store inside the fridge.

NUTRITION: calories 85, fat 5g, protein 2g, carbs 9g, sodium 71mg

577. Strawberry fluff

Cooking time 10 mins | Servings 6

INGREDIENTS:

- 1 oz strawberry gelatin
- 2 cup strawberry, quartered
- 8 oz sliced pineapple
- ¼ cup marshmallows
- 1 oz vanilla pudding mix
- 1 cup water
- 8 oz whipped topping

DIRECTIONS:

1. inside a large mixing bowl, combine the gelatin mix, followed by pudding mix, with water, then whisk until creamy and thickened. whisk in the whipped topping until well blended
2. fold in strawberries, followed by pineapple and marshmallows. place in the refrigerator until ready to eat. serve!

NUTRITION: calories75, fat 3g, protein 2g, carbs 12g, sodium 10mg

578. Super light tiramisu

Cooking time 15 mins | Servings 6

INGREDIENTS:

- 1 cup skimmed milk
- 3 oz ladyfingers
- 6 oz cream cheese
- 2 cup whipped topping, skimmed
- 1/3 cup black coffee, chilled
- 1 package vanilla pudding mix
- ½ teaspoon cocoa

DIRECTIONS:

1. slice the ladyfingers into half parts, then line the base of an 8-inches square glass baking tray with 1/2 of them.
2. dribble ladyfingers with ½ tbsp coffee. inside a large mixing bowl, beat the pudding mix with milk until thickened
3. whisk in the remaining coffee. include cream cheese, then beat until soft. distribute the pudding mixture uniformly over the ladyfingers.
4. put the remaining ladyfingers over the top of the pudding, then garnish with whipped topping.
5. dust with cocoa powder. refrigerate for 2-4 hours. Serve!

NUTRITION: calories 130, fat 5g, protein 5g, carbs 20g, sodium 80mg

579. Apple crisp

Cooking time 25 mins | Servings 6

INGREDIENTS:

- 6 apples, peel-cored, flaked
- ½ cup rolled oats
- 2 tbsp brown sugar
- 4 tbsp whole grain flour
- 1 tbsp sugar substitute
- ½ tsp ground cinnamon
- 2 tbsp margarine, half-skim

DIRECTIONS:

1. preheat oven to 400° F. coat a 9-inch microwave-safe pie plate with cooking spray.
2. in a large bowl, combine apples, 2 tbsp flour, sugar substitute, and cinnamon; mix well.
3. spoon into pie plate and cover with wax paper. microwave on high for about 5 to 8 minutes or until the apples are soft.
4. meanwhile, in a medium bowl, combine the remaining 2 tablespoons flour, the oats, and brown sugar; mix

well. with a fork, blend in margarine until crumbly; sprinkle over apples.

5. bake for about 20 to 25 minutes or until golden and bubbly. serve warm.

NUTRITION: calories 200, fat 4g, protein 2g, carbs 37g, sodium 260mg

580. Rich & creamy fudge

Cooking time 15 mins | Servings 8

INGREDIENTS:

- 1/4 cup margarine
- 1 tsp vanilla extract
- ½ cup diced nuts (optional)
- 2 oz dark chocolate
- 1 cup granulated splenda
- 8 oz cream cheese, half-skim

DIRECTIONS:

1. cover and 8-inches square baking tray with cooking spray. now melt margarine inside a saucepan on low flame. include the chocolate and stir unless melted.
2. remove from the heat and whisk in splenda with vanilla until well combined.
3. spill into a large mixing bowl. include cream cheese, then beat until soft. whisk in nuts, if needed, and spread into the baking tray.
4. refrigerate for 60-minutes or until the mixture is set.

NUTRITION: calories 110, fat 2g, protein 4g, carbs 23g, sodium 60mg

581. Apple-caramel crunch balls

Cooking time 35 mins | Servings 8

INGREDIENTS:

- 1/3 cup peanut butter, half-skim
- 1/4 cup margarine
- 1/3 cup dried apples, thinly diced
- 2 tbsp thinly diced walnuts
- ½ tsp apple-pie spice
- 1 tbsp caramel syrup, no-sugar
- 1/4 cup honey
- 2 cup crumbled wheat cereal

DIRECTIONS:

1. combine the peanut butter with margarine, plus honey inside a large saucepan. cook, constantly stirring, on medium flame until the combination comes to a simmer. remove from the heat.
2. stir in the cereal, apples, followed by walnuts, including apple pie spice, unless thoroughly combined. cover and allow to cool for 35-mins into a small-sized bowl. split the mixture into 18 equal portions.
3. form mixture into balls with slightly damp hands. refrigerate for 16 minutes, or until set, over a baking tray lined with waxed paper. dribble caramel sauce over the balls. chill for at least 20-mins before serving, or store wrapped in the refrigerator.

NUTRITION: calories 53, fat 4g, protein 2g, carbs 10g, sodium 75mg

582. Protein cheesecake

Cooking time 15 mins | Servings 8

INGREDIENTS:

- 8 oz cottage half-skim
- 2 egg whites
- ½ tsp vanilla powder
- 1 tbsp stevia
- 1 tsp vanilla concentrate
- 1 serving strawberry jell-o
- Water

DIRECTIONS:

1. preheat your oven to about 325°F. place the strawberry jell-o within the freezer after preparing it according to the box directions. blend cottage cheese with egg whites in a blender until creamy.

2. pour the prepared mixture into a mixing bowl and stir in the vanilla, followed by stevia, then the vanilla extract.
3. move the batter within a shallow nonstick skillet and cook for 26-mins. switch off the oven; however, keep the prepared cake in it to cool. discard the cheesecake from the oven until it is cooled.
4. once the jell-o becomes set, add it on the top of the cheesecake. allow the cake to set in the refrigerator for at least 10-12 hours before serving.

NUTRITION: calories 223, fat 18g, protein 22g, carbs 16g, sodium 160mg

583. Peanut butter cookies

Cooking time 15 mins | Servings 8

INGREDIENTS:

- 1 cup peanut butter sugar-free
- 1 egg
- 2/3 cup erythritol
- ½ tsp baking soda
- ½ tsp vanilla essence

DIRECTIONS:

1. preheat the oven to about 350°F and cover a cookie sheet with parchment paper. place aside. include the erythritol in a blender, then blend until it is powdered. place aside.
2. include all the items into a standard mixing bowl, then mix unless a smooth, shiny dough emerges. roll about 2-tbsp of dough among your palms to shape a ball, then put on the cookie sheet lined with parchment paper. repeat unless all the dough has been utilized. you can have 13-14 cookies.
3. straighten the cookies with a fork to make a crisscross design across the top. now bake for 13-15 mins, depending on the size of the cookies.
4. now remove the cookies from the oven; let them cool for 26-mins on the cookie sheet, then move them to a wire rack for another 16-mins. serve it.

NUTRITION: calories 72, fat 5g, protein 2g, carbs 11.6g, sodium 65mg

CHAPTER 13 Sauces, Dips and Dressings

584. Cranberry Sauce

Cooking time: 5 mins | Servings: 2

INGREDIENTS:

- 2 cups fresh cranberries, or frozen cranberries
- 1 tbsp granulated stevia
- ¾ cup water

DIRECTIONS:

1. In a 4-quart saucepan set over medium heat, mix together the cranberries, stevia, and water. Cook for 1 minute, stirring constantly until the stevia dissolves. Bring to a boil. Cook for about 5 mins more, or until the skins burst.
2. To a food processor or blender, transfer the cooked cranberries. Pulse gently for about 30 seconds.
3. Serve warm or chilled.

NUTRITION: calories 15, fat 0g, protein 0g, carbs 3g, sugars 1g, fiber 1g, sodium 0mg

585. Tofu and Lemon Sauce

Cooking time 5 mins | Servings 2

INGREDIENTS:

- 1 pound firm tofu, drained, cut into 8 pieces
- ¼ cup plain nonfat Greek yogurt
- 1 tsp stone-ground mustard
- 3 tbsp freshly squeezed lemon juice
- 1 tbsp coarsely chopped fresh cilantro
- 1 garlic clove, minced
- ¼ tsp salt
- ¼ tsp paprika

DIRECTIONS:

1. Prepare a steamer.
2. In steamer basket, place the tofu. Steam for 3 to 5 mins. Set aside.
3. In a blender, purée the yogurt, mustard, lemon juice, cilantro, garlic, salt, and paprika.
4. Add in 1 piece of tofu at a time and blend until smooth. Continue until all the tofu is blended in.
5. Serve warm.

NUTRITION: calories 39, fat 2g, protein 5g, carbs 0g, sugars 0g, fiber 0g, sodium 65mg

586. Pepper Sauce

Cooking time 20 mins | Servings 4 cups

INGREDIENTS:

- 2 red hot fresh chiles, seeded
- 2 dried chiles
- ½ small yellow onion, roughly chopped
- 2 garlic cloves, peeled
- 2 cups water
- 2 cups white vinegar

DIRECTIONS:

1. In a medium saucepan, combine the fresh and dried chiles, onion, garlic, and water. Bring to a simmer and cook for 20 mins, or until tender. Transfer to a food processor or blender.
2. Add the vinegar and blend until smooth.

NUTRITION: calories 2, fat 0g, protein 0g, carbs 0g, sugars 0g, fiber 0g, sodium 1mg

587. BBQ Sauce

Cooking time 15 mins | Servings about 3 cups

INGREDIENTS:

- 1¼ cup tomato salsa
- 1½ cup white vinegar
- 1 tbsp yellow mustard
- 1 tsp mustard seeds
- 1 tsp ground turmeric
- 1 tsp sweet paprika
- 1 tsp garlic powder
- 1 tsp celery seeds
- ½ tsp onion powder
- ½ tsp freshly ground black pepper

DIRECTIONS:

1. In a medium pot, combine the tomato salsa, vinegar, mustard, mustard seeds, turmeric, paprika, garlic powder, celery seeds, onion powder, and black pepper. Simmer over low heat for 15 mins, or until the flavors come together.
2. Remove the sauce from the heat and let cool for 5 mins. Transfer to a blender, and purée until smooth.

NUTRITION: calories 7, fat 0g, protein 0g, carbs 1g, sugars 1g, fiber 0g, sodium 12mg

588. Easy Peanut Sauce

Cooking time 0 mins | Servings 4

INGREDIENTS:

- ¼ cup peanut butter
- Juice of 1 lime
- 1 tbsp honey
- 1 minced garlic clove
- 1 tbsp reduced-sodium soy sauce
- 1 tbsp peeled fresh ginger, grated
- Pinch red pepper flakes

DIRECTIONS:

1. Put all ingredients in a medium bowl and whisk until well blended.

NUTRITION: calories 120, fat 8g, protein 4g, carbs 9g, sugars 7, sodium 138mg

589. Creamy Lemon Sauce

Cooking time 3 to 5 mins | Servings 2 cups

INGREDIENTS:

- 1 cup heavy cream
- 1 tbsp unsalted butter
- 2 tbsp Parmesan cheese, shredded
- 1 tsp freshly squeezed lemon juice
- ¼ tsp garlic powder

DIRECTIONS:

1. Add all ingredients to a saucepan and cook over medium-low heat for about 3 to 5 mins, stirring frequently, or until the sauce is heated through.
2. Remove from the heat to a bowl. Let it cool for a few mins before serving.

NUTRITION:

calories 55, fat 5g, protein 3g, carbs 1g, fiber 0g, sugars 0g, sodium 40mg

590. Greek Tzatziki Sauce

Cooking time 0 mins | Servings 6

INGREDIENTS:

- 1 medium cucumber, peeled and grated
- ¼ tsp salt
- 1 cup plain nonfat Greek yogurt
- 2 garlic cloves, minced
- 1 tbsp freshly squeezed lemon juice
- 1 tbsp olive oil
- ¼ tsp freshly ground black pepper

DIRECTIONS:

1. In a colander, sprinkle the cucumber with the salt. Set aside.
2. In a medium bowl, combine the yogurt, garlic, lemon juice, olive oil, and pepper.

3. Using your hands, squeeze as much water from the grated cucumber as possible. Transfer the cucumber to the yogurt mixture and stir well. Cover and refrigerate for 2 hours, if desired, to let the flavors merge.
4. Store in the refrigerator in an airtight container for up to 5 to 7 days.

NUTRITION: calories 48, fat 3g, protein 4g, carbs 3g, sugars 2g, fiber 0g, sodium 104mg

591. Roasted Tomato Salsa

Cooking time 1 hour | Servings 1 cup

INGREDIENTS:

- 1 pound tomatoes (about 6 large), papery husks removed, rinsed
- ½ large onion, quartered
- 3 serrano chiles, halved lengthwise, seeded
- 1 tbsp olive oil
- 1 tsp kosher salt
- 1 cup (loosely packed) fresh cilantro leaves

DIRECTIONS:

1. Preheat the oven to 375°F.
2. In an 8-inch square baking dish, combine the tomatillos, onion, chiles, oil, and salt. Roast for 1 hour or until the vegetables are very soft. Remove from the oven and let cool slightly.
3. Transfer everything from the baking dish to a food processor and add the cilantro. Purée until almost smooth. Pour the salsa into a glass jar and store, covered, in the refrigerator for up to 1 week.

NUTRITION: (2 tbsp) calories 33, fat 2g, protein 1g, carbs 4g, sugars 2g, fiber 1g, sodium 187mg

592. Beet Yogurt Dip

Cooking time 45 to 60 mins | Servings 6

INGREDIENTS:

- ½ pound red beets
- ½ cup plain nonfat Greek yogurt
- 1 tbsp olive oil
- 1 tbsp freshly squeezed lemon juice
- 1 garlic clove, peeled
- 1 tsp minced fresh thyme
- ½ tsp onion powder
- ¼ tsp salt

DIRECTIONS:

1. Preheat the oven to 375°F.
2. Wrap the beets in aluminum foil and bake for 45 to 60 mins until the beets are tender when pierced with a fork. Set aside and let cool for at least 10 mins. Using your hands, remove the skins and transfer the beets to a blender.
3. To the blender jar, add the yogurt, olive oil, lemon juice, garlic, thyme, onion powder, and salt. Process until smooth. Chill for 1 hour before serving.

NUTRITION: calories 49, fat 2g, protein 3g, carbs 5g, sugars 2g, sodium 121mg

593. Quick Pesto

Cooking time 0 mins | Servings 1 cup

INGREDIENTS:

- 3 garlic cloves, peeled
- 2 cups packed fresh basil leaves
- ½ cup freshly grated Parmesan cheese
- 1/3 cup pine nuts
- ½ cup olive oil
- Kosher salt and freshly ground black pepper, to taste

DIRECTIONS:

1. With the motor running, drop the garlic cloves through the feed tube of a food processor fitted with the steel blade. Stop the motor, then add the basil, Parmesan, and pine nuts. Pulse a few times until the pine nuts are finely minced.

2. With the motor running, add the olive oil in a steady stream and process until the pesto is completely puréed. Season with salt and pepper.
3. Store, covered, in the refrigerator for up to 2 weeks.

NUTRITION: (1 tbsp) calories 94, fat 10g, protein 2g, carbs 1g, sugars 0g, fiber 0g, sodium 71mg

594. Guacamole

Cooking time 0 mins | Servings 6

INGREDIENTS:

- 2 large avocados
- 1 small, firm tomato, finely diced
- ¼ white onion, finely diced
- ¼ cup finely chopped fresh cilantro
- 2 tbsp freshly squeezed lime juice
- ¼ tsp salt and pepper

DIRECTIONS:

1. Cut the avocados in half, remove the seeds, and scoop out the flesh into a medium bowl.
2. Using a fork, mash the avocado flesh. Mix in the tomato, onion, cilantro, lime juice, and salt. Season with black pepper.
3. Serve immediately.

NUTRITION: calories 82, fat 7g, protein 1g, carbs 6g, fiber 3g, sodium 84mg

595. Chimichurri

Cooking time 0 mins | Servings 4

INGREDIENTS:

- ½ cup parsley
- ¼ cup olive oil
- ¼ cup fresh cilantro, stems removed
- Zest of 1 lemon
- 2 tbsp red wine vinegar
- ½ tsp sea salt
- 1 garlic clove, minced
- ¼ tsp black pepper

DIRECTIONS:

1. Process all the ingredients in a food processor until smooth.
2. Store in an airtight container in the fridge for up to 2 days or in the freezer for 6 months.

NUTRITION: calories 124, fat 13g, protein 0g, carbs 1g, fiber 0g, sodium 150mg

596. Ranch Dressing

Cooking time 0 mins | Servings 8 to 10

INGREDIENTS:

- 8 oz fat-free plain Greek yogurt
- ¼ cup low-fat buttermilk
- 1 tbsp garlic powder
- 1 tbsp dried dill
- 1 tbsp dried chives
- 1 tbsp onion powder
- 1 tbsp dried parsley
- Pinch freshly ground black pepper

DIRECTIONS:

1. In a shallow, medium bowl, combine the Greek yogurt and buttermilk.
2. Stir in the garlic powder, dill, chives, onion powder, parsley, and pepper and mix well.
3. Serve with animal protein or vegetable of your choice, or place in an airtight container.

NUTRITION: calories 29, fat 0g, protein 3g, carbs 3g, sugars 2g, fiber 0g, sodium 23mg

597. Italian Dressing

Cooking time 0 mins | Servings 12

INGREDIENTS:

- ¼ cup red wine vinegar
- ½ cup olive oil
- ¼ tsp salt
- ¼ tsp freshly ground black pepper
- 1 tsp dried Italian seasoning
- 1 tsp Dijon mustard

- 1 garlic clove, minced

DIRECTIONS:

1. In a small jar, combine the vinegar, olive oil, salt, pepper, Italian seasoning, mustard, and garlic. Close with a tight-fitting lid and shake vigorously for 1 minute.
2. Refrigerate for up to 1 week.

NUTRITION: calories 81, fat 9g, protein 0g, carbs 0g, sugars 0g, fiber 0g, sodium 52mg

598. Creamy Avocado Dressing

Cooking time 0 mins | Servings 1 cup

INGREDIENTS:

- 1 large avocado, peeled and pitted
- ½ cup plain Greek yogurt
- ¾ cup fresh cilantro
- 1 tbsp water
- 2 tsps freshly squeezed lime juice
- ⅛ tsp garlic powder
- Pinch salt

DIRECTIONS:

1. Process the avocado, yogurt, cilantro, water, lime juice, garlic powder, and salt in a blender until creamy and emulsified.
2. Chill for at least 30 mins in the refrigerator to let the flavors blend.

NUTRITION: (¼ cup) calories 92, fat 6g, protein 4g, carbs 4g, fiber 2g, sodium 52mg

599. Greek or Italian Vinaigrette

Cooking time 0 mins | Servings 4

INGREDIENTS:

Greek

- ¼ cup olive oil
- 3 garlic cloves, minced
- 1 tbsp freshly squeezed lemon juice
- 1 tbsp red wine vinegar
- 1 tsp dried marjoram
- 1 tsp dried oregano
- ¼ tsp sea salt

Italian

- ¼ cup olive oil
- 2 tbsp red wine vinegar
- 1 tsp Dijon mustard
- 2 tsps Italian seasoning
- 1 garlic clove, finely minced
- 1 tbsp minced shallot
- ¼ tsp sea salt

DIRECTIONS:

1. Stir together all ingredients in a medium bowl until completely mixed and emulsified.

NUTRITION: calories 129, fat 14g, protein 0g, carbs 1g, fiber 1g, sugars 0g, sodium 76mg

600. Tahini Dressing with Honey

Cooking time 0 mins | Servings 1 cup

INGREDIENTS:

- ½ cup water
- ¾ cup unsalted tahini
- 1/3 cup freshly squeezed lemon juice
- 3 tbsp honey
- ½ tsp salt

DIRECTIONS:

1. Mix together the water, tahini, lemon juice, honey, and salt in a medium bowl, and stir vigorously until well incorporated.
2. Store the leftover dressing in an airtight container in the fridge for up to 2 weeks and shake before using.

NUTRITION: (2 tbsp) calories 168, fat 13g, protein 4g, carbs 10g, sugars 8g, sodium 148mg

CHAPTER 14 28-DAY MEAL PLAN

MEAL PLANNING is essential to your diet and to saving money. As follows the main benefits of it:

Saves money: When you meal plan for the week, your grocery trips will become more focused, and your cart will be filled with foods that you planned to buy instead of foods that you picked up on impulse. Meal planning can also help limit the number of times that you get food delivered or dine out; cooking at home is usually a less expensive option.

Saves time: At first, meal planning might feel more time-consuming, but we promise that once you get in the habit, it will become much faster and easier. Planning your meals ahead of time will also help reduce the time you spend thinking about and coming up with meals during the week. Plus, this can help cut back on your grocery store trips – a huge timesaver too!

Provides more variety: When you sit down and think about what you want to purchase or cook in advance, this will help you vary the cuisine, flavors, and recipes.

Creates less stress: Meal planning takes the guesswork away and gives you a plan for what to cook for the week.

Ensures healthier eating: When you plan your meals, you are in better control of the ingredients you put in your body. Although you don't have to cook every meal to be healthy, meal planning does provide great motivation to get back to the kitchen. At To Taste, we believe cooking is one of the best ways to take control of your health!

Prevents food waste: Meal planning promotes conscientious grocery shopping and helps you pay better attention to a food's shelf life. When you plan ahead and stick to a list, you are less likely to buy extra foods that may go bad.

As follows a complete monthly meal plan to suit all types and tastes. You will find all the recipes included in the cookbook with their index number.

Day	Breakfast	Lunch	Dinner	Dessert
1	Pumpkin-Peanut Butter Muffins #1	Lemony Spinach-Tofu Bake #257	Zucchini Boats #263	Peach Crumb Cobbler #544
2	Vegetable Omelet #11	Garlic Fettuccine #334	Lemon Pepper Salmon #421	Pineapple Pear Medley #545
3	Greek Yogurt Bowl #49	Grilled Vegetables on Hummus #258	Italian Pasta with sauce #282	Spiced Baked Apples #546
4	Crepe Cakes #54	Curried Rice with broccoli #343	Sweet Potato Kale Chickpea Bowl #259	Maple Oatmeal Cookies #547
5	Zucchini Bread #55	Black Bean Enchilada #259	Simply Sole Piccata #426	Peach and Almond Meal Fritters #548
6	Walnut Granola #56	Beef Burrito Bowl #524	MushroomStuffed Turkey #512	Peach Berry Parfaits #30
7	Tex-Mex Omelet #13	Ratatouille #262	Cajun Catfish #408	Blackberry Yogurt Ice Pops #550
8	Yogurt Sundae #61	Salmon with Spicy Honey #366	Tofu and Bean Chili #264	Chocolate Almond Butter Fudge #551
9	Apple and Bran Muffins #62	Cauliflower Steaks #265	Fettuccine with Peppers and Broccoli #338	Pineapple Nice Cream #552
10	Coconut and Berry Oatmeal #63	Mushroom Pesto Flatbread Pizza #266	Coconut Lime Chicken #451	Grilled Peach and Coconut Yogurt Bowls #553
11	Cranberry Grits #65	Broccoli Beef Stir-Fry #526	Tempeh Wraps #274	Creamy Strawberry Crepes #554
12	Huevos Rancheros #67	Stuffed Squash with Cheese and Artichokes #267	Blueberry Chicken Salad #128	Flourless Orange Bundt Cake #555
13	Coconut Pancakes #68	Kale Mushroom Bread Pudding #268	Beans and Brown Rice #271	Avocado Chocolate Mousse #556
14	Spanakopita Omelet #68	Squash and broccoli salad #125	Chicken Rigatoni #128	Cottage Cheese Almond Pancakes #66
15	Greek Toast # 7	Chickpea Coconut Curry #269	Creole Chicken #505	Frozen Chocolate Peanut Butter Bites #558
16	Shrimp with Scallion Grits #71	Turkey Taco #518	Orange Scallops #440	Apple Crunch #559

17	Brussels Sprouts Egg Scramble #47	Quinoa Salad #178	Rainbow Rice Casserole #341	Goat Cheese-Stuffed Pears #560
18	Blueberry Muffins #39	Asian Rice #340	Jambalaya #442	Gingerbread Soufflés #561
19	German Pancakes #10	Coconut Chicken Curry #502	Spinach Mini Quiches #273	Crispy Apple Chips #562
20	Broccoli and Mushroom Frittata #18	Veggie Lo Mein #339	Grilled Cod #353	Blackberry Soufflés #563
21	Apple and Pumpkin Waffles #64	Spiced Tilapia #351	Miso pork and apple soup #196	Carrot Cupcakes #564
22	Breakfast Bagels #12	BBQ Salad #151	Lentil and lemon soup #220	Lemon Squares #575
23	Mediterranean Toast #14	Beans and Rice #271	Slow chicken curry #452	Apple crisp #579
24	Scrambled Eggs #29	Egg Celery Salad #140	White Fish Soup #357	Strawberry fluff #577
25	Chia Seeds Breakfats #23	Salmon Meal #371	Jambalaya #442	Bakery squares #573
26	Healthy Granola Bowl #28	Spicy Beef salad #154	French onion soup #197	Vanilla custard #568
27	Pita and Bacon #70	Sweet potato bowl #259	Crispy Fish Fillet #395	Melon Pearl Medley #545
28	Walnut Granola #56	Chicken Pho #199	Vegetable Lentil Soups #201	Peach crumb #544

Appendix 1 Conversions Chart

VOLUME EQUIVALENTS (LIQUID)

US STANDARD	US STANDARD	METRIC (APPROX.)
2 tablespoons	1 fl. oz.	30 mL
¼ cup	2 fl. oz.	60 mL
½ cup	4 fl. oz.	120 mL
1 cup	8 fl. oz.	240 mL
1½ cups	12 fl. oz.	355 mL
2 cups or 1 pint	16 fl. oz.	475 mL
4 cups or 1 quart	32 fl. oz.	1 L
1 gallon	128 fl. oz.	4 L

OVEN TEMPERATURES

FAHRENHEIT (F)	CELSIUS (C) (APPROX.)
250°	120°
300°	150°
325°	165°
350°	180°
375°	190°
400°	200°
425°	220°
450°	230°

VOLUME EQUIVALENTS (DRY)

US STANDARD	METRIC (APPROX.)
⅛ teaspoon	0.5 mL
¼ teaspoon	1 mL
½ teaspoon	2 mL
¾ teaspoon	4 mL
1 teaspoon	5 mL
1 tablespoon	15 mL
¼ cup	59 mL
⅓ cup	79 mL
½ cup	118 mL
⅔ cup	156 mL
¾ cup	177 mL
1 cup	235 mL
2 cups or 1 pint	475 mL
3 cups	700 mL
4 cups or 1 quart	1 L

WEIGHT EQUIVALENTS

US STANDARD	METRIC (APPROX.)
½ ounce	15 g
1 ounce	30 g
2 ounces	60 g
4 ounces	115 g
8 ounces	225 g
12 ounces	340 g
16 ounces or 1 pound	455 g

Appendix 2 Index

A

Apple; 5; 6; 7; 9; 12; 14; 43; 44; 50; 64; 67; 80; 89; 118; 188; 190; 198; 234; 235; 241; 242; 250; 251; 257; 258; 259; 260
Apricot; 14; 238; 257
Artichoke; 5; 6; 8; 42; 61; 97; 259; 261
Asparagus; 7; 9; 10; 11; 76; 82; 134; 141; 149; 178; 180; 260; 261
Avocado; 6; 7; 13; 14; 41; 45; 72; 81; 101; 103; 115; 177; 188; 233; 247; 251; 257; 259; 261

B

Barley; 147
Bean; 6; 7; 8; 9; 10; 11; 72; 81; 84; 112; 113; 115; 151; 163; 250; 259; 261; 262
Beans; 8; 9; 10; 11; 104; 118; 140; 146; 162; 176; 251; 259; 260
Beef; 6; 8; 13; 74; 102; 103; 109; 218; 219; 220; 250; 251; 252; 257; 258; 260; 261; 262
Beet; 5; 6; 7; 14; 52; 68; 69; 77; 246; 257
Berries; 5; 6; 8; 37; 39; 45; 67; 96
Berry; 4; 5; 6; 13; 33; 43; 44; 66; 71; 230; 250; 251; 257; 258; 261
Black Bean; 99
Black Cod; 167
Blackberry; 7; 13; 14; 82; 231; 235; 250; 251; 258
Blueberry; 36; 237
Broccoli; 4; 5; 6; 7; 9; 10; 12; 13; 26; 30; 40; 60; 66; 69; 74; 78; 87; 93; 140; 144; 146; 197; 208; 220; 250; 251; 258; 259; 261
Broccoli Cheese Quiche; 26
Brussels Sprouts; 5; 7; 11; 38; 87; 176; 251; 258; 260
Butternut; 8; 9; 95; 104; 129; 262
Butternut Squash; 95

C

Cabbage; 6; 7; 8; 9; 12; 13; 59; 68; 75; 76; 78; 83; 90; 107; 133; 198; 199; 225; 257; 260; 261; 262
Calamari; 151
Carrot; 6; 7; 8; 14; 73; 75; 95; 97; 100; 105; 236; 251; 258; 259
Carrots; 5; 9; 10; 50; 51; 129; 132; 148
Catfish; 10; 11; 152; 153; 171; 179; 250; 258
Cauliflowe; 94
Cauliflower; 5; 7; 8; 9; 10; 12; 54; 94; 101; 115; 120; 122; 124; 125; 136; 139; 141; 158; 198; 250; 258; 261
Celeriac; 8; 98
Cheese; 4; 5; 6; 8; 9; 10; 12; 13; 26; 37; 45; 55; 62; 63; 73; 96; 116; 124; 127; 142; 188; 233; 251; 258; 259; 260; 261
Chestnut; 6; 68
Chia Seeds; 31
chicken; 12; 18; 20; 23; 32; 38; 48; 51; 52; 53; 62; 66; 67; 70; 71; 73; 84; 89; 90; 91; 92; 96; 98; 99; 100; 101; 102; 106; 107; 108; 110; 133; 143; 144; 146; 152; 162; 163; 170; 172; 175; 177; 183; 184; 188; 189; 190; 191; 192; 193; 194; 195; 196; 197; 200; 201; 202; 203; 204; 205; 206; 207; 208; 209; 210; 211; 212; 213; 217; 224; 251
Chicken; 5; 6; 7; 8; 12; 13; 32; 38; 48; 51; 52; 62; 66; 67; 70; 71; 83; 90; 92; 96; 102; 188; 189; 190; 191; 192; 193; 194; 195; 196; 197; 200; 201; 203; 205; 206; 207; 208; 209; 210; 211; 212; 213; 251; 252; 258; 259; 260; 261
Chicken and Vegetable; 38
Chicken Rolls; 193
Chickpea; 8; 9; 113; 117; 130; 250; 251; 258; 261
Chicory; 98
Chocolate; 13; 14; 231; 233; 239; 250; 251; 257; 258; 259

Coconut; 4; 5; 8; 9; 12; 13; 14; 34; 44; 46; 98; 100; 117; 186; 189; 209; 213; 237; 251; 258; 259; 260; 262
Cod; 150; 151; 156; 163; 164; 170; 172
Corn; 56; 71
Crab; 5; 6; 7; 9; 55; 61; 86; 94; 135; 259
Cranberry; 5; 6; 14; 44; 68; 69; 70; 244; 251; 259
Cucumber; 6; 7; 13; 63; 76; 77; 81; 226; 259; 260

D

Daikon; 69
Duck; 13; 215; 257

E

Egg; 4; 5; 6; 11; 26; 33; 38; 70; 162; 251; 258; 261
Eggplant; 7; 9; 10; 90; 121; 126; 136; 147; 259; 261
Eggplants; 9; 128
Eggs and Beans; 134

F

Feta; 77
Figs; 49; 74
Fruits; 26

G

Goat Cheese; 5; 7; 14; 42; 82; 234; 251; 257; 258; 259

H

Haddock; 160; 174
Halibut; 11; 176; 177; 259

K

Kale; 5; 6; 7; 8; 9; 10; 12; 53; 56; 83; 103; 117; 129; 142; 208; 250; 251; 258; 260; 261; 262
Kiwi; 26

L

Lamb; 8; 13; 107; 108; 218; 226; 227; 228; 260; 261
Lentil; 5; 7; 8; 38; 91; 97; 251; 252; 260

M

Melon; 27
Monk-fish; 173
Mushroom; 4; 8; 9; 13; 30; 114; 116; 117; 122; 124; 137; 214; 251; 258; 260
Mushrooms; 4; 5; 6; 10; 11; 13; 27; 34; 55; 59; 61; 155; 165; 227; 259; 260
Mushrooms Tofu; 34
Mussels; 12; 185; 260

O

Okra; 139
Onion; 6; 7; 9; 10; 60; 89; 92; 93; 135; 152; 160; 258; 259
Onions; 131

P

Papaya; 6; 70
Peach; 4; 6; 7; 8; 13; 33; 58; 81; 95; 229; 230; 231; 249; 250; 251; 252; 259; 260; 261
peaches; 236
Pear; 6; 7; 13; 66; 77; 78; 85; 86; 229; 249; 260; 261
Peas; 57
Pepper; 4; 5; 6; 7; 8; 11; 14; 30; 40; 53; 54; 58; 59; 75; 80; 90; 94; 106; 110; 175; 197; 244; 249; 257; 259; 260; 261
Peppers; 4; 9; 10; 13; 30; 128; 140; 141; 143; 144; 210; 250; 259; 260; 261
Pineapple; 6; 11; 13; 22; 71; 167; 231; 249; 250; 259; 260
Pork; 7; 8; 12; 13; 89; 106; 190; 218; 223; 224; 225; 226; 258; 259; 260; 261
Potatoes; 5; 7; 9; 50; 56; 78; 258
Pumpkin; 4; 5; 7; 8; 14; 25; 39; 44; 92; 98; 99; 104; 236; 249; 251; 257; 260; 261

Q

Quinoa; 7; 9; 13; 82; 92; 118; 130; 213; 251; 258; 261; 262

R

Rice Milk; 36

S

Salmon; 7; 10; 11; 80; 82; 151; 153; 155; 157; 158; 162; 163; 164; 165; 166; 169; 171; 175; 176; 249; 250; 252; 259; 260; 261

Sardine; 5; 11; 52; 170
Sardine Fish; 170
Sausage; 4; 5; 12; 25; 40; 206; 261
Scallops; 6; 10; 11; 63; 159; 174; 180; 182; 251; 257; 260; 261
Sea Bass; 10; 11; 161; 169
Shrimp; 5; 6; 10; 11; 12; 47; 53; 61; 69; 156; 157; 158; 168; 172; 181; 183; 186; 251; 258; 260; 261
Shrimps; 6; 8; 11; 62; 105; 162
Sole; 159
Spelt; 7; 83
Spinach; 4; 5; 6; 7; 8; 9; 10; 11; 31; 42; 66; 86; 112; 119; 129; 137; 138; 145; 162; 249; 251; 258; 260; 261
Sweet Potato; 8; 9; 104; 108; 113; 123; 137; 250; 260; 261
Sweet Potatoes; 131

T

Tempeh; 9; 119; 251; 261
Tilapia; 10; 11; 150; 160; 162; 175; 251; 258; 259
Tofu; 4; 8; 9; 14; 31; 99; 112; 115; 123; 244; 249; 250; 259; 260; 261
Tomato; 6; 7; 8; 9; 14; 65; 81; 84; 103; 106; 121; 246; 259; 260; 261
Tomatoes; 4; 5; 10; 29; 51; 142; 258; 261
Tomatoes Eggs; 29
Trout; 11; 178; 179; 259; 262
tuna; 154
Tuna; 5; 10; 11; 48; 49; 53; 150; 152; 153; 154; 165; 167; 169; 171; 174; 178; 179; 259; 260; 262
turkey; 190
Turkey; 8; 12; 13; 101; 195; 201; 202; 203; 205; 206; 213; 214; 215; 216; 217; 250; 251; 258; 259; 260; 262

W

White Bean; 132
White Fish; 152

Y

Yogurt; 5; 13; 14; 39; 43; 231; 246; 249; 250; 251; 257; 258; 259; 262
Yucca; 134

Z

Zucchini; 5; 6; 7; 8; 9; 10; 38; 41; 52; 58; 59; 73; 80; 115; 130; 133; 142; 146; 249; 250; 259; 260; 262

Made in the USA
Monee, IL
04 November 2021

81449018R00142